PIRANDELLO'S THEATRE OF LIVING MASKS

THE DA PONTE LIBRARY SERIES

PIRANDELLO'S THEATRE OF LIVING MASKS

New Translations of Six Major Plays

by Umberto Mariani and
Alice Gladstone Mariani

UNIVERSITY OF TORONTO PRESS
Toronto Buffalo London

© University of Toronto Press Incorporated 2011
Toronto Buffalo London
www.utppublishing.com
Printed in Canada

ISBN 978-1-4426-4211-9

Printed on acid-free, 100% post-consumer recycled paper
with vegetable-based inks.
The Lorenzo Da Ponte Italian Library

Library and Archives Canada Cataloguing in Publication

Pirandello, Luigi, 1867–1936
Pirandello's theatre of living masks: new translations of six major plays /
Umberto Mariani, Alice Gladstone Mariani.

(Lorenzo Da Ponte Italian library)
Includes bibliographical references and index.
ISBN 978-1-4426-4211-9

1. Pirandello, Luigi, 1867–1936 – Translations into English. I. Mariani,
Umberto, 1927– II. Mariani, Alice Gladstone III. Title. IV. Series:
Lorenzo da Ponte Italian library series

PQ4835.I7A277 2011   852'.912   C2011-901880-2

Publication of this book assisted by the Istituto Italiano di cultura, Toronto.

This book has been published under the aegis and with financial assistance of:
Fondazione Cassamarca, Treviso; the National Italian-American Foundation;
Ministero degli Affari Esteri, Direzione Generale per la Promozione
e la Cooperazione Culturale; Ministero per i Beni e le Attività Culturali,
Direzione Generale per i Beni Librari e gli Istituti Culturali, Servizio
per la promozione del libro e della lettura.

University of Toronto Press acknowledges the financial assistance to its publishing program of the Canada Council for the Arts and the Ontario Arts Council.

 Canada Council   Conseil des Arts   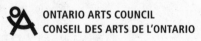 ONTARIO ARTS COUNCIL
for the Arts   du Canada   CONSEIL DES ARTS DE L'ONTARIO

University of Toronto Press acknowledges the financial support for
its publishing activities of the Government of Canada through the Book
Publishing Industry Development Program (BPIDP).

Contents

PIRANDELLO'S THEATRE OF LIVING MASKS

Introduction

Umberto Mariani

The 'Pirandellian' Characters

In virtually every major work of Pirandello's maturity, like those in this collection, a fundamental ethical and psychological opposition recurs between those characters who reject the values and conditions to which their bourgeois society seeks to bind them – whom, for convenience, we will call 'the Pirandellian characters' – and those who embody the values of that society, its customs, its prejudices, its complacent self-assurance, its claim to superior knowledge and wisdom, whom we will call the bourgeois characters. This is the opposition through which the 'Pirandellian' characters reveal themselves to us. It is an opposition that also affects the very structure of the plays.

By the end of the nineteenth century, the world these 'Pirandellian' characters represent has lost the sense of stability and self-confidence the bourgeois world had been enjoying; they are beset by doubts about their identity, about the possibility of ever being able to communicate it to others, to establish a normal relationship with their society; they have lost the sense of a community of thought and belief – and they suffer from, and protest dramatically against, this loss.

By the turn of the century the bourgeoisie of Europe, and of Italy in particular, was losing the position of power it had previously enjoyed. The politicized trade union movements were rising on the left and the industrial baronies on the right. Bourgeois intellectuals, whose participation had been vital during the recent struggle for the unification of the country and its political aftermath, saw their role becoming increasingly irrelevant.

The bourgeois world, which had once seemed solid and secure, indeed complacent, in the principles and institutions that ruled social behaviour and, especially, confident in its faith in the omnipotence of scientific progress, had not kept its promises. Scientific positivism had not produced any progress in the world of ethical and social intercourse. If an objective reality existed, it could not be known, especially outside the field of the exact sciences. The moral principles of the bourgeois world had often revealed themselves as merely hypocritical masks for the justification of oppressive customs or plain convenience. The old values and ideals now appeared empty and were rejected, together with the unified vision of reality which that society had fostered.

Once that common vision of reality ceased to be held, the certainties and assumptions regarding one's individual identity were bound to collapse also. So, together with the experience of the disintegration of the social reality on whose assurances they had been raised, the Pirandellian characters must also confront a disintegration of confidence in the stability of the essential inner self and in their personal worth.

They take the stage to proclaim the drama of that loss of their unity, of the certainty of their knowledge of their own truth, of its communicability. However, unlike the characters of many dramatists who came after Pirandello, who are resigned to the impossibility of attaining that truth, the unassailable knowledge of that reality, and have made peace with the chaos of formlessness, the Pirandellian characters do not accept their loss; they protest against it as an unjust privation; they feel the need for unity, consistency, self-assurance, for an existence supported by a system of truer values and ideals, the need to know one's identity and to communicate what one is, the need to identify with, to integrate into, a stable society and enjoy its recognition. They assert it as a fundamentally human and irrepressible need, as a birthright, all the while knowing that their loss is final, that their need will never be satisfied. But they resent this: they cannot resign themselves to formlessness and insignificance. Although they know they will never arrive at an acceptable solution, they do not cease to search for it, to declare their need for it, even to pursue unsatisfactory solutions, so strong is their longing for a reality that can be shared. The Six Characters, for instance, seeking a definitive artistic form because they consider it the most effective means of communication, having failed to obtain it from their creator, seek at least a very temporary expressive form in the acting of a theatrical company. They must realize that there they are pursuing only compromises, unsatisfactory goals, because the satisfactory ones are unattainable.

This traumatic discovery of an irreparable loss is the existential condition of Pirandello's characters and the cause of their insoluble conflict with life. Thus their author's works are permeated with compassion for the plight of humanity in the modern world, the victim of that traumatic loss, and by a condemnation of the false values and social myths through which the bourgeoisie masked its moral void. Pirandello's inspiration springs from a profound ethical source.

He created a new idea of what he called 'humour,' attributing to the 'humorist' writer a particular awareness of reality, of the tragic predicament of humanity in our time. The humorist's inspiration and compassion are born of the awareness of what is tragic in life before it becomes the theme of artistic creation, and the Pirandellian characters are the expression of their creator's moral torment confronting it.

Besides trying to unmask the social myths of the bourgeois world, the Pirandellian characters argue with the artistic forms that had represented and celebrated them, especially the bourgeois comedy that had dominated the Italian and European stage for more than half a century. At times, as in *Six Characters*, they radically oppose those forms; more often they embody recognizable situations and people of a bourgeois reality in order to decry their hollowness, to protest their alienated and alienating qualities. They present themselves to a public very familiar with the forms and contents of bourgeois drama in order to show its mechanical nature, the rigidity of its outworn structures, the bankruptcy of its conventional dénouements, and to demonstrate the validity of new experimental forms. If the tragedy of the characters is insoluble, then the new theatre must remain open and not offer artificial solutions; may propose non-conclusions, even suppress that fraudulent third act, even expand the conventional physical space of the stage to include the orchestra, the auditorium, the lobby, and the people in them – the representatives of 'real life' – the adjacent streets, any place where an audience might gather.

Liolà

The presence of many strong naturalistic elements in this play should not deceive us into seeing it, as it has often been seen in the past, as a thematically immature regression to such models of Italian naturalism as the best known works of Verga. Pirandello could not have done such a thing more than twelve years after the publication of so original and typically Pirandellian a work as *The Late Mattia Pascal. Liolà* makes very deliberate and skilful use of some plot elements of Italian naturalism, as it does of elements of the commedia dell'arte, of Renaissance comedy – like Machiavelli's *Mandrake* – and classical comedy, both Roman and Greek. Although Tuzza, who makes love with Liolà to spite Mita, reminds one clearly of Verga's Santuzza, who makes love with Turiddu to spite Lola, other motifs are not exclusive to Sicilian naturalism – for example, the motif of the marriage between a young woman and a rich old man, frequently found in Renaissance and classical comedy, or that of the hiring of day labourers in the village square which appears in the parables of the New Testament.

The fact is that the few things that Liolà and other characters do because they are Sicilian are either not important to the thematic development of the play or are used in a uniquely Pirandellian and 'humoristic' way, while the things Liolà does because he is a 'Pirandellian' character would not be different if the action took place elsewhere, and are what really count in the development of the character and his function in the play.

Liolà is not a naturalistic character but a great new invention, vividly alive, 'humoristically' complex, and altogether functional in regard to the themes of the play. He embodies two human characteristics that deeply influence the development of those themes, characteristics that may seem opposite but are actually complementary: the gaiety of a carefree man and the astuteness of a wise one. Liolà is joyous, lively, lighthearted. Wherever he goes in his radiant joy, everyone is happy; the young women go a little crazy. Only the old fogies think of him as irresponsible, dangerous, someone to stay away from. Attractive to others, he is content with himself as well.

But Liolà is not exclusively happy-go-lucky. If Liolà were only cheerful and lighthearted, he would not have been so for long; he would very probably have become the object of some tragic settling of accounts. The most important characteristic of Liolà is his awareness and the astuteness that follows from it. He knows the ways of the world, the value of the hypocritical conventions of society, and he exploits them.

If a carefree soul alone would cause him nothing but trouble, and awareness alone would destroy his contentment, an awareness that engenders shrewdness makes him a happy man. He uses his knowledge of 'the rules of the game' to avoid being oppressed by society, to beat it at its own game. Thus he goes through life singing, inspiring affection, making use of every possible circumstance to foster his success, even circumstances that might be damaging, like the existence of that nestful of illegitimate children, playing and singing with them in a display of simplicity and fatherly love.

Whereas lightheartedness makes him attractive, his shrewdness makes him dangerous. Even his mother, always eager to defend him against gossip, is very explicit about the danger the young women who buzz around him run. Though he makes the dutiful gesture of asking for Tuzza's hand, he is very glad when his offer is rejected. The manner in which the offer is tendered, his wish to be told by Tuzza herself before witnesses that she does not want him, are telling indications of his cleverness and intuitive penetration: when he sees Uncle Simone go into the house where Tuzza has taken refuge alone, in an instant he foresees all the possible consequences of the situation and conceives his plan of action in support of his childhood friend, Mita. All his actions derive from his knowledge of the ways of the world, of society's outrageous deception and hypocrisy, of which he is unwilling to become a victim.

He contends that in such a hypocritical society there are no moral or immoral actions in an absolute sense, as society would have us believe, but only in a relative one: when someone stabs you in the back and you refuse to strike back, to fight one injustice with another, you are thinking in absolute terms, your action is unjust only in absolute terms; in his view the end more than justifies the means. Any means is justified to battle against the hypocrisy and deceptions of a society that attaches such importance to appearances and compromises every moral principle while trying to impose absolute moral principles. See how the dishonour of an illegitimate pregnancy or the stigma of sterility is redeemed in this society; see whether marriages are founded on love or on the question of inheritance; see how convenience and authority can put a lid on a can of lies and impose it as truth. This hypocrisy is condemned in the play as a means society uses to oppress its most defenceless members. Liolà rejects this claim to and imposition of an absolute morality in a world marked everywhere by clearly relativistic practices, and Pirandello, through his original character, suggests a new, positive code of behaviour, a call to consistency as a possible redemption from the hypocrisy of the absolute moralists. The moral dimension of social behaviour can be more authentic if social behaviour is consistent with the moral relativism that actually prevails. If society puts great value on appearances, then it must stop preaching absolute moral principles; let it value appearances, but admit that it does so, and stop trying to conceal reality with its absolutist moral smokescreen.

Liolà knows what kind of person he is, admits it openly, accepts the consequences of his behaviour (the children, even marriage, if necessary), and does not hide the fact that he exploits the hypocrisy of those who value appearances but do not want to admit it. Dissimulation can be practised as a Machiavellian virtue when it is necessary to achieve a just, 'relatively' moral end. It must be recognized as such and admitted. An enormous injustice (Mita's situation) may be righted by consistency within pretence. Dissimulation is the mask everybody is more or less compelled to wear in life; those who are aware of it, and admit it, might succeed in using it to laudable ends, re-establishing justice, albeit a relative one. Unlike the Pirandellian protagonists of the other plays considered here, Liolà himself, the joyous, supremely self-assured manipulator of his society, does not suffer. But those who interact most closely with him do.

If the old ways of social behaviour cause a great deal of injustice and suffering, the process of transforming them generates just as much. *Liolà* is inspired by the feeling for the suffering born of the fundamental opposition of the recalcitrant Pirandellian characters and the society by which they are oppressed. And this is the 'humoristic' aspect of this supposedly 'joyful' play: there is a great deal of suffering around Liolà, especially for Tuzza, Mita, and Uncle Simone. Simone is not the comical figure he might superficially seem; he wants not only a son, but also redemption from the stigma of sterility; he wants public recognition of his fatherhood; and he finds and imposes it through the process of suffering typical of the most 'humoristic' Pirandellian figures – a process that includes the more or less conscious adoption of the despised relativistic logic and ethics of his antagonist, Liolà.

Following the development and resolution of this comedy closely and comparing them to the dénouement of traditional comedy, one realizes how different *Liolà*'s development and outcome are.

Finally, the play is built around a powerful protagonist, hardly an epigone of naturalism, but a highly imaginative creation, perfectly suited to his function, capable not only of asserting a vision but of translating his view into dramatic action through his magnificent ability to manipulate situations, events, human destinies. The action he stage-manages dramatizes the central themes of the play: the dialectical opposition between what seems and what is; the contradictions in social behaviour, and the oppression of the individual those contradictions cause when absolute principles are imposed or when people try erroneously to hang on to them.

Right You Are

In *Right You Are, if You Think You Are* the opposition between appearances and reality, as well as between the individual and society, is dramatized chiefly in the conflict that arises between a group of three Pirandellian characters and the familiar group of conventional, self-righteous bourgeois characters. When the first group act upon their relativistic view of reality, they profoundly disturb the latter, whose prying and intolerance unleash a virtual 'inquisition' upon the nonconformists.

Pirandello's stage directions as well as his dramatic dialogue reflect the profound inner differences between the groups. The unsettling, unseemly struggle is staged in a familiar, decorous middle-class drawing room, and the voices of the opposed groups are sharply contrasted. Smug, comfortable, closed-minded, complacent masters of a world in which everything is as it should be, the bourgeois characters, convinced of the existence of absolute truth, pursue it relentlessly. Their victims have arrived at a truth of their own through years of suffering and patient adjustment, and now are determined to defend their hard-won conquest.

Laudisi, unconnected to either group of antagonists, is the detached chorus, representing the ideas of the author. His is a multiple dramatic function, part author, part director, part puppeteer; he projects, in intellectual terms, the contrast played out in the dramatic action between the Pirandellian and the bourgeois characters.

To the inquisitors the existence of objective, absolute truth is not problematic; they have never questioned the assumption that it exists and is attainable. Laudisi agrees that some truths can be known, truths involving mathematical and scientific facts; but he seeks to convince them that in the realm of human emotions, of personal opinions and beliefs, of the value of moral principles and behaviour, truth can never be absolute: it is subjective, personal, relative, and may be known only in those terms. It is a known fact that Mrs Frola cannot enter her daughter's home, that Mr Ponza allows her to communicate with her daughter only from a distance. But the reason behind these facts is totally different in the minds of the two Pirandellian characters, sincere as both are. Meanwhile, Laudisi's relatives and their guests cannot admit that both may be right.

So, the dramatic action consists of an obstinate search for one absolute, objective truth, and it dramatizes the subjectivity of truth, and of the difficulty of communicating one's own truth to others. All the elements of the work are designed to achieve this end.

The action that takes place in the typical middle-class parlour is made to seem perfectly recognizable, as are the inquisitors we meet first, with their bourgeois mentality and prying gossip, with their acritical assumption that an objective truth both exists and can be established. But Pirandello immediately introduces into this world contrasting forces that precipitate the dramatic action: the behaviour impelled by the bourgeois mentality is presented simply, in the documentary manner characteristic of positivistic realism; and Pirandello cleverly heightens the tension in the characters in search of an objective truth by presenting them with a dilemma so absolutely simple as to appear absolutely resolvable: whether Mrs Ponza is or is not the daughter of Mrs Frola. The action, however, reaches a 'surprise' ending, a resolution dictated entirely by the development of the play, but unexpected and unsatisfactory for the investigators and also, in general, for its early audiences, accustomed to the predictable endings of the bourgeois theatre.

The bourgeois investigators, and the audience, are led step by step to their perception of the simple nature of the dilemma by a process that must inevitably stimulate and justify their mounting curiosity, indignation, and determination.

The technique of heightening suspense is accompanied by the maintenance of a reasonable degree of verisimilitude in the presentation of the dramatic events, all sufficiently plausible, at least until Mr Ponza contradicts Mrs Frola with an equally plausible but different explanation. Each of the two in turn presents such a plausible version of the facts as to put in doubt the version just furnished by the other.

Each clarification elicits further curiosity and calls for further explanations, simply because the two versions continue to be contradictory and include an increasingly clear and persistent reciprocal accusation of madness. Pirandello brilliantly dramatizes the characters' attachment to the reality they have created for themselves, and which they feel the need to defend even if it means hurting each other, despite their awareness that they need each other in their common struggle against the inquisitorial group.

The verisimilitude of the development of the action, and its background, is an important part of Pirandello's subversive dramatic strategy, designed to make the bourgeois characters (and the audience?) feel at home in their own environment.

Those very elements of verisimilitude and the posing of a problem apparently so simple in a context apparently so close to 'normal' impel the bourgeois characters towards a need for a definitive explanation. But the 'conclusive' explanation, when it finally comes, vindicates the position of the Pirandellian characters, not least because the two separate truths they persist in maintaining have been presented with such plausibility that they demand acceptance; the carefully crafted aura of verisimilitude in the dramatic action forces on us the reality of truths that do not coincide.

It is clear that under the sustained realism of the surface the disturbing critical consciousness of the 'humorist' writer is continually at work. The awareness of the artist, who, particularly through the character of Laudisi, pauses to contemplate the spectacle of life that is before him and to perceive the futility of much of human behaviour, invites the audience to share his perception of the suffering it causes.

From an initial position of detachment, Laudisi is compelled to become increasingly involved in the action, to the point where he takes it into his own hands. However, what for him is mostly a vision of reality and an intellectual attainment, for the non-conforming neighbours has been a conquest that cost them dearly in a long torment patiently endured. They remain defensive against whatever threatens to deny and destroy the reality, the individual truth, they have so painfully built.

And though they know they will never reach an objective, absolute truth, they need support and confirmation of the subjective, temporary truth they do achieve, to break their isolation, to overcome the anguish of their solitude; they need the acceptance of their own truth by others. The consensus of others is needed to keep their own truth alive.

In reality this is everyone's drama. But those who believe in one absolute, objective, communicable truth are not aware that it is theirs as well; while the Pirandellian characters are intensely aware that it is their fundamental drama: to communicate their own perception of their identity, their own truth, and to seek recognition. Their problem lies in the fact that their truths do not coincide.

Not only in her appearance in the final moments, but throughout the play, Mrs Ponza is presented as the projection of the two distinct truths of Mr Ponza and Mrs Frola, and thus in her final statement she has no hidden individual identity to reveal; she furthers and brings to its necessary conclusion her sole function in the play: she is, and speaks as, the person the others believe her to be. Given the opportunity to define herself definitively, she defines herself as the others had defined her; she compels the audience to accept the reality of subjective truths, although she achieves no greater success than the other 'Pirandellian' characters do with the inquisitors, for whom she clarifies nothing.

Six Characters in Search of an Author

Approaching *Six Characters* by way of Pirandello's earlier masterpieces makes its major themes easier to understand. But it is clear from the outset that this is a far more complex play than the preceding ones, and far more original in form vis-à-vis the bourgeois theatre Pirandello turned against. The theme of the nature of artistic creation – of the relationship between art and everyday reality, the staging of a play, and even the process of its creation – is put on stage. The themes, the plots, the familiar conventions of the bourgeois theatre – still employed, albeit with subversive intent, in *Right You Are* – are utterly rejected. It is a revolutionary play, and it was perceived as such when it was first performed in 1921 in Rome, and later in Milan, Paris, and throughout the world, where it was justly to become Pirandello's best-known play.

We are presented with a group of characters, born of the author's imagination and developed to the point of being charged with a kind of independent life, although, not having been given definitive artistic form, they are unfinished, still in a developing stage. But they already have a drama, that is, a ruling passion, which colours their vision of reality, conditions their thoughts and behaviour, obsesses them – makes them, that is, dramatic characters.

Unfortunately, the drama in which they think they are characters resembles too closely in plot and spirit certain late-nineteenth-century romantic plays, especially of the bourgeois theatre of the turn of the century that Pirandello had decidedly rejected.

A wealthy, self-styled intellectual makes the gesture of reaching out for 'normalcy' by marrying an ordinary woman. A son is born, and the father immediately delivers him, in the bourgeois mode of the time, to a healthy countrywoman to nurse. So the 'ordinary' mother is unoccupied in their large house, and seems more able to communicate with the husband's down-to-earth secretary than with the husband himself, who, noticing their affinity, decides to rid himself of this 'ordinary' wife by favouring their union. The two set up house in another part of town, where a daughter is born. The Father keeps an eye on the new family for a while. Occasionally he meets the Stepdaughter on her way home from school and presses some little present on her, arousing suspicion in the parents, who move away leaving no trace behind. Unfortunately – some years and two more children later – the secretary dies and poverty takes his place. The Mother brings the family back and takes in sewing jobs for Madame Pace, a modiste, who behind her workshop runs a secret prostitution business. Every time the Stepdaughter, now eighteen, comes to deliver her mother's work, Madame Pace complains about the quality of the work and cuts the payment, while trying to make her understand that both complaints and cuts would stop if she would lend herself to Madame's other business. The Stepdaughter agrees in order to save her mother constant humiliation. And one day one of Madame Pace's clients is the now fiftyish Father; his attempt to undress the Stepdaughter is interrupted by the Mother, whose suspicions about her daughter's fate have brought her to the atelier to put an end to the sordid trafficking. The Father, having thus rediscovered the little family, takes them out of the squalor of their rented room and brings them home, where the first son, now twenty-two, treats the Mother he has never known and the bastards who have invaded his home with 'sullen indifference,' and the Father, the author of these surprises, with 'repressed anger.' The one who suffers most intensely from this rejection is the Mother, and the intensity of her grief is felt by the two younger children as if through physical contact, for they clutch her hands constantly without uttering a word, observing everything with wide eyes. Finally the intensity of the gnawing torment they sense in their mother overcomes them. The girl drowns herself in the garden fountain and the boy shoots himself. While the Mother pursues her first son from room to room, 'her arms stretched out to him,' imploring understanding, the older daughter leaves to become a streetwalker.

While the characters call this their 'painful drama' on various occasions, their author has evidently seen it for what it is, something of an old-fashioned tearjerker, material typical of the bourgeois theatre, the kind of literature Pirandello rejected from the very beginning of his creative career. Therefore, the author has decided not to give definitive artistic form to such a story and its characters.

And they resent that denial, because definitive artistic form would have meant not just the gift of life, but also immortality. They must instead be content with having been created originally as mortal characters who walk and talk in the author's study, but are not yet alive. A true character is a creature of the imagination, a form of communication that lives only in the act of communicating. In order to live, therefore, these characters, rejected by their creator and thus deprived of a desired immortal life, are in search of any occasion to communicate, that is, to live, even if 'only for a moment': a compromise, to be sure, with immortality, but certainly better than nothingness. Paying a visit to an acting company engaged in a rehearsal might forward their quest; and when they realize that the prompter might put down their parts in shorthand, they even begin to think that the director might take the place of the author, put together a script, give them definitive artistic form, the immortality denied them by their creator.

But inevitably they soon realize that without definitive artistic form it is virtually impossible for them to communicate, that is, to live wholly, even 'only for a moment': they can live only in brief fragments.

The very nature of this particular theatrical company further complicates things: it is accustomed to performing conventional, sentimental, romantic plays of the turn-of-the-century bourgeois theatre. The company cannot even begin to understand the new 'Pirandellian' theatre they are rehearsing or the one the six characters bring them.

Thus, on the one hand, director and actors become interested in the family story of the six, since it is the very stuff of turn-of-the-century, bourgeois, sentimental theatre; but on the other hand they will never understand the complex nature of these 'characters,' the problems they embody as 'characters.' They will even mistake them for 'persons' who, having lived their strange story in real life, now want to put it on the stage. For the acting company, the different nature of the characters, their differing consciousness of being 'characters' and not persons, or of having a role in their play, remains an utterly unfathomable matter.

The six characters are different both because among them some are primary figures, some secondary, and because they must perform different functions. But their most important difference is in the degree of awareness of their nature as characters and the needs inherent in that nature: needs they all feel, but of which they are not all equally aware and to satisfy which, therefore, they do not all struggle with the same intelligence and sense of urgency.

As characters in their turn-of-the-century sentimental family melodrama, they were rejected by their creator, who did not cast their story in definitive artistic form. But while rejecting them as characters in that tearful bourgeois play, he has cast them in another play, a deeper, more modern play, the play of the rejected characters in search of an author, whose real drama is the urgent need for human communication and the difficulty of achieving it.

Each to differing degrees, the six are conscious of being rejected characters in search of an author, but they must not discover that this, and not their family misadventure, is their real drama; they must continue to believe that the drama that makes them characters, creatures of art, potentially capable of achieving immortality, is the family drama that did not get written and that they want to act out. They must do so because, if they were to discover that the drama which makes them immortal is instead their search for an author, and that the definitive artistic form they are seeking has been granted them in this 'other' play, they would no longer suffer from rejection.

Instead, conscious of both rejection and search, but unconscious that their real drama consists precisely in this situation, the six characters live this drama with the passion with which any authentic character must live its drama. And it is in the passionate experience of this drama that they develop and express the complex Pirandellian themes of this play, both in their collective effort to project their family drama as an interesting one and in the individual effort of each character to make his or her own idea of the drama prevail, to influence the final shape the script (if there is going to be one) might take – that is, in their individual efforts to find their author, to achieve definitive artistic form.

The language of the play reflects the distinction between the two dramatizations. Being an old-fashioned, turn-of-the-century melodrama, the family misadventure is presented in the familiar naturalistic language of the bourgeois theatre, but the language of the play alters when the six characters interrupt the presentation of their family story and take on the role of 'Pirandellian' characters in search of understanding from their uncomprehending audience (the Director and his actors). They become characters trying to explain their essence as creations of art, imagined by their author and rejected, cast into the limbo of formlessness, deprived of an immortality they feel is their due. And as soon as, fired by this passion, they assume this role, their language rises to new levels of conceptual coherence, capable of expressing the awareness of the artist, the mystery of artistic creation, and the problems of its genesis, of its translation into formal expression, of its communication to an audience. Although it deals with complex aesthetic questions, the language here, spoken as it is by the characters, possesses the dynamism, the immediacy, the vivid imagery of animated conversation in its pervasive use of images, references, and examples that are immediate and concrete. And it is when the characters live their 'role' as characters, aware of the possibility of definitive artistic form, aggrieved at not having achieved it, searching for a way to communicate their drama, rather than when they present their family story, that the new themes of the Pirandellian theatre are developed.

Pirandello himself in his renowned 'post-preface' gives us the essence of his major themes:

The delusion of mutual understanding, irremediably based on the empty abstraction of words; the multiple personality of every individual, deriving from all the possibilities of being present in each one of us; and finally the inherent, tragic conflict between life, which constantly moves and changes, and form which fixes it immutably.

Beneath these themes lies the larger, inclusive one of the human need for communication and the difficulty, if not the impossibility, of satisfying it. To convey one's own individual human reality is rendered difficult both by the inescapable subjectivity of one's own perception of oneself and the reality around one, and by the very nature of language itself. Inevitably even that definitive artistic form would be subject to endless interpretive betrayals in the moment of communication.

But in addition to their complaint about the interpretive shortcomings of the actors, the six characters are also aware that the definitive artistic form they pursue so intelligently and persistently will never succeed in rendering wholly the multiplicity of the individual, nor the flow, the dynamic pulse of real life; art tends to freeze, to contract, to simplify life.

Human beings are always dissatisfied with these limitations, but in their irrepressible need to communicate and to be understood, they accept as inevitable the need for a crystallizing form, however inadequate, as the only means by which to reveal themselves to others.

By using dramatic characters as characters, not people, Pirandello explores on another level a basic theme of all his work, the fundamental human need to communicate and the difficulty of satisfying it, for characters, as we have said, being artistic creations, means of communication, can live only in the act of communicating.

Henry IV

Like most of the author's major plays, *Henry IV* centres on a 'Pirandellian' character – that is, a character tormented, persecuted, insulted by a philistine society which is insensitive and ignorantly self-assured, which makes its own laws and imposes them on everything; a society that makes arbitrary value judgments on individual behaviour, on human liberty, on the definition of sanity and madness; a complacent bourgeois society that thinks it is pursuing the common good by allowing the madman to hold court, while actually keeping him shut up as dangerous and isolated so they do not have to listen to his disturbing truths, and at most providing him with the 'help' of a scientific charlatan, to whom, instead, it accords authority and respect; a society in which Henry IV, a thinker, a serious man, hence 'a man of sorrows,' was therefore already considered strange before the pageant in which he was the victim of a provoked accident that caused his madness.

It is clear, however, that Henry IV is seen throughout by his creator as more human than his enemies, because of his suffering and the penetrating power of his thought. An extraordinarily human – though solitary – hero, misunderstood by a group of complacent bourgeois, one lone man, as in some classical tragedies (Aeschylus' Prometheus, Sophocles' Philoctetes, etc.), condemned to experience the ingratitude and insensitivity of his society.

Henry IV is unlike the classical heroes, however, in that his relentless thought has led him to a thoroughly modern, pessimistic appreciation of the absurdity of each man's illusion about his freedom and sanity. Confronted by the tragic choice of surviving by compromising his nature as a hero, and thus condemning himself to obscurity, or asserting his heroic nature even if it means physical death, the classical tragic hero chooses the heroic, tragic end. Henry IV, awakening after twelve years of darkness, clearly aware of the loss of so many years of youth, faced with the possibility of re-entering everyday reality, of trusting himself to the casual surge of the instincts, the chaos of human passions, to the mutable and uncontrollable life that his adversaries foolishly think they are able to control, chooses survival. He chooses to control his world by continuing voluntarily to wear the mask that chance had imposed on him, the mask that the rest wear unawares.

His humanity does not suffer for this unheroic choice. His is not the heroic humanity of the protagonist of earlier tragedy, but that of a twentieth-century hero – vulnerable, unjustly excluded, driven to alienation. Nor does Henry's role as a main character suffer. But although the author's celebration of a final, unrecognized wisdom acquired through the experience of profound suffering given witness in the play strongly recalls King Lear as well as Prometheus and Philoctetes, Henry IV is as different from the Shakespearean hero as he is from the heroes of Greek tragedy. His stature in this play in no way derives from the status of a king who retains his essential majesty even when most deeply stricken by misfortune, nor is he attended by the sacred aura of heroes touched by fate or the furies, like Prometheus enchained, or Oedipus at Colonus, or Lear in the storm. He dominates precisely in his character as an ordinary mortal, whose costume recalls if anything that of the Son of Man before Pilate; it is that of a mock emperor, of a man who has been beaten and insulted by a cruel joke, of a poor mortal who has looked into the depths of truth in a way others did not or could not, and who has found it frightening enough to shrink from it, as behooves a man who shares our common weakness – the very opposite of the exceptional heroism of the protagonist of earlier tragedy.

And if Henry knows that he has behaved like a weak human being, he also knows that others wear a mask for the same reason, even if unknowingly, and thus fault his weakness unjustly. Hence he is trying to open their eyes to their own hypocrisy, and they resent him for it and try to shut him up again, calling him insane. Yet the only means remaining to him to fight his persecutors is the strength of his passionate thought, his passionate search for truth that may explain and authenticate his suffering – suffering that society, far from recognizing in itself and pitying, scorns and rejects as illness.

While unwittingly wearing a mask of its own, this society derides Henry's consciously chosen assumption of a mask, as if the deception consciously devised in order to escape insanity were not a serious business and certainly more justifiable than the mask its members wear perhaps for the same purpose, although unawares. This society pretends to be free and in control of reality, while it is actually controlled by many things: the uncontrollable events of life; the social conventions that dictate dress and behaviour; the recluse himself whom they want to control and lock up as insane and who continually shows them that they are controlled by him, shaking like reeds before him.

Certainly he is given several chances to choose: ten years earlier, when he had regained sanity, he had chosen to fake a continuing insanity; towards the end of the second act he chooses to reveal his sanity; after the killing of Belcredi he will have to choose again whether to go on faking insanity or to face the consequences of his action as a sane man. But each time it is the conscious choice of a man who has learned a terrible wisdom from the spectacle of a world seen from eight centuries away.

Henry IV is always the same intense, deeply serious man who both before and after the fall can stare into the depths of human feelings and draw back disconcerted. He has the consciousness and the experience of a historical character who can judge the world of the present, see the reality of the human predicament, from the rich experience of eight centuries of history. This is, in fact, a drama of modern and 'Pirandellian' consciousness.

Explaining to his councillors the advantage of contemplating the maddening spectacle of twentieth-century humanity from the distance of eight centuries and seeing its vanity, its misery, its insanity, Henry is proposing that they do more or less what the dramatist tries to do and invites his audience to do through his play. Contemporary life is seen as an uncontrollable agony, because it is in flux; history is seen as an extraordinarily orderly universe, knowable because it is fixed and completed, as the completed work of art was seen in *Six Characters.*

Henry IV equals *Six Characters* and the other masterpieces of Pirandello's maturity not only in its thematic richness, but also in the extraordinarily organic development of its action and the complex rhythm of its dramatic tension, which is made to coincide more or less with the tension and fear that its dominating hero arouses in the other characters and, empathetically, in the audience.

The first scene has a comic tone that seems to put the audience at ease. But as the scene progresses we realize that the comedy of the councillors is rather macabre, and begin to feel the same uneasiness experienced by Bertholdt, the new councillor, as he becomes aware of the real nature of his new job. The strangeness of the situation has by now seized us, and we are ready for the second scene, the visit, which is to furnish us with the historical background of the case. The scene is long, but psychologically very vivid, especially in the outbursts of sincerity and irony of Matilde Spina and her lover, Belcredi; it successfully conveys the complexity and human depth of the main character, and increases our desire to see him in person. This happens in the third scene, which is extremely intense emotionally, and develops a dramatic tension that seems on the verge of exploding at any time, because of the behaviour of the hero, who keeps all of them holding their breath.

The second act also begins in a relaxed mood: the visitors are discussing their impressions of the meeting with the 'madman.' Tension starts mounting again when Matilde begins to insist that she has been recognized; there is talk of a plan for a decisive encounter, designed to snap the madman out of his fixations, and Frida, who is to play an important part in it, appears dressed as the Marchioness of Tuscany, very nervous and full of fears about her role; the expert, Landolfo, reveals one of the 'madman's' fixations: that Henry IV in the days of Canossa cherished a secret love for the Marchioness, the hostess of his arch-enemy, the pope. Thus the tension is high when in the following scene the visitors come again before the 'madman,' pretending to take leave of him. From him we know we can expect anything, that he will keep all of them holding their breath, as in the first act, with the command of the situation that he enjoys. And this he does, tyrannizing over everybody. We wait for the rage to explode at any moment. Informed by Landolfo of his fixation, we hear a threatening ring in any allusion he makes to Matilde's daughter, who should be his wife, since Matilde is dressed as his mother-in-law. We feel the tension mount, up to the final scene when Henry IV reveals his sanity to his councillors and valets. Then all terror leaves the stage in spite of Henry's attempt to maintain it by threatening to continue to be as tyrannical with the visitors, and if necessary with his attendants, as he has been up to now. We are no more convinced by his threats than are the councillors, who, in fact, against his specific orders, inform the visitors of Henry's regained sanity, offstage, during the first scene of Act Three.

Thus at the beginning of the third act, the tension that would otherwise pervade the scene, with the two live portraits and Frida's visible fear, is just not there. Only after the first scene does the atmosphere again become charged. Henry IV admits that he is cured, but becomes threatening: sane now, he starts playing Henry IV as before, vomiting accusations against his visitors, particularly his rival Belcredi, working himself up, so that he might at any time take for himself that just revenge which everyone feared he might take when he was mad; the explosion finally comes when he sees that any desired understanding is impossible, that an attempt is being made to keep him in the position of perpetrator of the original joke rather than its victim. Blinded by rage, he loses control and commits an act of summary justice against his rival, after which he will have once again to make a choice: probably he will choose to take refuge again in his assumed madness and remain in the world of isolation that is by now familiar to him.

This rhythmic progression from minimal to maximal tension within each act is very frequent in Pirandello. And it effects a similar progression in the play as a whole, so that the opening is always calm and light, and the last scene the most dramatically tense. This element contributes greatly to an expressive unity: through it, all the action, all the thematic developments converge on the non-cathartic conclusion of the play and find there their ultimate meaning.

Each in His Own Way

Each in His Own Way, the second play of Pirandello's 'theatre trilogy,' returns to and develops further some of the themes, situations, and innovative theatrical techniques first brought into play in *Six Characters*; it is at least equal in importance to the earlier work in the revolution Pirandello effected in the theatre of our time.

In *Six Characters* the supposedly rejected family melodrama served as an occasion for another drama, the drama of characters in search of their author, that is, of definitive artistic form, the most powerful form of communication, without which it is impossible for them to 'live.' In *Each in His Own Way*, Pirandello creates a supposedly 'real life' event reported in the daily press, the suicide of the sculptor Giacomo La Vela following the discovery of an affair between his fiancée, Amelia Moreno, and Baron Nuti, his sister's fiancé; the playwright has translated this event for the stage into the Giorgio Salvi–Delia Morello–Michele Rocca affair. Although it is not rejected, like the family melodrama of *Six Characters*, as a sentimental, late-nineteenth-century bourgeois situation, which it actually is, the 'real life' event functions similarly as the occasion for a deeper drama, one that focuses on the theme of 'the continual reversals of our convictions and feelings,' the uncertainty and instability of our vision of ourselves and of the world around us. And while the six characters were unable to leave the stage in spite of their loud protestations, constrained to act their parts when their drama was to be played out, here the stage couple and the 'real' one, while denigrating and abhorring each other when not in each other's presence, must embrace and depart together, to everyone's dismay, when their face-to-face meeting compels them to act out their destined roles.

Each in His Own Way also develops the Pirandellian chorus character further. Here he reappears at first as a single character, Diego Cinci, who, unlike the imperturbable Laudisi, is immersed in the dramatic event, living it as passionately as all the others, a victim himself of the contradictions he illustrates. But unlike the others, he is able to 'see himself living,' as he sees the others, and is capable of explaining himself to himself and the others to themselves, revealing their hidden motives, acting as their conscience.

In *Six Characters* a number of parallels express the dichotomy between artistic creation and its actual communication: the characters of the family melodrama and those of the real drama of the characters in search of their author; the Pirandellian characters and the actor-characters who are to perform the family melodrama and who for the Pirandellian characters represent the public, the audience. In *Each in His Own Way* the parallels are multiplied. Being a *comédie à clef*, it has in the background the 'persons' of the La Vela–Moreno–Nuti affair and the characters-as-persons

Moreno and Nuti of the 'intermezzi,' acted out by the actors who play the roles of Rocca and Morello, who, in her role as an actress and not in her role as a character, yet because she has played the character, is slapped in the face by the character-as-person Moreno. There are also the spectator-characters who during the 'intermezzi' criticize the quality of the play and the acting, discussing and passing judgment on the characters, or, as Diego Cinci does, on the logic, or lack of it, of the dramatic event that has taken place, and the one that is taking place before their eyes.

The characters of *Each in His Own Way* live the drama of incompleteness that goes on uninterruptedly in everyone's life – the drama of insecurity, inconsistency, uncertainty, of doubt about oneself and others, of a continuing shifting of convictions.

Delia Morello and Michele Rocca live the contradiction of attraction and rejection, a tragic condition of willing and not willing, believing and disbelieving, a condition shared by all the characters of the play, whether they are conscious of it like Diego Cinci or unaware like his friends, because in everyone, 'humoristically,' a character and its opposite, and many intermediate characters, exist simultaneously.

One of the major themes of this drama is in fact that of appearance and reality, already developed in *Right You Are* and *Six Characters*, of the subjectivity of our perceptions and beliefs, and hence of our need to find them corroborated by others. A sub-theme that flows from this, and is more strongly dramatized in the present work, is that of uncertainty and contradiction, which dominate the life of all its characters.

Engaging in a fictional imitation of the 'real life' reported in the daily papers, Pirandello expresses the human problem of the subjectivity of perception and the difficulty of communication, of the mutability of our convictions, in a novel and unpredictable dramatic action, in an intensely vivid and innovative theatre.

Finally, a new theme is developed here as well, introduced but not fully explored in *Six Characters*: the relationship between the truth of artistic reality and that of real life, dramatized especially in the extraordinary 'intermezzi' in which the characters of the event from 'real life' encounter both the characters of the play based on it and the actors who portray them, when the lobby becomes the stage on which the characters of art can meet those of life. A superbly original theatrical imagination has put the relation between art and life on stage, before our astonished eyes.

But apart from its theatrical originality, the drama and the poetic unity of this work are grounded firmly in its central human predicament: every character is caught up in the same fundamental conflict – between uncertainty about oneself and others, about the reality in which one moves, and the intense although unconscious need to be anchored in some certainty. Life is seen as an 'incessant fluctuation between contradictory terms.' The characters are placed between two contrasting realities of daily life, and this shared inner drama of them all gives the action a sense of necessity and precision,

This dramatic economy is already at work in the first scenes, which immediately establish the atmosphere of uncertainty, doubt, and shifting convictions on the one hand, and of an anxious need for certainty and stability on the other. The first act opens with three dialogues. A young man cannot extract the certainty he is seeking from an older man; two young ladies exchange dramatic doubts about their own deepest feelings; then Diego Cinci asserts to a group of friends the impossibility of maintaining certitudes. All the characters who become involved in the action of this drama are caught up in the same conflict, so that they are never sure of their own convictions, or their own reality, nor can the others formulate a firm opinion of them; all are driven to a constant alteration of their ideas, to the repeated revelation of themselves in a new light, when they thought they had finally succeeded in expressing themselves and being perceived with a certain finality, including the protagonists of the lively exchanges in the lobby.

In this obsessive nightmare nobody understands or agrees with or influences anyone else, to the ironic point that when one person has altered and is ready to agree with another, the latter has moved to the opinions of the former. Each character emerges from one illusion of certainty and enters another: the protagonists of the actual event (Moreno–Nuti), the protagonists of the theatrical translation (Morello–Rocca), those who discuss the actual event (Doro–Francesco–Diego, etc.), the spectators who discuss its theatrical translation. The dramatic intensity of the play strengthens its perceptions: that art understands the persons of real life better than they can understand themselves; that art reveals the truth in an ever-changing, illusory world; that only art achieves that stable form which life – chaotic, shifting, inchoate – yearns for.

As the play develops, the relationship between art and life emerges as its central theme. In the last 'choral intermezzo' this relationship is effectively dramatized by bringing together and mixing art and life, getting the 'audience' to take part in the action on the stage, abolishing the separation through noisy, action-filled scenes rather than abstract discussion.

The last intermezzo is the missing 'third act.' The theme of the relationship between artistic truth and the truth of real life, repeatedly hinted at
from the initial stage directions, becomes increasingly clear until in the
final 'intermezzo' it emerges as the primary and conclusive theme of the
play. All the action that develops the earlier themes, and that in this sense
we might well consider concluded with the end of the second act, with the
embrace of Morello and Rocca under the horrified eyes of Francesco and
his guests, is also integral to the development of the major theme carried
by the four primary characters. The four protagonists of the bloody event
must first live the drama of uncertainty, doubt, and instability with the
secondary characters. Like the latter they experience the illusion of finding the explanation of their own actions and motivations, only to come to
understand at last the falseness of their interpretation.

Both protagonists and non-protagonists must first live the drama that
drives them to the edge of madness, the drama of beliefs shifting between a truth just discovered and the next one. And the brilliant actor
who has played the part of Diego Cinci warns at the end that it is a permanent condition which is going to repeat itself forever, that once outside
the door of the theatre, god knows how many more discoveries those two
who have just left together had still to make.

Once the dramatic experience of the uncertainty and instability of
convictions has been lived through and exhausted, the play can bring to
the fore the theme of the relationship between art and life and carry this
theme to its dramatic conclusion in the last 'intermezzo,' intermingling
the characters of the world of art and those of daily reality, abolishing the
separation between art and life the better to dramatize their difference.

The Mountain Giants

The bleak outcome of *Each in His Own Way* is the conclusion of another
of Pirandello's dramatic masterpieces as well as his last, unfinished one,
a final play on the nature of art as an expression of human creativity, of
the highest, most divine of human activities, which is nevertheless probably destined for incomprehension or rejection.

The central concern of *The Mountain Giants* is the problem of the
communicative ends of the theatre and of art in general. But it explores
the role of art not exclusively in terms of its power and permanence as
a means of communication, but as a life avocation, and perhaps even
as a means of renewal and salvation. For, if the dramatist's vocation is
of a communicative rather than a solipsistic nature, and he pursues it

faithfully, expressing to others the truths which, though subjective, are the fruits of his passionate search, then he has realized his calling, has made an important contribution to human life.

The Mountain Giants contrasts two ways of viewing the essence and the ends of art in the now-familiar context of a clash between two ways of viewing reality and thereby shaping human behaviour, represented by the Pirandellian characters on the one hand and the self-righteous and philistine world of the bourgeoisie on the other.

The clash between the Pirandellian characters and the philistinism of the bourgeois world occurs in two separate phases. Before the action begins, the dwellers in 'Villa Scalogna' have long since rejected an ungrateful and insensitive world and taken refuge in a solitary villa abandoned because it is supposedly haunted. The theatrical company that reaches the villa at the opening of the play has been dwindling in numbers, energy, and means, its members having endured the frustration and suffering of two years of vain efforts to overcome public indifference to what they believe to be a splendid poetic script; but they are still searching for the audience the Scalogna dwellers have long abandoned, because they still passionately cherish the idea of the essentially communicative function of art, the idea that poetry 'must live among people.' At the end of the play some of the Scalogna group and all their guests will again face the obtuseness and deafness of the outside world, with even worse consequences, since it is no longer the world of the Victorian bourgeoisie but a world of industrial capitalism and of anonymous masses enslaved to consumerism.

Another clash, between two ways of conceiving the nature and ends of poetry, underlies the entire play, a clash between those who earlier chose to abandon the attempt to breach the philistinism of the bourgeois world and have immersed themselves in the solipsism of an art that reaches no one beyond its creators, and their guests, who have exhausted themselves in the effort to bring poetry 'among people,' but still reject the attitude of the others, because of their fundamental, irrepressible human need for communication.

They also reject the view of art of Cotrone, the leader of the Scalogna group, because of the irrational character of his poetry and the detachment he claims to be content with. Cotrone contends that reason is the death of poetry. He argues for the suppression of reason in favour of a return to a child's innocence and openness. The Pirandellian characters, by contrast, consumed by the need to understand, to search for truth, to get to the root of their suffering, refuse to give up the quest.

The attempt to explain reality rationally responds to an irrepressible human need in them, as irrepressible as the need to communicate, however meagre the results may be.

Throughout this play Pirandello also explores the potential of the stage space, which he had so boldly liberated in *Six Characters;* he makes use of it in imaginative and revolutionary ways, as an integral element of his dramatic language.

In *The Mountain Giants* Pirandello poses the question of the nature and function of art, examines its ostensibly contradictory tendencies, the lusory and solipsistic as opposed to the communicative, and asks whether the choice of the Scalogna group means an enhancement or an impoverishment of the essence of the work of art and of humanity. He concludes that it entails an impoverishment of both, the loss of an essential human dimension, which man is already in danger of losing in a mass industrial society.

Yet after siding with Ilse in insisting on the essence and function of art as communication, Pirandello, in the sketchy outline we have of the unfinished fourth act, intended us to witness the destruction of this kind of poetry at the hands of the helots of modern society, perhaps to suggest that unfortunately only another kind of art, an art which is merely play, an art stripped of all vital communicative function, may be able to survive in that mass society.

The Mountain Giants explores the nature of art as a quest no longer for renewal but for a kind of last lifeline, for a final kind of certitude, as to whether the truth of a work of art can be created – or discovered – and communicated. The outcome of this quest is dismaying: just as the human need for communication, though irrepressible, remains extremely difficult if not impossible to satisfy, so the communicative impulse of poetry, though essential and inalienable, is blunted by its target – a humanity progressively more resistant to art and deaf to its messages.

Liolà

A Country Comedy

1916

Characters

NINO SCHILLACI *called* LIOLÀ
ZIO [UNCLE][1] SIMONE PALUMBO
ZIA [AUNT] CROCE AZZARA *his cousin*
TUZZA *daughter of Aunt Croce*
MITA *the young wife of Uncle Simone*
CARMINA *called* LA MOSCARDINA
GESA *Mita's aunt*
ZIA [AUNT] NINFA *Liolà's mother*
Three young peasant girls CIUZZA, LUZZA, NELA
Liolà's three 'goldfinches' TININO, CALICCHIO, PALLINO
Other local men and women

In the countryside around Agrigento; the time is the present.

ACT ONE

(*An area covered by a tin roof between the farmhouse, the storeroom, the stable, and the oil press shed of Zia Croce Azzara. In the background a view of the countryside, with clumps of prickly pears, almond, and Saracen olive trees. On the right, under the covered area, the door of the farmhouse, a rustic stone seat, and a monumental oven. On the left, the storeroom door, the window of the oil press shed, and another window with an iron grate. Rings attached to the walls to tie the animals to. It is September, almond-shelling time.*

---

1 'Zio' and 'zia' literally mean uncle and aunt, but in some regions, as in this case, they are used as the informal equivalent of Mr and Mrs.

Tuzza, Mita, Gesa, Carmina–La Moscardina, Luzza, Ciuzza, and Nela are
sitting on two corner benches. They are shelling the almonds by hitting each one
with a stone on another stone they hold on their knees. Uncle Simone is watching
them, sitting on a large chest turned upside down. Aunt Croce comes and goes.
Sacks, baskets, chests, and nutshells are strewn on the ground. As the curtain
rises, the women are singing 'The Passion' as they shell.)

CHORUS.
  And Mary outside the gates
  The terrible flogging heard:
  'Oh pity his tender flesh,' she cried,
  'And do not strike so hard.'
ZIA CROCE (*coming through the storeroom door with a basket of almonds*).
  Come on, come on, girls, these are the last! With God's help, we're
  all done shelling for this year.
CIUZZA. Bring them to me, Zia Croce.
LUZZA. To me!
NELA. To me!
ZIA CROCE. If you're quick, you may catch the last mass.
CIUZZA. Oh, right! Which mass at this hour?!
NELA. It takes time to get into town…
LUZZA. And to get dressed…
GESA. Do you really need to dress up to hear holy mass?
NELA. Do you want us to go to church dressed for the stable?
CIUZZA. If I can make it, I'll get to it, even dressed this way.
ZIA CROCE. Good girls, meanwhile keep wasting time talking!
LUZZA. Come on, let's sing, let's sing.
CHORUS.
  'Oh John, take me to Him!'
  'But Mary, you cannot walk!'
ZIO SIMONE (*interrupting the chorus*). Once and for all, enough of this
  'Passion'! You've been driving me crazy all morning! Shut up and
  shell!
LUZZA. Oh come on, you know we always sing while we shell the
  almonds!
NELA. What an old grouch!
GESA. It should be on your conscience, the sin we're committing for
  you working on the holy Sabbath!
ZIO SIMONE. For me? For Zia Croce, you mean.

ZIA CROCE. Oh yeah! What a nerve! He's been after me for three days, about these almonds he wants to sell! God only knows what could have happened to him, if I didn't get them to him right away!

ZIO SIMONE (*complaining, ironically*). Oh, sure, they're going to make me rich.

MOSCARDINA. Oh, Zio Simone, don't forget your promise to treat us to a glass of wine, when we're through!

ZIA CROCE. A 'promise'? It's in the contract! Don't you worry!

ZIO SIMONE. What contract, cousin? A contract, for a couple of shells? Are you serious?

ZIA CROCE. So, now you go back on your promise, huh? After you made me fetch the women to shell nuts on a Sunday? No, no, cousin, you don't pull this kind of thing with me. (*Turning to Mita*) Come on, Mita, run, run get a good half-gallon of wine for everyone here to drink to the health and prosperity of your husband! (*The women approve, clapping: 'yeah, yippee, yay!'*)

ZIO SIMONE. Thanks, cousin! You're really very generous!

ZIA CROCE (*to Mita*). Aren't you moving?

MITA. Not unless he orders me to!

ZIA CROCE. Do you have to wait for his order? Aren't you the boss, too?

MITA. No, Zia Croce, he's the boss!

ZIO SIMONE. I can tell you this – next year, if I'm tempted again to buy fruit before the harvest, I'll have these eyes of mine ripped right out first.

CIUZZA. He's already thinking about next year!

LUZZA. As if everyone didn't know how it is with almonds!

NELA. One year the trees are loaded, the next – nothing!

ZIO SIMONE. The almonds, sure. But it's not just the almonds! The entire vineyard's been hit by blight! And go take a look: all the new growth on the olives's been burned by the drought, it's pitiful!

MOSCARDINA. Good God, always complaining, rich as you are! So you looked at the trees, made an estimate, and you were wrong! Why not think, after all, your loss was a gain for your cousin who's a widow and your niece who's an orphan? and forget about it!

CIUZZA. Money that stays in the family...

LUZZA. You can't take it with you, you know...

MOSCARDINA. If you had children... Ooops, sorry! (*She claps her hand over her mouth. The other women look stunned. Zio Simone glares down at them; then, catching sight of his wife, takes his anger out on her.*)

ZIO SIMONE (*to Mita*). Get outta here, you good-for-nothing, get outta here! (*And, since Mita, mortified, does not move, he comes over to her, yanks her up, grabs her shoulders, and shakes her:*) See? See what you're good for? only so everybody can pick on me! Get outta here! Go on home right away – go on! Or, Christ, I'll wind up doing something crazy this morning! (*Mita goes off through the rear, mortified, sobbing. Zio Simone kicks the chest he was sitting on and enters the storeroom.*)

ZIA CROCE (*to Moscardina*). Damn it, woman, can't you watch your tongue?

MOSCARDINA. I don't know, he just made me say it!

CIUZZA (*as if naively*). Why is it such a disgrace for a man not to have children?

ZIA CROCE. You be quiet! This is not a subject for young ladies.

LUZZA. What's so wrong?

NELA. It's simply that God's decided not to give him any!

LUZZA. So why's he always picking on his wife about it?

ZIA CROCE. Come on, will you stop it? Keep shelling those nuts!

CIUZZA. We're done, Zia Croce.

ZIA CROCE. Then go and mind your own business. (*The three girls withdraw to the rear around Tuzza, who has not said a word, visibly angry. They try to get her to talk, but she puts them off with a shrug. So, two of them, one by one, move towards Zia Croce, Gesa, and Carmina to hear what they are whispering about, and return to report it to the other two, who laugh, gesturing to them to keep it low.*) My friends, he's driving me nuts. He's been here all day long, harping on it, morning to night, on the same string...

MOSCARDINA. About the child that isn't coming? How does he expect to get it?

GESA. If complaining were enough...

ZIA CROCE. No, he complains – let's be fair – he complains about his stuff, all that nice stuff, that'll end up in other people's hands when he dies. He can't accept that!

MOSCARDINA. Let him complain, Zia Croce! As long as he complains, you've got reason to smile, it seems to me!

ZIA CROCE. Because of the inheritance, you mean? I don't even think about it, my friend. He has more relatives than I have hair on my head.

MOSCARDINA. Still, a lot or a little, according to how closely related people are, a part of it will come to you too, right? I'm sorry for your niece, Zia Gesa, but the law's the law: if there are no children the husband's property...

GESA. Let the devil carry him off, him and all his stuff! Do you want her to die, my niece, for the sake of all that stuff? The poor soul, unlucky since the day she was born: left by her mother when she was still in swaddling clothes, and then an orphan at three, with her father dead, too! I brought her up, God only knows how! If she had a brother, at least, you can bet the old man wouldn't treat her that way – I assure you! It's a wonder he doesn't trample her under his feet! Did you see? (*She starts crying.*)

MOSCARDINA. It's true. Poor Mita! Who would have foreseen it, four years ago! Everybody thought her marriage to Zio Simone Palumbo was such a stroke of luck! I dunno! 'Plums and cherries are fine indeed' (but, if you have no bread...).

ZIA CROCE. Just a moment! Are you saying that after all it wasn't a stroke of luck for Mita? Come on, come on! A nice girl, Mita, I don't deny it. But really not even in her dreams could she have expected to become my cousin's wife!

GESA. Still, I'd like to know who begged your cousin to marry my niece. Not me, for sure – much less Mita.

ZIA CROCE. You know very well that Zio Simone's first wife was a real lady...

MOSCARDINA. And he cried for her, to tell the truth, he really cried for her when she died!

GESA. O sure! for all the children she was able to give him!

ZIA CROCE. What children could you expect her to give him; poor thing, she was that thin (*raising her little finger*), hung on to life by her teeth! You can't deny that, once he was a widower, he had plenty of candidates for a new wife. Beginning with me; if he'd asked for my daughter, I would've given her to him. He didn't want to put anyone from his family or even from our neighbourhood in the place of his dead wife. He took your niece only to have a son, and for no other reason.

GESA. Pardon me, what do you mean by that? That he has failed because of my niece? (*At this point Luzza, who has drawn close to hear, turning around to signal to the others, bumps into Zia Croce, who grabs her and pushes her angrily towards her friends, who start shouting and laughing.*)

ZIA CROCE. Damn it, how nosy you are! I told you to keep away, you're such a bunch of gossips!

MOSCARDINA (*resuming their talk*). Mita's really beautiful, blooming, fresh as a rose, just bursting with health!

ZIA CROCE. That doesn't mean anything. In some cases...

GESA. Are you serious, Zia Croce? Dear God, put them side by side and I defy anybody to tell me which one of the two's at fault!

ZIA CROCE. I beg your pardon! If he's harping so much on this question of the child, it seems to me that he knows he can have one! Or he'd keep quiet!

GESA. He can thank God that my niece is a honest woman, and so it's not possible to have a test! But you can be sure, Zia Croce, not even a saint from heaven would stand the way this old man mistreats her, the way he humiliates her in front of everybody. The Virgin Mary herself, pushed that far, would yell, 'So, you really want a child from me? Just you wait, I'll give it to you in no time!'

MOSCARDINA. Oh, no, God forbid! She'd never...

GESA (*correcting herself immediately*). Who? my niece?

MOSCARDINA. That would be a mortal sin!

GESA. She'd rather lie down and die than do such a thing, my niece!

MOSCARDINA. A real pearl, if there ever was one, wise even as a child – I don't mean to put anyone else down, but she's really the best...

ZIA CROCE. I never denied that.

CIUZZA (*from the rear, as she sees Zia Ninfa crossing in front of the shed with Tinino, Calicchio, and Pallino*). Ah, here comes Zia Ninfa with Liolà's three goldfinches!

LUZZA AND NELA (*clapping*). Zia Ninfa! Zia Ninfa!

CIUZZA (*calling*). Tinino! (*Tinino runs to her and jumps into her arms.*)

LUZZA (*calling*). Calicchio! (*Calicchio runs to her and jumps into her arms.*)

NELA (*calling*). Pallino! (*Pallino runs to her and jumps into her arms.*)

ZIA NINFA. Please, girls, let them be! They've made my head spin like a reel. And see how late for mass I am! They've made me!

CIUZZA (*to Tinino*). Who do you love?

TININO. You! (*kissing her*).

LUZZA (*to Calicchio*). And you, Calicchio?

CALICCHIO. You! (*kissing her*).

NELA (*to Pallino*). And you, Pallino?

PALLINO. You! (*kissing her*).

MOSCARDINA. The wolf's children are born with teeth!

GESA. Poor Zia Ninfa, she looks like a hen with her chicks!

ZIA NINFA. Three poor innocent children, without a mother...

MOSCARDINA. And thank God there are only three of them! Since his rule is to keep all the kids women dish out to him – only three? – they could be thirty!

ZIA CROCE (*indicating the girls with her eyes*). Please, neighbour, watch what you say!

MOSCARDINA. I meant no harm. In fact, it means he's good-hearted.

ZIA NINFA. He says he wants a whole clutch of them; teach them all to sing – then into a cage and off to town to sell them.

CIUZZA. You in a cage, Tinino, like a goldfinch? Do you know how to sing?

MOSCARDINA (*caressing Pallino's hair*). Is this the child of Rosa from Favara?

ZIA NINFA. Who, Pallino? Would you believe, I can't remember myself! No, I think Tinino was Rosa's child.

CIUZZA. No, no, not Tinino! He's my child, Tinino!

GESA. Sure! You'd be in quite a jam if it were true!

ZIA NINFA (*resentful*). What makes you say that?

MOSCARDINA. Liolà's wife?

ZIA NINFA. You shouldn't say such things, Carmina. There's never been a more dutiful and loving son than my Liolà.

MOSCARDINA. Loving? And how! If he sees a hundred of them, he wants them all.

ZIA NINFA. It means he's not yet found the one... (*looking at Tuzza meaningfully*) the right one for him. – Come on, come on, let me go, girls! (*Approaching Tuzza*) What's wrong with you, Tuzza? Don't you feel well?

MOSCARDINA. She's been pouting all morning, Tuzza.

TUZZA (*rudely*). Nothing's wrong with me! Nothing!

ZIA CROCE. Leave her alone, Zia Ninfa. She had a temperature during the night.

GESA. I'm coming with you, Zia Ninfa, if we're all done here.

MOSCARDINA. You'll be in town in time for the rich ladies' mass!

ZIA NINFA. Please don't talk to me about the rich ladies' mass! Do you know that last Sunday I wasn't able to follow it? The devil kept tempting me. My eyes were fixed on the ladies' fans. I started looking at those fans and I couldn't see the mass any more.

CIUZZA. Why? What did you see in those fans?

LUZZA. Tell us, tell us!

ZIA NINFA. The devil, my girls! As if he'd sat down beside me to show me how the ladies fanned themselves. See how they did it. (*She sits and all the others surround her.*) The unmarried young ladies like this (*moving her hand as if fanning herself very fast and talking equally fast, her back straight and stiff*): 'I'll have him! I'll have him! I'll have him! I'll have him! I'll have him!' The married ladies like this (*moving her hand with slow, grave, satisfaction*): 'I have him! I have him! I have him!' While the poor widows (*moving her hand in disconsolate abandonment, from her chest to her lap*): 'I had him and I don't any more! I had him and I don't any more! I had him and I don't any more!' (*All laugh*) Even though I kept crossing myself, I couldn't chase away the temptation.

CIUZZA, LUZZA, NELA (*together, making the gesture of fanning themselves*). Oh yes, oh yes! I'll have him! I'll have him! I'll have him! I'll have him! I'll have him!

MOSCARDINA. Look how happy they are, just look at them! (*The voice of Liolà is now heard from a distance as he returns from town in his cart, singing.*)

LIOLÀ. It's twenty-two days and more, my love I haven't seen;
And I've been barking; like a mad dog on a chain...

GESA. That's Liolà, coming back in his cart.

CIUZZA, LUZZA, NELA (*running across the front of the shed with the children still in their arms*). Liolà! Liolà! Liolà! (*Shouting joyously, they wave to him to come closer.*)

ZIA NINFA. Come on, girls, put those children down, or that lunatic will never let me get to my mass!

LIOLÀ (*entering, festively dressed in a green velvet suit with a short jacket and bell-bottom trousers, a sailor's cap, English style, on his head, with two ribbons dangling from the back*). Huh, these children have found their mothers already! But three mothers is too many! (*Taking and setting on the ground first Tinino, then Calicchio, and last Pallino*)
And this is LI, and this is O, and here's LÀ
And the three of them make LIOLÀ!
(*While the girls laugh and applaud, he goes up to his mother.*) And you, how come, still here?

ZIA NINFA. Oh no. I'm going, I'm going...

LIOLÀ. Into town at this hour? Come on! Forget the mass for today. – Zia Croce, *benedicite!*

ZIA CROCE. Benedicite, son! And keep your distance!

LIOLÀ. And what if I wanted to get closer?

ZIA CROCE. I'd get myself a rolling pin and hit you on the head.

CIUZZA (*approvingly*). To let the crazy blood out! Yes, good idea!

LIOLÀ. You'd like that, huh? You'd like it, if she let the crazy blood out of my head, right? (*He grabs her in jest.*)

LUZZA AND NELA (*pulling on him to defend their friend*). Hey, keep your hands to yourself!

MOSCARDINA. What a lunatic! Leave him alone, girls! Don't you see how he's all decked out?

CIUZZA. Oh, yes! Fancy dress! How come?

LUZZA. What a dandy!

NELA. Where's this Englishman come ashore from?

LIOLÀ (*strutting like a peacock*). Am I handsome, or what? I'm getting married!

CIUZZA. To what she-devil from hell?

LIOLÀ. To you, little beauty. Don't you want me?

CIUZZA. Good Lord, I'd rather take the fire and brimstone!

LIOLÀ. Then to you, Luzza! Come on, if I should really ask you...

LUZZA (*quick*). I'd refuse you!

LIOLÀ. You would?

LUZZA (*stamping her foot*). Damn right!

LIOLÀ. You're all playing stuck-up because you know I'm not going to ask you, none of you three: otherwise as soon as I whistle (*he whistles*), like that, you'd be flying to me! But what do you want me to do with three butterflies like you? A little pinch, a little squeeze; even so it'd be a waste of time! You're not my type.
A queen in beauty and in merit she
Who'd bind my heart and mind must be.

CIUZZA, LUZZA, NELA (*applauding*). Hurrah for Liolà. Sing us another one, Liolà!

GESA. He reels them off like hail Marys.

MOSCARDINA. Another one, come on! Don't make us beg you!

THE GIRLS. Yes, yes, another one!

LIOLÀ. Here I am. I've never made people beg me! (*setting his three 'goldfinches' in a circle around him*): Pay attention, you three.
My poor old brain's
a weather vane:
The wind it blows and 'round it goes.
And as I turn, the world it turns,
And turns and seems
And turns and seems
Like a carousel, it seems, it turns.
(*Humming a dance tune, he turns in a circle, beating his hands and feet in time to the music, while the children jump around him. Then he stops and starts singing again*):
Today, my dear, for you I pine,
I'm mad for love, I've lost my mind.

But next day, dear, you'll see –
Don't wait for me,
Don't wait for me.
My poor old brain's a weather vane,
The wind it blows and 'round it goes with me.
(*He hums his dance tune, and the children whirl around, as above. The girls laugh and applaud. But Zia Croce is annoyed.*)

MOSCARDINA. Good! Is that the way you're going to look for your queen?

LIOLÀ. And who says I haven't already found her, and that she doesn't know why I'm laughing and singing this way? Pretending is a virtue. If a man can't pretend, he can't rule.

ZIA CROCE. Enough, enough, children! Let's cut it out now! I have a lot of cleaning up to do here!

MOSCARDINA. And Zio Simone's promise? He has to give us a drink!

ZIA CROCE. What, drink now? Forget it, after what you let out of your mouth!

MOSCARDINA. Oh, this is just grand! Do you know, Liolà, why Uncle Simone doesn't want to give us the drink he promised? Because I told him he has no children to leave his inheritance to!

CIUZZA. Tell me if that's a good reason!

LIOLÀ. Let me handle this. (*Going to the storeroom door, he calls*) Zio Simone! Zio Simone! Come here, please! I've got good news for you.

ZIO SIMONE (*coming out of the stockroom*). What d'you want, you goddam crook?

LIOLÀ. They've passed a new law, just the thing for us. I mean, to thin out our population. Listen. If you've got a sow that gives you twenty piglets, you're rich, right? I mean, if you sell them, the more piglets she makes you, the richer you are. The same for a cow, the more calves she produces. Now think of a poor man, with these women of ours who, God help us, no sooner you touch them, right away they've got morning sickness. A real problem, right? Well, the government has thought it all out. It passed a law that from now on the children may be sold. They can be bought and sold, Zio Simone. And me, look (*showing him the three children*), I can set up shop. Do you want a child? I can sell one to you. Here, this one (*getting hold of one*). Look how sleek he looks! Well fed! Must weigh forty pounds! All muscle! Take him, take him! Feel how heavy he is! I'll sell him to you for nothing: for a barrel of Concord wine! (*The women laugh, while the old man, offended, draws back.*)

ZIO SIMONE. Get outta here, cut it out, I don't like to joke about such things!

LIOLÀ. But I'm not joking. I'm talking seriously! Buy one, if you don't have any, and stop going around this way, with all your feathers ruffled, like a sick capon!

ZIO SIMONE (*infuriated, while the women laugh again*). Let me go, let me go. Or, by God, I don't know what I might do!

LIOLÀ (*restraining him*). No, sir. Stay here, and don't take offence! We're all good neighbours, a bunch of peasants, helping each other out. I'm prolific, and you are not...

ZIO SIMONE. So, I'm not? You know that, right? I'd like to show you!

LIOLÀ (*pretending to be frightened*). Show me? No, God forbid! You want to show me a miracle? (*pushing one after another of the three girls towards him*). Try it with this one, here! Or this one! Or this one!

ZIA CROCE. Ay, yai, children! Where d'you think you are? Stop this joke! I don't like it!

LIOLÀ. No harm done, Zia Croce. We're in the country: some of us live on the hill, some in the dales. Zio Simone lives down in the dales: kinda old, flabby, weak; if you poke him with a finger, it leaves a mark.

ZIO SIMONE (*lunging at him with his arm raised*). You filthy... I'll leave a mark on you! (*Liolà avoids the blow. Zio Simone is about to fall. Liolà steadies him by holding his arm.*)

LIOLÀ. Now, now, Zio Simone, you must drink iron-fortified wine!

CIUZZA, LUZZA, NELA. What's that? What's iron-fortified wine?

LIOLÀ. What is it? You take a piece of iron, get it red hot and stick it in a glass of wine, and send it down! Works wonders. You should thank God, Zio Simone, that they haven't dispossessed you yet.

ZIO SIMONE. They're going to dispossess me too?

LIOLÀ. And why not? They can pass that law tomorrow too. Listen. Here's a piece of land. If you stand there looking at it, what does it produce? Nothing. Like a woman. She doesn't make children for you. Well, I come to this piece of land of yours, I hoe it, I fertilize it, I dig a hole, I throw a seed into it: a tree comes up. Who has the earth given that tree to? To me! You come along and say no, that it's yours. Why yours? Because the land is yours? But does the land know, Zio Simone, who it belongs to? It gives the fruits to whoever works it. You take them because you clamp your foot on it, and because the law is on your side. But the law might be changed tomorrow, then you'll be pushed out with one hand. And the land will stay; I throw my seed into it and there you are: my tree is leafing out!

ZIO SIMONE. I see you're good with words.

LIOLÀ. Who, me? No. Don't be afraid of me, Zio Simone. I don't want
anything from you. I leave it to you to rack your brains over your
money, and to go around with your eyes darting from one side to the
other like a snake.

Last night I slept beneath the sky,
For shelter only stars on high;
A scrap of land was all my bed,
A thistle pillow 'neath my head.
Hunger, thirst, or cares that wring
The heart? Not mine, for I can sing!
I sing, my heart knows ecstasy,
Mine all the earth and all the sea.
May all enjoy good health and sun,
May I have the girls – the pretty ones!
And curly headed babies too,
And a little old mother just like you.

(*He embraces and kisses his mother, while the girls, moved, applaud; then
turning to Zia Croce*) Come on, come on. What else is there to do,
Zia Croce? Carrying the shelled almonds to Zio Simone's storeroom?
Ready! Let's go, girls, let's hustle, Zio Simone will give us a drink
afterwards! (*He enters the storeroom, then from the threshold starts loading
the sacks of almonds on the women's shoulders.*) Come on, who goes first?
Here's one for you, Nela! Go! Here, Ciuzza, go! For you, Luzza, go!
Here's one for you, Moscardina, you can do it! For you this little one,
Zia Gesa! And this, the biggest one, I'll take! Let's go, girls! Let's go,
Zio Simone!

ZIO SIMONE (*to Zia Croce*). I'll be back with the money a little later,
cousin.

ZIA CROCE. There's no hurry, cousin. Whenever's convenient.

LIOLÀ (*to Zia Ninfa*). You come after me with the children. I'm sure we
can sell him at least one. (*He goes out with the women and Zio Simone.
When everybody has left, he comes back.*) Please wait for me, Zia Croce,
I'll be back, I need to tell you something.

ZIA CROCE. Me? (*Tuzza jumps up, angrily.*)

LIOLÀ (*turning to look at her*). What's gotten into you?

ZIA CROCE (*also turning to look at her daughter*). Yeah. What's that supposed to mean?

LIOLÀ. Nothing, Zia Croce. It must have been a cramp. Never mind. I'll
be back in a moment. (*He goes off carrying his sack.*)

TUZZA (*at once, angrily*). Listen, I don't want him! I don't! I don't!

ZIA CROCE (*dumbfounded*). You don't want him? What are you talking about?

TUZZA. You'll see. He'll come to ask for my hand. I don't want him!

ZIA CROCE. Are you crazy? Who in the world is asking you to take him? But tell me: how can he have the nerve to come to ask for your hand?

TUZZA. I'm telling you, I – don't – want – him!

ZIA CROCE. Answer my question, you wicked thing. You went with him? So it's true! Where? When?

TUZZA. Don't shout like that in front of everybody!

ZIA CROCE. Shameless, shameless! You've thrown yourself away! (*Seizing her by the arms and staring into her eyes*) Tell me! Tell me! Come inside! Inside! (*She drags her inside the house and shuts the door. Crying and shouting are heard from within. Meanwhile from the distant farmhouse of Zio Simone singing and the sound of cymbals are heard. Soon after, Zia Croce comes out badly upset, clutching her head and, like a madwoman, unconscious of what she is doing, she starts putting the shed in order, muttering angrily.*) Oh God! On the Sabbath! on the holy Sabbath! What'll we do now? I'll kill her, I'll kill her! Hold me back, Lord, or I'll kill her! She has the nerve to say it's my fault, the hussy! Me, because I took it into my head to marry her to Zio Simone – and so, she says, I put the idea into her head too. (*Going back to the door*) But even if it were true, was that a good reason for you to go with that hoodlum?

TUZZA (*coming to the door, dishevelled and bruised, but proud and defiant*). Yes, yes, yes.

ZIA CROCE. Stay inside, you jailbird! Don't come near me right now, or, by God, I'll…

TUZZA. Will you let me talk, or not?

ZIA CROCE. Look at her, the nerve of her! She wants to talk!

TUZZA. First you yell, 'Talk, talk,' and when I wouldn't, slaps and punches. Now that I want to talk…

ZIA CROCE. What more can you say? Isn't it enough what you've told me?

TUZZA. I want to tell you why I went with Liolà.

ZIA CROCE. Why? Why? Because you're a shameless tramp, that's why!

TUZZA. No. But because when Zio Simone married that little saint, Mita, instead of me, I knew she and Liolà were courting.

ZIA CROCE. So what? What did Liolà have to do with it any more, once Mita was married to Zio Simone?

TUZZA. He had lots to do with it; because even after four years of marriage, he was still fluttering around her like a moth around a lamp. I wanted to take him away from her!

ZIA CROCE. Ah, so that's the reason?

TUZZA. Yes, that's the reason! How many things was that ragamuffin beggar supposed to have? Both a rich husband and a merry lover?

ZIA CROCE. You fool, you! Don't you understand that this way you've harmed only yourself? Now your only choice is to marry –

TUZZA (*immediately*) – What? Marry him? A husband who would be mine and everybody else's as well? I'm not crazy! I'd rather be ruined. But you know why? Because now I can dump my bad luck on the one who was the cause of it. If I'm ruined, so is she. That's what I wanted to tell you.

ZIA CROCE. But how? My God, I think she's gone crazy!

TUZZA. No, I'm not crazy! See, Zio Simone…

ZIA CROCE. … Zio Simone? …

TUZZA. … has been telling me for quite a while now he's sorry he didn't marry me instead of Mita. (*As she is talking, she begins to smooth and rearrange her hair, while her eyes sparkle with malice.*)

ZIA CROCE. I know, he told me too. But do you perhaps… ?

TUZZA (*pretending to be horrified*). No! What? Me, with my uncle?

ZIA CROCE. Well, then, what do you mean to do? I don't get you!

TUZZA. How many relatives does Zio Simone have? More than we have hairs on our head, right? (*pointing to the hair she is braiding*). And no children. Well. It couldn't be done before, it can be done now.

ZIA CROCE (*shocked*). Would you try to make him believe that the child … ?

TUZZA. Not make him believe! It won't be necessary. I'll throw myself at his feet and confess everything.

ZIA CROCE. And then?

TUZZA. Then he'll make all the others believe – and his wife first of all – that the child is his. It'll be enough for him, to get it this way – just to have the satisfaction.

ZIA CROCE. You're a devil! A real devil! You want everybody to believe…?

TUZZA. If I'm lost, now that I've done the damage with that guy…

ZIA CROCE (*interrupting her quickly*). Get inside, get inside: here he comes with Liolà! (*Tuzza goes indoors quickly.*) Ah, My Lady of Sorrows, how will I manage now? How? (*Taking the broom, she starts sweeping up the almond shells left on the ground, pretending to be very busy.*)

LIOLÀ (*entering with Zio Simone*). Please, Zio Simone, give the money to your cousin and go, because I've got to speak to Zia Croce now.

ZIA CROCE. You're giving orders? Who are you to tell my cousin to go away? For your information, my cousin can make himself at home here. Please, please, go in, cousin: Tuzza is inside.

ZIO SIMONE. May I give the money to her?

ZIA CROCE. If you want to. And if you don't, that's fine too. You're the boss, and can do whatever you please. Go in and let me hear what this crazy guy has to tell me.

ZIO SIMONE. Don't pay any attention to him, cousin, or he'll make your head spin like mine. He's really crazy! (*As he enters the farmhouse, Aunt Croce closes the door.*)

LIOLÀ (*almost to himself*). Oh, yes, I can see it now...

ZIA CROCE. What are you saying?

LIOLÀ. Oh, nothing. I had a little speech prepared, but now, I don't know, I think... I think there is no need for it any more. You say I'm crazy. Zio Simone says I'm crazy. And now I see that you're both absolutely right! Just think, I wanted to sell him a son! A son, to him! He wants one free; and it seems to me he's already found the way to get one free.

ZIA CROCE. What're you saying? What are you raving about?

LIOLÀ. I saw your daughter jump a foot in the air when I told you I wanted to come back to talk to you...

ZIA CROCE. I noticed it too. And so?

LIOLÀ. And now I see the way you invite Zio Simone into the house, turning on the charm, flattering him – He hangs around here from morning to night...

ZIA CROCE. Is it your place to give orders in my house, about Zio Simone coming or going?

LIOLÀ. Not giving orders, Zia Croce. I only came to do my duty. I don't want people to say that I didn't live up to it.

ZIA CROCE. And just what might it be, this duty of yours? Let's hear.

LIOLÀ. Here it is, right away. But you know it already. I'm no tame bird, Zia Croce. I'm a bird on the wing. Here today, there tomorrow: in the sunlight, in the rain, in the wind. I sing and I'm drunk; and I don't know which makes me more drunk, the singing or the sunlight. Still, here I am: trimming my own wings and locking myself into a cage. I'm asking for your daughter's hand.

ZIA CROCE. You? Humph, I see you really *are* out of your mind. My daughter? You want me to give my daughter to a guy like you?

LIOLÀ. I ought to thank you, Zia Croce, and kiss your hand for this answer. But mind, it has to be your daughter herself who gives it. Not for my sake, but for hers.

ZIA CROCE. My daughter? Look, I'd rather send her to the gallows than give her to you! Understand? To the gallows. Tell me, isn't it enough you've ruined three poor girls?

LIOLÀ. Oh, come on, Zia Croce, stop it. I haven't ruined anybody, ever!

ZIA CROCE. Three children! Were they born all by themselves? You're like those snakes that fool the cows into suckling them!

LIOLÀ. Oh, be quiet. You know very well where those sons came to me from! Everybody knows! Those girls were the roving kind. It's a sin to force a well-guarded door; but someone who takes a beaten path… No one, in fact, I can assure you, would've hesitated to kick aside any obstacle on that kind of road. But I didn't do that. Three poor innocent creatures… they live with my mother and wouldn't be in the way, Zia Croce. Boys, when they grow up, as you know, in the country, the more hands there are, the richer we are. I'm a good worker, farm-hand, day labourer: I harvest, I prune, I mow the hay; I do everything and never botch things up: I'm like an Easter oven, Zia Croce, I could feed an entire village.

ZIA CROCE. Very nice, my boy; now go find somebody else to make this pretty speech to: it has no effect on me.

LIOLÀ. Zia Croce, don't say that. Now look here – I don't want to do anybody wrong, but by the same token I don't want anybody to do wrong by using me! I want your daughter herself to tell me, in front of Zio Simone, that she doesn't want me.

ZIA CROCE. She doesn't want you! She doesn't want you! She herself told me a moment ago, right here! She said it over and over. She doesn't want you!

LIOLÀ (*to himself, pinching his lip with two fingers*). Ah, so it's true? (*He is about to rush the door, but Zia Croce gets there first and plants herself before him; the two stare at each other for a moment.*) Zia Croce!

ZIA CROCE. Liolà!

LIOLÀ. I want Tuzza to tell me, understand? Tuzza with her own mouth, and in front of Zio Simone!

ZIA CROCE. See here! Tuzza has nothing more to say to you. I'm telling you, and that's enough! Go on, get out of here, you'll be better off.

LIOLÀ. Oh, sure, I'll be, yes; but somebody else won't be: you know what I mean! Look here, Zia Croce, you won't pull this off! (*Holding an arm under her nose*) Smell!

ZIA CROCE. Get away, what d'you want me to smell?

LIOLÀ. Don't you smell it?

ZIA CROCE. Yes, I smell the spoiled meat you are!

LIOLÀ. No, you smell the spoiler I am! I don't lose a game just because the cards are shuffled badly, remember that! For now, I'll take this mouthful of straw, and say goodbye.

ZIA CROCE. Oh, yes, good. Get away from here, and stay away, far away.

LIOLÀ (*chewing on the straw, laughing, makes a long round so he can pass Tuzza's door. He sings, laughing derisively after each line*).

Right now nobody even knows (heh, heh, heh).

But let her climb, and down she goes (heh, heh, heh).

With nothing left but a broken no - o - o - se... (*a longer sneering laugh*) See you, Zia Croce! (*He exits stage rear. Zia Croce remains deep in thought. Soon after, the door of the farmhouse opens and Zio Simone and Tuzza come out: the latter, worn out by weeping – real or pretended – the former upset and dismayed. They remain silent for a while, for Zia Croce has signalled them not to talk.*)

ZIO SIMONE (*in a low voice*). What did he say? What did he want?

LIOLÀ (*in the far distance*).

With nothing left but a broken no - o - o - se...

ZIO SIMONE (*to Tuzza*). Ah, was it with him? (*Tuzza hides her face in her hands.*) But... tell me: does he know?

TUZZA (*quickly*). No, he doesn't know anything! Nobody knows anything!

ZIO SIMONE. Ah, good. (*To Zia Croce*) Only on that condition, cousin: that nobody knows! Then, the son... is mine!

LIOLÀ (*from even farther away*).

With nothing but a broken no - o - o - se...

CURTAIN

ACT TWO

(*Another section of town: on the left, halfway between the front and back of the stage, Gesa's small, rustic house. The front and a bit of the left side of it can be seen. A small front door leads into the garden, fenced in, from the corner of the house to the stage lights, by a row of dry blackberry bushes, with a passageway in the centre, as if it were a gate. On the left side of the house another door is seen, the street door. On the right side of the stage, Liolà's house, with front door and two windows. A narrow country road divides the garden hedge from the house of Liolà.*)

As the curtain rises, Gesa is sitting in her garden peeling potatoes over a large tin colander held between her knees. Liolà's three children are around her.)

GESA. Are you really a good boy, Pallino?

PALLINO. Yes, good.

CALICCHIO. Me too!

GESA. You too?

TININO. And me too, me too!

GESA. But who's the best of you three?

PALLINO. Me, me!

CALICCHIO. No, me! me!

TININO. No, no, me! me! me!

GESA. All three, all three! One as good as the other! Pallino's the tallest, you can't deny that! So, Pallino, listen, could you go fetch me there – right there, see? – (*indicating a point in the garden, to her right, off stage*) three little onions?

PALLINO. Yes, yes. (*He starts running.*)

GESA. Wait!

CALICCHIO. Me too! Me too!

TININO. Me too!

GESA. Quiet, quiet, one little onion each! one each! Pallino'll show you where.

ALL THREE (*running towards the place indicated*). Yes, yes, yes.

GESA. Slowly! Only three! Good, that's it, that's it! That'll do! (*The three boys return, each carrying a small onion.*) Yes, it's true, one's just as good as the other. (*At this point the voice of Zia Ninfa is heard from Liolà's house, calling in a tone that must be habitual to her.*)

ZIA NINFA. Pallino, Calicchio, Tinino.

GESA. They're here with me, Zia Ninfa. Don't worry.

ZIA NINFA (*showing her face at the door*). Buzzing around you like flies. Come in, come in, now.

GESA. Let them be, Zia Ninfa. They're no bother. In fact they're helping me.

ZIA NINFA. If they bother you, chase them away!

GESA. Don't worry, they're very quiet with me, like three little turtles.

ZIA NINFA. All right (*going back into her house*).

GESA. Otherwise, your dad, when he gets home… – tell me, what does your dad do?

PALLINO (*very serious*). He teaches us to sing.

GESA. And doesn't he slap you on the rear, if you're not good and drive grandma crazy? (*Ciuzza comes down the lane from the back, stops, and looks over the hedge.*)

CIUZZA. Please, Zia Gesa, would you have a bit of garlic to lend my mother?

GESA. Yes, Ciuzza, come in, come in, (*points to the door at her back*) go help yourself.

CIUZZA (*pushing the gate and entering*). Thank you, Zia Gesa. Are these boys always here with you? So cute! Who wouldn't like to be a mother for them?

GESA. You would with all your heart, I bet!

CIUZZA. For God's sake, Zia Gesa, please!

GESA. Oh, sure. For God's sake! Who could doubt it?

CIUZZA. But tell me something. Liolà... (*Luzza and Nela come down the lane also. They too look over the hedge.*)

LUZZA. Zia Gesa, may we come in? Oh look, Ciuzza's here too!

GESA. (Here're the other two!)

NELA. We've come to help you, Zia Gesa! Are you peeling potatoes?

GESA. You want to help me? God bless you. So helpful! (It's as if there were birdlime all over this garden.) Come in, come in. But he isn't back yet (*maliciously alluding to Liolà*).

NELA (*pretending not to understand*). Who, Zia Gesa?

GESA. Who? Don't act like a dummy!

LUZZA (*sitting on her heels in front of Gesa*). Here, hand them to me. I have a penknife, I'll help you peel.

GESA. Not that way. Go on, Pallino, go get her a chair!

NELA. I'll go, I'll go, Zia Gesa! (*She goes and returns with three chairs.*)

GESA. Look, how beautiful! All three sitting here, just to help me! I'd hate to think that your mother's home waiting for that clove of garlic, Ciuzza.

CIUZZA. 'Course not. She needs it for tonight.

GESA. Well, it seems evening already to me! Do as if he were already here (*again alluding to Liolà*).

CIUZZA (*also pretending not to understand*). Who, Zia Gesa?

GESA. The cat! my dear. Don't you act like a dummy too!

LUZZA. D'you mean Liolà?

GESA. Oh, I'm really sly, didn't you know?

CIUZZA. I meant to ask you, Zia Gesa, if it's true that Zia Croce's Tuzza didn't want him.

GESA (*herself pretending not to understand this time*). Didn't want... who?

LUZZA (*while the others laugh*). Now *you're* acting like a dummy!

NELA. I heard it was the mother, Zia Croce.

LUZZA. You don't know about it?

CIUZZA. No, they say it was Tuzza herself.

NELA. Tuzza? But if... (*covering her mouth*), come on, don't make me talk.

LUZZA. But what about him? What's Liolà saying. We'd like to know!

GESA. From me you'd like to know? Go ask him!

CIUZZA. I'd like nothing better!

LUZZA. Me too!

NELA. Me too, me too!

CIUZZA. He thought that any woman, as soon as he crooked his finger, would throw herself from her window to his feet!

GESA. Not you, though, none of you three!

LUZZA. Who's thinking about him?

CIUZZA. Who's looking for him?

NELA. Who wants him!

GESA. Oh, I can see that!

LUZZA. Just because we're here asking you... ?

NELA. We're here because we'd like to hear how he sings when he's angry!

CIUZZA. He must be boiling mad, I can imagine it!

LUZZA. What does he do? Has he been singing?

GESA (*covering her ears*). Girls, girls, what d'you want from me? Zia Ninfa's over there, ask her whether he's been singing.

ZIA NINFA (*coming to the door, as if hearing a call*). What's this? Do you have cicadas in your garden, Zia Gesa?

LUZZA, CIUZZA, NELA (*all together, embarrassed*). Nothing, nothing, Zia Ninfa! – Good evening, Zia Ninfa! – (Oh, she's heard us)!

GESA. Worse than cicadas, Zia Ninfa. More like wasps! They've come to me because they want to know...

LUZZA, CIUZZA, NELA. No, nothing! – It's not true! – It's not true!

GESA. ... yes, it is! whether Liolà's been singing in a rage because Zia Croce's Tuzza didn't want him for a husband.

ZIA NINFA. My son? Who said that?

LUZZA, CIUZZA, NELA. Everybody, everybody! – And this time it's true! – Don't you deny it, Zia Ninfa!

ZIA NINFA. I don't know a thing about it! But, even if it were true, Tuzza did the right thing, and her mother, Zia Croce, was even more right,

if she didn't let him have her. As a mother, I wouldn't trust a man like Liolà with a dog of mine, let alone a daughter! Keep away from him, girls! Keep away! The blackest sins, he's done them all! You should keep away from him as if he were the devil! Besides, with these three little ones, here… – Come on, children, come on home!
(*Moscardina's voice is heard from down the lane before she comes into view, her arms in the air.*)

MOSCARDINA. My Lord, my Lord! What things! Things you couldn't believe! There're no limits any more!

CIUZZA. It's Moscardina. Do you hear how she's shouting?

NELA. What's the shouting about?

MOSCARDINA (*entering the garden*). What a disaster, what a disaster, Zia Gesa, in your niece's house!

GESA (*jumping up*). My niece? What's happened to her? Tell me!

MOSCARDINA. She's like one of the three Marys, clutching her head in her hands!

GESA. Why? Why? Mother of God! Let me go! Let me go! (*running down the lane, turning and disappearing on the left*).

THE OTHERS (*all together*). What's happened to Mita? Tell us! What happened?

MOSCARDINA. Zio Simone, her husband… (*looking at them, she breaks off*).

THE OTHERS (*immediately, prodding her*). Well? – Tell us! – What did he do?

MOSCARDINA. He's taken up with his niece!

THE OTHERS (*at once*). With Tuzza? – Is it possible? – Imagine that! – My God! What're you saying?

MOSCARDINA. Just that! And it seems that Tuzza is already… (*making a gesture secretly to Zia Ninfa that means 'pregnant'*).

ZIA NINFA (*horrified*). Oh, Virgin Mary, help us!

LUZZA, CIUZZA, NELA. What d'you mean? – Tuzza? – Seems what? What's she done?

MOSCARDINA. Off with you, off! These aren't things for you to hear! Off!

ZIA NINFA. But is it true? is it true?

MOSCARDINA. He himself, Zio Simone, has gone to boast about it to his wife!

ZIA NINFA. He had the nerve to say that?

MOSCARDINA. Yes – that it wasn't true they had no children because of him; and that if he had married his niece, he would've had not one but three children by now!

CIUZZA (*to Zia Ninfa*). But, pardon me, hasn't Tuzza been going around with your son, Liolà, up until yesterday, Zia Ninfa?

ZIA NINFA. I told you I don't know anything about it.

MOSCARDINA. Oh, Zia Ninfa, let's not tell stories! You can't deny it! Who'd swallow such a thing, that Zio Simone by himself... Mother and daughter together have pulled the wool over the old man's eyes!

ZIA NINFA. What?! what?!

MOSCARDINA. All lies?

ZIA NINFA. That my son was involved, yes!

MOSCARDINA. Zia Ninfa, I'd give both my hands, first one and then the other!

CIUZZA. Me too!

LUZZA. Me too!

NELA. Everybody knows it!

ZIA NINFA. Everybody, and not me!

MOSCARDINA. Only because you don't want to know it! Come on!

LUZZA. Ho, here comes Mita, Mita with her aunt! (*Mita, crying, all dishevelled, is coming down the lane with Zia Gesa, who runs from stage rear to the hedge and back again, shouting, hands on her hips, while the women in the garden try to comfort Mita.*)

GESA. Oh, my darling child, my child! May God strike him down! He dared hit her, the dirty old man, the murderer! Dirty old man! Criminal! On top of everything else, he hit her! He grabbed her by her hair and dragged her through the house! The crook! let me through, let me through! I'm going into town! I'm putting her into your hands, my good neighbours! I'm going to get justice! To jail! He'll go straight to jail!

MOSCARDINA. That's right, yes, yes! Go to the township lawyer!

ZIA NINFA. Not to the township lawyer, to an attorney! Listen to me, an attorney!

GESA. I'm going to both! To jail with him, the dirty old blasphemer! He had the nerve to say that Tuzza's child is his, as true as the blood of Christ is in the cup on the church altar!

ZIA NINFA (*covering her ears*). What things are going on, my God!

GESA. To jail with those two shameless bitches too, mother and daughter! Let me go! It'll be night by the time I get into town – it doesn't matter, I'll sleep at my sister's. You're safe here in your own house in the meantime, with these good neighbours around. Lock up well, both doors. I'm leaving. To jail with them! Criminal! Shameless bitches! ... (*Still shouting, she disappears at the end of the lane.*)

MOSCARDINA. Even separated you've the right to living expenses, don't you worry!

ZIA NINFA. What do you mean, separated! What're you saying! You'd be giving in to their wishes! You're the wife and you've got to remain the wife!

MITA. Oh, no, no, enough! I'm not going back to him, that's for sure! Even if they kill me!

ZIA NINFA. But don't you understand that that's just what they want?

MOSCARDINA. Sure! Mother and daughter go there to the old man's as the mistresses of the house, and make all the other relatives eat garlic!

MITA. Then you want me to let myself be trampled underfoot? No, no, there's nothing left between us, Zia Ninfa! He's gotten what he wanted from someone else and now they want me dead, the three of them!

MOSCARDINA. Dead? Easier said than done! There's the law, darling! Your aunt's run to town for that very reason!

MITA. What law! Four years I've suffered. D'you know what he had the nerve to shout in my face? That I shouldn't dare say anything bad about his niece! Yes! Because, he says, she's an honest woman!

ZIA NINFA. Honest! That's what he said?

MOSCARDINA. It's incredible, incredible!

CIUZZA (*to Luzza and Nela*). Honest, eh! honest!

MITA. Yes, exactly that! Because she took up with him. And he's going to leave her everything, he says, because she gave him proof, he says, that it wasn't his fault, but mine. And that the law, in fact, ought to find a remedy for a poor man like him who happens to fall in with a girl like me! Oh, Zia Ninfa, my heart kept telling me not to marry him! And I wouldn't have accepted him, if I hadn't been...

MOSCARDINA. ... helpless, poor little orphan, it's true...

MITA. ... dependent on my aunt, whom I couldn't disobey! I was so peaceful and happy, here, in this little house, and this little garden. You can vouch for that, Zia Ninfa, you saw me every day. But God will surely punish the people who did this to me.

MOSCARDINA (*resolute*). Liolà must speak up, Zia Ninfa!

ZIA NINFA. Liolà again! Will you girls stop talking about my son?

MOSCARDINA. Come on, girls, tell her if it is not true!

CIUZZA, LUZZA, NELA. Yes, it's true! It's true! It was him! it was him!

MITA. I know that Liolà was fond of me, when I was living here, Zia Ninfa. Was it my fault if, being a minor, they married me to somebody else?

ZIA NINFA. But can you really believe that Liolà has done this to you out of spite, after four years?

MOSCARDINA. No, not that, I·don't believe that either. But if he's an honest man, Liolà must go and tell that dirty old man to his face what a trap those two disgusting creatures, mother and daughter, have set to ruin this poor woman! That's what your son must do, Zia Ninfa, if he has any conscience! Shame those two shameless bitches and upset their plot against a poor innocent woman! (*Evening has come, and Liola's voice is heard. He is coming home, singing.*)

LIOLÀ.

Now all my friends they say
A man who marries will pay…

MOSCARDINA. Ah, here he's on his way home, singing! *I'll* talk to him now. *I'll* tell him.

CIUZZA, TUZZA, NELA (*leaning over the hedge and calling*). Liolà! Liolà! Liolà!

ZIA NINFA. Come, come here, my son.

MOSCARDINA. Here, here, Liolà!

LIOLÀ (*to Moscardina*). At your service, Ma'am! (*Then to the girls*) Oh, the little doves are here!

MOSCARDINA. Let the little doves be! Come here! Look who's here: Mita!

LIOLÀ. Oh, Mita. What's up?

MOSCARDINA. What's up is, you've got to act on your conscience, Liolà! Here's Mita crying and it's your fault!

LIOLÀ. My fault?

MOSCARDINA. Yes, because of what you did with Zia Croce's Tuzza.

LIOLÀ. Me? What did I do?

MOSCARDINA. Mother and daughter want Zio Simone to believe that the child…

LIOLÀ. The child? What child?

MOSCARDINA. Ah, you're asking us? Tuzza's child!

LIOLÀ. Tuzza's? What're you saying? So Tuzza is… (*makes the gesture that means 'pregnant'*)?

ZIA NINFA. Off with you, girls. Go on, go! Do me this favour!

LUZZA. Oh, God in heaven, her and her 'go, go…'

CIUZZA. And her 'these discussions that aren't fit for us girls'!

LIOLÀ. To tell the truth I don't get the gist of this discussion either.

MOSCARDINA. Oh, yes, go on playing dumb. The innocent one! Well, will you girls get out of here? I can't talk with you hanging around!

CIUZZA. All right, we're leaving, we're leaving! Good evening, Zia Ninfa.

LUZZA. Good evening, Mita.

NELA. Good evening, Carmina.

LIOLÀ. And me? Not even a little goodbye for me?

CIUZZA. Get out of here, you hypocrite!

LUZZA. Rat! Pig!

NELA. What nerve! (*All three go off at the end of the lane.*)

MOSCARDINA (*immediately, with resolution*). Tuzza's child is yours, Liolà!

LIOLÀ. Oh, come on, stop it! It's become a real vice, around here! Every girl who starts getting queasy in the morning – who did it? – Liolà!

MOSCARDINA. Are you denying it?

LIOLÀ. I'm telling you to stop it! I know nothing about it!

MOSCARDINA. Then why did you go to ask Zia Croce Azzara for Tuzza's hand?

LIOLÀ. Oh, that's why? I was still waiting to hear what I had to do with it!

MOSCARDINA. See, you can't deny it any more!

LIOLÀ. Well, it was just as a joke. Just in passing...

MOSCARDINA (*to Zia Ninfa*). D'you hear him, Zia Ninfa? Now it's your turn to talk to him, as a mother: With me the young gentleman is turning it into a laughing matter, while there's a poor woman here in tears. Look at her! If you've got any conscience...

LIOLÀ. Yes, I see she's in tears, but why?

MOSCARDINA. Why, you say? (*Turning to Zia Ninfa and stamping her foot*) You talk to him!

ZIA NINFA. Because Zio Simone, it seems...

MOSCARDINA. (Oh, finally a word out of her!) It seems? He's even beaten her!

ZIA NINFA. Yes, because he says he doesn't have any use for her any more, now that he's about to get a son, he says, by his niece...

LIOLÀ. Ah, so it was him, Zio Simone? Good grief, he went with his niece?

ZIA NINFA (*indicating Liolà for Moscardina*). See? My son is sincere. If it were the way you say...

MOSCARDINA (*ignoring her, turning to Liolà*). You expect me to swallow that... you who never wanted to hear about marriage...

LIOLÀ. Me? Who told you that? Never wanted to hear about it? Why, every five minutes...

MOSCARDINA. Ah, just as a joke!

LIOLÀ. No! With all my heart! It's not my fault, pardon me, if then not one woman wants me. All of them want me – and none of them want

me. For five minutes, yes. As soon as I pop the question... A priest
should be running up to us in a hurry with holy water. Instead
nobody runs – and the marriage evaporates. Hmm, so, then Tuzza...
Well, you can't say that Zia Croce hasn't chosen her son-in-law with
great care! Long live Zio Simone! He's finally succeeded, then! What
a rooster... A little old, but made of good stuff, you can see that...
And of course Tuzza... With this fine trick she got ready for Mita
here... Well, poor Mita, you must be patient! What else can you do?

MOSCARDINA (*with rage*). That's all you have to say? Is that all? Let me
out of here! I get so angry! I've got to get out of here! Arguing with
people who trample their conscience under their feet! (*She exits
angrily, waving her arms.*)

ZIA NINFA. She's really crazy! Conscience, she says! Of course, if she
believes so stubbornly that things are the way she sees them!

LIOLÀ. Pay no attention! Go, go, put these kids to bed. Look there.
Tinino's fallen asleep already. (*The child, in fact, has fallen asleep, face
up, on the ground. The others are dozing sitting up.*)

ZIA NINFA. Ah, yes, poor child, look at him! (*Running to him, she leans
over him and calls*) Tinino, Tinino... (*To Liolà*) Come on, pick him up
and put him in my arms. (*Liolà bends over, makes the sign of the cross over
the sleeping child, then whistles to wake him up; but, seeing that the child does
not wake, he hums the dance motif we heard earlier, clapping his hands;
Tinino then rises, as do his two little brothers, rubbing their eyes with their
small fists; they begin to dance, and all three, thus dancing, accompanied by
their father who continues to sing and clap his hands, go into the house.*)

MITA (*rising*). I'm going in too, Zia Ninfa, good night.

ZIA NINFA. If you need me, my child, as soon as I put these children to
bed, I'll come back to you.

MITA. No, thank you. I'll shut myself in for the night. Good night to you
too, Liolà. (*Zia Ninfa goes into her house.*)

LIOLÀ. Are you staying here for the night?

MITA. My aunt went into town.

LIOLÀ. Has she gone to lodge a complaint?

MITA. She said she was going to a lawyer.

LIOLÀ. Really. Does that mean that you don't want to go back to your
husband any more?

MITA. There is nothing left between us. Good night.

LIOLÀ. Oh, how foolish you are, Mita.

MITA. We can't all be shrewd like you, Liolà. It means that God will have
to look after me.

LIOLÀ. God, oh yes! He should. He did it once. But no matter how good you might be, how devout, how observing of all his commandments, you surely don't dare to compare yourself with the Virgin Mary!

MITA. Me? You're blaspheming!

LIOLÀ. Pardon me, if you say that God must look after you! How? Through the power of the Holy Spirit?

MITA. Go away, go. It's better that I retire for the night. I can't stay here to hear such irreverent talk.

LIOLÀ. Irreverent? No, I'm just telling you that God can't help you in this matter...

MITA. But I didn't mean what you mean!

LIOLÀ. And what do you mean? He's going to help you with the scenes Moscardina came here to make? or your aunt running uselessly into town? Shouts, banging, beatings, lawyers, a separation? ... or by getting me involved? sending me to shout in Zio Simone's face that Tuzza's child is mine? Childish stuff! Things that you and I could have thought of when we used to play husband and wife in this little garden, and once in a while got into a fight and ran to your aunt or my mother to say who'd been the worst offender, remember?

MITA. Yes, I remember. But it wasn't my fault, Liolà! (I just told your mother too.) Only God knows whom I really loved when I got married...

LIOLÀ. I know it too, Mita, whom you loved. But now it doesn't matter. You got married, and that's it!

MITA. I only mentioned it because you asked whether I remembered...

LIOLÀ. Now we're talking about something different. You're wrong and your husband is right.

MITA. *I'm* wrong?

LIOLÀ. Yes, if you'll pardon me; you lost... how many years? four? five? That's your fault! Your husband got tired. You knew, when you got married, that he was marrying you in order to have a child. Did you give him a child? No. Wait – today, tomorrow – in the end he got busy and found somebody else who's going to give it to him instead of you.

MITA. But if God didn't want to grant me this favour?

LIOLÀ. Well, if you're waiting for figs to fall into your lap! Did you really expect it from God himself? And then you accuse *me* of blaspheming! Go, go ask Tuzza by whom she is having her child.

MITA. By the devil, I say!

LIOLÀ. No, by Zio Simone!

MITA. By the devil, by the devil!

LIOLÀ. By Zio Simone!

MITA. You dare say that in front of me? It's outrageous, Liolà!

LIOLÀ. That's why I tell you you're a fool! (*Resuming his argument*) Look: Let's do what Moscardina says to do: I go to Zio Simone – better, I tie a bell around my neck and go around shouting throughout the countryside and the streets of the town: *Ding, dong, Zio Simone's child is mine! Ding, dong, Zio Simone's child is mine!* Who'd believe it? Oh, yes, perhaps everybody would. But not him, he'll never believe it, because he doesn't want to! Try to convince him, if you can! And, after all, come on, let's be fair! Do you think Tuzza's child will be born with a sticker on his forehead – *Liolà!* – Even the mother herself doesn't know certain things! Even if they cut his throat, you can be sure, he won't admit that the child isn't his! Nor do I have the means to make him recognize that it's mine! But you yourself, you yourself, if you're not really a fool, you yourself, before anybody else, should tell him that he's right.

MITA. That the child is his?

LIOLÀ. Yes, yes: his, his! And that it's your fault, not his, that so far he hasn't had one by you! Witness the fact that now he's getting a child by Tuzza, and that just as he can get one by Tuzza today, he can get one by you tomorrow!

MITA. But how?

LIOLÀ. How? I'm telling you how! The same way he's having one by Tuzza now!

MITA. Oh, no! Not that! Never!

LIOLÀ. Well, good night, then! Be quiet and quit crying! Who do you turn to? Why do you run away? Who are you blaming? These people are teaching you how to go about it, and you refuse to learn. You're letting Tuzza commit the outrage, not me! That's why I've denied it, and am denying it! For your sake, for your sake I'm denying it, for your good, and because there's no other way now to overturn their trick and their anger! Do you think you're the only one who's been burned by it? Only God knows what I had to swallow! When I went there to do my duty as a honest man, and before my very eyes that wicked mother got your husband to go into the room where Tuzza was! I saw it all like in a picture, their betrayal! I saw you, Mita, and what was going to happen to you, and I swore to myself that they weren't going to have it their way! I sealed my lips, and waited for this moment! No, no, this outrage mustn't stand, Mita! It's you that must punish them! God Himself commands you to! That shameless slut must not use me to ruin you! (*He's put his arm around her waist, as he says these last words.*)

MITA (*trying to free herself*). No, no... leave me alone, I'll never do that... No, no, I don't want to, I don't want to... (*Suddenly she stops, frightened, straining to hear.*) Wait, ssst, wait! I hear footsteps. Who's coming?

LIOLÀ. Let's go in, let's go in right away!

MITA. No, it's him... it's him, yes, my husband. It's his step... Run, run away, for pity's sake! (*In one jump Liolà is at the door of his house; Mita runs noiselessly into her aunt's house, closing the door very quietly. Zio Simone appears at the end of the lane holding a little lamp attached to a short chain; he gets to the street door of the little house and knocks repeatedly.*)

ZIO SIMONE. Zia Gesa! Zia Gesa! Please open, it's me. (*Hearing Mita's voice from inside*) Oh, it's you? Open up... I say, open up! Open up or I'll tear the door down! No, I've got to tell you something. Yes, I'll go, but open up first! (*The door opens and Zio Simone enters. Liolà from his doorway peers out, trying to fathom the darkness and the silence. Then he withdraws, hearing the garden door opening.*)

MITA (*going into the garden and calling*). Zia Ninfa! Zia Ninfa! (*then, turning towards her husband who is coming out of the house with the lantern in his hand*): No! I told you no, I'm not coming! I don't want to live with you any more! Zia Ninfa! Zia Ninfa!

ZIO SIMONE. Are you calling for help?

ZIA NINFA (*running out of her house and entering the garden*). Mita, Mita! What is it? ... Oh, it's you, Zio Simone!

MITA (*from behind Zia Ninfa*). *You* tell him, Zia Ninfa, for God's sake, tell him to leave me alone!

ZIO SIMONE. You're my wife, you've got to come with me!

MITA. No, no! I'm not your wife any more. No! Go look for your wife where she is, in the house of your filthy cousin!

ZIO SIMONE. Shut up, shut up, or by God you'll feel the back of my hand again!

ZIA NINFA (*protecting Mita*). That's enough, Zio Simone. Come on, let her get it all off her chest, at least, for God's sake!

ZIO SIMONE. No, she's got to keep her mouth shut! She couldn't be a mother, she can at least be a wife; and not dirty her mouth saying bad things about my relatives.

ZIA NINFA. But let's be fair, Zio Simone, don't you expect too much? The poor thing's hurt by what you did to her!

ZIO SIMONE. I did nothing to her! I did something good for her, when I took her in from the street and put her in a place she didn't deserve.

ZIA NINFA. What a man! You think this is the way to persuade her to come back to you?

ZIO SIMONE. Zia Ninfa, I'd never have shown any disrespect to the blessed memory of my dead wife, if it weren't for the fact that I didn't know whom to leave all I had to! All I had, all I sweated blood for, in the rain, in the scorching sun!

ZIA NINFA. All right. But is that this poor girl's fault, for God's sake?

ZIO SIMONE. It might not be her fault, but she's got no right to fault the one who's doing now what she's failed to do!

MITA (*to Zia Ninfa*). Do you hear him? (*to Zio Simone*). What more do you want from me, then? Go to the one who can do it for you, and leave me in peace. I don't know what to do with your name or your possessions!

ZIO SIMONE. You're my wife, I told you, and she's my niece. What's happened happened, and I don't want to hear one more word about it. I need a woman to help me in the house, Zia Ninfa.

MITA. And I'd rather go roaming around the countryside at night!

ZIA NINFA. Come on, give her a little time to calm down, Zio Simone: you've hit her a pretty hard blow. Have a bit of patience! You'll see that Mita will calm down and return home.

MITA. He can wait all he wants! I'll never go back!

ZIA NINFA. You see, he's come all the way here to take you home. He told you that it's all over, and that he won't go to Zia Croce's any more. Right, Zio Simone?

ZIO SIMONE. I won't go there any more, but when the child is born, I'll bring him home.

MITA. There, do you hear him? And then the mother will come to the house to order me around.

ZIA NINFA. No, why?

MITA. With the excuse that she's the mother. Will I be able to shut the door in her face? And you expect me to stand such an outrage? Or should I also prepare their bed in my own house with my own hands? Do you have the heart, after all this, to make me go back to him?

ZIA NINFA. Me? What have I got to do with it, my girl? I certainly can't keep you here with me! I'm saying this for your own good.

ZIO SIMONE. Come on, let's go. It's nighttime!

MITA. No! If you don't go, I'll run and throw myself off the bridge!

ZIA NINFA. Listen to me, Zio Simone. Let her stay here, at least for this one night. Little by little, if you're nice she'll come around, and you'll see by tomorrow... tomorrow she'll come home. You can be sure.

ZIO SIMONE. But why does she want to stay here tonight?

ZIA NINFA. Because, among other things, she must watch over her aunt's house – her aunt's gone into town...

ZIO SIMONE. ... to file a complaint against me?

ZIA NINFA. Well, never mind! It was done on the spur of the moment, in that first fit of rage! Go, go home to sleep, it's late. Mita will shut herself in the house. (*To Mita*) Go, lead your husband out first; then lock the front door, then this one. Good night. Good night to you too, Zio Simone. (*Zio Simone is the first to enter the cottage, forgetting the lantern in the garden. Mita enters after him and shuts the little door.*)

ZIA NINFA (*crossing the garden and the lane*). I think Zia Gesa has given the lamb to the wolf to take care of. (*In front of her door she sees Liolà looking and speaks to him in a low voice.*) Get inside, get inside, son. Don't make things worse...

LIOLÀ. Ssst. Wait... I want to see how it all ends... Go, go to sleep...

ZIA NINFA. Be careful! Be sensible! (*She goes in. Liolà shuts the door and quickly enters the garden, crouching behind the hedge; he creeps silently to the corner of the house, where he straightens up, pressed against the wall. All of a sudden the little door opens and Mita, seeing Liolà, cries out but immediately stifles her cry and turns towards her husband to prevent him from coming out.*)

MITA. I told you no! Go away, or I'll call Zia Ninfa again! Go away!

ZIO SIMONE (*from inside the cottage*). All right, I'll go, I'll go. Take it easy. (*Mita enters the house, leaving the little door ajar. So, while Zio Simone goes out through the street door, Liolà, pressing himself against the wall, moves to the side door, enters, and closes it at once. Zio Simone's exiting one door and Liola's entering the other must take place at the same moment. But as soon as the street door closes, Zio Simone turns around and says*) Oh, my lantern... I left my lantern... where? in the garden? Oh, yes, I'll go around this way... (*He comes down the lane, enters the garden through the little gate, picks up the lantern, and makes sure that it is lit well.*) In the dark, here in the country, it is dangerous, you could really go and break your horns... (*He walks slowly up the lane.*)

CURTAIN

ACT THREE

(*The same scene as in Act One. It is the season of the grape harvest. Crates and baskets are visible near the storeroom door. Tuzza is sitting on the stone bench sewing garments for the baby she is expecting. Zia Croce, wearing a large shawl around her shoulders and a kerchief on her head is coming forward from the rear.*)

ZIA CROCE. They're all rich these days! No one wants to come.

TUZZA. You should've known!

ZIA CROCE. I didn't go to invite them over for dinner! They're filthy, worse than the town dump; they haven't got even a handful of straw to sleep on, and look at this, I give them a chance to earn some bread, and this one's arm hurts, that one's leg...

TUZZA. I told you not to go beg them!

ZIA CROCE. It's just envy, it's eating them alive, and they all act like they're too good for the work! So I have to go all the way into town and hire regular workers for a handful of grapes, or the wasps will get them all. Has the wine press been cleaned up?

TUZZA. Yes, yes, it's all set to go.

ZIA CROCE. The baskets are here, ready, everything's ready, but no workers. Only Liolà, he's the only one who's promised to come.

TUZZA. So, you really insist on asking him?

ZIA CROCE. On purpose, silly! To show nothing's changed.

TUZZA. But even the stones know about it by now!

ZIA CROCE. Not through him, though – he's been denying it all along, they tell me! And I'm grateful. I'd never have thought he'd do that. And if he denies it, let the others sing till they burst, like cicadas.

TUZZA. Okay! But I'll tell you this, I'm going to shut myself up in the house and I won't even stick my nose outside. I can't bear the sight of him anymore!

ZIA CROCE. Oh, *now* you say so! Now you can't bear the sight of him! You tramp! Meanwhile it's been days since your uncle's come by.

TUZZA. He's sent word that he isn't feeling well.

ZIA CROCE. If he were here, I'd've gotten out of this harvesting fix. But this child is coming some day soon! I can't wait any longer! When his child is here – now that he's claimed it so publicly as his own – his wife'll have a hard time keeping him away! His home'll be here. Your home is where your children are. (*Moscardina comes in at this point, flushed and happy.*)

MOSCARDINA. May I come in, Zia Croce?

ZIA CROCE. Oh, it's you, Moscardina?

MOSCARDINA. Yep, it's me. I wanted to let you know they're coming. All of them!

ZIA CROCE. Oh, what's happened? Why're you so happy?

MOSCARDINA. Yes, I am, I'm really happy, Zia Croce.

ZIA CROCE. You're red as a pepper! Did you run all the way?

MOSCARDINA. I always run, Zia Croce. You know the saying: 'A hen that pecks fast here and there, of food will always get her share.' Besides, it's harvest time! You'll see, all the girls are happy!

ZIA CROCE. How come? I saw them a moment ago, they were all sulky. Not a one wanted to come. Now they're all happy and raring to go?

TUZZA. If I were you, I'd refuse now, and go into town and get a regular crew.

ZIA CROCE. No, I'd much rather clear up any bad feeling between neighbours. But I *would* like to know why everyone's so happy...

MOSCARDINA. Maybe because they heard that Liolà's coming. That Liolà, believe me, Zia Croce, he's something... something... He seems to have made a pact with the devil!

ZIA CROCE. Has he been up to some of his old tricks again?

MOSCARDINA. I don't know. But the fact is he makes us all so happy. He's busy doing things and dreaming up a hundred others. And wherever he is, the girls are happy to go! There, d'you hear? He's singing. He's coming along, singing, with the girls and the three children dancing around him. Look, look! (*A rustic chorus is heard, in fact, led by Liolà. Then Liolà comes into view, with Ciuzza, Tuzza, and Nela, other peasant men and women, and his three 'finches,' and starts improvising tapping his feet in time.*)

LIOLÀ.
Ullarallà
Press hard, those grapes with Liolà!
Press hard, press hard!
The harder you press, you'll see,
The stronger the wine will be!
Stronger than last year's, Liolà

CHORUS.
Ullarallà! Ullarallà!

LIOLÀ.
Every turn,
You'll quickly learn,
Done with a will,

Gives a barrelful!
A barrel so fine,
One gulp of that wine
Can do me in,
My head will spin!
Ullarallà! Ullarallà!

CHORUS.
Ullarallà! Ullarallà!

LIOLÀ. Dear Zia Croce, here we are again! (*The workers are laughing, dancing, clapping.*)

ZIA CROCE. My, my! How jolly you all are! A real cheery bunch! What kind of miracle is this?

LIOLÀ. No miracle, Zia Croce. 'Seek and ye shall find, and keep on and ye shall win!' (*The girls laugh.*)

ZIA CROCE. What does it mean?

LIOLÀ. Nothing, just a saying.

ZIA CROCE. Oh yes? Then listen: 'All this song and dance ain't worth a whistle.'

LIOLÀ (*quickly*). But 'the piper must be paid.'

ZIA CROCE. It's only fair! Plain dealing. The same pay as last year, right?

LIOLÀ. Of course, never mind. I said that only to show you I knew your saying and its follow-up too.

ZIA CROCE. Let's get to work, then. Girls, take the baskets. And pick carefully – it goes without saying.

LIOLÀ. I brought the children along to pick any leftover grapes.

ZIA CROCE. As long as they don't climb the branches when they can't reach.

LIOLÀ. No danger of that! They learned at their daddy's school. The high bunch you can't reach by hand – leave it there, and don't say it's sour (*another laugh from the girls*). Why're you laughing? You don't know the old fable about the fox?... Enough! Is everything ready at the wine press?

ZIA CROCE. Yes, yes, everything's ready.

LIOLÀ (*picking up the crates and baskets and distributing them to the girls and young men*). Let's go, then. Come on, take this... here! Take these. And let's sing as we go. Ullarallà! Ullarallà! (*He exits stage rear with the whole crew singing.*)

ZIA CROCE (*shouting after them*). Start from the bottom, girls, go from row to row, move on up little by little. And keep an eye on the

children! (*Then to Tuzza*) You go down with them! Get busy! Do I
have to look after our affairs all by myself?

TUZZA. No, no. I told you, I won't go!

ZIA CROCE. God knows what a mess those starving girls will make out
there! And did you see the look on their faces? What a glint in their
eyes?

TUZZA. I saw, I saw.

ZIA CROCE. For that crazy guy! (*Then, looking offstage, she sees Zio Simone*)
Oh, here comes your uncle... Look, he's moving his legs as if they
weren't his own... He must be really sick! (*Zio Simone comes into view,
looking very grumpy.*)

ZIO SIMONE. Good morning, dear cousin. Good morning, Tuzza.

TUZZA. Good morning.

ZIA CROCE. Aren't you feeling well, cousin? What ails you?

ZIO SIMONE (*scratching his head under his cap*). Problems, cousin,
problems.

ZIA CROCE. Problems? What problems can you have?

ZIO SIMONE. Not myself, actually... In fact, I...

ZIA CROCE. Is your wife sick, maybe?

ZIO SIMONE. Well... She says... She says that... well...

ZIA CROCE. Well, what? Speak up. I've got the workers out picking, and
I've got to watch what they're doing.

ZIO SIMONE. Have you started harvesting?

ZIA CROCE. Yes, just now.

ZIO SIMONE. Without telling me anything?

ZIA CROCE. You haven't been around for two days! In fact I had quite a
rough time with all these vipers in our neighbourhood! They didn't
want to come. Then all of a sudden, who knows why, they all came,
and now they're down there with the crates.

ZIO SIMONE. You're always in a big hurry, cousin!

ZIA CROCE. A hurry, me? What do you mean, hurry? The wasps were
eating the whole thing...

ZIO SIMONE. I'm not just talking about the harvest... I'm talking about
other things too... I'm talking about myself too... I don't see the
advantage of breaking your neck instead of letting time do its thing!

ZIA CROCE. Oh, come on, can you tell me what's eating you? Spit it out!
I see you're keen on blaming something on me...

ZIO SIMONE. Not you, cousin, not you! I blame myself, myself!

AUNT CROCE. For being in a hurry?

ZIO SIMONE. Exactly, being in a hurry.

ZIA CROCE. Hurry to do what?

ZIO SIMONE. Do what? D'you think all this is easy for me? Yesterday my friend Nicola Randisi came to see me!

ZIA CROCE. Oh, yes. I saw him walking by...

ZIO SIMONE. ... did he stop to talk?

ZIA CROCE. No, he went straight on by...

TUZZA. They all go straight on by, all the people who pass here now!

ZIO SIMONE. They go straight on by, my child, because, seeing me here, people imagine... imagine things that aren't so, thank God, nor ever were so. Our conscience is clean, but, unfortunately, appearances...

ZIA CROCE. Okay, okay, Zio Simone. We know – and we should have thought of it before – that all envious people would react this way. Now that we think of it... (*To Tuzza*) You too, fool!

ZIO SIMONE. Yes, cousin. But all those who go straight on by here, come to say nasty things right in my face!

ZIA CROCE. Can you *finally* tell me what the devil this friend of yours, Cola Randisi, came to tell you?

ZIO SIMONE. He came to tell me just that: 'Such a damn hurry!' if you really want to know. Right in front of my wife he swore people've had children not after four years of marriage, but even after fifteen.

ZIA CROCE. Well, I was dying to hear what he could've told you to make you so worried! And tell me, what'd you answer him? Fifteen years? Sixty plus fifteen, what's that? Seventy-five, I think. Listen, cousin: nothing at sixty, and a child at seventy-five?

ZIO SIMONE. Who told you, nothing at sixty?

ZIA CROCE. Those are the facts, cousin.

ZIO SIMONE. No, cousin. The facts are... (*hesitating*).

ZIA CROCE. What facts?

ZIO SIMONE. That at sixty, yes.

ZIA CROCE. What?

ZIO SIMONE. Yes, yes. Just so.

ZIA CROCE. Your wife?

ZIO SIMONE. She told me this morning.

TUZZA (*biting her fingers*). Ah! Liolà!

ZIA CROCE. She's tricked you!

TUZZA. That's why those vipers were all so happy! 'Seek and ye shall find, and keep on and ye shall win!'

ZIO SIMONE. Come on, don't go around saying that stuff now!

ZIA CROCE. Do you really have the cheek to think the child is yours?

TUZZA. Liolà! Liolà's tricked him! He's tricked him, and he's tricked me, the bastard!

ZIO SIMONE. Don't go around saying that, don't...

ZIA CROCE. So that's how you watched over your wife, you old fool?

TUZZA. And I told him! A hundred times I told him, to watch out for Liolà!

ZIO SIMONE. Uh-oh, careful! don't talk about Liolà now, because I ordered my wife to shut up when she threw the same accusation in my face about you, and it was true!

ZIA CROCE. And now it's not true? Now it's not true about your wife, you old cuckold?

ZIO SIMONE. Cousin, don't get me all riled up, or...

ZIA CROCE. Oh go on, get away! As if we didn't know...

ZIO SIMONE. ... what?

ZIA CROCE. ... what you know too, and better than anybody else!

ZIO SIMONE. All I know is, I never had anything to do with your daughter here: it was an act of charity, nothing else. But with my wife, I was there, I was there!

ZIA CROCE. Yes, for four years, and nothing came of it! Go on, go and ask now who was 'there' with your wife!

TUZZA. 'An act of charity!' What a nerve!

ZIA CROCE. Yeah, sure! After he boasted to everybody, to his own wife, that the child was his, to have that satisfaction, knowing he couldn't get it any other way!

TUZZA (*suddenly changing her attitude*). Enough, enough! Stop shouting, now! Enough!

ZIA CROCE. Oh, no, my dear! You don't expect me to take it meekly, do you?

TUZZA. What else do you want to do? If he was willing to take mine, even knowing whose it was, imagine if he won't recognize his wife's as his own...

ZIO SIMONE. ... and it is mine! mine! mine! And whoever dares say anything against my wife better watch out... (*Mita, extremely calm, comes in from stage rear.*)

MITA. Hey, what's all the noise about?

TUZZA. Go away, Mita, go away, don't make me angry!

MITA. Me, make you angry? I'd never do that!

TUZZA (*lunging to get hold of her*). Get her away from me! Get her away!

ZIO SIMONE (*getting in between the two*). Watch it, I'm right here!

ZIA CROCE. How dare you come here? Go on! Get out of here!

MITA (*gesturing towards her husband*). Look who's saying 'dare'!

ZIO SIMONE. No, don't you get mixed up in this, my dear wife! Go back home and let me defend you!

MITA. No, wait, I want to remind Tuzza about an old saying: 'She who is late but doesn't fail can't be called a failure.' I've been late, yes, but I haven't failed. You went ahead, and I followed you.

TUZZA. Yes, you did, on the very same path!

MITA. No, dear, mine's straight and true, yours is crooked and false.

ZIO SIMONE. Don't get all upset this way, my dear wife! Don't you see, they're doing it on purpose, to get you angry? Go, go, listen to me, go home, go home!

ZIA CROCE. Look at him! Listen to him! 'My dear wife!'

TUZZA (*to Mita*). You're right! You're right! You did better than me! You got the facts, I only got the words!

MITA. Just words? I don't think so!

ZIA CROCE. Yes, words, words! Because we're not deceitful, though we seem to be! You are, though you don't seem to be!

ZIO SIMONE. Enough, I say! That's enough!

ZIA CROCE. See? Now you have your husband to protect you, though he's deceived! While my daughter didn't try to deceive her uncle: no, she threw herself at his feet crying, like Mary Magdalene!

ZIO SIMONE. That's true! that's true!

ZIA CROCE. There, you see? He says it himself! He who's the cause of all the trouble, just so he could boast before you, before the whole town…

MITA. And you let him, Zia Croce? Look at him! At the cost of your daughter's honour? But the deceit, yes, is just where it doesn't seem to be: in my husband's money, which you wanted to get your hands on even if it cost you your shame!

ZIO SIMONE. Enough! enough! enough! Instead of all this useless talk and fighting that gets us nowhere, let's look for a way out now, that we can all agree on. We're all in the family!

ZIA CROCE. Way out? What way out are you going to find, you old fool? We're all in the family, he says. You'd better find a way out of all the damage you did to my daughter, for the satisfaction you wanted to get out of it!

ZIO SIMONE. Me? I've got to think of my own child now. His father will take care of yours. Liolà won't dare deny to my face that the child is his.

TUZZA. Which one?

ZIO SIMONE (*astounded by the question that hit him like a knife in the back*). What d'you mean, which one?

MITA (*quickly*). Yours, of course, dear girl! Which one do you think it could be? I have my husband here, who can't have any doubt about me.

ZIO SIMONE. Will you stop? Will you stop, the two of you, mother and daughter? Now that my wife's decided to give me such a consolation, she shouldn't have to listen to this. Let me talk to Liolà. (*The choir of the grape harvesters is heard from afar, coming gradually nearer.*)

TUZZA. Oh no, stop! Don't you dare talk to him on my behalf! I forbid you to!

ZIO SIMONE. You'll take him, because it's the right thing to do. Only he can give you the position of a wife and his child a legitimate birth. *I'll* do the persuading, by whatever means my heart may dictate. Here he comes. Let *me* talk to him (*Liolà returns with the harvesters, singing a harvesting chorus. As soon as they all come under the shed, carrying their full baskets as if in triumph, and see Mita and Zio Simone, and the contorted faces of Zia Croce and Tuzza, they stop short and break off their song. Only Liolà goes on singing, as if unawares, and proceeds to the window of the winepress room to empty his basket.*)

ZIA CROCE (*going towards them*). Enough, enough! Empty your baskets, girls, and throw them over there. I'm in no state to watch over your work, right now.

LIOLÀ. Why? What happened?

ZIA CROCE (*to the women*). Go on, go, I'm telling you! Maybe I'll call you back later.

ZIO SIMONE. You come here, Liolà! (*At the back of the stage Moscardina, Ciuzza, Luzza, Nela, and the other women surround Mita and congratulate her lavishly on the consolation she has given them all. Tuzza, watching them, is consumed with rage: slowly she backs away to the door of the house and plunges inside.*)

LIOLÀ. You want me? Here I am.

ZIO SIMONE. Cousin, you come here too.

LIOLÀ (*with a commanding air*). Zia Croce, over here!

ZIO SIMONE. Today's a special day and all of us must celebrate.

LIOLÀ. And sing, too. Not the way Zia Croce says, 'song and dance ain't worth a whistle.' If they're made of wind, they're my kind; because the wind and I, Zio Simone, are brothers.

ZIO SIMONE. We know it, we all know you as a breezy butterfly! But now it's time to settle down, dear boy.

LIOLÀ. Settle down? You're killing me!

ZIO SIMONE. Listen to me, Liolà. First of all I must share with you the consolation that God has finally decided to grant me...

ZIA CROCE. Listen, listen to this marvellous piece of news, you who know nothing about it!

ZIO SIMONE. I thought I told you to let me do the talking...

LIOLÀ. Let him do the talking!

ZIA CROCE. Oh, yes, talk, talk! Sure it was *God* who granted you this!

ZIO SIMONE. Yes, ma'am, the favour that after four years my wife has finally decided...

LIOLÀ. Oh, yes? Really? Your wife? I'll whip you up a poem on the spot!

ZIO SIMONE. Wait, wait! What kind of poem!

LIOLÀ. Allow me to go and drink her health, at least!

ZIO SIMONE. Wait, I said, for God's sake!

LIOLÀ. Oh, don't get angry! You must be in seventh heaven, and you get angry? Come on, I have it on the tip of my tongue!

ZIO SIMONE. Leave the poem alone, I said; you have something else to do here, now.

LIOLÀ. Me? I can't do anything else, Zio Simone!

ZIA CROCE. Right... Sure... He can't do anything else, the poor thing! (*Going up to him and seizing his arm, she mutters to him between her teeth:*) You've ruined my daughter twice, you devil!

LIOLÀ. Me? Your daughter? You dare say this to me in front of Zio Simone? *He*'s ruined your daughter twice, not I!

ZIA CROCE. No, you, you!

LIOLÀ. Him! him! Zio Simone! Let's not shuffle the deck in the middle of a hand, Zia Croce! I came here asking honestly for the hand of your daughter, never imagining that...

ZIA CROCE. Oh, no? After what you did with her?

LIOLÀ. Me? Zio Simone!

ZIA CROCE. Right, Zio Simone! Sure, Zio Simone!

LIOLÀ. You tell her, Zio Simone! You want to deny it, now, and unload the kid on me? Are you kidding? I've thanked God a hundred times for saving me from the net I swam into not suspecting a thing. Stand back, Zio Simone! What kind of old man are you, anyway? Having a kid by your niece wasn't enough for you? One by your wife, too? What's driving you? The flames of hell, or the divine fire? the devil? Mount Etna? God keep all the girls!

ZIA CROCE. Oh, sure! All the girls better watch out for him!

ZIO SIMONE. Liolà, don't make me talk! Don't force me to do what I don't want to do! You see that no sin was committed between me and my niece! – nor ever could be! It was only that she threw herself at my feet, sorry for what she'd done with you, confessing the state she was in: My wife knows all that now: And I'm ready to swear before the holy sacrament and in front of everybody that my boast was a lie, about the child, that's really yours!

LIOLÀ. And by this you mean that I should now marry Tuzza?

ZIO SIMONE. You can and you must, Liolà, because, I swear by God and the Holy Mother, she's been only yours and nobody else's!

LIOLÀ. Hey, hey, hey, you're running too fast, Zio Simone! Yes, I meant to, before. As a matter of conscience, only. I knew if I married her all my songs would die in my heart. Tuzza did not want me then. The barrel full and the wife drunk? Zio Simone, Zia Croce, you can't have both things at the same time! Now that your trick has failed? No, no. Thank you, but no! (*Taking the hands of two of the children*) Let's go, let's go, boys! (*He starts walking away, then turns back.*) I can do this as an act of conscience, yes. Turn and turn, I see that there's one child too many here. Well, I have no problem with that. My mother will have a bit more work to do. You can tell Tuzza, Zia Croce, if she wants to give the child to me, I'll take it!

TUZZA (*who has been crouched in a corner, her eyes flashing, on hearing these last words lunges towards Liolà with a knife in her hand*). Oh, yeah? The child? Take this, instead! (*All shout, flinging up their arms and running to restrain her. Mita, about to faint, is supported and comforted by Zio Simone. Liolà, alert, has seized Tuzza's arm, and strikes her fingers with his other hand until the knife falls to the ground. Laughing, he reassures everybody that it was nothing.*)

LIOLÀ. Nothing, nothing… it's nothing… (*As soon as Tuzza has dropped the knife, he puts a foot on it, and repeats, with a burst of grand laughter*) Nothing! (*He bends down to kiss the head of one of the children; then, seeing a thread of blood on his chest*) A little scratch, just grazed me…

(*He touches the blood with a finger; then goes to touch it to Tuzza's lips*)
Here, taste it! Sweet, huh? (*To the women who are restraining her:*)
Let her go, let her go! (*He looks at her; then looks at the three children,
puts his hands on their small heads and says, turning to Tuzza*)
No more tears! No sorrow's sting!
Three and one make four.
When it's born, give me your
Child, I'll teach him too to sing.

CURTAIN

Right You Are, If You Think You Are

(also known in English as
It Is So, If You Think So)
A Parable in Three Acts

1917

Characters

LAMBERTO LAUDISI

MRS FROLA

MR PONZA *her son-in-law*

MRS PONZA

MR AGAZZI *a counsel in the provincial government.*

AMALIA *his wife and Laudisi's sister*

DINA *their daughter*

MRS SIRELLI

MR SIRELLI

The provincial Prefect

CENTURI *Chief of Police*

MRS CINI

MRS NENNI

A servant in the Agazzis' household

Other ladies and gentlemen

In a provincial capital. The time is the present.

ACT ONE

(*The living room in the home of Counsel Agazzi. Main door to the rear, side doors to the right and left.*)

Scene One
Amalia, Dina, Laudisi

(*As the curtain rises, Lamberto Laudisi, visibly irritated, is pacing the drawing room. Forty-ish, slender, elegant in an unobtrusive way, he is wearing a purple morning jacket with black lapels and cuffs.*)

LAUDISI. So, he's gone to take the matter up with the Prefect?

AMALIA (*grey hair, in her mid-forties; her ostentatiously self-important manner is due to the position her husband occupies in society. She gives you to understand, however, that, were it completely up to her, she would act her part and behave quite differently on many occasions*). Well, Lamberto, because he works under him!

LAUDISI. Under him in the Prefect's office, not here at home!

DINA (*nineteen; has the air of one who thinks she understands everything better than Mom, and even Dad; although this air of hers is softened somewhat by a certain youthful grace*). But he's taken a place for his mother-in-law right next to us, on the same landing!

LAUDISI. Wasn't that allowed? There was a small apartment available and he rented it for his mother-in-law. Did he need your permission? Or is a mother-in-law obliged to come and pay her respects (*heavy, drawing it out, intentionally*) to the wife and daughter of her son-in-law's boss?

AMALIA. Who's saying obliged? It was we, instead, Dina and I, who went to call on this lady, and we weren't received.

LAUDISI. And what's your husband gone to the Prefect to do? To impose an act of courtesy through the authorities?

AMALIA. A justified act of reparation, if anything! You don't leave two ladies standing like two pegs in front of your door.

LAUDISI. It's an abuse of power! Can't people choose to be left alone in their own homes any more?

AMALIA. Oh, well, if you choose to ignore the fact that it was we who were trying to be courteous to a stranger!

DINA. Come on, Uncle, calm down! Let's be frank, if you must. Here, let's admit that we were being courteous out of curiosity. But don't you think it's natural?

LAUDISI. Oh, natural, sure, for people like you who have nothing to do!

DINA. No, Uncle dear. Look, here you are, totally ignoring what others are doing around you. Okay. Here I come. And here, right on this little table in front of you, utterly non-cha-lant-ly – or better yet, with the sinister look of that man – I put, well, what? let's say a pair of the cook's shoes.

LAUDISI (*explosively*). What have the cook's shoes got to do with it?

DINA (*promptly*). There, see? You start wondering! It seems odd to you, and right away you're asking me why.

LAUDISI (*startled, with a cool smile, but soon regaining his composure*). Dear girl! You're very clever, but don't forget you're talking to me... You come here and put the cook's shoes on the little table in order to arouse my curiosity; and surely, since you've done it for that specific purpose, you can't reproach me if I ask you 'Why the cook's shoes just here, sweetheart?' But you've got to prove to me that this Mr Ponza – this boorish country lout, as your father calls him – has taken a place for his mother-in-law next to us, on purpose!

DINA. All right! He might not have done it on purpose. But you can't deny that this gentleman is living in such a strange way that he's made the whole town curious. Listen: he gets here, rents a small apartment on the top floor of that huge dark building at the edge of town overlooking the truck gardens... Have you ever seen it? I mean, inside?

LAUDISI. Have *you* gone to see it, by any chance?

DINA. Yes, Uncle dear! With mother. And not only us, you know? Everyone's gone to see it. There's a courtyard – so dark! it looks like a well – with an iron railing, way up there, of the long top floor balcony, with lots of little baskets hanging from it on strings.

LAUDISI. So?

DINA (*astounded and indignant*). He's stuck his wife away up there!

AMALIA. And his mother-in-law here, next to us!

LAUDISI. In a beautiful little apartment, the mother-in-law, in the centre of town!

AMALIA. Thanks! And he forces her to live apart from her daughter?

LAUDISI. Who told you that? Why can't she herself, the mother, have wanted it, so she'd have more freedom?

DINA. No, no, Uncle dear! Everybody knows it's him!

AMALIA. Listen – it's logical that a daughter, when she gets married, leaves her mother's home and goes to live with her husband, even in a different city. But when a poor mother who can't live away from her daughter follows her, and in the city where she's a stranger too is forced to live apart – come on, you must admit that's not so easy to understand any more!

LAUDISI. Oh sure! What dull imaginations you've got! (Like a pair of mud turtles!) Does it take so much to imagine that, either through

her own fault, or his own fault – or even nobody's fault – they might
be so incompatible that, even under those conditions…

DINA (*interrupting, amazed*). What do you mean, dear Uncle?
Incompatible mother and daughter?

LAUDISI. Why mother and daughter?

AMALIA. Because, it's not the two of them! They're always together, he
and she!

DINA. Mother-in-law and son-in-law! That's why everybody's wondering!

AMALIA. He comes here every evening to keep the mother-in-law
company.

DINA. During the day too. Once or twice a day.

LAUDISI. Do you suspect they might be making love, mother-in-law and
son-in-law?

DINA. No, what're you saying? A poor little old lady!

AMALIA. But he never brings her daughter! He never takes her daughter
with him, to see her mother!

LAUDISI. The poor thing might be sick, she might not be able to leave
the house.

DINA. What are you saying? She goes there, the mother…

AMALIA. She goes there, yes! Just to see her from a distance! Everybody
knows, it's the absolute truth – this poor mother is forbidden to go
up to see her daughter!

DINA. She can talk to her only from the courtyard!

AMALIA. From the courtyard, you understand?

DINA. Talks to her daughter, who comes out on the long balcony, up
there, as if from the sky! This poor little old lady goes into the courtyard, pulls on the basket rope, a bell rings up there, her daughter
comes out, and she speaks to her from down there, from that well,
twisting her neck around like this, imagine! And she doesn't even see
her, blinded by the light up there. (*A knock is heard at the door, and the
servant comes in*).

SERVANT. Excuse me.

AMALIA. Who is it?

SERVANT. The Sirellis, with another person.

AMALIA. Oh, let them in. (*The servant bows and exits*).

Scene Two
The Sirellis, Mrs. Cini, and the previous characters

AMALIA (*to Mrs. Sirelli*). My dear Mrs. Sirelli!

MRS. SIRELLI (*plump. red-cheeked, still young, attractive, decked out with overdone provincial elegance; burning with restless curiosity, sharp with her husband*). I took the liberty of bringing along my good friend, Mrs Cini, who wanted very much to meet you.

AMALIA. So nice to meet you. Please sit down. (*She introduces the others.*) This is my daughter, Dina. And my brother, Lamberto Laudisi.

MR SIRELLI (*bald, forty-ish, fat, greased hair, pretensions to elegance, shiny, squeaky shoes, greeting everyone*). Mrs Agazzi, Miss Agazzi. (*He shakes hands with Laudisi.*)

MRS SIRELLI. Ah, Mrs Agazzi, we're coming here as to the source. We're two poor women thirsty for news.

AMALIA. News about what, ladies?

MRS SIRELLI. But about that blessed new secretary of the Prefect's office. It's all they're talking about in town!

MRS CINI (*a silly old woman, full of avid malice poorly concealed by an affectation of naïveté*). We're all dying to know, just dying…

AMALIA. But we don't know any more than anyone else, believe me, Mrs Cini!

SIRELLI (*to his wife, triumphantly*). Didn't I tell you. No more than I do – maybe even less than I do! (*Then, turning to the others*) The reason that poor mother can't go to visit her daughter, for instance, do you really know what it is?

AMALIA. I was just talking about that with my brother.

LAUDISI. I think you've all gone mad!

DINA (*quickly, so they will not pay attention to her uncle*). Because the son-in-law won't let her, they say.

MRS CINI (*whining*). That's not all, young lady!

MRS SIRELLI (*following up*). That's not all! He's doing more!

SIRELLI (*first making a gesture to get their attention*). Fresh news, just now confirmed: (*almost a hiss*) he keeps her locked up!

AMALIA. The mother-in-law?

SIRELLI. No, Mrs Agazzi, the wife!

MRS SIRELLI. The wife, the wife!

MRS CINI (*whining*). Locked up!

DINA. D'you hear, dear Uncle? And you're trying to defend him…

SIRELLI (*amazed*). What? You're defending such a monster?

LAUDISI. I'm not trying to defend anything! I'm just saying that your curiosity (I beg the ladies' pardon) is unbearable, if only because it's pointless.

SIRELLI. Pointless?

LAUDISI. Pointless, pointless, my dear ladies!

MRS CINI. That we want to know?

LAUDISI. Know what? What can we really know about other people? who they are, what they are, what they do, why they do it?

MRS SIRELLI. By asking around, seeking information...

LAUDISI. But in that case you, if anyone, ought to know the latest – with a husband like yours, always so well informed!

SIRELLI (*trying to break in*). Excuse me, excuse me...

MRS SIRELLI. Oh no, my dear, that's the truth! (*Turning to Amalia*) The truth, my dear lady, is that with my husband who's always claiming to know everything, I never get to know anything.

SIRELLI. Well, of course! She's never satisfied with what I tell her! She always doubts a thing could be the way I told it. In fact, she insists that things can't possibly be the way I told her. She even goes so far as to claim the very opposite, on purpose!

MRS SIRELLI. Well, come on, with the kind of stuff you're always telling me...

LAUDISI (*laughing loudly*). Ha, ha, ha. Let *me* answer your husband, dear lady. How do you expect your wife to be satisfied with the things you tell her, if you, quite naturally tell them the way they are for you?

MRS SIRELLI. The way they can't possibly be!

LAUDISI. Oh no, dear lady, bear with me when I say that in this you're quite wrong! As far as your husband is concerned, you can be sure things are the way he says they are.

SIRELLI. But it's the way they are in reality! Exactly the way they are!

MRS SIRELLI. Absolutely not! You're always wrong!

SIRELLI. Believe me, *you*'re always wrong, not me!

LAUDISI. No, no, my friends! Neither of you is wrong. Allow me. I'll prove it to you (*rising and coming to the centre of the drawing room*). Both of you, here, you see me. You do see me, right?

SIRELLI. Of course!

LAUDISI. No, no! not so fast, my friends. Come here, come here.

SIRELLI (*looks at him grinning, perplexed, a bit disconcerted, as if unwilling to lend himself to a game he does not understand*). Why?

MRS SIRELLI (*urging him, irritation in her voice*). Go on over, go!

LAUDISI (*to Sirelli, who has approached him hesitantly*). You see me? Take a better look. Touch me.

MRS SIRELLI (*to her husband who is hesitating, as before, to touch him*). Go on, touch him!

LAUDISI (*to Sirelli, who has raised his hand to touch him briefly on the shoulder*). That's it, good. You're sure you're touching what you see, right?

SIRELLI. I should hope so.

LAUDISI. You can't doubt your own eyes, of course! Go back to your seat.

MRS SIRELLI (*to her husband, standing stupefied before Laudisi*). It's pointless to stand there blinking! Go back to your seat now!

LAUDISI (*to Mrs Sirelli, when her husband has gone back to his seat*). Now, if you don't mind, come here, dear lady. (*Immediately forestalling her*) No, no, here, I'll come to you. (*He stands before her and goes down on one knee.*) You see me, right? Please raise your little hand and touch me. (*As Mrs Sirelli puts her hand on his shoulder, he bends to kiss it.*) Dear little hand!

SIRELLI. Hey, what the...

LAUDISI. Never mind him! Are you sure too that you're touching what you see? You can't doubt your own eyes. But, for heaven's sake, don't tell your husband, nor my sister, nor my niece, nor the Mrs here...

MRS CINI (*eagerly*). Cini...

LAUDISI. Cini... how you see me, because all four of them'll tell you that you're quite wrong, while you're not a bit wrong! Because I really am the way you see me. But that does not eliminate the fact, my dear lady, that I'm also the way your husband, my sister, my niece, and the Mrs here...

MRS CINI (*eagerly*). Cini...

LAUDISI. Cini... see me – that they too, are not wrong at all.

MRS SIRELLI. But how? Do you change from one to the other?

LAUDISI. I surely do, my dear lady! And you don't, perhaps? You don't change?

MRS SIRELLI (*quickly*). Oh no, no, no. I assure you, in my view, I don't change a bit!

LAUDISI. Nor do I, in my own view, believe me! And I say that you're all wrong if you don't see me the way I see myself! Yet that doesn't eliminate the fact that we're both making quite a presumption – me as well as you, dear lady.

SIRELLI. But what's the point of all this quibbling?

LAUDISI. You don't see the point? marvellous! I see you all getting worked up in this attempt to know who other people really are, and how things really are, as if other people and things were this or that in themselves.

MRS SIRELLI. Then, according to you one can't ever know the truth?

MRS CINI. If we can't believe even in what we see and touch any more!

LAUDISI. Oh, please, do believe in it, dear lady! I only say: respect what others see and touch also, even when it's the opposite of what you see and touch.

MRS SIRELLI. Oh, come now! I'm turning my back on you – I'm not speaking another word to you. I'm not going to let you drive me crazy!

LAUDISI. Enough, enough. Go on talking about Mrs Frola and Mr Ponza. I won't interrupt you any more.

AMALIA. Oh, thank God! And it would really be better, Lamberto dear, if you were to go into the other room.

DINA. Yes, Uncle dear, the other room. Go on, go on!

LAUDISI. No, why? it's great fun to listen to you. I'll keep quiet, don't worry. At most I'll laugh inside a little, and you'll excuse me if a louder laugh escapes me now and then.

MRS SIRELLI. Just think we came here to find out something... But dear Mrs Agazzi, isn't your husband this Mr Ponza's superior?

AMALIA. The office is one thing, the home's quite another, dear Mrs Sirelli.

MRS SIRELLI. Of course, of course! But haven't you ever tried to see the mother-in-law, next door?

DINA. We sure have, twice, dear Mrs Sirelli!

MRS CINI (*with a start, then avidly intent*). Ah, so! So you've spoken to her?

AMALIA. We were not received, my dear Mrs Cini!

SIRELLI, MRS SIRELLI, MRS CINI. Oh! What?!

DINA. Even this morning...

AMALIA. The first time we were left at the door for more than fifteen minutes. Nobody came to open it, and we couldn't even leave a card. Today we tried again...

DINA (*with a gesture expressing terror*). *He* came to the door!

MRS SIRELLI. Yes, what a face! It's really a nasty face! He scared the entire town with that face of his! And then, with that black suit on all the time... All three of them are wearing black, even the wife, right? the daughter?

SIRELLI (*annoyed*). But nobody's ever seen the daughter! I told you a thousand times! Probably she wears black too... They're from a little village in Marsica...

AMALIA. – yes, destroyed, totally, it seems...

SIRELLI. – totally, razed to the ground, by the recent earthquake.

DINA. They say they've lost all their relatives.

MRS CINI (*anxious to get back to the interrupted story*). Well, so then he came to the door?

AMALIA. So, the minute I saw him there, with that face of his, I was practically speechless... could barely tell him that we'd come to call on his mother-in-law. Nothing, you know? Not even thanks.

DINA. Well, he *did* bow.

AMALIA. But just like this, barely a nod.

DINA. The eyes, you should tell them about. The eyes of a wild animal, not of a man!

MRS CINI (*as above*). So then what did he say?

DINA. He was all wrought up...

AMALIA. ... yes, all flustered... he said his mother-in-law was indisposed... thanked us for the courtesy... and he stayed there on the threshold, waiting for us to leave.

DINA. We were mortified!

SIRELLI. What a rude hick! Oh, but that's him, for sure, you know? Maybe he's keeping the mother-in-law locked up too!

MRS SIRELLI. Some nerve! Do that to his superior's wife!

AMALIA. Oh, but this time my husband really got angry, he took it as a serious lack of respect, and he's gone to protest to the Prefect, demanding an apology.

DINA. Oh, just in time, here's Daddy!

Scene Three
Counsel Agazzi and the previous characters

AGAZZI (*fifty years old, unkempt, red hair, bearded, gold-rimmed spectacles, authoritarian, irritable*). Oh, Sirelli, old man. (*Approaching the sofa, bows and shakes hand with Mrs Sirelli*) Dear Mrs Sirelli.

AMALIA (*introducing Mrs Cini*). My husband, Mrs Cini.

AGAZZI (*bowing and shaking her hand*). Very pleased. (*Then turning almost solemnly to his wife and daughter*) Be aware that Mrs Frola will be here shortly.

MRS SIRELLI (*clapping for joy*). Ah, she's coming? coming here?

AGAZZI. You bet she is! Could I tolerate such an open insult to my house, my women folk?

SIRELLI. Way to go! We were just saying the same exact thing!

MRS SIRELLI. And that it would have been a good idea to use this opportunity...

AGAZZI. ... to call to the Prefect's attention everything they're saying about this gentleman? Don't worry, that's just what I did!

SIRELLI. Oh good, good!

MRS CINI. Things you'd never dream of! unheard of!

AMALIA. Really savage! Did you know he keeps them both locked up?

DINA. No, mother, we still don't know that about the mother-in-law!

MRS SIRELLI. But the wife, yes, no doubt about it!

SIRELLI. And the Prefect, what did he say?

AGAZZI. Oh, yes... Well... he was very... very struck by it...

SIRELLI. Oh, thank goodness!

AGAZZI. He'd heard some talk too, and... and he too sees this as a good chance to clear up this mystery, to get to know the truth.

LAUDISI (*bursting into a loud laughter*). Ha, ha, ha, ha!

AMALIA. That's just what we need now, your laughter!

AGAZZI. And why is he laughing?

MRS SIRELLI. Because he says that it's impossible to discover the truth!

Scene Four
Servant, the previous characters, and later Mrs Frola

SERVANT (*coming to the door and announcing*). Excuse me. Mrs Frola.

SIRELLI. Oh, here she is!

AGAZZI. Now we'll see if it's impossible, dear Lamberto!

MRS SIRELLI. This is wonderful! Oh, I'm just so happy!

AMALIA (*rising*). Shall we show her in?

AGAZZI. No, please, stay seated. Let her come in first. Sit down, sit down, everyone. You all must stay seated. (*To the servant*) Show her in. (*The servant exits. A moment later Mrs Frola enters, and everybody rises. Mrs Frola is a neat little old lady, modest, very pleasant, her eyes full of an enormous sadness, tempered by a constant sweet smile.*)

AMALIA (*going forward to meet her, extending her hand*). Please, do come in, Mrs Frola. (*Holding her hand, she introduces the others*) Mrs Sirelli, a good friend of mine. Mrs Cini. My husband. Mr Sirelli. My daughter, Dina. My brother, Lamberto Laudisi. Please have a seat.

MRS FROLA. I'm so sorry... I apologize for putting off paying my respects until today. You, dear Mrs Agazzi, you've so kindly honoured me with your visit, when it was my place to come here first.

AMALIA. Oh, dear Mrs Frola, between neighbours it doesn't matter who's first. Especially since you're here alone, a stranger, and, you know, might have needed...

MRS FROLA. Thank you, thank you. You're so kind.

MRS SIRELLI. *Are* you alone in town?

MRS. FROLA. No, I have a married daughter, who came to live here a short time ago too.

SIRELLI. Your son-in-law is the new secretary of the Prefect's office, Mr Ponza, isn't he? ·

MRS FROLA. Yes, yes, he is. And I hope the Counsel will be so kind as to pardon me, and my son-in-law too.

AGAZZI. To tell the truth, dear lady, I was somewhat offended...

MRS FROLA (*cutting in*). ... you were right, you were right! But you must excuse him! Believe me, our tragedy has left us so distraught...

AMALIA. Oh, yes, you were victims of that terrible disaster!

MRS SIRELLI. Did you lose any relatives?

MRS FROLA. Oh, all of them. Every one, Mrs Sirelli. There's almost no trace left of our village: it's left there in the midst of the countryside, a heap of ruins, abandoned.

SIRELLI. Yes, we heard!

MRS FROLA. I had only one sister left, with a daughter, still unmarried. The thing was much worse for my poor son-in-law: his mother, two brothers, a sister, and brothers-in-law, sisters-in-law, two nephews.

SIRELLI. A massacre!

MRS FROLA. And they're disasters you'll never get over! You're dazed!

AMALIA. Oh, of course!

MRS SIRELLI. From one moment to the next! You could go out of your mind!

MRS FROLA. You just can't think straight any more. You neglect things... unintentionally, of course, Counsel.

AGAZZI. Oh please, no more, dear Mrs Frola.

AMALIA. In fact, it was because of all that had happened to you that my daughter and I called on you first.

MRS SIRELLI (*dying to get to the point*). Yes! Knowing that you were so alone! ... Although, pardon me; dear Mrs Frola, if I dare ask... how come, with your daughter here in town, after a disaster like that, which... (*becoming a little shy, after such smooth sailing*) it seems to me, would make the survivors feel the need to be together...

MRS FROLA (*completing the sentence herself to ease Mrs Sirelli's embarrassment*). ... how come I'm living all alone, is that it?

SIRELLI. Right, there you are. It does look strange, to tell the truth.

MRS FROLA (*sadly*). Eh, I understand. (*Then, as if she were searching for a way out*) But, you know, I'm of the opinion that when a son or a daughter gets married, they should be left to themselves, to live their own life, I mean.

LAUDISI. Excellent! Very true! Which by its very nature must be a new life, with new relationships with the wife or the husband.

MRS SIRELLI. But pardon me, Laudisi, not to the point of shutting your mother out of one's own life!

LAUDISI. Who's talking about shutting anyone out? We're speaking – if I've understood correctly – of a mother who understands that her daughter cannot and should not stay tied to her as before, now that she has a different life of her own.

MRS FROLA (*with intense gratitude*). There you are, that's just the way it is! Thank you! That's just what I wanted to say.

MRS CINI. But I imagine your daughter must come here... must come here often to keep you company.

MRS FROLA (*very uncomfortable*). Oh... yes... we see each other, sure...

SIRELLI (*quickly*). But your daughter never leaves home! Or at least nobody's ever seen her!

MRS CINI. Maybe she has to mind the children!

MRS FROLA. No, no children, not yet. And perhaps, by now, she'll never have any. She's been married seven years already. She has work to do at home, of course. But that's not the reason. (*Smiling sadly, she adds, attempting another way out*) We women, you know, we're accustomed, in our small villages, to stay at home.

AGAZZI. Even when there's a mother to visit? A mother who doesn't live with us any longer?

AMALIA. But maybe Mrs Frola goes to visit her daughter herself!

MRS. FROLA (*immediately*). Oh, sure, of course! I go to see her once or twice a day.

SIRELLI. And once or twice a day you climb all those stairs, up to the top floor of that huge house?

MRS FROLA (*turning pale, yet still trying to hide the torture of this interrogation beneath a smile*). Oh, no. I don't really climb up. You're right, sir. It'd be too much for me. I don't go up. My daughter comes to the rail above the courtyard and... and we see each other, and talk.

MRS SIRELLI. Is that all? You never see her any closer?

DINA (*putting her arm around her mother's neck*). I'm a daughter, and I wouldn't expect my mother to climb five or six flights of steps for my sake; but I wouldn't be satisfied to see her and talk to her from a distance like that, without hugging her, holding her close to me.

MRS FROLA (*visibly upset, embarrassed*). You're right! Oh yes, I ought to explain. ... I wouldn't like you to think something untrue about my daughter – that she doesn't have sufficient feeling for me, sufficient consideration. Nor something untrue about me, her mother... Five or six flights of steps can't be an obstacle to a mother, no matter how old and tired she is, when up there she has the reward of holding her own daughter close.

MRS SIRELLI (*triumphantly*). Ah, there you are! As we were just saying, dear Mrs Frola, there must be a reason!

AMALIA (*pointedly*). You see, Lamberto? There *is* a reason!

SIRELLI (*quickly*). Your son-in-law, right?

MRS FROLA. Oh, but for heaven's sake, don't think badly of him. He's such a fine young man! You people can't imagine how good he is! What tender, delicate feelings he has for me, how thoughtful he is! Let alone the love and concern he has for my daughter. Believe me, I couldn't have wished for a better husband for my daughter!

MRS SIRELLI. Well... what then?

MRS CINI. Then he can't be the reason!

AGAZZI. Of course not, it's inconceivable that he forbids his wife to go to visit her mother, or the mother to go up to his house to spend a little time with her daughter!

MRS FROLA. He doesn't forbid it, no! I didn't say that he forbids it! It's ourselves, Counsel, my daughter and I. We refrain of our own free will, believe me, out of consideration for him.

AGAZZI. Pardon me, but how could he be offended? I don't see...

MRS FROLA. Not offended, Counsel. It's a feeling... a feeling, my dear ladies, that's hard to understand, maybe, but once you've understood, it's no longer difficult – believe me – to put up with, although there's no question it does demand a heavy sacrifice from me and my daughter.

AGAZZI. You must admit it's pretty strange, dear Mrs Frola, all this you're telling us.

SIRELLI. Right, and enough to arouse quite a bit of legitimate curiosity.

AGAZZI. And even, perhaps, a certain amount of suspicion.

MRS FROLA. Against him? Please don't say that! What kind of suspicion, Counsel?

AGAZZI. Oh, nothing, don't be upset, please. I only said one might have suspicions.

MRS FROLA. No, no! What about? Our arrangement functions perfectly! We're happy with it, very happy, both my daughter and I.

MRS SIRELLI. Is it jealousy, perhaps?

MRS FROLA. Towards her mother? Jealousy? I don't think you can call it that. Although I don't know for sure. You see, he wants his wife's heart all for himself, to the point that he wants even the love that my daughter must feel for her mother (and he doesn't deny that, not at all!) to reach me through him, that's all!

AGAZZI. Oh! Pardon me, but I think that's downright cruel!

MRS FROLA. No, no, not cruel! don't say cruel, Counsel! Believe me, it's something else! I seem unable to express myself... It's nature, that's it. But, no... Perhaps, oh God, perhaps it's a kind of sickness, if you prefer. It's a kind of fullness of love... closed in... that's it, yes, exclusive – in which the wife must live without ever going out, and into which nobody else may enter.

DINA. Not even her mother?

SIRELLI. Quite selfish, I'd say!

MRS FROLA. Perhaps. But a selfishness that gives all of itself, its entire world, to one's own wife! The selfishness would be mine, essentially, if I should try to forcibly open that closed world of love, knowing that my daughter lives happily in it, adored so deeply! That should be enough for a mother, my dear ladies, shouldn't it? ... After all, I see my daughter, I speak to her... (*with a gesture indicating that what she's going to say is confidential*). The basket I pull up and down in that courtyard always carries a few little words about the events of the day... That's enough for me... And besides, I've grown accustomed to it... or, if you like, resigned! I don't find it so painful any more.

AMALIA. Well, after all, if they're happy...

MRS FROLA (*rising*). Oh, yes! I told you. Because he's so good... believe me! He couldn't be any better! We all have our weaknesses, and we must bear with each other. (*She shakes hands with Amalia.*) Dear Mrs Agazzi. (*She shakes hands with Mrs Sirelli and Mrs Cini, then with Dina, then turning to Mr Agazzi:*) I hope you've pardoned me...

AGAZZI. Oh, dear Mrs Frola, what're you saying? We 're extremely grateful for your visit.

MRS FROLA (*nodding to Mr Sirelli and Laudisi, then turning to Amalia*). No, please, stay here, dear Mrs Agazzi. Don't bother...

AMALIA. No, dear Mrs Frola, of course I'll see you out. (*Mrs Frola exits accompanied by Amalia who returns immediately.*)

SIRELLI. No way! Are you satisfied with that explanation?

AGAZZI. What explanation? God knows what mystery's at the bottom of all this!

MRS SIRELLI. And God knows how hard it must be for the heart of that poor mother!

DINA. But for her daughter too, my God! (*A pause*)

MRS CINI (*shrilly from the corner of the room where she has crept to hide her tears*). Her voice was trembling with tears!

AMALIA. Yes! When she said she'd climb six flights just to hold her daughter close!

LAUDISI. What struck me was her attempt – in fact I'd say her determination – to protect her son-in-law from any suspicion!

MRS SIRELLI. What? My God, she couldn't find a way to excuse him!

SIRELLI. Excuse what? Violence? Brutality?

Scene Five
Servant, all the preceding characters, then Mr Ponza

SERVANT (*appearing at the door*). Sir, there's a Mr Ponza asking to be received.

MRS SIRELLI. Oh! Him! (*general surprise, and a flutter of anxious curiosity – indeed, almost of panic*).

AGAZZI. Received by me?

SERVANT. Yes sir, that's what he said.

MRS SIRELLI. Please, receive him in here, Counsel. I'm a little scared, but I'm dying to see him close up – the monster!

AMALIA. What could he want?

AGAZZI. We'll see. Sit down, sit down, everyone. You must stay seated. (*To the servant*) Show him in. (*The servant bows and leaves. A moment later Mr Ponza enters. Stocky, dark-skinned, almost savage-looking, dressed entirely in black; thick, black hair, low forehead, thick, black moustache; clenches his fists constantly, speaks with an effort, in fact with barely contained violence; at intervals dries his brow with a black-bordered handkerchief. When he talks, his eyes remain hard, fixed, and grim.*) Come in, come in, please, Mr Ponza! (*Introducing him*) The new secretary, Mr Ponza: my wife, Mrs Sirelli, Mrs Cini, my daughter, Mr Sirelli, my brother-in-law, Laudisi. Please be seated.

PONZA. Thanks. Just one moment, and I'll be out of your way.

AGAZZI. Do you want to talk to me in private?

PONZA. No, I can... I can say this in front of everybody. In fact... it's my duty to make an open statement... it's my duty.

AGAZZI. Are you referring to the visit of your mother-in-law? You can save yourself the trouble, because...

PONZA. … not that, Counsel. In fact I want you to know that Mrs Frola, my mother-in-law, would certainly have called on you before your wife and daughter had the kindness to call on her, if I hadn't done everything in my power to prevent it – since I can't allow her to pay or receive calls.

AGAZZI (*with haughty resentment*). Pardon me, but why?

PONZA (*with growing anger despite his efforts to control himself*). My mother-in-law has certainly talked to you about her daughter; she's told you that I forbid her to see her, to go up to my apartment, right?

AMALIA. No, no, she has shown nothing but respect and goodwill towards you!

DINA. She said nothing but good things about you!

AGAZZI. And that it's she who refrains from going up to her daughter's home, out of regard for your feelings – which frankly we must say we don't understand.

MRS SIRELLI. In fact, if we were to say exactly what we think of it…

AGAZZI. Yes, it seems cruel to us. Let's be plain, really cruel!

PONZA. I am here to clear up this very point, Counsel. That woman's condition is really pitiful. But mine is no less pitiful, if only because I'm forced to excuse myself, to spell out for you the tragedy that only… only an act of force like this could compel me to reveal. (*He pauses a minute to look at them all, then he says slowly and very distinctly*) Mrs Frola is insane.

ALL (*starting*). Insane?

PONZA. For the last four years.

MRS SIRELLI (*with a shriek*). Oh, my God. But she doesn't look it!

AGAZZI (*dumbfounded*). What do you mean, insane?

PONZA. She doesn't look it, but she's insane. And her insanity lies in the belief that I don't want to let her see her daughter. (*In an outburst of atrociously painful, savage emotion*) What daughter, in the name of God? Her daughter died four years ago!

ALL (*in consternation*). Died? … Oh! … What? … Died?

PONZA. Four years ago. That's why she went mad.

SIRELLI. Then the one who lives with you?

PONZA… I married her two years ago; she's my second wife.

AMALIA. And Mrs Frola thinks that she's still her daughter?

PONZA. It's been her good fortune, in a sense. She saw me going by in the street with this second wife of mine, from the window of the room where they kept her shut in. She thought she was seeing her daughter, alive, and started smiling, trembling; she emerged suddenly from the gloomy desperation she'd fallen into, only to find herself in this other obsession. She was elated at first, blissfully happy, then gradually she grew more calm; but she gets upset, as you saw, yet she herself has chosen a kind of resignation. At the same time, she's content, as you could see. She simply persists in her belief that it's not true her daughter is dead, but that I want to keep her all to myself and won't let her see her daughter. It's as if she were cured. So much so that to look at her, she doesn't seem insane any more.

AMALIA. Not at all, not at all.

MRS SIRELLI. Yes, she did actually say she's happy this way.

PONZA. She says that to everybody. And she shows great affection and gratitude to me. Because I try to go along with her, as much as I can, even at great sacrifice. I'm forced to maintain two households. I compel my wife, who fortunately lends herself to it very charitably, to constantly confirm her illusion that she's her daughter. She comes to the window, talks to her, writes to her. But charity, duty, ladies and gentlemen, have limits! I can't force my wife to live with her. Meanwhile, the poor woman must live as if in prison, under lock and key, afraid that she might come into the house. Yes, the old woman is calm, and has such a gentle disposition, but you understand, of course, my wife would shudder from head to foot at the inevitable caresses the old woman would lavish on her.

AMALIA (*starting, with horror and pity*). Oh, of course, poor lady, imagine such a thing!

MRS SIRELLI (*to her husband and Mrs Cini*). So, d'you hear? She's the one who wants to be locked up!

PONZA (*to cut it short*). You understand, Counsel, that I could not have allowed her to visit here, except under orders.

AGAZZI. Oh, yes, I understand, now. Everything's explained.

PONZA. It's better if people in a tragic situation like this keep to themselves. But since I was forced to send my mother-in-law here, I was also obliged to come and make this statement. I mean, out of respect for the post I occupy, so that the town would not suspect a public official of such an enormity – that out of jealousy, or anything else, I'm preventing a poor mother from seeing her daughter. (*He rises.*) I beg the ladies' pardon for having unintentionally distressed them. (*He bows.*) Counsel! (*He bows to Laudisi and Sirelli.*) Gentlemen! (*He leaves through the main door.*)

AMALIA (*astounded*). So then... she's insane!

MRS SIRELLI. The poor lady! Out of her mind.

DINA. So, that's why. She thinks she's the mother, and the other's not her daughter! (*She hides her face in her hands in horror.*) My God!

MRS CINI. Who could ever have imagined it?

AGAZZI. Yet... from the way she was talking...

LAUDISI. ... you'd already guessed it?

AGAZZI. No... but, it's true that... she herself didn't know how to explain it!

MRS SIRELLI. Of course, poor thing. She's irrational!

SIRELLI. However – yet pardon me – it's strange, for someone who's insane! She was certainly irrational. But the way she was trying to explain why her son-in-law doesn't want her to see her daughter, to find excuses for him, to comply with the excuses she found herself...

AGAZZI. Oh, but don't you see, that's the real proof she's insane! She keeps trying to find excuses for her son-in-law, and can't find a convincing one.

AMALIA. Right! She kept saying one thing, then taking it back.

AGAZZI (*to Sirelli*). And if she weren't crazy, do you think she could accept those conditions – being allowed to see her daughter only at a window, with the excuse she comes up with – that morbid love of a husband who wants his wife all to himself?

SIRELLI. Okay, but does that prove she's crazy, that she accepts it? And is she really resigned to it? It all seems strange to me, very strange. (*To Laudisi*) And what's your opinion?

LAUDISI. My opinion? I have none!

Scene Six
Servant, all of the preceding, then Mrs Frola

SERVANT (*knocking, then appearing in the doorway, uneasy*). Excuse me, Mrs Frola is back.

AMALIA (*appalled*). Oh, God, what d'we do now? What if we can't get rid of her?

MRS SIRELLI. Of course, now that we know she's insane!

MRS CINI. Lord, Lord! Who knows what she'll tell us this time! I'm dying to hear her!

SIRELLI. I'm curious too. I'm not at all sure she's crazy!

DINA. Of course, Mother! There's nothing to be afraid of. She's so calm!

AGAZZI. We must see her, of course. Let's hear what she wants. If necessary, we'll take measures. But be seated, please, be seated. We must all be in our seats. (*To the servant*) Show her in. (*The servant leaves.*)

AMALIA. Help me, for heaven's sake! I don't know how to speak to her any more! (*Mrs Frola comes in. Amalia rises and goes to meet her, visibly frightened. The others look at Mrs Frola with fear.*)

MRS FROLA. May I come in?

AMALIA. Please, come in, come in. My friends are still here, as you can see...

MRS FROLA (*sad but pleasant, smiling*). ... who are looking at me – as you are – dear Mrs Agazzi, like a poor madwoman, right?

AMALIA. No, my dear lady, what're you saying?

MRS FROLA (*with deep sorrow*). Ah, better the rudeness of leaving you outside the door, as I did that first time! I never thought you'd come back and force me to pay you this visit – I'd foreseen all these unfortunate consequences!

AMALIA. No, believe me, we're glad to see you again.

SIRELLI. Mrs Frola is troubled over something... we don't know what... let her talk.

MRS FROLA. Didn't my son-in-law leave just a moment ago?

AGAZZI. Yes, but he came... to see me, to... to talk with me about office matters!

MRS FROLA (*hurt, dismayed*). Oh, this pitiful lie you're telling me, so I won't be upset...

AGAZZI. No, no, dear lady. You can be sure I'm telling you the truth.

MRS FROLA (*as above*). Was he calm, at least? Did he speak calmly?

AGAZZI. Yes, of course, calm, very calm, wasn't he? (*Everybody nods, in agreement.*)

MRS FROLA. Oh, God, you people are trying to reassure me, while I, on the contrary, want to reassure you about him!

MRS SIRELLI. But what about him, dear lady? We just told you that...

AGAZZI. ... he talked to me about office matters...

MRS FROLA. But I can see how you're all looking at me! Please bear with me. I'm not doing this for myself. From the way you're looking at me, I know he came here to prove something I'd never have revealed for all the gold in the world! You'll all agree that a little while ago I wasn't able to answer your questions – which, believe me, were very painful for me – and I gave you an explanation about our family that couldn't satisfy anybody. I admit that! But could I tell you the real

reason? Or could I have told you – as he goes around saying – that
my daughter died four years ago, and that I'm a poor madwoman
who thinks she's still alive, and he doesn't want to let me see her?

AGAZZI (*amazed by Mrs Frola's tone of deep sincerity*). Oh... but what? Your
daughter?

MRS FROLA (*immediately, anxiously*). See? it's true! Why are you trying to
hide it? He told you that...

SIRELLI (*hesitating, but observing her closely*). Yes... in fact, he said...

MRS FROLA. Of course, I know what he said! And I know how deeply it
upsets him to have to say that about me! It's a real tragedy, Counsel,
which through terrible privation and suffering we've been able to
deal with... by agreeing to live the way we live. I understand, of
course, that it must attract attention, must seem suspicious, even
scandalous. But on the other hand, if he's an excellent employee...
zealous, scrupulous... You've certainly had occasion to see that.

AGAZZI. No, to tell the truth, I haven't had the opportunity yet.

MRS FROLA. For heaven's sake, don't judge from appearances! He's very
good – all his superiors have said so. So why torture him with this
inquiry into his family, his tragedy? As I said, we've managed, and, if
word got around, it could ruin his career.

AGAZZI. But no, dear Mrs Frola, stop worrying so much. Nobody wants
to torture him.

MRS FROLA. My God, how could you expect me not to worry, when I see
him forced to give everybody an absurd... a horrible explanation!
Can you really believe that my daughter is dead? that I'm crazy? that
the one he's living with is his second wife? It's a need he feels, believe
me, it's a compulsion to say that! It was the only way to restore his
serenity, his trust. But he himself is aware of the enormity of what
he's saying, and, when he's forced to say it, he gets all worked up,
terribly upset. You've seen him!

AGAZZI. Well, yes, he was... he was a bit worked up.

MRS SIRELLI. Oh, God! But what? Then, he's the one?

SIRELLI. Of course, it must be him! (*Triumphant*) Ladies and gentlemen,
I told you!

AGAZZI. Come on! Is it possible? (*keen agitation all around*).

MRS FROLA (*at once, clasping her hands*). No, for heaven's sake, ladies and
gentlemen! What are you thinking of? It's only that one subject you
bring up! Just think of it: would I leave my daughter alone with him,
if he were really mad? Of course not! Besides, you can have all the
proof you need at the office, Counsel, where his work is impeccable.

AGAZZI. Oh, but you must explain how things stand – and very clearly too, dear Mrs Frola. Is it possible that your son-in-law came here to trump up such a story?

MRS FROLA. Yes, sir, certainly, I'll explain the whole thing. But you must have pity on him, Counsel.

AGAZZI. But what do you mean? The story of your daughter's death isn't true?

MRS FROLA (*horrified*). Oh, no, God forbid!

AGAZZI (*shouting, very irritated*). But then he's the one who's mad!

MRS FROLA (*begging*). No, no... look...

SIRELLI (*triumphant*). Oh yes, by God, it must be him!

MRS FROLA. No, look! Look! He's not, he's not insane! Let me explain! You've seen him: he's so strong physically, violent... When he got married, he was seized by a real frenzy of love. He almost came close to destroying my daughter, who was somewhat frail. On the advice of the doctor, and of all the relatives – including his (who are all gone now, poor things) – they had to take his wife away from him secretly and put her in a clinic. He was already a little deranged, of course, due to that... excessive love of his, so when he found her gone, he was overcome by despair; he was raving, he thought his wife had actually died, he wouldn't listen to reason; he insisted on dressing in mourning, did lots of crazy things, and it was impossible to shake his conviction. So much so that when, after only a year, my daughter had recovered completely and was brought back to him, he said no, that she wasn't the same one, no, no – he looked at her, no, she wasn't the same one. Oh, my dear ladies, what a terrible thing! He went up close to her, he seemed to recognize her, and then again no, no... and in order to make him take her back, with the help of friends we had to fake a second marriage.

MRS SIRELLI. Oh, so you're saying that this is why...

MRS FROLA. Yes, but not even he believes it any more! He needs to convince other people, he can't help it! To feel sure himself, you understand? Maybe because, from time to time, he's seized with fear that his darling wife may be taken away from him again. (*In a low voice, smiling confidentially*) That's why he keeps her under lock and key, all for himself. But he worships her, I'm sure of it! And my daughter is happy. (*She rises.*) I must leave. I'd hate it if he were to come back to my place right away and find me gone, if he's that upset. (*She sighs sweetly, her hands clasped.*) We must be patient! My poor darling must pretend to be someone else, not herself; and I...

ah,… I must pretend to be crazy, my dear ladies. But what can you
do? As long as he's calm! Please don't bother, I know the way out.
Goodbye, ladies and gentlemen, goodbye. (*Bowing, she withdraws
quickly through the main exit. All the others remain standing, astounded,
staring at each other. Silence.*)

LAUDISI (*moving to the centre of the group*). All staring at each other, eh?
The truth?! (*Exploding in loud laughter*) Ha! Ha! Ha! Ha!

CURTAIN

ACT TWO

(*The study in the home of Counsel Agazzi: antique furniture; old paintings on
the walls; a curtained doorway on the back wall. Another curtained doorway
stage left opens into the drawing room. Stage right a large fireplace, on its mantel
a large mirror; a telephone on the desk; also a small sofa, easy chairs, other
chairs, etc.*)

Scene One
Agazzi, Laudisi, Sirelli

(*Agazzi is standing near his desk, speaking on the telephone. Laudisi and Sirelli,
seated, are looking at him, waiting.*)

AGAZZI. Hello! … Yes. … Is this Centuri? … Well? Yes, very good. (*After
listening for quite a while*) Excellent! What are you saying? Is that
possible? (*After listening again for quite a while*) I understand, but if you
search a little harder… (*Again after a long pause*) But it's very strange
that there's no way… (*Another pause*) I understand, yes… I understand. (*Pause again*) Okay, take care… See you. (*He puts down the
receiver and comes forward.*)

SIRELLI (*anxious*). Well?

AGAZZI. Nothing.

SIRELLI. Nothing can be found?

AGAZZI. Everything scattered: municipal building, archives, records
office.

SIRELLI. What about the testimony of some survivors at least?

AGAZZI. There's no knowledge of any survivors; and if there were any,
it's very difficult to trace them now.

SIRELLI. So all we can do is to believe either one or the other without any proof?

AGAZZI. Unfortunately, yes.

LAUDISI (*rising*). Want my advice? believe both of them.

AGAZZI. Sure, and how can we do that?

SIRELLI. ... when one's saying white and the other is saying black?

LAUDISI. Then don't believe either of them.

SIRELLI. You're joking. We have no proof, no factual data, but the truth must be on one side or the other!

LAUDISI. Factual data! What would you get from those?

AGAZZI. Well, for instance, the death certificate of the daughter, if Mrs Frola is the crazy one – unfortunately it can't be found, nothing can be found any more – But it must have existed. Some day it could be found – then, once it's found, it would be clear that the son-in-law is right.

SIRELLI. Could you deny the evidence, if some day such a document were put in front of you?

LAUDISI. Me? I haven't denied anything! Far from it! You're asking for factual data, for documents, so you can either accept or deny – not me! I have no use for them, because, as far as I am concerned, reality lies not in them but in the minds of those two, and I've got no access to their minds, except for whatever they choose to tell me.

SIRELLI. Fine! Aren't they saying that one of them is crazy? Either she is or he is? There is no escape from that! Which one is it?

AGAZZI. That's the question!

LAUDISI. First of all, it's not true that both of them say that. He says it, Mr Ponza, about his mother-in-law. Mrs Frola denies it, about both herself and him. At most, she says, his thinking was a bit impaired at one time, by excessive love. But now, he's in perfect mental health.

SIRELLI. Ah, so like me you lean towards what she says, the mother-in-law?

AGAZZI. No doubt about it, if you accept what she says you can explain everything.

LAUDISI. But if you accept what he says, the son-in-law, you can explain everything just as well.

SIRELLI. But then – neither one is crazy? Look, one of them has to be, for God's sake!

LAUDISI. But which one? You can't say which one, just as nobody else can, and not so much because these factual data you're looking for

have been obliterated – dispersed or destroyed – by some kind of
accident – a fire, an earthquake – no! But because they themselves
have obliterated those factual data, in their minds, don't you understand? and they've created, she about him and he about her, a fantasy
that has all the solidity of reality – a fantasy in which they live by now
in perfect, tranquil harmony, quite calmly. And that reality of theirs
can't be destroyed by any document, because they're living inside it,
feeling it, touching it! At most the document might be of some use to
you, to satisfy your foolish curiosity. But you have no document, and
now you're condemned to the exquisite torture of having before you
both the illusion and the reality, and being unable to distinguish one
from the other!

AGAZZI. Philosophy, old man, philosophy! We'll see, now we'll see if it is
impossible!

SIRELLI. We've heard first one, then the other; now if we get the two of
them to confront each other, don't you think we'll be able to find out
what's fantasy and what's reality?

LAUDISI. As long as you let me ask your permission to keep laughing to
the end.

AGAZZI. All right, all right. We'll see who has the last laugh. Let's stop
wasting time! (*Going to the door stage left, he calls out*) Amalia, Mrs Sirelli,
come here, come here!

Scene Two
Amalia, Mrs Sirelli, Dina, and all the above

MRS SIRELLI (*to Laudisi, shaking her finger at him*). You still here? Still at
it?

SIRELLI. He's incorrigible!

MRS SIRELLI. How come you're not dying to get to the bottom of this
mystery like the rest of us? It's driving us all crazy! I haven't slept all
night!

AGAZZI. Please, my dear lady, don't get him started!

LAUDISI. Pay attention to my brother-in-law, instead. He'll help you get
to sleep tonight.

AGAZZI. So, let's decide: you ladies'll go to Mrs Frola's...

AMALIA. Will she let us in?

AGAZZI. Well, I should think so!

DINA. It's our duty to return the visit.

AMALIA. But if he doesn't let her either pay visits or receive any?

SIRELLI. Yes, before! When nobody knew anything yet. But now that she's been forced to speak out, and she's explained in her own way the reasons for his reserve...

MRS SIRELLI (*continuing*). ... perhaps she'd really like to tell us something about the daughter.

DINA. She's so nice! I've no doubts, you know: he's the crazy one!

AGAZZI. No rush! Let's not rush to judgment. So, listen to me. (*Looking at his watch*) You'll stay there a short time, fifteen minutes at most.

SIRELLI (*to his wife*). Please, pay attention!

MRS SIRELLI (*furious*). Why me?

SIRELLI. Because once you start talking...

DINA (*to forestall an altercation*). Fifteen minutes, fifteen minutes, I'll make sure.

AGAZZI. I'll get over to the Prefect's office and will be back here at eleven. Let's say in twenty minutes.

SIRELLI (*eagerly*). And me?

AGAZZI. Wait a moment. (*To the women*) A little before that, with some excuse or other, you'll invite Mrs Frola to come here.

AMALIA. What... what excuse?

AGAZZI. Any excuse! Something will come up in the conversation. D'you think you won't find one? Aren't you women? With Dina there and Mrs Sirelli...? Of course you'll go into the living room (*going to the door stage left, opens it wide and draws the curtain aside*). This door must stay this way – wide open, this way! So you can be heard talking from this room. I'll leave these papers on my desk. I'm supposed to take them with me. Some office business I have set up for Mr Ponza to take care of. I pretend to forget to take them with me, and on that pretext I bring him back here with me. Then...

SIRELLI (*as above*). But what about me? When am I supposed to come?

AGAZZI. A few minutes after eleven, when the ladies are already in the living room, and I'm in here with him. You're coming to pick up your wife. You have yourself shown into this room. Then I'll ask the ladies to please come into the study too...

LAUDISI (*cutting in*). And the truth shall be revealed!

DINA. But uncle dear, when they confront each other...

AGAZZI. Never mind him, for God's sake. Go, go. There's no time to waste!

MRS SIRELLI. Yes, let's go, let's go. (*To Laudisi*) You I'm not even going to say goodbye to!

LAUDISI. Well, I'll say goodbye on your behalf, Mrs Sirelli! (*He shakes his own hand.*) Good luck! (*Amalia, Dina, and Mrs Sirelli depart.*)

AGAZZI (*to Sirelli*). We have to go too, eh? Right.

SIRELLI. Yes, let's go. Goodbye, Lamberto.

LAUDISI. Goodbye, goodbye. (*Agazzi and Sirelli leave.*)

Scene Three
Laudisi alone, later the servant

LAUDISI (*moves around the study for a while, laughing and shaking his head, then stops in front of the large mirror on the mantelpiece, looks at his reflection, and speaks to it*). Oh, there you are! (*He greets it with two fingers, winking slyly, and sneers*) Well, old man. Who's the crazy one, me or you? (*He points a finger at his reflection, which of course points a finger at him. After another malicious smile:*) Well, I know... I say you and you point to me. Come on, surely face to face the two of us know each other pretty well! The unfortunate thing is, the others don't see you the way I do! And in that case, old man, what becomes of you? I'm talking about me, the one who's seeing and touching myself in front of you... so you, as far as others see you, what becomes of you? You're a phantom, old man, a phantom! And yet, see these crazy people? Instead of paying attention to the phantom they carry around with them, inside themselves, they're running, bursting with curiosity, after somebody else's phantom! And they think it's a different thing. (*The servant, entering, is startled by the last words Laudisi has addressed to the mirror. Then he calls out:*)

SERVANT. Signor Lamberto.

LAUDISI. Well?

SERVANT. There are two ladies: Mrs Cini and another one.

LAUDISI. Asking for me?

SERVANT They asked for Mrs Agazzi; I told them she's visiting Mrs Frola, next door, so they...

LAUDISI. So they?

SERVANT. They looked at each other; they got all excited, clapped their hands, gloves and all: 'Oh yes? really?' and asked if anyone at all was at home.

LAUDISI. And you certainly answered that nobody was home.

SERVANT. I answered that you were.

LAUDISI. Me? No. Maybe the one they know!

SERVANT (*even more astounded*). What're you saying?

LAUDISI. Well, do you think it's the same one?

SERVANT (*as above, attempting a weak smile, open mouthed*). I don't understand.

LAUDISI. Who are you speaking to?

SERVANT (*stunned*). What? Who am I speaking to? To you.

LAUDISI. And are you sure I'm the same one those ladies are asking for?

SERVANT. Well... I wouldn't know... They said: Mrs Agazzi's brother...

LAUDISI. Good boy! Ah... Well, yes, then it's me, it's me. Show them in, show them in. (*The servant withdraws, turning several times to look back at Laudisi, as if he can't believe his eyes.*)

Scene Four
Laudisi, Mrs Cini, Mrs Nenni

MRS CINI. May I come in?

LAUDISI. Come in, come in, dear Mrs Cini.

MRS CINI. I was told that Mrs Agazzi is not in. And I've brought my friend with me, Mrs Nenni (*she introduces her: an even sillier and more affected old lady, just as avidly curious but more wary, frightened*), who wants so much to meet Mrs...

LAUDISI (*quickly*). ... Frola?

MRS CINI. No, no: your sister!

LAUDISI. Oh, she'll come, she'll be here soon. Mrs Frola as well. Please, sit down (*he invites them to sit on the small sofa, then sits down amiably between the two of them*). May I? It does seat three comfortably. Mrs Sirelli is next door too.

MRS CINI. Yes, the servant told us.

LAUDISI. All arranged, you know. It's going to be such a scene, such a scene! Any moment now, at eleven o'clock, right here!

MRS CINI (*befuddled*). Arranged? But what?

LAUDISI (*playing up the mystery, first by solemnly crossing his two index fingers, then by his tone of voice*). The encounter. (*With a gesture of admiration*) A great idea!

MRS CINI. What... what encounter?

LAUDISI. Of the two of them. First he'll come in here.

MRS CINI. Mr Ponza?

LAUDISI. Yes, while she will be taken in there (*pointing to the living room*).

MRS CINI. Mrs Frola?

LAUDISI. Exactly. (*Conveying a sense of mystery as above, first by an explicit gesture, then by his tone of voice*) But then, both of them in here, facing each other; and all of us around them, to see and hear. A great idea!

MRS CINI. In order to find out... ?

LAUDISI. ... the truth! But we know it already! All that's left is to unmask it.

MRS CINI (*surprised and visibly anxious*). Oh, we know? Who is it then? Which one of the two? Who is it?

LAUDISI. Let's see. Take a guess. Who do *you* say it is?

MRS CINI (*overjoyed, hesitant*). Well... I... Well...

LAUDISI. Him or her? Let's see... Take a guess... Come on!

MRS CINI. I... I say it's him!

LAUDISI (*looks at her briefly*). It's him.

MRS NENNI (*delighted*). Him! ... Well, we women all said so!

MRS CINI. And how did they find out? Proof was discovered, right? factual data.

MRS NENNI. Through the police, right? That's just what we were saying! Impossible that they couldn't get to the bottom of it through the Prefect's office!

LAUDISI (*gestures for them to lean closer to him, then in a mysterious tone, in a low voice, enunciating each syllable distinctly*). The certificate of the second marriage.

MRS CINI (*as if she'd been punched on the nose*). The second?

MRS NENNI (*very upset*). What? What? The second marriage?

MRS CINI (*regaining her composure, annoyed*). But then... then he would be right?

LAUDISI. Ah, yes! Factual data, my dear ladies: the second marriage certificate, it makes things quite clear.

MRS NENNI (*almost in tears*). But then *she's* the crazy one?

LAUDISI. Oh, yes! So it seems.

MRS CINI. What? A moment ago you said he's the one, now you say she is?

LAUDISI. Yes. But only because the document, my dear lady, this second marriage certificate, could very well be – as Mrs Frola assured us – a fabrication, right? drawn up fraudulently, with the help of friends, to go along with his fixation that his wife wasn't the same woman, but another.

MRS CINI. Ah, then, a document... with no value?

LAUDISI. Well, that is... With the value, my dear ladies, with the value that anyone wants to attribute to it! Aren't there also the little notes that Mrs Frola says she gets from her daughter every day in the little basket, there in the courtyard? Those little notes do exist, right?

MRS CINI. Yes, and so?

LAUDISI. And so? Documents, my dear lady! Documents, even these little notes! But according to the value you want to attribute to them! Mr Ponza says they're fake, written to go along with Mrs Frola's fixation.

MRS CINI. But then, oh Lord, we know nothing with certainty!

LAUDISI. What do you mean nothing?! Why nothing? Let's not exaggerate! Pardon me, the days of the week, how many are there?

MRS CINI. Well, seven.

LAUDISI. Monday, Tuesday, Wednesday...

MRS CINI. ... Thursday, Friday, Saturday...

LAUDISI. ... and Sunday! (*Turning to the other woman*) And the months of the year?

MRS NENNI. Twelve!

LAUDISI. January, February, March...

MRS CINI. All right, we get it! You are trying to make fun of us!

Scene Five
All the above and Dina

DINA (*enters running through the door at the rear of the stage*). Uncle, please... (*seeing Mrs Cini, she stops short*). Mrs Cini, you here?

MRS CINI. Yes, I came with Mrs Nenni...

LAUDISI. ... who wants so much to meet Mrs Frola.

MRS NENNI. No, please.

MRS CINI. He keeps making fun of us! My dear Dina! He's mixed us up completely. Like when a train comes into a station: tun-tun, tun-tun, and never stops hitting the switches! We're totally confused!

DINA. Oh, he's very naughty just now, even with his own family! Be patient. I don't need anything any more. I'm going to tell mother that you're here: it'll be enough. Oh, uncle, if you'd just heard her, what a darling little old lady! How she talks! How kind she is! And what a sweet place, everything neat and clean, everything just right, the white doilies on the furniture... She's shown us all the notes from her daughter.

MRS CINI. Yes, but... if as Mr. Laudisi was telling us...

DINA. And what does he know about them? He hasn't read them!

MRS NENNI. Couldn't they be fake?

DINA. What do you mean, fake? Pay no attention to him! How could a mother be fooled by the words of her own daughter? The last one, from yesterday... (*she is interrupted by the sound of voices coming from the living room, through the open door*). Ah, they're here, for sure. (*She goes to the living room door to look in.*)

MRS CINI (*running after her*). With her? With Mrs Frola?

DINA. Yes, come, come. We must all be in the living room. Is it eleven yet, uncle?

Scene Six
All the above and Amalia

AMALIA (*entering from the living room door, agitated*). We could not go through with this! There's no more need for proof!

DINA. Sure! I think so too! It's pointless, now.

AMALIA (*upset and anxious, greeting Mrs Cini, quickly*). My dear Mrs Cini.

MRS CINI (*introducing Mrs Nenni*). Mrs Nenni, who's come with me to…

AMALIA (*greeting Mrs Nenni quickly too*). Pleased to meet you. (*Then:*) There is no doubt any more! He's the one!

MRS CINI. It's him, isn't it? It's him.

DINA. If only the poor lady could be spared this trick, by catching father in time!

AMALIA. Yes! We got her in here! I feel as if I were betraying her!

LAUDISI. Yes! It's shameful. You're right! Especially since it's beginning to seem evident that she must be the one! Absolutely she is!

AMALIA. She's what? What are you saying?

LAUDISI. She is, she is.

AMALIA. Oh, please!

DINA. We are absolutely sure of just the opposite, now!

MRS CINI AND MRS NENNI (*overjoyed*). Yes? Yes, eh?

LAUDISI. Just because you people are so certain, that's why!

DINA. Let's go, come on, let's go in there. Don't you see he's teasing?

AMALIA. Yes, let's go, let's go, dear ladies. (*She stands at the door stage left.*) Please, do go in. (*Mrs Cini, Mrs Nenni, Amalia exit; as Dina is about to leave…*)

LAUDISI (*calling to her*). Dina!

DINA. I don't want to listen to you! No! No!

LAUDISI. Close that door, if you think proof is unnecessary now.

DINA. And father? He left it open this way on purpose. He must be about to come with that man. If he found it closed… You know how daddy is…

LAUDISI. But you'd explain (you especially) that it's no longer necessary to keep it open. Aren't you convinced?

DINA. More than convinced!

LAUDISI (*with a challenging smile*). Then close it!

DINA. You want to have the pleasure of seeing me still in doubt. I'm not closing it, but only in deference to daddy.

LAUDISI (*as above*). D'you want me to close it?

DINA. On your own responsibility!

LAUDISI. But I'm not blessed with your conviction that he's the crazy one.

DINA. Then come into the living room, listen to her talk as we have, and you won't have any doubts either any more. Are you coming?

LAUDISI. Yes, I'm coming. And I can close the door too. On my own responsibility.

DINA. Ah, you see? Even before you hear her talk!

LAUDISI. No, my dear. It's because I'm sure that your father too, at this moment, thinks, like you, that this proof is pointless.

DINA. Are you sure?

LAUDISI. Oh yes! He's speaking to Ponza! He's surely convinced that she's the crazy one. (*Goes to the door resolutely.*) I'm closing it.

DINA (*quickly stopping him*). No. (*Then regaining her composure*) Sorry... if that's what you think... let's leave it open...

LAUDISI (*with his usual laughter*). Ha, ha, ha!

DINA. I mean for daddy's sake!

LAUDISI. And daddy will say for your sake! Let's leave it open. (*From the adjoining living room comes the sound of the piano, an old song full of sweet, sad grace, from 'Nina Mad for Love' by Paisiello.*)

DINA. It's her, d'you hear? She's playing, she's playing!

LAUDISI. The old lady?

DINA. Yes, she said that her daughter, before, always played this old song. D'you hear how sweetly she plays it? Let's go, let's go. (*Both leave through the door at the left.*)

Scene Seven
Agazzi, Ponza, and later Sirelli

(*After Laudisi and Dina have left the room, the stage remains empty for a time; the piano music is heard from the next room. Mr Ponza enters through the central door with Counsel Agazzi, and, hearing that music, is profoundly shaken. His agitation gradually increases throughout the scene.*)

AGAZZI (*just outside the rear door*). Please, do go in. (*After showing Mr Ponza in, he enters too and goes towards his desk to get the papers he has intentionally forgotten there.*) Here, I must have left them here. Please have a seat. (*Mr Ponza remains standing, looking with agitation towards the living room, from where the piano music is coming.*) Here they are, in fact. (*Taking the papers, he approaches Mr Ponza, leafing through them*) It's a knotty question, as I told you, that's dragged on for years. (*He too turns to look towards the living room, annoyed by the piano music*) What's this damn music! Just now! (*In turning he makes a gesture of annoyance, as if saying to himself: 'How stupid those women are!'*) Who's playing? (*He goes to look through the door of the living room; seeing Mrs Frola, he makes a gesture of surprise*) Oh, look!

PONZA (*approaching, convulsive*). In God's name, is it her? Is she playing?

AGAZZI. Yes, your mother-in-law! How well she plays!

PONZA. So, you've dragged her here again, and make her play?

AGAZZI. I don't see what harm there can be!

PONZA. No, no, please! Not this music! It's the music her daughter used to play!

AGAZZI. Oh, perhaps it hurts you to hear her play?

PONZA. Not me, not me! It hurts *her*! It hurts her terribly! Didn't I explain to you, Counsel, and to the ladies, what that poor lady is going through?

AGAZZI (*trying to calm the increasing agitation of Ponza*). Yes, yes... but see here...

PONZA (*continuing*). She must be left in peace! She cannot receive or pay visits! I'm the only one... I'm the only one who knows how to deal with her! They're ruining her, ruining her!

AGAZZI. No, no. My wife and daughter also know, surely... (*He stops suddenly as the music in the drawing room ceases; a round of applause is heard.*) There, see, you can hear... (*From the inner room the following dialogue is heard clearly.*)

DINA. You can still play very well, dear Mrs Frola.

MRS FROLA. I? Oh, no, my Lina, you should hear my Lina, how well she plays it!

PONZA (*shaking, wringing his hands*). Her Lina! Do you hear? Her Lina, she says!

AGAZZI. Ah, yes, her daughter.

PONZA. But she's saying 'she plays! ... she plays'! (*Again from inside the inner room:*)

MRS FROLA. No, she can't play any more, since that time! And maybe that's what hurts her most, poor thing!

AGAZZI. It seems natural to me... She believes her daughter's still alive...

PONZA. But she mustn't be made to say such things! She mustn't, she mustn't say that... Did you hear? 'Since that time'... She said, 'Since that time.' On that piano, of course! She doesn't know! On my poor dead wife's piano! (*At this point Sirelli appears; hearing Ponza's last words and noticing his extreme exasperation, he stops, stunned. Agazzi, equally upset, motions to him to approach.*) Please, ask the ladies to come in here! (*Sirelli, keeping his distance from Ponza, approaches the door and summons the ladies.*)

PONZA. The ladies? In here? No, no! Rather...

Scene Eight
Mrs Frola, Amalia, Mrs Sirelli, Dina, Mrs Cini, Mrs Nenni, Laudisi, and all the above.

(*The ladies enter, summoned by the visibly agitated Sirelli; they are frightened. Mrs Frola, seeing her son-in-law in such agitation, trembling like an animal, is terrified. Attacked by him with extreme violence during the following scene, she will from time to time glance at the others significantly. The following scene develops rapidly and in extreme agitation.*)

PONZA. You here? Here again? What did you come for?

MRS FROLA. I came... Please be patient...

PONZA. You've come to talk again... What did you say? What did you say to these ladies?

MRS FROLA. Nothing! I swear! Nothing!

PONZA. Nothing? What do you mean, nothing? I heard you! And this gentleman heard you too! (*Pointing to Agazzi*) You said 'she plays'! Who plays? Lina plays? You know damn well that your daughter died four years ago!

MRS FROLA. Yes, my dear! Please be calm! Yes, yes!

PONZA. And 'She can't play any more, since that time'! Of course she can't play any more since that time! How can she play if she's dead?

MRS FROLA. Yes, of course! Didn't I say exactly that, dear ladies? I said she can't play any more since then! How can she, if she's dead?

PONZA. So why are you still thinking of that piano, then?

MRS FROLA. Me? No, I don't think of it any more! Not any more!

PONZA. I broke it into pieces! And you know it! When your daughter died! So that my second wife wouldn't touch it – she can't play anyway! You know my wife doesn't play.

MRS FROLA. Of course, if she can't play! of course!

PONZA. And what was your daughter's name, Lina was her name, right? Now tell these people what my second wife's name is! Tell all these people, because you know it perfectly well! What's her name?

MRS FROLA. Giulia! Her name's Giulia! Yes, yes, it's true, ladies and gentlemen, her name's Giulia!

PONZA. Giulia, then, not Lina! And don't try to wink while you say her name's Giulia!

MRS FROLA. Me? No, no, I didn't wink!

PONZA. I saw you! You winked! I saw you perfectly well! You want to ruin me! You want to make these people think that I want to keep your daughter all to myself, still, as if she weren't dead (*breaking into horrible sobs*). As if she weren't dead!

MRS FROLA (*running up to him immediately, with infinite tenderness and humility*). Me! No, no, my dear son! Calm down, please! I never said such a thing... Isn't it true? Isn't it true, dear ladies?

AMALIA, MRS SIRELLI, DINA. Yes, yes! She never said that! She's always said that her daughter's dead!

MRS FROLA. It's true. I said she's dead! Of course! And that you're always very good to me! (*To the ladies*) Isn't it true? Isn't it true? Me? Ruin you? Compromise you?

PONZA (*drawing himself up, with intensity*). But meanwhile you go around looking for a piano in other people's homes, to play your daughter's songs on them, and saying that Lina plays them this way, and even better!

MRS FROLA. No, it was... I did it... just... just to see if...

PONZA. You can't! You mustn't! How can you think of playing again what your dead daughter used to play?

MRS FROLA. You're right, yes! Oh, poor thing... poor thing! (*Moved, she starts to cry.*) I'll never do it again! I'll never do it again!

PONZA (*turning on her with terrific force*). Go! Go away! go away!

MRS FROLA. Yes... yes... I'm going, I'm going... Oh, my God! (*As she withdraws, crying, she makes pleading gestures to everybody to be considerate to her son-in-law.*)

Scene Nine
All the above except for Mrs Frola

(*All remain motionless, gripped by pity and terror, looking at Ponza. But as soon as Mrs Frola has left, he changes at once, and calmly, resuming his normal demeanour, simply says:*)

PONZA. I beg your pardon, ladies and gentlemen, for the sad spectacle I had to expose you to, in order to undo the evil that, unwittingly, unintentionally, out of pity, you're doing to this unhappy
woman.

AGAZZI (*dumbfounded, like the others*). What? You faked all that?

PONZA. I had to, ladies and gentlemen! Don't you understand, this is
the only way to keep her illusion? I've got to shout the truth to her, as
if it were a crazy fixation of mine! Please pardon me, and allow me to
run to her now. I must. (*He leaves quickly through the rear door. Again
they all remain motionless, astounded, silent, looking at each other.*)

LAUDISI (*moving centre stage*). So there we are, ladies and gentlemen, the
truth's been revealed! (*He bursts into laughter*) Ha! ha! ha! ha!

CURTAIN

ACT THREE

(*The same room as in Act Two*)

Scene One
Laudisi, Servant, Chief of Police Centuri

(*Laudisi is sprawling in an easy chair, reading. Through the door on the left into
the living room comes the confused sound of many voices. The servant at the rear
door is showing in Chief of Police Centuri.*)

SERVANT. Please go in. I'll go tell the Counsel immediately.

LAUDISI (*turning his head and seeing Centuri*). Oh, the Commissioner!
(*He jumps up and calls back the servant who is about to leave.*) Pssst! Wait.
(*To Centuri*) Any news?

CENTURI (*about forty, tall, stiff, frowning*). Yes, some.

LAUDISI. Oh, good! (*To the servant*) Never mind calling my brother-in-
law. I'll call him myself in a while (*indicating with a movement of his
head the door on the left. The servant bows and leaves*). You've performed
a miracle! You're going to save the town! Do you hear? Hear how
they shout? Well: solid news?

CENTURI. From someone we've been able to locate…

LAUDISI. … from the same village as Mr Ponza? People in the town?
People who ought to know what they're talking about?

CENTURI. Yes, indeed, some factual data. Not a lot, but solid.

LAUDISI. Very good, very good. For instance?

CENTURI. Here are the communications I received. (*Taking from the inner pocket of his jacket an open yellow envelope containing a sheet of paper, he gives it to Laudisi.*)

LAUDISI. Let's see, let's see! (*He takes the sheet from the envelope and starts reading it silently, now and then uttering 'ahs' and 'ehs' in different tones, at first of satisfaction, then of doubt, then of commiseration, finally of full disappointment.*) No, no! There's nothing here! Nothing solid at all, Commissioner!

CENTURI. It's all we were able to gather.

LAUDISI. But this leaves all the doubtful points exactly where they were! (*Looks at him, then with sudden resolve:*) Do you really want to do a good deed, Commissioner? Render a meaningful service to the citizens for which God will certainly reward you?

CENTURI (*looking at him in perplexity*). What service? I wouldn't know what you mean!

LAUDISI. Here, look. Sit down here, please (*pointing to the desk*). Tear away this half sheet of 'information' that says nothing, and there, on the other half, write some precise and solid information.

CENTURI (*dumbfounded*). Me? How can I do that? What information?

LAUDISI. Anything you please! In the name of these two villagers you were able to trace... For the good of all! To restore tranquillity to the entire town! Do they want the truth, any truth? it doesn't matter which, as long as it's factual, categorical! Well, give it to them!

CENTURI (*forcefully, getting angry, offended*). How do I give it to them, if I don't have it? Do you want me to falsify a document? I'm surprised that you dare propose such a thing to me! I say 'surprised,' but I could say something much stronger! Come, do me the favour of announcing my presence to the Counsel.

LAUDISI (*with a gesture of defeat*). Your servant, sir, at once. (*Going to the living room door, he opens it. Immediately the volume of the noise in the living room increases. But as soon as Laudisi crosses the threshold, the noise ceases immediately. Laudisi's voice is then heard announcing:*) Ladies and gentlemen, Commissioner Centuri is here, with solid news from people in the know! (*Cheers and applause greet this statement. Centuri, worried, knowing that the information he brings is not sufficient to satisfy the expectations aroused...*)

Scene Two
Centuri, Agazzi, Sirelli, Laudisi, Amalia, Dina, Mrs Sirelli, Mrs Cini, Mrs Nenni, many other ladies and gentlemen

(*They all rush in through the door on the left. Agazzi at their head, clapping and shouting:* Well done, well done, Centuri.)

AGAZZI (*with outstretched hands*). Dear Centuri! I kept saying it was impossible you wouldn't be able to get to the bottom of it!

ALL. Bravo! Bravo! Let's see! Let's see! The proof, now! Who is it? Who is it?

CENTURI (*befuddled, confused*). No... please... dear Counsel...

AGAZZI. Ladies and gentlemen, please! Quiet down!

CENTURI. I did my best, yes, but if Mr Laudisi told you in there...

AGAZZI. ... that you are bringing solid information!

SIRELLI. ... precise factual data!

LAUDISI (*strong, resolute, cutting in*). ... not much, yes, but precise! From people who could be traced! From the same village as Mr Ponza! Someone who is in the know!

ALL. Finally! Ah, finally! Finally!

CENTURI (*shrugging his shoulders and handing the sheet to Agazzi*). Here it is, dear Counsel.

AGAZZI (*unfolding the sheet of paper as all the others rush up and crowd around*). Let's see, let's see!

CENTURI (*in an offended tone, approaching Laudisi*). But you, Mr Laudisi...

LAUDISI (*promptly, loudly*). Let him read it, please! Let him read it!

AGAZZI. Ladies and gentlemen, a bit of patience! Don't crowd me, stand back! I'm reading, I'm reading! (*A moment of silence ensues. And then, in the silence, Laudisi's voice is heard very clearly.*)

LAUDISI. But I've already read it!

ALL (*leaving Agazzi and rushing up to Laudisi*). Oh, yes? Well. What does it say? What do we know?

LAUDISI (*slowly and clearly*). It's certain, irrefutable, on the word of a person from Mr Ponza's village, that Mrs Frola has spent time in a clinic!

ALL (*regretful and disappointed*). Oh!

MRS SIRELLI. Mrs Frola?

DINA. Then she's the one?

AGAZZI (*having finished reading, shouts, waving the sheet in the air*). No, no, it doesn't say that at all here!

ALL (*leaving Laudisi and rushing up to Agazzi, shouting*). Ah! What? What does it say? What does it say?

LAUDISI (*to Agazzi, loudly*). Yes, it specifically says: 'the signora'!

AGAZZI (*more loudly*). Not at all! This person says 'he thinks,' but he's not sure at all! And anyway, he doesn't know whether it was the mother or the daughter!

ALL (*relieved*). Ah!

LAUDISI (*countering*). But it must be her, the mother! No doubt about it!

SIRELLI. What! It's the daughter, ladies and gentlemen! The daughter! ...

MRS SIRELLI. ... as Mrs Frola herself told us, after all! ...

AMALIA. ... yes! Sure! when they took her away from her husband without telling him...

DINA. ... and put her in a clinic!

AGAZZI. Besides, this informant isn't even from their village! He says he used to go there often... that he doesn't remember well... that he thinks he heard people say so...

SIRELLI. Aha, mere hearsay, then!

LAUDISI. But, excuse me, if you're so convinced that Mrs Frola is right, why're you still searching? Put a stop to it, once and for all! He's the insane one, and that's that!

SIRELLI. Yes! but the Prefect, old boy, is of the opposite opinion, and has complete confidence in Mr Ponza!

CENTURI. Yes, it's quite true. The Prefect believes Mr Ponza. He told me so!

AGAZZI. Because the Prefect hasn't yet spoken to the lady next door!

MRS SIRELLI. Of course! He 's spoken only to Ponza!

SIRELLI. And besides, there are others here who share the Prefect's opinion!

ONE GENTLEMAN. I for one, I do, yes sir! Because I'm aware of a similar case: of a mother who goes insane because of her daughter's death, and believes that her son-in-law won't let her see her daughter. Just like this case!

ANOTHER GENTLEMAN. No, no. In that case there is also the fact that the son-in-law is still a widower and has no one in the house with him. While in our case, this Mr Ponza has a woman in the house with him...

LAUDISI (*struck by a sudden thought*). Oh, my God! Gentlemen, did you hear? Here's the solution! My God, Columbus's egg! (*Patting the shoulder of the second gentleman*) Well done, bravo, dear sir. Did you hear?

ALL (*perplexed, not having understood*). What is it? What is it?

SECOND GENTLEMAN (*dumbfounded*). What did I say? I don't know...

LAUDISI. What do you mean, what did you say? You've solved the problem! Just wait a minute, gentlemen! (*To Agazzi*) The Prefect, is he expected here?

AGAZZI. Yes, we're expecting him... But why? Explain.

LAUDISI. It's pointless for him to come here to speak to Mrs Frola. Until now he's believed the son-in-law; once he speaks to the mother-in-law, he too will no longer know which one to believe! No, no! The Prefect must do something else at this point, something that only he can do!

ALL. What? What?

LAUDISI (*beaming*). What? Didn't you hear what this gentleman said? Mr Ponza has 'a woman' with him in his house! His wife!

SIRELLI. Question the wife? Oh yes, yes!

DINA. But the poor thing is kept in a virtual prison!

SIRELLI. The Prefect must use his authority to get her to speak!

AMALIA. Of course, she's the only one who can tell the truth!

MRS SIRELLI. Oh no! She'll say what her husband wants her to say!

LAUDISI. Of course, *if* she were to speak in his presence!

SIRELLI. She ought to speak alone with the Prefect!

AGAZZI. And the Prefect has the authority to insist that the wife reveal to him alone how things really are. Of course, of course! Don't you think so, Centuri?

CENTURI. Oh, no doubt, if the Prefect wants to!

AGAZZI. It's really the only way! He ought to be told, it'll save him the inconvenience of coming here now. Why don't you go do that, Centuri?

CENTURI. Yes sir. Goodbye. Ladies and gentlemen (*he bows and leaves*).

MRS SIRELLI (*clapping her hands*). Oh, yes! Bravo Laudisi!

DINA. Well done, well done, dear uncle! What a good idea!

ALL. Bravo! Bravo! Yes, it's the only way! The only way!

AGAZZI. Oh, yes! How could we not have thought of it?

SIRELLI. Of course. Nobody's ever seen her! As if she didn't exist, that poor thing!

LAUDISI (*as if struck by a new idea*). Oh! But… excuse me… are you sure that she does exist?

AMALIA. Lamberto! For God's sake!

SIRELLI (*pretending to laugh*). Do you want us to doubt her very existence?

LAUDISI. Well, not so fast! You yourselves say that nobody's ever seen her!

DINA. Come on, Mrs Frola sees her and speaks to her every day!

MRS SIRELLI. Besides, he confirms it, the son-in-law!

LAUDISI. All right! But just think for a moment. To be strictly logical, only a phantom should be living in that house.

ALL. A phantom?

AGAZZI. Come on, stop being a smart aleck for once!

LAUDISI. Let me finish: the phantom of a second wife, if Mrs Frola is telling the truth. Or the phantom of her daughter, if he, Mr Ponza, is telling the truth. What we must find out, ladies and gentlemen, is whether this phantom to one or the other is also a real person in herself. Which, at this point, might very well be doubtful.

AMALIA. Oh, sure! You'd like to see all of us go as crazy as you are!

MRS NENNI. My God, I'm all goose pimples!

MRS CINI. I don't know what pleasure you get from frightening us this way!

ALL. No, no! He's joking! He's joking!

SIRELLI. She's a woman of flesh 'n blood, you can bet your life on that! And we'll make her talk! We'll make her talk!

AGAZZI. After all, it was your idea to make her talk to the Prefect!

LAUDISI. Yes, it was, if there's really a woman up there. I mean, any woman. But mark my words, ladies and gentlemen, there can't be any woman up there. There isn't any. At least *I* doubt, now, that there is one.

MRS SIRELLI. My God, you really do want to drive us crazy!

LAUDISI. Well, we'll see, we'll see!

ALL (*speaking at once*). But if she's been seen by other people too! ... If she comes to look down into the courtyard! ... She writes her those notes! ... He's doing it on purpose, to make fun of us!

Scene Three
All the above and Centuri

CENTURI (*arrives amidst the general agitation announcing excitedly*). The Prefect! The Prefect!

AGAZZI. What? Here? What did you do, then?

CENTURI. I met him on his way here, together with Mr Ponza.

SIRELLI. Oh, with him?

AGAZZI. Oh, God, no! If he's coming with Mr Ponza, he'll go to Mrs Frola next door! Please, Centuri, stand outside the door and ask him from me to please come here first, for a moment, as he promised.

CENTURI. Yes sir. You can count on me. I'm on my way. (*He leaves hastily through the rear door.*)

AGAZZI. Ladies and gentlemen, please withdraw into the living room for a while.

MRS SIRELLI. But please, tell him clearly! It's the only way, the only way!

AMALIA (*at the living room door*). Please, ladies.

AGAZZI. You, Sirelli, please stay; and you too, Lamberto. (*All other ladies and gentlemen leave through the door on the left. Then to Laudisi:*) But let me do the talking, please.

LAUDISI. I don't care a bit. In fact, if you want me to go too...
AGAZZI. No, no! It's better if you're here. Ah, here he is.

Scene Four
Agazzi, Sirelli, Laudisi, the Prefect, Centuri

THE PREFECT (*sixty-ish, tall, fat, an air of superficial affability*). Agazzi, old
man! Oh, you here, too, Sirelli? Laudisi, my dear fellow! (*Shaking
hands with everyone*)
AGAZZI (*inviting him to sit with a gesture*). Pardon me if I made you stop
by here first.
THE PREFECT. It was my intention, as I promised you. I'd have come
afterwards, certainly.
AGAZZI (*seeing Centuri still standing behind the Prefect*). Please, Centuri,
come, come sit here.
THE PREFECT. And you, Sirelli – I hear you're one of the people most
wrought up – in a fever, they say – over this gossip about our new
secretary.
SIRELLI. Oh no, Your Excellency, the whole town's at least as upset as
I am.
AGAZZI. That's true. Yes, everyone's very upset.
THE PREFECT. Well, I for one don't see the reason for it!
AGAZZI. Because you haven't had occasion to be present at certain
scenes, as we have. His mother-in-law lives right next door.
SIRELLI. Pardon us, Your Excellency, you haven't heard this poor lady yet.
THE PREFECT. That's just where I was going. (*To Agazzi*) I promised you
to listen to her here in your house, as you suggested. But the son-in-
law himself came to beg, to implore me – to put an end to all this
gossip – to go to her house. Excuse me, but do you think that he'd
ever have requested such a thing, if he weren't more than sure such a
visit would prove what he claims is true?
AGAZZI. Of course, because in front of him that poor lady...
SIRELLI (*quickly continuing*). ... would have said what he wants her to,
Your Excellency! And there's the proof that she's not the one who's
insane!
AGAZZI. We witnessed exactly that, here, yesterday!
THE PREFECT. Oh, yes, dear man, because he makes her believe that *he's*
the insane one! He's forewarned me of that. And in fact, how could
the poor woman go on in her illusion otherwise? It's a martyrdom,
believe me, a martyrdom for the poor man!

SIRELLI. Oh, sure! But what if she's the one who gives *him* the illusion that her daughter's really dead, so that he can feel sure his wife isn't going to be taken away from him again! In which case you can see, Your Excellency, that the martyr would be Mrs Frola and not Mr Ponza!

AGAZZI. This is what we're in doubt about. Have you had such doubts...

SIRELLI. ... the doubts we've all had?

THE PREFECT. Doubts? Not quite; it seems to me that you don't have even the shadow of a doubt! As, I must confess, I don't... on the opposite side. But what about you, Laudisi?

LAUDISI. Pardon me, Your Excellency. I promised my brother-in-law I wouldn't open my mouth.

AGAZZI (*abruptly*). Oh, come on, what are you saying! If you're asked a question, answer! I told him not to talk, only because for the last two days he's been enjoying himself making things even murkier!

LAUDISI. Don't you believe it, Your Excellency. The opposite is true. I did my best to clear things up.

SIRELLI. Oh, sure. D'you know how? Insisting that it's impossible to arrive at the truth – and now raising the notion that in Mr Ponza's home there is a phantom living, not a woman!

THE PREFECT (*enjoying this*). What? What? How nice!

AGAZZI. For God's sake! Don't you see it's useless to listen to him?

LAUDISI. And yet, Your Excellency, you were invited to come in here because of me.

THE PREFECT. Because you think so too, that I ought to speak to the lady next door?

LAUDISI. Of course not! You're perfectly right to believe what Mr Ponza says.

THE PREFECT. Ah, good! So you too believe that Mr Ponza...

LAUDISI (*quickly*). No. Just as I'd like all these people to believe what Mrs Frola says, and put an end to it!

AGAZZI. Do you get it now? Do you think that's any way for a sane person to talk?

THE PREFECT. If you'll allow me. (*To Laudisi*) According to you, then, one can believe what Mrs Frola says too?

LAUDISI. Definitely! Every single thing she says. And the same for him!

THE PREFECT. But then, pardon me...

SIRELLI. But they're saying the exact opposite!

AGAZZI (*irritated, resolutely*). Please, listen to me! I do not lean, I don't want to lean, so far, in either direction. He might be right, she might be right. We must get to the bottom of it. And there's only one way.

SIRELLI. And he's the one who suggested it! (*pointing to Laudisi*)

THE PREFECT. Oh yes? Let's hear it then!

AGAZZI. Because we don't have any other factual proof, this is the only thing we have left: you must exercise your authority to obtain the confession of Mr Ponza's wife.

THE PREFECT. Of Mrs Ponza?

SIRELLI. But not in the presence of her husband, of course!

AGAZZI. So she'd be able to tell the truth!

SIRELLI. ... whether she's the daughter of Mrs Frola, as we think she well might be...

AGAZZI. ... or his second wife, who's willing to play the part of Mrs Frola's daughter, as Mr Ponza would like us to believe...

THE PREFECT. ... and as I do definitely believe! Yes, I think it's the only way too. Believe me, the poor fellow wants nothing better than to convince everybody that he's right. He's been very very agreeable to my suggestions. He'll be even happier than all of you! And you'll be set at ease right away! Please, Centuri (*Centuri rises*). Go and call Mr Ponza next door. Ask him, from me, to come here a moment.

CENTURI. At once, sir! (*He bows and leaves through the rear door.*)

AGAZZI. Of course, if he's willing!

THE PREFECT. You'll see, he'll agree at once! It'll all be over in fifteen minutes! Right here in front of you!

AGAZZI. What? Here? In my home?

SIRELLI. You believe he'll be willing to bring his wife here?

THE PREFECT. Leave it to me! Yes, right here. Because, otherwise, I know that you'll continue to think that I...

AGAZZI. ... of course not, what're you thinking of? please!

SIRELLI. ... never!

THE PREFECT. Oh, come on. Knowing that I'm so sure truth is on his side, you'll think that to put a lid on the thing, since he's a public functionary... No, no. I want you to hear it too. (*To Agazzi*) What about your wife?

AGAZZI. She's in the next room, with some other ladies...

THE PREFECT. Ah, you've established a real nest of conspiracy here...

Scene Five
Centuri, Ponza, and the above

CENTURI. May I come in? Here's Mr Ponza.

THE PREFECT. Thank you, Centuri. (*Ponza appears on the threshold.*) Come in, come in, dear Ponza. (*Ponza bows.*)

AGAZZI. Please, have a seat. (*Ponza bows again and sits.*)

THE PREFECT. You know these gentlemen... Mr Sirelli... (*Ponza rises and bows.*)

AGAZZI. Yes, I've introduced him already. My brother-in-law, Laudisi. (*Ponza bows.*)

THE PREFECT. I asked you in, dear Ponza, to tell you that here, with these friends of mine... (*He stops short, observing that, as soon as he started to speak, Ponza has been visibly disturbed and upset*) Is there something you want to say?

PONZA. Yes. That I intend to ask for a transfer this very day.

THE PREFECT. But why? Only a moment ago you were talking to me, so agreeable to everything...

PONZA. But I've been made the object, Your Excellency, of such outrageous harassment!

THE PREFECT. Oh, come now! Let's not exaggerate!

AGAZZI. Harassment? Do you mean, from me?

PONZA. From everybody! That's why I'm leaving! I'm leaving, Your Excellency, because I cannot bear this cruel, relentless inquisition into my private life, which will end up jeopardizing – in fact, destroying forever – a work of charity that has cost me great suffering and sacrifice! I honour that poor old woman more than my own mother, and I was forced, here, yesterday, to attack her so cruelly, so violently. And just now I found her, next door, so discouraged, so distressed...

AGAZZI (*calmly, interrupting*). That's strange! Because with us she has always spoken with the utmost calm. *You're* the one who's shown all the distress up to now, Mr Ponza... and you're showing it now too!

PONZA. Because you have no idea of what you are making me go through!

THE PREFECT. Come now, come now, calm down, dear Ponza! What's the matter? I am here for you! And you know with what confidence and sympathy I've listened to your reasons! Isn't that so?

PONZA. I beg your pardon. It's true. And I am very grateful to you, Your Excellency.

THE PREFECT. So then, you honour this poor mother-in-law of yours like your own mother? Well, just consider, these friends of mine are so eager to know everything because they have so much feeling for Mrs Frola too.

PONZA. But they're killing her, Your Excellency! And I've told them so more than once!

THE PREFECT. Please, be patient. You'll see that they'll stop just as soon
as the whole thing is cleared up. Right now, in fact! It won't take
much. You have in your possession the simplest and surest way of
removing all doubts whatsoever from the minds of these gentlemen.
Not from mine, for I don't have any.

PONZA. But they don't want to believe me, no matter what!

AGAZZI. That's not true. When you came here, after your mother-in-
law's first visit, to tell us she was insane, we all believed you, though
we were surprised. (*To the Prefect*) But right after that, Mrs Frola came
back, you see? ...

THE PREFECT. ... yes, yes, I know, you told me. (*He turns to Ponza and
continues*)... and she gave those explanations you yourself have been
trying to give your mother-in-law. You must bear with us, if a gnawing
doubt arises in those who listen to the poor lady after listening to
you. Faced with what your mother-in-law says, these gentlemen, you
see, don't think they can be sure of what *you've* told them, dear
Ponza. So it's clear. You and your mother-in-law... well... ought to
step aside for a moment! You're sure you're telling the truth, as I am;
so you surely can't have anything against its being reasserted here,
now, by the only person who can confirm it, besides the two of you.

PONZA. And who's that, may I ask?

THE PREFECT. Your wife, of course!

PONZA. My wife? (*Forcefully, indignantly*) Oh, no! Never, Your Excellency!

THE PREFECT. And why not, may I ask?

PONZA. Bringing my wife here for the satisfaction of those who refuse to
believe me?

THE PREFECT (*quickly*). No, for *mine*! Do you have any difficulty with
that?

PONZA. But, Your Excellency... No! Not my wife! Let's leave my wife out
of it! Surely you can believe me!

THE PREFECT. Oh, no. Look, I too am beginning to believe that you're
trying to do your best not to be believed!

AGAZZI. Especially since you tried every way you could to prevent your
mother-in-law from coming here to talk – even at the cost of a double
act of rudeness to my wife and daughter.

PONZA (*exploding in exasperation*). But what do you people want from
me? In the name of God! Isn't it enough you got the poor old lady
here? No, you want my wife here too? Your Excellency, I cannot bear
this act of violence! My wife will not leave my home! I won't bring her
to anybody's feet! It's enough for me that *you* believe me! And,

besides, I'm on my way right now to submit my application to be
transferred from here! (*He rises.*)

THE PREFECT (*pounding his fist on the desk*). Just a moment! First of all,
Mr Ponza, I won't tolerate your taking that tone with one of your
superiors and with me – so far I've spoken to you with great courtesy
and deference. Secondly, I repeat to you that now this obstinacy of
yours is beginning to give me some second thoughts too. You're
refusing to provide proof that *I*, not others, am requesting of you; it's
in your own interest, and I see absolutely nothing wrong in it. Both
I and my colleague here are perfectly capable of receiving a lady...
or, if you prefer, coming to your place...

PONZA. Are you forcing me, then?

THE PREFECT. I repeat that I'm requesting it for your own good. As your
superior, I could also give you an order!

PONZA. All right. All right. If that's how it is, I'll bring my wife here, to
put an end to this thing! But who'll assure me that the poor lady next
door won't see her?

THE PREFECT. Oh, yes. Since she's here right next door...

AGAZZI (*quickly*). We could pay a visit to your wife ourselves.

PONZA. No! I'm saying it to warn you people. That you'd better not spring
another surprise on me that would have terrible consequences!

AGAZZI. You can rest assured, as far as we're concerned!

THE PREFECT. Or, if you like, at your convenience, you may bring your
wife to my office.

PONZA. No, no... the sooner, the better... I'll stand on guard over there
myself. I'm going right away, Your Excellency, then it'll be over with,
all over with! (*He leaves hurriedly through the rear door.*)

Scene Six
All the above, minus Ponza

THE PREFECT. I must confess I wasn't expecting that opposition on his
part.

AGAZZI. And you'll see, he'll make his wife say what he wants her to say!

THE PREFECT. Ah, no. You can rest assured about that: I'll interrogate
his wife myself!

SIRELLI. If you don't mind my saying so, he seems as exasperated as
ever!

THE PREFECT. It's the first time... I assure you... it's the first time I've
seen him behave this way. Maybe the idea of bringing his wife here...

SIRELLI. ... of letting her out of prison...

THE PREFECT. ... oh, that... the fact that he keeps her as if in prison can be explained without assuming that he's mad.

SIRELLI. Pardon, Your Excellency, you haven't heard the poor lady next door yet.

AGAZZI. Yes, she says he keeps her that way for fear of his mother-in-law.

THE PREFECT. But it might not be that; he might just be jealous.

SIRELLI. Pardon me, to the point of not even keeping a maid? He forces his wife to do all the housework herself!

AGAZZI. And he goes to do the shopping himself, every morning!

CENTURI. That's true, sir. I saw him myself! He has a boy help him take the stuff home...

SIRELLI. ... and always keeps him from coming in!

THE PREFECT. Heavens, gentlemen, these are things he himself has deplored, talking to me.

LAUDISI. Irreproachable information service!

THE PREFECT. He does it to economize, Laudisi. He has to maintain two households!

SIRELLI. No, we're not talking about that! Pardon me, Your Excellency, can you believe that a second wife would put up with that...

AGAZZI (*continuing*). ... the most humble housework...

SIRELLI (*continuing*). ... for the sake of a person who used to be her husband's mother-in-law, and is a perfect stranger to her?

AGAZZI. Come on, come on! Doesn't it seem a bit too much to you too?

THE PREFECT. Yes, too much...

LAUDISI (*interrupting*). ... for any ordinary second wife!

THE PREFECT (*quickly*). Okay, let's admit it. It *is* too much. But even that, pardon me, can be explained very easily if not as generosity, then as jealousy. And that he *is* jealous – sane or insane – seems to me beyond discussion. (*At this point a clamour of confused voices is heard from the living room.*)

AGAZZI. What's happening in there?

Scene Seven
The above and Amalia

AMALIA (*coming in hurriedly and in consternation through the door on the left, announcing*). Mrs Frola! Mrs Frola is here!

AGAZZI. No! My God, who asked her to come?

AMALIA. No one! She came on her own!

THE PREFECT. No! For God's sake! Not now! Get her to go away!

AGAZZI. Instantly! Don't let her in here! It must be prevented at all costs! If he found her here, he'd think it was a real set-up!

Scene Eight
The above, Mrs Frola, and all the others

(*Mrs Frola comes in trembling, weeping, a handkerchief in her hand, appealing brokenly to the crowd around her, who are all visibly upset.*)

MRS FROLA. Ladies and gentlemen, please I beg of you! Please, dear Counsel, tell them yourself!

AGAZZI (*coming forward, very irritated*). I am telling you, Mrs Frola, to withdraw at once! You cannot stay here right now!

MRS FROLA (*confused*). Why? Why? (*To Amalia*) I'm turning to you, my good lady...

AMALIA. But you see... The Prefect is here...

MRS FROLA. Oh, it's you, Your Excellency. Please! I wanted to come to see you!

THE PREFECT. No, dear Mrs Frola, please be patient. At this moment I can't see you. It's imperative that you leave! That you leave here immediately!

MRS FROLA. Yes, I'll go! I'll go this very day! I'll leave, Your Excellency! I'll leave forever!

AGAZZI. No, dear Mrs Frola. Just do us the favour of withdrawing to your apartment next door for a moment! Please do us this favour. Later you'll be able to speak to the Prefect!

MRS FROLA. But why? What is it? What is it?

AGAZZI (*losing his patience*). Because your son-in-law is about to return! That's why, do you understand?

MRS FROLA. Oh yes? Well, then, yes, yes, I'll leave, I'll leave right away! I only wanted to beg you all – have mercy! – stop what you're doing! You think you're helping me, but you're doing so much harm! I'll be forced to leave if you go on this way, to leave this very day, so that he'll be left in peace! What do you want from him, what do you want from him now? What is he coming here for? Oh, Your Excellency!

THE PREFECT. Nothing, dear Mrs Frola. Please don't worry, and leave, please!

AMALIA. Come on, dear Mrs Frola! Please, be good!

MRS FROLA. Oh, my God. Mrs Agazzi, you people are going to deprive me of the one good thing, the only comfort I have left: to see my daughter, at least from a distance! (*She starts to cry.*)

THE PREFECT. But who's telling you that? There's no need for you to leave the city! We're only suggesting that you withdraw now, just for a moment. Don't worry so much!

MRS FROLA. But I'm so worried about him, Your Excellency! I came here to plead with you all for his sake, not my own!

THE PREFECT. Yes, yes, fine! And you can ease your mind about him too, I assure you, everything will be all right now.

MRS FROLA. But how? I see everyone dead set against him here!

THE PREFECT. No, dear Mrs Frola! It isn't true! I am here to protect him! Don't worry!

MRS FROLA. Ah, thank you! It means you understand...

THE PREFECT. Yes, yes, Mrs Frola, I understand...

MRS FROLA. I've told these people so many times: it's a tragedy we've been able to overcome, we mustn't go back.

THE PREFECT. Yes, yes, Mrs Frola. I told you, I understand!

MRS FROLA. We're content to live the way we do, my daughter is content. So... take care of this, please, take care of it. Otherwise I'd be forced to leave! And never see her again, even from a distance... please leave him in peace, please! (*At this point there is a movement in the crowd; all gesture; some look towards the door; some suppressed voices are audible.*)

VOICES. Oh my God! Here she is, here she is!

MRS FROLA (*noticing the consternation and confusion, trembling, moans in perplexity*). What is it? What is it?

Scene Nine
All the above, Mrs Ponza, Ponza

(*The crowd parts to let Mrs Ponza through. She comes forward stiffly, in mourning dress, her face hidden by a thick, black, impenetrable veil.*)

MRS FROLA (*with a heartrending shriek of wild joy*). Ah! Lina! Lina! Lina! (*She rushes up and clings to the veiled woman, with the hunger of a mother who for years and years has been unable to embrace her daughter. But immediately we hear offstage the shouts of Mr Ponza, who now rushes onto the stage.*)

PONZA. Giulia! Giulia! Giulia! (*Mrs Ponza, hearing his cry, stiffens in the arms of Mrs Frola, who holds her tightly. Coming on the scene, Mr Ponza is at once aware of his mother-in-law so passionately embracing his wife, and furiously assails the culprits.*) Ah, I said this would happen. You cowards took advantage of my good faith!

MRS PONZA (*turning her veiled head, solemnly and sombrely*). Don't be afraid, both of you! Don't be afraid! Just go now!

PONZA (*softly, lovingly to Mrs Frola*). Let's go, yes, let's go...

MRS FROLA (*who has detached herself from the embrace of her own accord, trembling, immediately echoes him, humbly, tenderly*). Yes, yes... let's go, dear, let's go... (*Their arms around each other, both weeping in their different ways, they withdraw, whispering affectionately. Silence. Having followed them with their eyes until they have disappeared, all turn now, moved and amazed, to the veiled lady.*)

MRS PONZA (*looks at all of them through her veil, then says solemnly and sombrely*). What else can you want from me after all this, ladies and gentlemen? There is a tragedy here, as you can see, that must remain hidden – only that way can the remedy our compassion has shown us do its work.

THE PREFECT (*moved*). But we want to respect your compassion, dear lady. We would just like you to tell us...

MRS PONZA (*speaking slowly and distinctly*). ... what? the truth? the truth is only this: that I am the daughter of Mrs Frola, yes...

ALL (*with a sigh of relief*). ... ah!

MRS PONZA (*immediately, as above*). ... and the second wife of Mr Ponza...

ALL (*stunned and disappointed, softly*). ... oh! how can it be?

MRS PONZA (*immediately, as above*). ... yes. And for myself, nobody! nobody!

THE PREFECT. Oh, no, for yourself, dear Mrs Ponza, you must be either one or the other!

MRS PONZA. No, ladies and gentlemen. For myself, I am whoever I'm thought to be. (*She looks at everyone through her veil for a moment; then she withdraws. Silence.*)

LAUDISI. Behold, ladies and gentlemen, how truth speaks! (*He glances about with derisive defiance.*) Are you happy now? (*He bursts into laughter.*) Ha! ha! ha! ha!

CURTAIN

Six Characters in Search of an Author

The characters in the play to be written

THE FATHER

THE MOTHER

THE STEPDAUGHTER

THE SON

THE BOY

THE LITTLE GIRL

(*The latter two have non-speaking parts*)

(*Evoked later*) MADAME PACE

The actors in the theatrical company

THE DIRECTOR

THE LEADING LADY

THE LEADING MAN

THE SECOND FEMALE LEAD

THE INGÉNUE

THE JUVENILE LEAD

OTHER ACTORS AND ACTRESSES

THE STAGE MANAGER

THE PROMPTER

THE PROPERTY MAN

THE SCENE SHIFTER

THE DIRECTOR'S SECRETARY

THE DOOR KEEPER

WORKERS AND STAGE HANDS

Daytime, on the stage of a theatre

N.B. *The play has no act or scene divisions. The performance is interrupted first – without the curtain being lowered – when the Director and the major character withdraw to decide on the scenery and the Actors leave the stage; and a second time when the Scene Shifter drops the curtain by mistake.*

(*The audience entering the theatre finds the curtain up, the stage as it would be during the day, without wings or scenery, almost dark, and empty, so as to have from the very beginning the impression of an unrehearsed play.*

Two sets of stairs, on the right and left ends of the stage, connect the auditorium and the stage.

On the stage the box that normally conceals the prompter is set to one side, next to the well in which he would stand.

On the opposite side, stage front, there is a desk and an easy chair with its back to the audience, for the Director.

There are two more desks, a larger and a smaller one, with a number of chairs around them, to be used, if needed, during the rehearsal. More chairs are set here and there, stage right and left, for the Actors, and a piano at the rear, to one side, almost hidden.

As the house lights are turned off, the Scene Shifter is seen entering through the stage door wearing navy overalls with a bag hanging from his belt, taking some boards from a rear corner, setting them up front, and kneeling to nail them down. Hearing the hammering, the Stage Manager runs in from the door to the dressing rooms.)

STAGE MANAGER. Hey, what're you doing?

SCENE SHIFTER. What'm I doing? I'm nailing them down!

STAGE MANAGER. At this hour? (*Looks at his watch*) It's half past ten already. The Director will be here for the rehearsal soon.

SCENE SHIFTER. I gotta have some time to work too, don't I?

STAGE MANAGER. Yes, but not now.

SCENE SHIFTER. When, then?

STAGE MANAGER. When rehearsal's over. Come on, take all your stuff away and let me get the scene ready for the second act of *Role Playing*.

(*The Scene Shifter, fuming, grumbling, picks up the boards and goes out. Meanwhile, through the stage door, the Actors of the theatrical company begin to arrive, men and women, first one, then another, then two together, etc.: nine or ten, as many as are needed to take part in the rehearsal of Pirandello's play*, Role Playing, *scheduled for this day. They come in, greet the Stage Manager and wish each other 'Good morning.' Some head for their dressing rooms, some, including the Prompter, who holds the script rolled under his arm, remain on stage waiting for the Director to start the rehearsal. In the meantime, either seated in groups or standing, they exchange a few words: one lights a cigarette, another complains about the part assigned to him, one reads a bit of news aloud to the others from a paper. Both Actresses and Actors should wear light-coloured, cheerful, theatrical clothing, and this first improvised scene ought to be played with great spontaneity and liveliness. At a certain point one of the Actors might sit down at the piano and strike up a dance tune, and the youngest Actors and Actresses start dancing.)*

STAGE MANAGER (*claps his hands to call them to order*). Come, come, stop that! Here comes the Director!

(*The music and dance stop suddenly. The Actors turn to look out over the auditorium. The Director enters through the door from the lobby, wearing a top hat, carrying a walking stick under his arm, a huge cigar in his mouth. He comes down the aisle between the seats and, greeted by the Actors, climbs to the stage by either of the two sets of steps. His Secretary hands him the mail: a few newspapers, and a package evidently containing a script.*)

DIRECTOR. Any letters?
SECRETARY. None. This is all the mail that came.
DIRECTOR (*hands him the script*). Take this to my dressing room. (*Then he looks around and turns to the Stage Manager.*) Hey, you can't see a thing in here. Please, get them to give us some light.
STAGE MANAGER. Right away. (*He goes off to give the order. Soon afterward the stage is lit with a vivid white light on the entire right-hand side where the Actors are. Meanwhile the Prompter has taken his place in his box, lit his small lamp and opened the script in front of him.*)
DIRECTOR (*clapping his hands*). Come on, come on, let's begin. (*To the Stage Manager*) Is anyone missing?
STAGE MANAGER. The Leading Lady is missing.
DIRECTOR. As usual! (*He looks at his watch.*) We're ten minutes late already. Make a note of it, please. So she'll learn to show up on time for rehearsal (*He has not finished his reprimand, when the Leading Lady's voice is heard from the rear of the auditorium.*)
LEADING LADY. No, no, please. I'm here! I'm here! (*She is dressed all in white, with a huge flamboyant hat on her head and a pretty little dog in her arms. She runs down the aisle between the seats and hurries up one of the staircases.*)
DIRECTOR. You've taken a vow to make people wait for you all the time.
LEADING LADY. Please, forgive me. It took me forever to get a cab to get here in time! But I see you haven't started yet. And I'm not on stage right away. (*Then calling the Stage Manager and handing the little dog over to him*) Please shut it in my dressing room.

DIRECTOR (*grumbling*). The doggie too! As if there weren't enough dogs around here already (*He claps his hands again and turns to the Prompter.*) O.K., come on, the second act of *Role Playing* (*he sits in his easy chair*). Attention, everybody! please! Who's on? (*Actors and Actresses clear the centre stage and sit down on the sides, except for the three who are to start the rehearsal and the Leading Lady who, paying no attention to the Director's question, sits down at one of the small desks.*)

DIRECTOR (*to the Leading Lady*). So you're in this scene?

FIRST ACTRESS. No.

DIRECTOR (*annoyed*). Then, for god's sake, get out of the way! (*The Leading Lady rises and goes to sit next to the other Actors who have already made room for her.*)

DIRECTOR (*to the Prompter*). Please begin.

PROMPTER (*reading from the script*). At the home of Leone Gala. An odd dining room-study.

DIRECTOR (*turning to the Stage Manager*). We'll use the red room.

STAGE MANAGER (*making notes on a sheet of paper*). The red one. Okay.

PROMPTER (*goes on reading*). Table set and desk with books and papers. Bookshelves and glass-doored cabinets with costly tableware. Door at rear leading to the Galas' bedroom. Side door on left leading to the kitchen. Main entrance on the right.

DIRECTOR (*rising and pointing*). So, remember: the main entrance over there. The kitchen over here. (*To the actor playing the role of Socrates*) You'll come in and exit this way. (*To the Stage Manager*) You'll set up the sliding doors back there, and put up the curtains (*he goes back to his seat*).

STAGE MANAGER (*making notes*). Okay.

PROMPTER (*reading as before*). Scene One. Leone Gala, Guido Venanzi, Filippo, also called Socrates. (*To the Director*) Should I read the stage directions too?

DIRECTOR. Yes, yes! I told you a hundred times.

PROMPTER. As the curtain rises, Leone Gala, wearing a chef's hat and apron, is beating an egg in a bowl with a wooden spoon. Filippo is beating another, he too dressed up as a chef. Guido Venanzi, seated, is listening.

LEADING MAN (*to the Director*). Excuse me, do I really have to put on a chef's hat?

DIRECTOR (*annoyed by the question*). Of course! It says so right there! (*pointing to the script*).

LEADING MAN. But, come on, it looks ridiculous, if you don't mind my saying so!

DIRECTOR (*jumping up in a rage*). Ridiculous, ridiculous! What can I do
if we don't get any good plays from France any more? And we're
reduced to staging Pirandello's, which nobody understands, purpose-
ly written to leave actors, critics, and public eternally dissatisfied?
(*The Actors laugh, so he gets up, goes up to the Leading Man and shouts*)
Yes, a chef's hat! And beat those eggs! Do you think those eggs you
are beating are all there is to it? No! You've got to portray the shell of
the eggs you're beating! (*The Actors laugh again and start making ironic
comments among themselves.*) Quiet! And pay attention when I explain
things! (*Turning to the Leading Man again*) Yessir, the shell! That is,
the empty form of reason without the content of blind instinct! You
are reason, your wife instinct, in a game of assigned roles, in which
you who are acting out your role are intentionally playing the puppet
of yourself. Understand?

FIRST ACTOR (*spreading his arms*). No, I don't.

DIRECTOR (*going back to his seat*). Neither do I! Let's go on, you'll be
pleased with the ending. (*In a confidential tone*) Please try to keep
yourself turned towards the audience, otherwise between the byzan-
tine dialogue and your voice not reaching the audience, we're done
for! (*He claps again.*) Pay attention, pay attention! Let's begin!

PROMPTER. Excuse me, may I please put my box in place? There's a
draft.

DIRECTOR. Yes, do, by all means!

(*The Doorkeeper of the theatre, wearing a cap with gold braid, has entered the
auditorium in the meantime. He goes down the aisle and up onto the stage to inform the Director of the arrival of the Six Characters, who have also entered the
auditorium and have been following him at a certain distance, somewhat confused and hesitant, looking all around.*

*Whoever wants to try to stage this play must employ every means possible to
achieve the effect of keeping the Six Characters distinct from the Actors of the company. The stage directions given as the six climb onto the stage will certainly help,
as will different lighting by means of appropriate spotlights. But the most apt and
effective way, we suggest, would be the use of special masks for the Six Characters.
Masks of a material not likely to go limp with sweat, yet light for those who wear
them, with openings made so as to leave the eyes, nostrils, and mouth free. This
will also interpret the deeper meaning of the play. For the Characters must not look
like ghosts but like created reality, immutable constructs of the imagination,
and thus more real and consistent than the inconstant 'naturalness' of the Actors.
The masks will help to give the impression of characters created by art and each*

fixed immutably in the expression of its fundamental emotion, that is, remorse *for the Father,* revenge *for the Stepdaughter,* scorn *for the Son,* grief *for the Mother, with fixed tears of wax in her dark eye sockets and on her cheeks, like those we see in the carved and painted images of the* Mater dolorosa *in churches. Their clothing should also be special; it should be simple, with the rigid folds and volume of a statue, almost, that is, giving no suggestion that it is made of material which could be bought in any shop in town, or cut and sewn by any ordinary tailor.*

The Father is around fifty, with a receding hairline, but not bald, red haired, a thick moustache bushed out over a mouth still young looking, often open in an uncertain and vacuous smile. Pale skinned, particularly his wide forehead; blue oval eyes, very bright and sharp. He wears light trousers and a dark jacket. His speech is generally mellifluous, but his outbursts can be harsh and sharp.

The Mother seems terrified and crushed by an unbearable burden of shame and disgrace. She wears a thick black widow's veil, and is humbly dressed in black. When she lifts the veil her face is still young, but seems made of wax; her eyes are always cast down.

The Stepdaughter, eighteen, is bold, almost impudent, very beautiful; she too is dressed in mourning, but is strikingly elegant. She displays annoyance with the timid, miserable, bewildered look of her fourteen-year-old brother, also wearing black, and an ardent tenderness towards her little sister, about four, in white with a black silk sash around her waist.

The Son is twenty-two, tall, almost rigid in his repressed anger at his father and sullen indifference towards his mother; he wears a purple overcoat and a long green scarf around his neck.)

DOORKEEPER (*cap in hand*). Pardon me, sir.

DIRECTOR (*abruptly, rudely*). What's the matter now?!

DOORKEEPER (*timidly*). There are some people here asking for you.
   (*Director and Actors turn, surprised, to look down from the stage into the auditorium.*)

DIRECTOR (*infuriated*). I'm rehearsing here! You know damn well nobody's allowed in here during rehearsal! (*Turning to the rear of the auditorium*) Who the hell are you? What do you want?

FATHER (*coming forward, followed by the others, up to the foot of one of the two sets of stairs*). We're here in search of an author.

DIRECTOR (*half-puzzled, half-angry*). Of an author? What author?

FATHER. An author, sir.

DIRECTOR. But there's no author here, because we're not rehearsing any new play.

STEPDAUGHTER (*gaily, briskly, climbing the steps quickly*). That's good, we can be your new play.

SOME OF THE ACTORS (*among the lively comments and the laughter of the others*). Listen to this! Get this!

FATHER (*following his Stepdaughter onstage*). Right. But if there's no author! (*To the Director*) Unless you'd like to be the author. (*The Mother, the Little Girl, whose hand she is holding. and the Boy climb the first steps of the stairs and stop there waiting. The Son remains below, morosely.*)

DIRECTOR. Is this some kind of joke?

FATHER. Not at all, sir. On the contrary, we bring you a painful drama.

STEPDAUGHTER. And could make your fortune!

DIRECTOR. Please, do me the favour of getting lost. We've got no time to waste on crazy people!

FATHER (*offended but speaking in his mellowest tone*). But sir, you know very well that life is full of endless absurdities, which – shamelessly – don't even need to look realistic, because they're real.

DIRECTOR. What the hell are you saying?

FATHER. I'm saying that it might really be crazy, yes indeed, to try to do the contrary – that is, to try to create realistic ones which look real; but – allow me to call this to your attention – if it is crazy, it's also the only reason for your craft. (*The Actors gesture angrily.*)

DIRECTOR (*rising and staring at him*). Oh, yes? You think people in our profession are crazy?

FATHER. Well, making what isn't real seem real – without any need for it, just as a play... Isn't it your job to give life on the stage to characters who are just dreamed up?

DIRECTOR (*quickly, giving voice to the rising indignation of the Actors*). I'll have you know, sir, that the acting profession is a most noble one! If today our new playwrights give us stupid plays to perform, and puppets instead of real people, I want you to know that we are very proud to have given life – here, on this very stage – to immortal works of art! (*The Actors, agreeing, approve and applaud their Director.*)

FATHER (*interrupting him and pursuing the idea with enthusiasm*). There you are! Exactly! To living beings, more alive than those who breathe and wear clothes! Less real, perhaps, but truer to life! We share the same opinion! (*The Actors look at each other, bewildered.*)

DIRECTOR. But, but... you just said...

FATHER. No, sorry, I just said it because you shouted to us that you have no time to waste on crazy people, while nobody knows better than you that nature uses the human imagination as a tool to carry on its creative work at a higher level.

DIRECTOR. Fine, fine. But what do you really mean to say?

FATHER. Nothing, sir. Just to show you that things can be born in many ways, in many forms: as a tree or a stone, as water or a butterfly – or a woman. And that one can also be born as a character.

DIRECTOR (*ironically, in feigned amazement*). And you, and these people around you, were born as characters?

FATHER. Exactly, sir. And alive, as you can see. (*The Director and the Actors burst into laughter as if in response to a joke. The Father is wounded.*) I'm sorry to see you laugh, because, as I said, we carry within us a painful drama, as you might guess from seeing this woman in the black veil. (*As he says this, he takes the hand of the Mother to help her up the last steps, and, still holding her hand, leads her with a certain tragic solemnity to the opposite side of the stage, which is lit immediately by a strange light. The Little Girl and the Boy follow the Mother; the Son, keeping his distance, comes up and goes to stand in the back. Then the Stepdaughter, who also stands apart, moves stage front and leans against the pillar. The Actors, first puzzled, then appreciative of so well executed a sequence, burst into applause as if they had been treated to a performance.*)

DIRECTOR (*first surprised, then outraged*). Oh, for god's sake, keep quiet! (*Turning to the Characters*) And you, get out of here! (*To the Stage Manager*) Damn it, clear the stage!

STAGE MANAGER (*going towards them, then stopping, as if restrained by some strange dismay*). Go on now, go.

FATHER (*to the Director*). But no... you see, sir, we...

DIRECTOR (*shouting*). We have work to do here, understand?

FIRST ACTOR. You can't come in here and pull a stunt like that...

FATHER (*resolute, coming forward*). I'm amazed at your disbelief! Aren't you accustomed to seeing them up here – alive, confronting each other, the characters created by an author? Just because the script that contains us isn't there? (*He points to the Prompter's box.*)

STEPDAUGHTER (*moving towards the Director, smiling, engagingly*). Please believe us, we are really six characters, and extremely interesting ones! even if we're lost.

FATHER (*edging her aside*). Yes, lost! Right! (*To the Director, quickly*) In the sense that the author who created us, live, then refused to, or physically could not, bring us into the world of art. And it was a real crime, sir, because he who has the good fortune to be born a live character, can laugh even at death. He will never die! The person, the writer, the tool of creation will die – his creature will never die! And to live forever one doesn't require extraordinary gifts, one needn't perform miracles. Who was Sancho Panza? Who was Don Abbondio? Yet they live forever, because – live seeds – they had the good fortune to find a fertile matrix, an imagination that was able to raise and nourish them, make them live forever!

DIRECTOR. All this is very fine! But what is it you want here?

FATHER. We want to live, sir!

DIRECTOR (*ironically*). Forever?

FATHER. No, sir; if only for a moment, in you.

ONE ACTOR. Hey, how about that?!

FIRST ACTRESS. They want to live in us!

THE YOUNG ACTOR. (*pointing to the Stepdaughter*). Be fine with me, if they gave me that one!

FATHER. Look here: the play is not yet written, (*to the Director*) but if you are willing, and your actors are willing, between us we can get it together right away!

DIRECTOR (*displeased*). What do you want to get together! We're not here to get things together, we're here to perform plays!

FATHER. Good, that's exactly why we came here to you.

DIRECTOR. And where's the script?

FATHER. It is in us, sir! (*The Actors laugh.*) The drama is in us, we are it. And we are as anxious to perform it as the passion within us spurs us on!

STEPDAUGHTER (*mockingly, with a malicious display of exaggerated impudence*). My passion, if you only knew, sir! My passion... for him! (*pointing to the Father and gesturing as if to embrace him, but bursting instead into strident laughter*).

FATHER (*angrily*). You keep quiet for now! And please don't laugh that way!

STEPDAUGHTER. No? Then with your permission – though I've only been an orphan for two months – you're going to see how I can sing and dance! (*Maliciously she sings a few bars of 'Prends garde à Tchou-Thin-Tchou' by Dave Stamper, arranged as a foxtrot or a slow one-step by Francis Salabert: the first stanza, accompanied by dance steps.*)

Les chinois sont un peuple malin,
De Shangaï à Pekin,
Ils ont mis des écriteaux partout:
Prenez garde à Tchou-Thin-Tchou!

(*The Actors, particularly the younger ones, while she sings and dances, as if drawn by a strange fascination, move towards her and raise their hands just a*

*little as if to grab her. She escapes them, and when the Actors burst into applause,
she seems indifferent to the disapproval of the Director.)*

ACTORS AND ACTRESSES (*laughing and applauding*). Brava, brava!
marvellous!

DIRECTOR (*angrily*). Quiet! Do you think you're at a variety show? (*He
takes the Father aside, with a certain degree of concern.*) Say, is she crazy?

FATHER. No, not crazy. Far worse!

STEPDAUGHTER (*running quickly to the Director*). Worse, worse! Eh,
something else, sir! Worse! Please, let's perform this drama right
away, so you'll see that at a certain point I – when this little darling
here (*she leads the child from the Mother to the Director*) – see what a little
beauty she is? – (*she picks her up and kisses her*) Sweetheart! (*she puts her
down and, almost against her will, continues emotionally*) Well, when God
suddenly takes this little darling from that poor mother, and this little
imbecile (*she pulls the Boy forward roughly by his sleeve*) does the stu-
pidest thing, like the idiot he is (*she pushes him back towards the Mother*)
– then you'll see me fly the coop! Yes! I'll fly away! And high time
too, believe me, high time! because after what's happened between
him and me (*she gestures towards the Father with a grotesque wink*), I can't
imagine staying with these people any longer, to witness the agony of
that mother on account of that guy there (*she points to the Son*).
– Look at him! Look at him! – indifferent, cold as ice, because he's
the legitimate son! Full of contempt for me, for him (*she points to the
Boy*), for the little one, because we're bastards. Understand? …
Bastards. (*She goes up to the Mother and embraces her.*) And this poor
mother, who is the mother of all of us, he refuses to recognize as his
mother too – and looks down his nose at her, as if she were the
mother of us three bastards only – coward! (*All this is said very quickly
in a state of extreme excitement; as she gets to the final 'coward,' she raises her
voice to stress the word 'bastards'; and lowers it on the 'coward,' saying the
word as if spitting it out.*)

MOTHER (*with extreme anguish, to the Director*). Sir, in the name of these
two little ones, I beg you… (*she sways, feeling as if she might faint*).
O my god…

FATHER (*running to support her, followed by almost all the Actors, bewildered
and dismayed*). A chair, please, a chair for this poor widow!

THE ACTORS (*running*). Is it true, then? Is she really fainting?

DIRECTOR. A chair, a chair, quickly! (*One of the Actors brings a chair. The
others move closer demonstrating concern. The Mother, seated, tries to prevent
the Father from lifting the veil that covers her face.*)

FATHER. Look at her, look at her, sir!

MOTHER. No, please, for god's sake, stop it!

FATHER. Let them see you! (*He raises her veil.*)

MOTHER (*standing up and shielding her face with her hands, desperately*). Sir, I beg you to prevent this man from carrying out his horrible intentions!

DIRECTOR (*surprised and confused*). Now I don't understand where we are any more. What it's all about? (*To the Father*) Is this your wife?

FATHER (*quickly*). Yes, sir, my wife!

DIRECTOR. How can she be a widow if you are alive? (*The Actors release all their bewilderment in noisy laughter.*)

FATHER (*wounded, sharply resentful*). Please, don't laugh! Don't laugh that way, for heaven's sake! This is precisely her drama, sir. She had another husband. Another man who ought to be here!

MOTHER (*with a cry*). No, no!

STEPDAUGHTER. Luckily for her, he's dead. Two months ago, as I told you. We're still in mourning, as you see.

FATHER. He's not here, but not because he is dead, see? He's not here because – please, look at her, sir, and you'll understand why right away! – Her drama could not consist of her love for two men, for whom she could feel nothing – except, perhaps, some gratitude (not towards me, towards him!). She's not a woman, she is only a mother! And her drama (a powerful one, sir, powerful) consists entirely in these four children of the two men she had.

MOTHER. I had? You have the nerve to say it was me who had them, as if I'd wanted them? It was him, sir! He gave me the other one, forced him on me. He made me, he made me go away with him.

STEPDAUGHTER (*impetuously, indignant*). It's not true!

MOTHER (*bewildered*). What do you mean, not true?

STEPDAUGHTER. It's not true! It's not true!

MOTHER. What can you know about it?

STEPDAUGHTER. It's not true! (*To the Director*) Don't believe her! Do you know why she's saying that? Because of him (*pointing to the Son*). She's saying it because she's tormented, consumed by the indifference of that son of hers – she wants to convince him that if she abandoned him when he was two, she did it because he (*pointing to the Father*) forced her to.

MOTHER (*forcefully*). He did, he forced me. As God is my witness! (*To the Director*) Ask him if it isn't true! Make him say it! She (*pointing to the Stepdaughter*) can't know the first thing about it.

STEPDAUGHTER. I know that with my father, as long as he lived, you were always happy and at peace. Deny it, if you can!

MOTHER. I don't deny it, no I don't…

STEPDAUGHTER. He was always so full of love and concern for you! (*Angrily, to the boy*) Isn't it true? Say it! Why don't you speak, you idiot!

MOTHER. Leave this poor child alone! Why do you want me to seem ungrateful? I don't mean to offend your father! I just wanted to make it clear that when I left my house and my son neither my guilt nor my pleasure were involved!

FATHER. It is true, sir. I was the one who made it happen. (*A pause*)

LEADING MAN (*to his companions*). Wow, what a spectacle!

LEADING LADY. And *they* are putting it on for *us*!

JUVENILE LEAD. For once!

DIRECTOR (*who is beginning to get very interested*). Let's listen, let's hear! (*As he speaks, he goes down one of the sets of stairs into the auditorium and remains standing in front of the stage, as if to take in the effect of the scene as a spectator.*)

SON (*without moving from his place, cold, ironic, speaking slowly*). Yes, listen to him now, see what philosophical insight! He'll speak to you about 'the Demon of Experimentation.'

FATHER. You're a cynical idiot! I've told you a hundred times! (*To the Director in the auditorium*) He mocks me because of this phrase I found to excuse myself.

SON (*scornful*). Phrases.

FATHER. Yes, phrases, phrases! As if everyone didn't take comfort – when there is something we can't explain, when something evil gnaws at us – in finding a word that means nothing, but brings us rest and peace!

STEPDAUGHTER. When there is remorse too! Especially remorse!

FATHER. Remorse? That's not true. I haven't put it to rest with words alone.

STEPDAUGHTER. With a little money too! Yes, yes, a little money too! With the fat sum he was about to offer me in payment, gentlemen. (*The Actors react with horror.*)

SON (*scornfully to the Stepdaughter*). That's contemptible!

STEPDAUGHTER. Contemptible? It was there, in a pale blue envelope on the mahogany desk, in Madame Pace's back shop. You know, sir, one of those madames who pretend to sell *robes et manteaux* in order to attract us poor daughters of respectable families to their *ateliers*.

SON. And she's bought the right to tyrannize over us all, with that money he was about to pay, and which later, luckily, he had no reason – mind you – to pay.

STEPDAUGHTER. Ah, but we came very close, you know! (*bursting into a laugh*).

MOTHER (*jumping up*). For shame, daughter! For shame!

STEPDAUGHTER (*vehemently*). Shame? It's my revenge! I am burning, sir, burning to relive that scene! The room… here the display rack of coats, over there the day bed, the mirror, a screen, and, in front of the window, that mahogany desk with the pale blue envelope with the hundred lire. I see it! I could pick it up! But you, gentlemen, should turn the other way – I'm almost naked! I no longer blush, because he's the one who blushes now! (*pointing to the Father*). But I assure you he was very, very pale, at that moment! (*To the Director*) Believe me, sir.

DIRECTOR. I've lost you completely.

FATHER. Of course! Badgered that way! Impose some order, sir, and allow me to speak, instead of listening to the disgrace this girl is trying so savagely to make you believe about me, without the necessary explanations.

STEPDAUGHTER. We're not telling stories here, no stories!

FATHER. But I'm not telling stories! I want to explain.

STEPDAUGHTER. Oh, sure, sure! Your way! (*The Director now climbs back on stage to restore order.*)

FATHER. But this is where the root of all evil lies! in words! We all have a world of things inside of us; each a world of his own! And how can we understand each other, sir, if in the words I use I put the meaning and value of things as they are within me; while those who listen inevitably invest my words with their own meaning and value from the world within themselves? We think we understand each other, but we never do! Look: my pity, all my pity for this woman (*points to the Mother*) she takes as the direst cruelty.

MOTHER. But you drove me away!

FATHER. There! Do you hear? She thought I was driving her away!

MOTHER. You're good with words, I'm not… But believe me, sir, that after he married me – why he married me, I don't know, I was a poor, humble woman –

FATHER. That's just why I married you, because I loved that humility in you, believing that… (*he stops at her gestures of denial, and throws up his hands in a gesture of exasperation, seeing the impossibility of making her understand, then turns to the Director*). See? No, she says no! (*Striking his forehead*) It's frightening. Her mental deafness is frightening! Heart, all heart for her children, but her brain – deaf, deaf, sir! It's enough to drive you crazy!

STEPDAUGHTER. Yes, but now ask him what good his intelligence was to us.

FATHER. If we could foresee all the evil that can come from the good we believe we're doing...

(*At this point the Leading Lady, who has been stewing watching the Leading Man flirting with the Stepdaughter, comes forward and asks the Director:*)

LEADING LADY. Excuse me, sir, are we going to go on with the rehearsal?

DIRECTOR. Yes, yes! Let me hear this now.

THE JUVENILE LEAD. This is really something new!

THE INGÉNUE. It's very interesting!

LEADING LADY. For those who're interested in it (*glancing at the Leading Man*).

DIRECTOR (*to the Father*). But you must explain things clearly. (*He sits down.*)

FATHER. Yes, I will. You see, sir, I had a poor employee, a secretary, a man devoted to me, who understood her perfectly (*pointing to the Mother*) with no trace of wrong, mind you! – good, humble, like her, incapable, either of them, not just of doing any wrong, but even thinking of it!

STEPDAUGHTER. So he thought of it for them, and did it too!

FATHER. It's not true! I meant to do them good – and myself too, yes, I confess! It had gotten to the point where I couldn't say a word to either of them without their immediately exchanging an understanding glance, without one looking immediately into the other's eyes for counsel on how to take my word so as not to anger me. This was enough, you understand, to keep me in constant state of rage, of unbearable exasperation.

DIRECTOR. Why didn't you get rid of that secretary?

FATHER. Of course, I did, sir! But then I saw this poor woman wandering around the house as if she were lost, like one of those stray animals that people bring home out of pity.

MOTHER. There was a different reason!

FATHER (*immediately turning to her, as if to anticipate her*). Our son, right?

MOTHER. He'd taken my son from my breast earlier, sir!

FATHER. But not out of cruelty! So he'd grow up healthy and strong, close to nature!

STEPDAUGHTER (*pointing to him ironically*). As you all can see!

FATHER (*immediately*). Well, is that my fault too, if he grew up that way?
I'd given him to a wet nurse in the country, sir, to a peasant woman
– I thought my wife wasn't strong enough, although she was from
humble stock. I did it for the same reason I'd married her. Whims,
I suppose, but what can you do. I've always had these damned
aspirations towards a certain solid moral health! (*The Stepdaughter
bursts into a peal of loud laughter.*) Please, make her stop! I can't bear it!

DIRECTOR. Stop it! Let me hear this, for god's sake! (*Again her laugh
breaks off immediately; at the Director's reproach she seems distant, rapt in
thought, remote. The Director again climbs down from the stage to get the
impact of the scene.*)

FATHER. I couldn't stand to have this woman (*pointing to the Mother*) at
my side any more. Not so much because of the boredom, the stifling
– really stifling – effect she had on me, but because of the sorrow –
the painful sorrow – I felt for her.

MOTHER. So he sent me away!

FATHER. Well provided with everything, to that man, yes – to free her
of me!

MOTHER. And free himself too of me!

FATHER. Yes sir, for myself too – I admit it. And a great deal of evil came
of it. But my intentions were good... and I did it for her good more
than mine, I swear! (*Arms crossed on his chest, he turns to the Mother.*)
Did I ever lose sight of you? Tell me. Did I ever lose sight of you, until
he took you away, from one day to the next, without my knowledge,
to another town? Foolishly disturbed by my interest, a pure interest,
sir, pure, with no ulterior motives. I took an amazingly tender interest
in the new little family she was raising. She (*pointing to the
Stepdaughter*) can confirm that.

STEPDAUGHTER. Oh, sure! I was a tiny little thing, you know? with
pigtails to my shoulders, and pantalettes longer than my skirt – this
little – when I used to see him in front of the school entrance when
I got out. He came to see how I was coming along...

FATHER. This is wicked! shameful!

STEPDAUGHTER. No, why?

FATHER. Shameful! shameful! (*excitedly, turning to the Director at once to
explain*) My house, sir, once she (*pointing to the Mother*) left, seemed
empty to me all at once. She was a nightmare, but she filled it. Alone,
I found myself moving through the rooms like a headless fly. That
one (*pointing to the Son*), raised away from home – I don't know – he

didn't seem mine any more, when he came back. Without a mother between him and me, he grew up by himself, apart, without any emotional or intellectual relation to me. So, strange as it seems, that is how it was; at first I grew curious about her little family, which owed its life to me, then gradually attracted to it. Thinking about it began to fill the void surrounding me. I felt the need to believe she was at peace, totally absorbed in the simplest cares of life, lucky to be far from the complicated torments of my soul. And to confirm it, I went to see that child coming out of school.

STEPDAUGHTER. Oh, sure! He used to follow me, smiling, and near home he'd wave goodbye – like this! I looked at him wide-eyed, uneasy. I didn't know who in the world he was! I told mother. She must have guessed right away who he was (*the Mother nods*). At first she kept me home from school for several days. When I went back, I saw him there at the door – ridiculous! – with a big package. He came up to me, caressed me, and took out of the package a big, beautiful Florentine straw hat with a garland of little roses around it – for me!

DIRECTOR. But all this is narrative!

SON (*scornfully*). Right, literature! literature!

FATHER. What do you mean, literature! This is life, sir! Feelings!

DIRECTOR. Maybe! But not performable!

FATHER. I agree, sir. Because all this came earlier. And I'm not saying all of it should be acted out. In fact, as you can see, she's (*pointing to the Stepdaughter*) no longer the little child with pigtails to her shoulders...

STEPDAUGHTER. And pantelettes down below her skirt!

FATHER. The drama starts now, sir! new, complex...

STEPDAUGHTER (*bold, fierce, coming forward*). As soon as my father died...

FATHER (*interjecting so as not to let her talk*). ... dire poverty, sir! They came back here, without my knowing it. So foolish of her (*pointing to the Mother*). She can hardly write, but she could have asked her daughter to write, or that boy, that they needed help!

MOTHER. You tell me, sir, if I could've imagined he had all these feelings for us.

FATHER. That's just what's wrong with you – you never understood any of my feelings!

MOTHER. After so many years and everything that happened...

FATHER. And is it my fault, if that man took you away – (*to the Director*) from one day to the next, I tell you... – because he'd found some sort of employment out there. I wasn't able to trace them, so, of course, my interest waned, for many years. The drama exploded, violent and unforeseen, on their return, when, unfortunately, driven by the misery of my flesh, still craving... – yes, it's misery, the misery of a man who's alone but who's avoided demeaning relationships, a man not old enough yet to be able to do without a woman, and not young enough to be able to go looking for one without shame. Misery? No! Horror, horror, because no woman can love him any more. And when you realize this, you should be able to do without it... But who's to say! we all wear our dignity on the outside, sir, in front of one another, but inside, we know very well what goes on, things we'd never confess! we give in to temptation, even though right after we may pick ourselves up, in a hurry to re-establish the integrity and solidity of our dignity, like putting a stone on a grave that hides and buries every sign of our shame, the very memory of it from our own eyes. We all do these things! Only we don't have the courage to talk about them!

STEPDAUGHTER. But the courage to do them, everybody has that!

FATHER. Everybody! But in secret. And so it takes more courage to talk about them! Because as soon as somebody does, that's it! He'll be called a cynic forever. But it's not true, sir. He's like everyone else. Better, even better. Because he's not afraid to reveal, with the light of reason, the blush of shame, there, in the human animal, who always closes his eyes so as not to see it. A woman, for instance, how does a woman act? She looks at us alluringly, seductively. You seize her! As soon as she's in your arms, she closes her eyes. It's the sign of her surrender. The sign by which she tells the man: 'Blind yourself, I am blind!'

STEPDAUGHTER. And when she doesn't shut them anymore? When she no longer feels the need to hide from herself, by closing her eyes, the blush of her shame, and sees instead, with dry, impassive eyes, the red shame of the man, who, though he feels no love, has made himself blind? Ugh, how disgusting then, how disgusting all these intellectual complications are, all this philosophy that first reveals the animal, then tries to save, to excuse it... I can't bear to listen to him, sir! Because when you're compelled to simplify life to that *animal* level, to discard all the 'human' baggage, all chaste aspirations, all pure feelings, idealism, duty, modesty, shame, then nothing causes more scorn and revulsion than a certain kind of remorse. It's all crocodile tears!

DIRECTOR. Let's get to what happened, let's get to the event, folks! This is only talk!

FATHER. Right, sir. Except that an event is like a sack: it doesn't stand up when it's empty. To make it stand up, first you have to put in the reasons and feelings that brought it about. I had no way to know that after the man had died over there, and they came back here in poverty, to provide for her children, she'd (*pointing to the Mother*) looked around for work as a seamstress and had gone to get work from that – from that Madame Pace!

STEPDAUGHTER. Fine ladies' tailoring she deals in, let me tell you. She appears to work for the finest clientele, but she's arranged things so that the best of her clients work for her instead... with no detriment to her more ordinary customers!

MOTHER. I hope you believe me, sir, if I tell you it didn't even cross my mind that that old witch gave me work because she had her eye on my daughter...

STEPDAUGHTER. Poor Mother! Do you know, sir, what that woman used to do when I brought back work my mother'd done? She'd point out the material that had been wasted, because she'd given the sewing to my mother. And docked the payment time after time. So – you understand – I ended up by paying for it myself, while my poor mother thought she was working her fingers to the bone for me and these two, sewing Madame Pace's stuff even at night !
(*The Actors express indignation.*)

DIRECTOR (*quickly*). And there one day you met...

STEPDAUGHTER (*pointing to the Father*). Him, yes sir, an old customer! You'll see what a scene to perform that is! Fantastic!

FATHER. As the Mother burst on the scene...

STEPDAUGHTER (*cutting in, maliciously*)... almost in time...

FATHER (*shouting*). No, in time, in time! Because, fortunately, I recognized her in time! And I took the whole family with me. Imagine my situation and hers, now, when we're face to face; – she, as you see her, and I, unable to look her straight in the eye!

STEPDAUGHTER. It's really a scream! But, sir, how can they expect me – 'afterwards' – to behave like a modest young lady, well brought up, virtuous, in line with his damned aspirations to 'solid moral health'?

FATHER. My whole drama lies in this, sir, in my awareness that while every one of us believes he is 'one,' he is instead 'many,' sir, 'many' in accord with all the possibilities of being that are within us: 'one' with this person, 'another' with that, all very different! And we have the illusion, meanwhile, that we're always being 'the same for everyone,' and always that same 'one' that we believe ourselves to be, in each of our acts. While it is not true, it is not true! And we realize it very well, when in one of our acts, by a most unfortunate accident, we remain suddenly suspended as from a hook: we realize, that is, that not all of ourselves is in that act, and therefore it would be a cruel injustice if we were to be judged solely on that act, to be kept hooked and suspended there, pilloried, for our entire life, as if our entire life consisted exclusively of that act. Now do you understand the malice of this young woman? She caught me in a place, in an act, in which she shouldn't have met me, in a role she shouldn't have seen me play, and she wants to stick me with an identity I never dreamed I could take on for her, in a fleeting, shameful moment of my life! This is it, sir, this is what torments me most. And you'll see, the play will be immensely more interesting because of it. Then there's the situation of the others! His... (*pointing to the Son*).

SON (*shrugging his shoulders contemptuously*). Leave me out. I've got nothing to do with it!

FATHER. What do you mean, nothing to do with it?

SON. I've got no role in it and I don't want to have any; you know that I'm not cut out to have any place among you people!

STEPDAUGHTER. Oh, we're common as dirt! ... and he's so refined! – But you can see, sir, that whenever I look at him to rivet him with my contempt, he lowers his eyes, because he knows how much harm he's done me.

SON (*barely looking at her*). Me?

STEPDAUGHTER. Yes, you! It's thanks to you I'm walking the streets! To you! (*The Actors express horror.*) Did you or didn't you, by your attitude, deny us not only the intimacy of a home, but even the kind welcome that puts guests at ease? We were the intruders, come to invade your kingdom of 'legitimacy'! Sir, I wish you could have seen some of the private little scenes between him and me! He says I've tyrannized over everyone. But, you see, it was just that attitude of his that led me to make use of the event he calls 'vile,' the event that allowed me to enter his house, with my mother, who is his mother too – as its mistress!

SON (*advancing slowly*). I'm everybody's fair game, you see? I'm an easy target. But just imagine a son who, one fine day, finds an insolent young lady, just like that, invading his quiet home, looking down her nose at him, asking for his father to whom she has something to say. Then he sees her coming back, with the same defiant attitude, in the company of that little girl, and treating his father – he's got no idea why – in a very questionable, demanding way, asking for money, in a tone that gives him to understand that he has to give it, he's under an obligation to give it…

FATHER. But I really am under an obligation: it's for your mother!

SON. And what do I know about it? When did I ever see her? When have I ever heard her mentioned? She shows up one day, with her (*pointing to the Stepdaughter*), with that boy and that little girl; and they tell me: 'Hey, know what? She's your mother too.' I can guess, from her (*pointing to the Stepdaughter again*) behaviour, the reason why they've come into the house this way from one day to the next… What I feel, sir, what I experience, I cannot and do not want to express. I could at most confide it in private, but I'd prefer not to, even to myself. My feelings cannot produce any action on my part. Believe me, sir, believe me, I'm an 'unrealized' character, dramatically, and I feel uneasy, downright ill, in their company. – Just count me out!

FATHER. But what're you saying? It's just because you're like that…

SON (*violently exasperated*). … and what do you know about what I'm like? When did you ever show any interest in me?

FATHER. Granted, granted! But isn't this a situation to consider too? This aloofness of yours, so cruel to me, to your mother, who, back in her home, sees you for the first time, all grown up, and doesn't know you, but knows you're her son… (*To the Director, indicating the Mother*) There, look, she's crying!

STEPDAUGHTER (*angry, stamping her foot*). Like the fool she is!

FATHER. And she (*to the Director, indicating the Stepdaughter*) can't stand it, of course! (*Referring to the Son again*) He says he's got nothing to do with it; instead the action hinges on him! Look at that boy, always clinging to his mother, scared to death, humiliated… He feels that way because of him. His situation may be the most painful of all. He feels like an outsider, more than the others, and, poor little thing, he's mortified, feels he's been taken in… out of charity… (*aside to the Director*) He's just like his father, humble, quiet…

DIRECTOR. Oh, but that isn't good! You don't know how awkward it can be to have children on the stage.

FATHER. Oh, but he'll free you of any awkwardness very soon! And that little girl too, who, in fact, is the first to go…

DIRECTOR. All right, then! I assure you that all this interests me very, very much. I feel, intuitively, that there's material here for a beautiful play!

STEPDAUGHTER (*trying to intervene*). With a character like me!

FATHER (*pushing her aside, very anxious as to the impending decision of the Director*). You be quiet!

DIRECTOR (*continuing, ignoring the interruption*). Something new, certainly...

FATHER. Totally new, sir!

DIRECTOR. It takes a bit of nerve, though – I mean – coming to dump it in front of me...

FATHER. Well, sir, having been born, as we were, for the stage...

DIRECTOR. Are you amateur actors?

FATHER. No, I say born for the stage because...

DIRECTOR. Well, now, you must have done some acting!

FATHER. No, sir, only that bit that each of us performs in the role he's assigned to himself in life, or that others have assigned to him. And in me, you see, it's a passion that, all by itself – as in all of us – becomes, as soon as we get worked up, a little theatrical...

DIRECTOR. Never mind, never mind! – You understand, dear sir, that without the author... I could direct you to someone...

FATHER. No, look... why don't *you* do it?

DIRECTOR. Me? What are you talking about?

FATHER. Yes, you, you! Why not?

DIRECTOR. Because I've never been an author!

FATHER. And why couldn't you be one now? It's no big deal. So many people do it! And your job is made much easier by the fact that we're here, all of us, alive in front of you.

DIRECTOR. That's not enough!

FATHER. What do you mean, not enough? Seeing us live our drama...

DIRECTOR. Sure. But you still need someone to write it down!

FATHER. No, only to take it down, from our live performance in front of you, scene by scene. It'll be enough to put down just an outline at first, and then try it out!

DIRECTOR (*tempted, climbing back up on the stage*). Well... it's kind of tempting... just for fun... we could actually try...

FATHER. Yes, sir. You'll see what fantastic scenes will come out of it! I can give you some idea right away!

DIRECTOR. It's tempting, it's tempting. Let's try. Come with me to my room. (*To the Actors*) You're free for a while, but don't go far. Be back here in fifteen, twenty minutes. (*To the Father*) Let's see, let's try... Maybe something really extraordinary may come of it...

FATHER. Of course! But it's better if they come too, right? (*gesturing towards the other Characters*).

DIRECTOR. Yes, come, come! (*He starts off, then turns to the Actors*) Please, be on time! In fifteen minutes! (*The Director and the Six Characters cross the stage and disappear. The Actors remain, astonished, looking at each other.*)

LEADING MAN. Is he serious? What is he trying to do?

JUVENILE LEAD. This is really crazy!

A THIRD ACTOR. He wants us to improvise a play off the wall?

JUVENILE LEAD. Yeah, like the actors of the commedia dell'arte!

LEADING LADY. Oh, if he thinks I'm going to take part in such a joke...

INGÉNUE. I won't either!

A FOURTH ACTOR. I'd like to know who those people are (*referring to the Six Characters*).

THE THIRD ACTOR. Who do you think they are? Lunatics, or con-men!

JUVENILE LEAD. And he's listening to them?!

INGÉNUE. What vanity! Now he's an author!

LEADING MAN. Unheard of! This is what the theatre is coming to, folks...

A FIFTH ACTOR. I'm enjoying it!

THE THIRD ACTOR. Well, let's just wait and see what comes of it.

(*Engaged in this kind of conversation the Actors clear the stage, some exiting through the rear door, some going to their dressing rooms. The curtain stays up. The performance is interrupted for about twenty minutes.*)

(*The sound of the buzzers tells the audience that the performance is about to continue. From the dressing rooms, the door, and the auditorium, Actors, Stage Manager, Scene Shifter, Prompter, and Property Man come onto the stage, and at the same time the Director and the Six Characters come out of the Director's dressing room. The house lights are turned down, the stage lights come on as before.*)

DIRECTOR. Come on, people. Are we all here? Please pay attention. We're set to go. Scene Shifter!

SCENE SHIFTER. Here I am!

DIRECTOR. Set up the drawing room right away. Just the two side walls and the backdrop with a door. Right away, please! (*The Scene Shifter runs to carry out the order, and while the Director talks to the Stage Manager, the Property Man, the Prompter, and the Actors about the coming performance, he sets up the sketchy scenery he has been directed to provide: two side walls and a backdrop with a door striped in pink and gold.*)

DIRECTOR (*to the Property Man*). Take a look and see if there is a daybed in the store room.

PROPERTY MAN. Yes, sir, there is the green one.

STEPDAUGHTER. No, not green! It was yellow, with flowers, fuzzy, very wide! Perfectly comfortable.

PROPERTY MAN. We don't have one like that.

DIRECTOR. It's not important! Get the one we have.

STEPDAUGHTER. What do you mean, it's not important? Madame Pace's famous little nest!

DIRECTOR. We're just rehearsing! Please don't interfere! (*To the Stage Manager*) See if there's a display case, long and low.

STEPDAUGHTER. The desk, the mahogany desk for the pale-blue envelope!

STAGE MANAGER (*to the Director*). There's that little one, gilded.

DIRECTOR. Go get it.

FATHER. A full-length mirror.

STEPDAUGHTER. And the screen! A screen, please. What do I do, otherwise?

STAGE MANAGER. Yes, Miss, we have lots of those, don't worry.

DIRECTOR (*to the Stepdaughter*). And some hangers, right?

STEPDAUGHTER. Yes, lots of them!

DIRECTOR (*to Stage Manager*). See how many are there and have them brought up.

STAGE MANAGER. Yes, sir, I'll take care of that! (*He runs to carry out the order and while the Director talks to the Prompter, Characters, and Actors, he gets the Stage Hands to carry in the pieces of furniture requested, disposing them as he sees fit.*)

DIRECTOR (*to the Prompter*). Take your place, please. This is the outline of the scenes, act by act (*handing him a few sheets of paper*). But now you've got to perform a minor miracle.

PROMPTER. Take shorthand?

DIRECTOR (*happily surprised*). Ah, beautiful! You can take shorthand?

PROMPTER. I may be a poor prompter, but shorthand…

DIRECTOR. Terrific! (*To a Stage Hand*) Go to my dressing room and get paper… a lot, all you can find! (*The Stage Hand leaves and returns soon after with a good sheaf of paper, which he hands to the Prompter.*) (*To the Prompter again*) Follow the scenes as they're performed, and try to set down the lines, at least the most important ones! (*To the Actors*) Clear the stage, folks! (*pointing to the left*) and pay strict attention!

LEADING LADY. But, do we have to…

DIRECTOR (*anticipating her*). You won't have to improvise, don't worry.

LEADING MAN. And what do we have to do?

DIRECTOR. Nothing! Just look and listen for now! Then each of you will
have your part written down. For now we'll just have a rehearsal. Do
the best we can. They'll act it out! (*pointing to the Characters*).

FATHER (*utterly surprised, in the midst of the confusion on stage*). Us? What
do you mean by a rehearsal?

DIRECTOR. A rehearsal, a rehearsal for them! (*pointing to the Actors*)

FATHER. But *we're* the characters...

DIRECTOR. Okay, you're the characters; but here, my dear fellow,
characters don't perform. Actors perform. The characters are
there, in the script – (*pointing to the Prompter's box*), when there is a
script!

FATHER. Exactly! And since there is none and you're lucky enough to
have the living characters in front of you...

DIRECTOR. Oh, great! So, you'd like to do it all yourselves? Perform,
face the audience... ?

FATHER. Yes, of course. Just as we are.

DIRECTOR. A nice spectacle you'd be, I assure you!

LEADING MAN. And what exactly would *we* be doing here, then?

DIRECTOR. You don't imagine you can act, do you? You'd make people
laugh... (*the Actors laugh, in fact*) There, see? They're laughing!
(*Remembering*) By the way, we've got to assign the roles. It's easy,
actually, they're self-evident. (*To the Second Female Lead*) You 'll play
the *Mother*. (*To the Father*) We must find her a name.

FATHER. Amalia, sir.

DIRECTOR. But that's your wife's name. We don't want to call her by her
real name!

FATHER. Why not, if that's her name... ? Oh, yeah, if this lady has to...
(*gesturing towards the Second Female Lead*) I see her (*indicating the
Mother*) as Amalia, sir. But you decide... (*He becomes increasingly
confused*) I don't know what to say any more... I'm already beginning
to hear... I don't know, my own words sound false, they sound
different...

DIRECTOR. Oh, don't worry, don't worry about this! We'll find the right
tone for them. And as for the name, if you like Amalia, let it be
Amalia, or we'll find another one. For the moment we'll assign the
roles this way: (*to the Juvenile Lead*) you the *Son*, (*to the Leading Lady*)
you, Miss, the *Stepdaughter*, of course.

STEPDAUGHTER (*highly amused*). What? what? Me, that one? (*bursting
into laughter*).

DIRECTOR (*irate*). What's there to laugh about?

LEADING LADY (*indignant*). Nobody's ever dared to laugh at me! Either
   I get respect or I'll go!
STEPDAUGHTER. No, I beg your pardon. I wasn't laughing at you.
DIRECTOR (*to the Stepdaughter*). You should feel honoured to be per-
   formed by...
LEADING LADY (*curtly, indignant*). ... 'that one'!
STEPDAUGHTER. I wasn't talking about you, believe me! I was talking
   about myself. I don't see myself in you, that's all. You don't... don't
   resemble me a bit!
FATHER. Yes, that's the problem, sir! Our expression...
DIRECTOR. ... What expression! Do you think you have it in you, your
   expression? Not at all!
FATHER. What? We don't have our expression?
DIRECTOR. Not at all! Your expression becomes real here, when the
   actors give it body and shape, voice and gesture. And, let me remind
   you, they've given expression to far more elevated subject matter,
   while yours is so low that if it holds up on the stage, it will be thanks
   to the merits of my actors, believe me...
FATHER. I don't want to contradict you, sir. But you must believe that it is
   a terrible pain for us who are as you see us, with this body, the way we
   look...
DIRECTOR (*cutting him off impatiently*). ... But the make-up will take care
   of that, my dear sir, the make-up!
FATHER. Well, but the voice, the gestures...
DIRECTOR. ... Oh, for pity's sake! you, as you, can't be here! Here it's
   the actor who plays you – and that's it!
FATHER. I understand, sir. But now I think I can guess why our author,
   who saw us this way, alive, didn't want to set us down in a script. I don't
   want to offend your actors, god forbid! But I think that to see myself
   played now... I don't know by whom...
LEADING MAN (*haughtily coming up to him, followed by the cheerful young
   Actresses, who are laughing*). By me, if you don't mind.
FATHER (*ingratiatingly, in honeyed tones*). Deeply honoured, sir (*bowing*), but
   I think that no matter how much the gentleman tries, with all his will
   and all his talent to take me into himself... (*he loses his train of thought*).
LEADING MAN. Go on, go on. (*The Actresses laugh.*)
FATHER. ... Well, I mean, your performance... even trying to resemble
   me with make-up,... with your height... (*all the Actors laugh*)... will
   hardly be a representation of me, as I really am. It'll instead be –
   apart from the looks – it'll be your interpretation of the way I am, the

way you feel I am – if you feel that – rather than the way I feel I am inside me. And I think whoever's called upon to judge us should take this into account.

DIRECTOR. Now you're worried about the judgment of the critics? And I was paying attention to what he was saying! Let the critics say what they want to. And let us think about getting the play together, if we can! (*Moving off and looking around*) Come on, come on! Is the scenery up? (*To Actors and Characters*) Please stand back. Let me see. (*Coming down off the stage*) Let's not waste any more time. (*To the Stepdaughter*) Do you think the set's all right this way?

STEPDAUGHTER. Well, I don't know. It's really not familiar.

DIRECTOR. Oh, come on! You can't expect us to build that back room of Madame Pace's down to the last details! (*To the Father*) You said a parlour with flowered wallpaper?

FATHER. Yes, white.

DIRECTOR. Well, it's not white, it's striped, but it doesn't matter! As for the furniture, we're okay, more or less! That little desk, please bring it forward a bit! (*The Stage Hands do so. To the Property Man*) Find an envelope, pale blue, if possible, and give it to the gentleman (*pointing to the Father*).

PROPERTY MAN. Like for a letter?

DIRECTOR AND FATHER. For a letter, a letter.

PROPERTY MAN. Right away! (*exiting*).

DIRECTOR. Come on, come on! The first scene is the young lady's. (*The Leading Lady comes forward*) No, no, you wait. I meant the young lady (*pointing to the Stepdaughter*), you just observe…

STEPDAUGHTER (*cutting in*). … How I live it!

LEADING LADY. I'll be able to 'live it' too, don't worry, as soon as I get started!

DIRECTOR (*his hands to his head*). No more talk, please! So, the first scene is between the young lady and Madame Pace. Oops… (*he is disconcerted, looks around, and goes up on the stage*), and this Madame Pace?

FATHER. She's not with us, sir.

DIRECTOR. Now what do we do?

FATHER. But she's alive, she's alive too!

DIRECTOR. Sure! But where is she?

FATHER. Well, let me tell you. (*Turning to the Actresses*) If you ladies would do me the favour of giving me your hats for a moment.

ACTRESSES (*a bit surprised, laughing a little, together*). … What? … our hats? … What're you saying? … Oh, look!

DIRECTOR. What do you want to do with the ladies' hats? (*the Actors laugh*).

FATHER. Nothing, just put them on these pegs for a moment. And if one of you would be so kind as to take your coat off too.

ACTORS (*as above*). ... The coat too? ... And then what? ... He must be crazy!

AN ACTRESS. ... But why? ... Only the coat?

FATHER. To hang them up, for a moment... Please do me this favour. Please?

ACTRESSES (*taking off their hats and one of them her coat too, still laughing, and going to hang them on the pegs*). ... And why not? ... There! ... This is really funny! ... Should we display them? ...

FATHER. Yes, exactly. Display them!

DIRECTOR. But may we know what for?

FATHER. Well, sir, maybe if we prepare the set properly, maybe, attracted by the tools of her trade, she might come among us... (*inviting them to look towards the door at the rear of the set*). Just look, look! (*The door opens and Madame Pace moves a few steps forward. She is an enormous fat old hag, wearing a garish carrot-coloured woollen wig with a bright-red rose on one side, Spanish style. Heavily made up, dressed with gauche elegance in a flaming red silk gown, a feather fan in one hand, the other holding up a lit cigarette between her fingers. As this apparition starts forward Actors and Director immediately rush from the stage with a shriek of fear, running down the stairs and heading for the aisle. The Stepdaughter instead runs up to Madame Pace humbly, as to one's boss.*)

STEPDAUGHTER (*running*). Here she is, here she is!

FATHER. It's her! Didn't I tell you? Here she is!

DIRECTOR (*overcoming his initial surprise, indignant*). What sort of trick is this?

LEADING MAN (*at almost the same moment*). What's going on, for pity's sake?

JUVENILE LEAD (*as above*). Where did she come from?

INGÉNUE (*as above*). They were keeping her in reserve!

LEADING LADY (*as above*). Magic tricks!

FATHER (*overcoming their protests*). Please! Why do you want to spoil – in the name of a vulgar factual reality – this prodigy of a reality which is born, evoked, drawn here, formed by the stage set itself? A reality which has a greater right to live here than you, because it's much truer than you. Which actress among you will play Madame Pace later? Well. Madame Pace is that woman! You must admit that the actress who plays her will be less true than that woman, who is herself in person! Look, my daughter has recognized her and gone right up to her! Please watch, watch the scene! (*Hesitantly, Director and Actors go back up to the stage. But already, during the Actors' protest and the Father's answer, the scene between the Stepdaughter and Madame Pace has begun, in very low voices – naturally, that is, in a way not possible on a real stage. Thus, when the Actors, asked by the Father to pay attention, turn to watch, they see Madame Pace who has already put her hand under the Stepdaughter's chin to make her raise her head, and hear her speak in a way that is totally unintelligible; they try to listen closely for a while, then, disappointed, almost immediately:*)

DIRECTOR. Well?

LEADING MAN. What's she saying?

LEADING LADY. Who can hear this way?

JUVENILE LEAD. Louder, louder!

STEPDAUGHTER (*leaving Madame Pace, who is smiling broadly with satisfaction, and coming before the group of Actors*). Oh sure, 'Louder'! Why louder? These aren't things you can say out loud! Only I could say them loudly, to shame him (*pointing to the Father*) and take my revenge! But for Madame it's different – it'd mean prison!

DIRECTOR. Oh, nice! Is that the way it is? But here you have to make yourself heard, dear! If even we on the stage can't hear, imagine when there's an audience in the theatre! You've got to create the scene. And after all, you can perfectly well talk loudly between yourselves, we're not going to be there listening as we are now. You have to imagine you're alone together in a room, in Madame Pace's back room, nobody hears you. (*The Stepdaughter, charmingly but smiling maliciously wags her finger – 'no' – several times.*) Why not?

STEPDAUGHTER (*in a low voice, mysteriously*). There's someone who'd hear us if she (*pointing to Madame Pace*) were to talk loudly!

DIRECTOR (*very distressed*). Someone else is going to jump out? (*The Actors ready themselves for another run down from the stage.*)

FATHER. No, sir, she's referring to me. It's me who 's supposed to be there, behind that door, waiting, and Madame knows it. In fact, please, allow me! I'll get over there, to be ready (*he starts moving*).

DIRECTOR (*stopping him*). No, wait! There are some theatrical conventions that must be respected here! Before you 're ready –

STEPDAUGHTER (*interrupting*). Yes, right away! Right now! I tell you I'm dying to live it, to see this scene! If he wants to be ready now, I'm more than ready!

DIRECTOR (*shouting*). But first the scene between you and her (*pointing to Madame Pace*) has to come out, loud and clear. Do you understand?

STEPDAUGHTER. Oh Lord, sir, she told me what you already know: that my mother's work was badly done again, that the material's wasted, and that I must be understanding if I want her to go on helping us in our poverty.

MADAME PACE (*coming forward with an air of great importance*). Eh, yeh, señor; porque yò nó quero aproveciarme... advantagiarme...

DIRECTOR (*almost terrified*). What? What? Is that the way she speaks? (*All the Actors burst out laughing loudly.*)

STEPDAUGHTER (*laughing too*). Yes, sir, that's the way she speaks, half her language, half ours, it's ridiculous!

MADAME PACE. Ah, no me par bon manners que you laugh de mi, se yo me fuerzo de hablar como puedo yor idioma, señor!

DIRECTOR. No, no, speak that way, speak that way, please, Madame! It's sure to be a hit! There's no better way to give the grossness of the situation some comic relief. Speak just like that! It's fine!

STEPDAUGHTER. Fine! Why not? Hearing certain propositions in such a language: it's sure to be a hit, because it sounds almost like a joke, sir. You laugh to hear her say there's an 'eldish señor' who'd like to 'amusarse con migo' – isn't that so, Madame?

MADAME PACE. Vieiito, yeh! Vieiito, linda; but meior para ti: que se no give gusto, te give prudencia!

THE MOTHER (*amid the astonishment and confusion of all the Actors, who had not been paying attention to her, and who now jump up at her cry to restrain her, for she has in the meantime torn the wig off Madame Pace and thrown it to the ground*). You witch! Witch! Murderer! My daughter!

STEPDAUGHTER (*running to restrain her mother*). No, no, mother! For god's sake!

FATHER (*running up too, at the same moment*). Be quiet, be quiet! Sit down!

MOTHER. Get her away from me, then!

STEPDAUGHTER (*to the Director, who also has run up*). It's impossible, it's impossible to have my mother here!

FATHER (*to the Director also*). They can't be together! That's why, when we came here, that lady wasn't with us! If they're together, of course, everything comes out too soon.

DIRECTOR. It's not important! This's only a first draft! Everything's useful for me to get the various elements even if they're a little mixed up. (*He turns to the Mother and leads her back to her seat*) Come on, my good lady, come on. Keep calm. Please sit down! (*The Stepdaughter returns to mid-stage and addresses Madame Pace.*)

STEPDAUGHTER. On with it, Madame, on with it.

MADAME PACE (*offended*). Ah no! Tank you! Yo aqui do nothing con tu madre present.

STEPDAUGHTER. Oh, come on, let in this 'eldish señor, porque se amusi con migo'! (*Turning to everyone, imperiously*) Come on, I've got to do this scene! Come on! (*To Madame Pace*) You can go now!

MADAME PACE. Ah, me go, me go... me go seguramente... (*She exits in a rage, collecting her wig and looking fiercely at the Actors, who applaud, laughing derisively.*)

STEPDAUGHTER (*to the Father*). And you make your entrance now! There's no need for you to go all the way around! Come here, as if you'd already made your entrance! See – I'm standing here, modest, my head low! Come on! Out with your voice! Say to me with a different voice, like someone coming from outside: 'Good morning, Miss'...

DIRECTOR (*already down off the stage*). Look at that! Are you the director, now? Or am I? (*To the Father who is looking at him, hesitant and perplexed*) All right, do it. Go to the back, without going out, and then come forward. (*The Father does so, almost frightened. Very pale, but already entering thoroughly into the reality of his created life. He smiles as he hurries forward from the rear, still unaware of the drama that is about to crash down upon him. The Actors are immediately intent upon the scene that now begins.*) (*To the Prompter in his box, speaking fast*) You pay attention now! Be ready to write!

The Scene

FATHER (*coming forward. In a different voice*). Good morning, Miss.

STEPDAUGHTER (*head low, barely containing her revulsion*). Good morning.

FATHER (*peeping at her under the hat that almost hides her face; realizing that she is very young, he exclaims almost to himself, partly with satisfaction, partly worried about compromising himself in a risky adventure*). Oh... But... I mean,... this isn't the first time that you've come here, is it?

STEPDAUGHTER (*as above*). No, sir.

FATHER. Have you been here before? (*The Stepdaughter nods affirmatively.*) More than once? (*He waits a bit for the answer. Again he peeps under her hat, smiles, and says:*) Well, then, come on... it shouldn't be so... Will you let me take off this sweet little hat?

STEPDAUGHTER (*immediately, to forestall him, but containing her revulsion*). No, sir, I can take it off myself. (*She does so in convulsive haste. The Mother, present at the scene with the Son and with the two young ones, who are always beside her, on the side of the stage opposite to the Actors, is on tenterhooks, and follows the words and actions of the two Characters with changing expressions, of pain, anger, anxiety, horror; sometimes she hides her face, sometimes she moans.*)

MOTHER. Oh, my god!

FATHER (*frozen for a long moment by the Mother's moan, then continuing in the same tone*). There, give it to me, I'll put it down. (*He takes the hat from her hands.*) But on such a sweet pretty little head as yours I'd like to see a prettier hat. You'll help me choose one from these on display later, won't you?

INGÉNUE (*interrupting*). Oh, oh, we'd better watch out, those are our hats!

DIRECTOR (*immediately, very angry*). Quiet, dammit! Stop trying to be funny! This is the big scene! (*To the Stepdaughter*) Go on, please!

STEPDAUGHTER (*continuing*). No, thank you, sir.

FATHER. Oh, come on, don't say no! You should accept it! I'll be offended… There are some pretty ones, look! Besides, Madame will be pleased! She puts them on display here for that purpose!

STEPDAUGHTER. No, sir, look, I couldn't even wear it.

FATHER. Do you mean, because of what they'd say at home, if you came back with a new hat? Come on! Don't you know how it is done? What to say at home?

STEPDAUGHTER (*nervous, impatient*). It's not that, sir! I couldn't wear it because I'm – as you see. You should have realized it by now! (*She indicates her black dress.*)

FATHER. Oh, yes – in mourning! It's true, I see. I beg your pardon. Believe me, I'm truly sorry.

STEPDAUGHTER (*making an effort to pluck up her courage and overcome both her indignation and revulsion*). Enough, enough, sir! I should be thanking you, not you feeling embarrassed or sorry. Please don't mind what I said. I myself… (*trying to smile, she adds*) have to forget that I'm dressed like this.

DIRECTOR (*interrupting, turns to the Prompter in his box and climbs onto the stage*). Wait, wait! Don't write that down! Leave out the last phrase! (*Turning to the Father and the Stepdaughter*) It's perfect, perfect! (*Then to the Father only*) Here you go on as we agreed! (*To the Actors*) Very nice, this scene with the hat, isn't it?

STEPDAUGHTER. But the best part is coming now. Why don't we go on?

DIRECTOR. Be patient for a moment! (*Again to the Actors*) Of course it has to be performed a bit lightly...

LEADING MAN. ... of course, free and easy...

LEADING LADY. ... Sure, nothing to it! (*To the Leading Man*) We can try it right now, can't we?

LEADING MAN. Sure... I'll go out to make my entrance! (*exits to be ready to come back in through the backdrop door*).

DIRECTOR (*to Leading Lady*). So, then, look – the scene between you and Madame Pace is over. I'll write it up later. Now you're... no, where are you going?

LEADING LADY. Wait, I'm putting my hat back on... (*She goes to get her hat from the hatstand.*)

DIRECTOR. Oh, yes, all right. So, you're standing here with your head down.

STEPDAUGHTER (*amused*). But she's not wearing black!

LEADING LADY. I'll be wearing black, and much more appropriately than you!

DIRECTOR (*to the Stepdaughter*). Be quiet, please! And watch! You'll learn something! (*He claps his hands*) Come on, come on! The entrance! (*He goes down off the stage again to take in an impression of the scene. The rear door opens and the Leading Man comes forward with the easy, playful manner of an old ladies' man. The Actors' performance will seem different from the very first phrases, without, however, giving the least impression of being a parody; instead, it will seem prettied up. Of course, the Stepdaughter and the Father, unable to recognize themselves at all in that actress and actor, will, when they hear their own words said, express in various ways – now with gestures, now with smiles, now with open protest – their surprise, amazement, pain, etc., as will be seen below. The Prompter's voice will be heard clearly from his box.*)

LEADING MAN. Good morning, Miss...

FATHER (*immediately, unable to restrain himself*). Oh nooo! (*The Stepdaughter, seeing the way the Leading Man has walked in, bursts out laughing.*)

DIRECTOR (*infuriated*). Keep quiet! And you stop laughing, once and for all! We can't get on with it this way!

STEPDAUGHTER (*approaching the proscenium*). Excuse me! It's only natural, sir! The young lady (*pointing to the Leading Lady*) stands there motionless; but if she's supposed to be me, I can assure you that if I heard a man saying 'Good morning' to me in that manner and in that tone of voice, I'd have burst out laughing, just as I did a moment ago!

FATHER (*also coming towards the Actors*). Yes, that's it, the manner, the tone...

DIRECTOR. What manner? What tone? Step aside now, and let me see the rehearsal!

LEADING MAN (*coming forward*). If I'm supposed to play an old man entering a house of ill repute...

DIRECTOR. Of course, don't mind them, for heaven's sake! Go on, go on, it's just fine! (*Waiting for the actor to begin*) So, then...

LEADING MAN. Good morning, Miss...

LEADING LADY. Good morning...

LEADING MAN (*imitating the Father's gesture of peeping under her hat, then, expressing first satisfaction, then apprehension*). Oh... but... I mean, this isn't the first time, I hope?

FATHER (*correcting him, unable to restrain himself*). Not 'I hope' – 'is it?' 'is it?'

DIRECTOR. He says 'is it,' question mark.

LEADING MAN (*pointing to the Prompter*). I heard 'I hope.'

DIRECTOR. All right, it's the same thing! 'Is it?' or 'I hope.' Go on, go on. Maybe a little more lightly... Wait, I'll show you. Watch... (*he goes up on the stage again, and performs the part, beginning from the entrance*) Good morning, Miss...

LEADING LADY. Good morning...

DIRECTOR. Oh... but... I mean... (*he turns to the Leading Man to show him how he has looked at the Leading Lady under her hat*). Surprise, fear, satisfaction. (*Then turning to the Leading Lady*) This isn't the first time that you've come here, is it? (*Again throwing an inquiring glance at the Leading Man*) Did you get it? (*To the Leading Lady*) And you say: No, sir. (*Again, to the Leading Man*). In a word – how can I put it? *Souplesse!* (*Again he descends from the stage.*)

LEADING LADY. No, sir...

LEADING MAN. Have you been here before? More than once?

DIRECTOR. No, no, wait. Let her (*pointing to the Leading Lady*) nod first. 'Have you been here before?' (*The Leading Lady lifts her head a little, lowering her eyes sadly to express revulsion, then, as the Director says 'Down,' she nods twice.*)

STEPDAUGHTER (*unable to resist*). Oh, my God! (*immediately she puts her hand over her mouth to restrain her laughter*).

DIRECTOR (*turning*). What is it now?

STEPDAUGHTER (*immediately*). Nothing! Nothing!

DIRECTOR (*to the Leading Man*). It's your line, go on.

LEADING MAN. More than once? Well then, come on, it shouldn't be so... Will you let me take off this sweet little hat? (*The tone of this last question and the gesture which accompanies it cause the Stepdaughter, who has been restraining herself with her hand over her mouth, to lose control. A loud laugh bursts from behind her fingers.*)

LEADING LADY (*indignant, going back to her seat*). I'm not going to stay here to be made a fool of by her!

LEADING MAN. Me neither. That's it!

DIRECTOR (*to the Stepdaughter, shouting*). Cut it out, will you?! Cut it out!

STEPDAUGHTER. I will, forgive me,... forgive me...

DIRECTOR. You're a rude little brat, that's what you are! A real smart aleck!

FATHER (*trying to intervene*). Yes, sir. It's true, it's true. But you must excuse her...

DIRECTOR (*going back up onto the stage*). Excuse what?! It's too much!

FATHER. Yes, sir. But believe me, believe me, it feels so strange...

DIRECTOR. Strange? What do you mean strange? Why strange?

FATHER. I admire your actors, sir, I admire them: this gentleman (*indicating the Leading Man*), the young lady (*gesturing towards the Leading Lady*), but certainly,... well, they're just not us...

DIRECTOR. Well, sure! How do you expect them to be 'you,' if they're actors?

FATHER. That's just it, actors! And both of them play our parts well. But believe me, to us it seems like something else, it's supposed to be the same, and yet it isn't!

DIRECTOR. What do you mean, it isn't? What is it, then?

FATHER. Something that... becomes theirs, and no longer ours.

DIRECTOR. But that's inevitable! I told you!

FATHER. Yes, I understand, I really do...

DIRECTOR. ... so, enough already! (*To the Actors*) This means that we'll rehearse among ourselves, alone, the way it should be done. It's always been a disaster for me to rehearse with the author present! They're never satisfied! (*Turning to the Father and the Stepdaughter*) Come on, let's start again with you, and let's see if you can stop laughing.

STEPDAUGHTER. Oh, I won't. I won't! For me the best part's coming now. Don't worry!

DIRECTOR. So, when you say: 'Please don't mind what I said. I too...' (*to the Father*) you've got to jump in immediately: 'I see, oh, I see,' and right away you've got to ask...

STEPDAUGHTER (*interrupting*). What? What does he ask?

DIRECTOR. The reason why you're in mourning!

STEPDAUGHTER. No, sir! Look: when I told him that I shouldn't think about being dressed like this, do you know what he answered? 'Oh, good! Then let's get rid of this nice little dress right away!'

DIRECTOR. Oh, fine! Really terrific! That'll bring the whole house down!

STEPDAUGHTER. But it's the truth!

DIRECTOR. What truth, pray tell me? This is a theatre! The truth... up to a certain point!

STEPDAUGHTER. And what do you mean to do, then?

DIRECTOR. You'll see, you'll see! Let me handle this now!

STEPDAUGHTER. No, sir! All my revulsion, all the reasons – one more cruel and nasty than the next – why I am the way I am, maybe you want to make a romantic, sentimental little mess out of all that, with him asking me why I'm in mourning and me in tears answering that my papa died two months ago? No, no, my dear sir! He's got to tell me what he told me: 'Then let's get rid of this nice little dress right away.' And I, with all that mourning in my heart, only two months old, I went over there, see? behind that screen, and with these fingers shaking with shame and revulsion, I unhooked my corset, my dress...

DIRECTOR (*running his hands through his hair*). For god's sake! What are you saying?

STEPDAUGHTER (*shouting, in great excitement*). The truth, the truth, sir!

DIRECTOR. All right, all right, it may be the truth... and I understand, I really do, how horrible it was for you. But even you've got to understand that all this can't be shown on stage!

STEPDAUGHTER. It can't? Well then, thank you very much, I'm out of here!

DIRECTOR. No, see here...

STEPDAUGHTER. I'm out of here! What can or can't be shown on stage was decided by the two of you in there. Thank you! I see it very clearly! He wants to go straight to performing (*stressing the next phrase*) his 'inner torment,' but I want to put on my drama! mine!

DIRECTOR (*annoyed, getting worked up*). Oh, come on, yours! It's not only yours, see? It's the others' too! His (*pointing to the Father*), your mother's! You can't have one character coming forward that much, upstaging everybody else, taking over the stage. All the characters must be kept within a harmonious framework, and act what can be acted! I know as well as you do that each person has a whole life inside him and would like to pour it all out. But the difficult thing is to pour out only what's necessary, with respect to the others, and, through that little, to suggest all the rest of a life that's left inside. How nice it would be, if each character could deliver a long monologue, or – even better – a long lecture, and dish out to the audience everything that's boiling in their cauldron! (*In a conciliatory, good-natured tone*) You've got to restrain yourself, Miss. And believe me, it's in your own best interest, because frankly all this destructive rage, this exasperation, this disgust, could make a bad impression, I tell you, frankly, when you've admitted yourself you'd been with others more than once at Madame Pace's, before him!

STEPDAUGHTER (*bowing her head, in a low voice, after a reflective pause*). It's true. But you've got to understand that for me all the others are... him too.

DIRECTOR (*not understanding*). What do you mean, the others are –?

STEPDAUGHTER. When a person commits a sin, sir, isn't the one responsible for all the sins that follow always the one who first caused the fall? Well, for me he is that one, even before I was born. Look at him, see if it isn't true!

DIRECTOR. Fine! And do you think for him the burden of his remorse is such a small thing? Give him a chance to express it.

STEPDAUGHTER. Pardon me, but how can he express all his 'noble remorse,' all his 'moral torments,' if you don't allow him first to experience the horror, one fine day, of finding in his arms... a grown woman and already a fallen one, whose mourning dress he proposed she take off... that little girl, sir, that little girl he used to go to see getting out of school? (*These last words are said in a voice trembling with emotion. The Mother, hearing her say these things, is overcome by a wave of irrepressible grief: her repressed moans break out at last in a flood of tears. Everyone is overcome by emotion. Long pause. As soon as the Mother gives signs that she has calmed down, the Stepdaughter, sombre and resolute, adds*) We're only here alone with each other now, with no audience. Tomorrow you'll present whatever spectacle you like of us, arranging it your own way. But do you really want to see the drama, see it burst out the way it really did burst out?

DIRECTOR. Yes, of course, I'd like nothing better, so I can use as much as possible of it!

STEPDAUGHTER. Then have my Mother led away.

MOTHER (*rising from her tears with a loud cry*). No, no! Don't allow it, sir! Don't allow it!

DIRECTOR. But, madam, it's only in order to see!

MOTHER. I can't bear it, I can't!

DIRECTOR. But why? Hasn't all this already taken place in the past?! I don't understand you!

MOTHER. No, it's taking place now, it's always taking place. My torment isn't over, sir! I'm alive and present, always, in every moment of my torment, which recreates itself, alive and present, always. But those two little children, have you heard them speak? They can no longer speak, sir! They keep on clutching my hands to keep my torment alive and present, but they in themselves no longer exist! And this one (*pointing to the Stepdaughter*) has run away, sir, has fled from me and is lost, lost... If I see her here before me, it's for the same purpose, the only purpose always, always – to recreate, alive and present, the torment I felt for her too!

FATHER (*solemnly*). The eternal moment, as I told you, sir! She (*pointing to the Stepdaughter*) is here to capture me, freeze me, keep me hooked and suspended for eternity, pilloried, in that single fleeting and shameful moment of my life. She can't give it up. And you, sir, can't really save me from it.

DIRECTOR. All right, I'm not saying that we shouldn't act it out. It'll be the nucleus of the entire first act, until we get to her surprise entrance... (*pointing to the Mother*).

FATHER. That's right. Because that's my sentence, sir. All our passions must lead to her final cry! (*he too points to the Mother*).

STEPDAUGHTER. It's still in my ears. That cry has driven me crazy! ... You can act me out as you like, sir; it doesn't matter! Even dressed, as long as at least my arms – only my arms – are bare, because, look, standing like this (*going up to the Father and leaning her head against his chest*) with my head leaning like this, and my arms like this around his neck, I could see a vein pulsing here on my arm; so, as if only that living vein revolted me, I shut my eyes tight like this, and, just like this, buried my head in his chest! (*Turning towards her mother*) Cry out, mama, cry out! (*with her head buried in the Father's chest, and with her shoulders raised as if to shut out her mother's cry, she says in a voice of strangled grief*) Cry out, as you did then!

MOTHER (*rushing forward to separate them*). No, my daughter, no, my daughter! (*and after tearing her away from him*) You brute, you brute, she's my daughter! Can't you see she's my daughter?

DIRECTOR (*backing all the way to the footlights at her cry, while the Actors express consternation*). Perfect! Absolutely perfect! Then the curtain falls! curtain!

FATHER (*running up to him, violently excited*). That's it, that's the way it really was, sir.

DIRECTOR (*filled with admiration and convinced*). Of course, and at this point we bring down the curtain! (*The Scene Shifter, hearing the Director shouting 'curtain,' lets the curtain drop, leaving the Director and the Father in front of it before the footlights. The Director, looking up with his arms raised*) What a moron! I say 'curtain' meaning that the act should end here, and he actually lets the curtain fall! (*To the Father, lifting the edge of the curtain to get to the stage again*) Yes, yes! Very good! Effect guaranteed! It has to end here! No doubt about it. This act'll be a success, I guarantee it! (*He goes behind the curtain with the Father.*)

(*As the curtain rises, we see that the earlier, sketchy scenery has been removed, and a small garden fountain has been set up. On one side of the stage the Actors are seated in a row, on the other the Six Characters. The Director is standing in the middle of the stage with his fist to his lips, as if meditating.*)

DIRECTOR (*shaking himself after a brief pause*). So, then: we come to the second act! Let me do it my way, okay? – as we arranged before. It'll go just fine!

STEPDAUGHTER. Our coming to his house (*pointing to the Father*) in spite of that guy! (*pointing to the Son*).

DIRECTOR (*impatient*). Okay! But let me do it, I said!

STEPDAUGHTER. As long as his spite is made plain!

MOTHER (*from her corner, shaking her head*). For all the good it did us…

STEPDAUGHTER (*turning to her abruptly*). It doesn't matter. The more grief for us, the more remorse for him!

DIRECTOR (*impatient*). I know all that! We'll bear it in mind, especially at the beginning.

MOTHER (*imploringly*). Please, make it very clear, sir, for the sake of my conscience, because I tried every possible way…

STEPDAUGHTER (*interrupting scornfully and completing the Mother's words*). … to placate me and persuade me not to act so spitefully towards him. (*To the Director*) Please, let her have her wish, let her, because it's true! I enjoy it so much, because it's so clear: the more she pleads, the more she tries to find a way to his heart, the more aloof, and 'above it all' he is. Marvellous!

DIRECTOR. Come, can we finally get started on the second act?

STEPDAUGHTER. I won't say another word! But, bear in mind that having it all take place in the garden, as you want to, won't be possible!

DIRECTOR. Why won't it be possible?

STEPDAUGHTER. Because he (*pointing to the Son*) keeps himself shut up in his room, isolated! And besides, the entire part of that poor lost boy there has to take place in the house, as I told you.

DIRECTOR. Oh, right! But on the other hand, you understand, we can't hang up captions, or change the scenery three, four times, every act!

LEADING MAN. They used to do it, once...

DIRECTOR. Yes, when the audience was like that child there, maybe!

LEADING LADY. And the illusion was easier to convey!

FATHER (*jumping up*). Illusion? Please, don't say illusion. Do not use that word which is so terribly cruel for us!

DIRECTOR (*astonished*). Oh, come on, why?

FATHER. Yes, cruel! really cruel! You ought to understand why!

DIRECTOR. And how should we say it, then? The illusion that has to be created here for the audience...

FIRST ACTOR. ... by our performance...

DIRECTOR. ... the illusion of reality!

FATHER. I understand, sir. But perhaps you can't understand us. Forgive me! Because, you see, here, for you and your actors, it's simply a matter – and rightly so – of a game.

LEADING LADY (*interrupting, indignantly*). What game?! We're not children! We're serious performers here.

FATHER. I'm not denying that. And I mean, in fact, the game of your craft, which has to create – as the gentleman says – a perfect illusion of reality.

DIRECTOR. Right, right!

FATHER. Now, just consider this: we, as characters, (*with a gesture that includes the other five Characters*) have no reality outside this illusion!

DIRECTOR (*confused, looking at his Actors, who also are perplexed and bewildered*). What do you mean by that?

FATHER (*after watching them for a moment, smiling faintly*). Yes, gentlemen! What other reality can we have? What for you is an illusion to create, for us is our only reality! (*Brief pause. He moves a step or two towards the Director and adds*) But, mind you, not only for us. Think of it. (*Looking him in the eye*) Would you be able to tell me who you are?

DIRECTOR (*disturbed, with a weak smile*). What do you mean who I am? I'm me!

FATHER. And if I told you that's not true, because you're me?

DIRECTOR. I'd answer that you're crazy! (*The Actors laugh.*)

FATHER. They're right to laugh, because right now we're playing (*to the Director*) and you can object that it's only in a game that the gentleman there (*pointing to the Leading Man*), who is 'himself,' has to be 'me,' who instead am I, 'this.' See how I've trapped you? (*The Actors laugh again.*)

DIRECTOR (*annoyed*). But we said this a little while ago! Are we starting all over again now?

FATHER. No, no. I didn't mean to say this, in fact. Instead I propose that you get out of this game (*looking at the Leading Lady as if to forestall her*), – I mean the game of your craft, of course – that you're used to playing here with your actors; and once again I ask you seriously: who are you?

DIRECTOR (*turning to the Actors, astonished and irritated at the same time*). Hey, but it takes a lot of nerve for someone who passes himself off as a mere character, comes and asks me who I am!

FATHER (*with dignity, but no arrogance*). A character, sir, can always ask a person who he is. Because a character really has a life of his own, distinguished by qualities of his own, so that he's always 'someone.' While a man – I'm not saying you necessarily – a man in general may be 'nobody.'

DIRECTOR. Right! But you're asking me that question, and I happen to be the Director, the head of the company! Understand?

FATHER (*in almost an undertone, with soft-spoken humility*). Only to find out, sir, if you, as you are now, really see yourself as you now see, for instance, from a distance, what you once were, with all the illusions you had then? with all the things, inside and outside of you, the way they seemed to you then – and were, really were for you? Well, sir, thinking of all those illusions long gone, of all the things that no longer 'seem' to you the way they 'were' then, don't you feel not just these stage boards, but the ground itself giving way under your feet, realizing that in the same way 'everything' you feel 'is' here and now, everything that's real for you today, is bound to reveal itself an illusion tomorrow?

DIRECTOR (*this sophisticated argument has left him dazed, he has not understood much of it*). Well? What are you getting at with all this?

FATHER. Oh, nothing, sir. Only to show you that if we (*again a gesture that includes himself and the other Characters*) have no other reality beyond illusion, it would be wise for you not to trust too much in yours, in this reality you breathe and touch in yourself today, because – like that of yesterday – it's bound to reveal itself an illusion tomorrow.

DIRECTOR (*trying his best to turn the thing into a joke*). Ah, very well! And I suppose you'll add that you, with this play you've come to act out here, are more true and real than me!

FATHER (*in all seriousness*). Oh, no question about it, sir!

DIRECTOR. Oh, really?

FATHER. I thought you'd understood it from the very beginning.

DIRECTOR. More real than me?

FATHER. But if your reality can change from one day to the next…

DIRECTOR. But we know that our reality can change, of course. It changes all the time, everybody's does!

FATHER (*with a cry*). But ours doesn't, sir, don't you see? That's the difference! It doesn't change, it can't change, or be different, ever, because it's been fixed – this way – 'this one' – forever – (it's a terrible thing, sir!). Our unchangeable reality should make you shudder when you come close to us!

DIRECTOR (*abruptly, confronting him with an idea that has suddenly popped into his head*). But I'd like to know when a character has ever been seen stepping out of his role and speaking for it, defending it, explaining it, the way you're doing? Can you tell me that? I've never seen one!

FATHER. You've never seen it because authors don't ususally disclose the laborious process of creation. Yet if the characters are alive, really alive, before their author, he does nothing but observe the words, the gestures, they suggest to him; he must want them to be the way they want themselves to be; he has to! When a character is born, he immediately acquires such independence even from his own author that he can be imagined by everybody in situations in which his author never thought of putting him, and takes on a meaning, at times, that his author never dreamed of giving him!

DIRECTOR. All right! I know all this!

FATHER. So why wonder at us? Think of the bad luck of a character born, alive, as I said, from the imagination of an author, who then wanted to deny him life, and tell me if this character, left as he is, alive and deprived of life, has no business doing what we're doing before you now, after having done it again and again before him, believe me, in order to convince him, to push him… appearing to

him, sometimes me, sometimes that girl (*pointing to the Stepdaughter*),
sometimes that poor mother...

STEPDAUGHTER (*coming forward as if in a reverie*). It's true, sir, I too,
I came too, to try to convince him, many times, in the melancholy
of that study of his, at dusk, when slouched in his easy chair, he
couldn't make up his mind to turn the light on and he let the
darkness invade the room, darkness teeming with us, who came to
tempt him... (*As if she were still seeing herself in that study and felt
bothered by the presence of the Actors*) Oh, if you all would just go away!
And leave us alone! Mother, there, with that son of hers... I with
that little girl... that boy, always alone... then I with him (*pointing to
the Father*), and then I by myself, alone... in that darkness (*starts
suddenly, as if she longed to grasp hold of herself in the vision she has of
herself, shining, alive, in that darkness*) Ah, my life! What scenes! what
scenes we came to suggest to him! I, I was the one who tried the
hardest to convince him!

FATHER. Yeah! But perhaps it was because of you, because of your
inordinate insistence, your inordinate excesses... !

STEPDAUGHTER. Most certainly not! He made me the way I am! (*coming
up to the Director to tell him in confidence, in a low voice*) I think instead
he was disheartened, scornful of the theatre, as the public usually
thinks of it and likes it...

DIRECTOR. Let's go on, let's go on, good Lord, and let's get to some
action, folks.

STEPDAUGHTER. Oh, but, it seems to me that you've got too much
action, when we come into his home! (*Pointing to the Father*) You said
you couldn't hang up captions or change scenery every five minutes!

DIRECTOR. Yes, that's just it. We've got to combine, group facts into
simultaneous, concise action, and not the way you want it – first to
see your little brother come back from school and wander like a
ghost through the rooms, hiding behind the doors to brood over an
idea, in which – how did you put it? –

STEPDAUGHTER. ... he's shrivelling up, sir! He's shrivelling up
completely!

DIRECTOR. I never heard that expression! Okay!: 'growing only in his
eyes,' right?

STEPDAUGHTER. Yes sir, there he is! (*pointing to the boy beside his mother*).

DIRECTOR. Very good! And then, at the same time you'd like the little
girl playing, carefree, in the garden. One in the house, the other in
the garden. Now, is that possible?

STEPDAUGHTER. Oh, in the sun, sir, how happy she was! It's my only recompense, her happiness, her enjoyment in that garden. Taken away from the poverty, the squalor, of the horrible room where all four of us had been sleeping – and me with her – me, think of it!, with the horror of my contaminated body, next to her, and she holding me so tightly in her loving, innocent little arms. In the garden, as soon as she saw me, she'd run to take my hand. She didn't care about the big flowers, she went to find all the 'itty bitty' ones and wanted to show them to me, with such joy, such joy! (*Overcome by the memory, she bursts into tears and cries desperately, dropping her head onto her arms, which are flung out on the desk. Everyone is overcome by emotion. The Director approaches her in an almost fatherly way, and to comfort her, tells her:*)

DIRECTOR. We'll have the garden, we'll have the garden, don't worry. You'll see, you'll like it. We'll group the various scenes there. (*Calling a Stage Hand by name*) Hey, let down some trees! A couple of small cypresses here in front of the pool! (*Two cypresses are lowered from above. The Scene Shifter runs to steady them with nails. To the Stepdaughter*) Just temporary for now, to give the idea. (*Calling the Stage Hand's name again*) Now give me a bit of sky.

THE STAGE HAND (*from above*). What?

DIRECTOR. A bit of sky! A backdrop, coming down here, behind the pool! (*A white backdrop is seen coming down from above*) Not white! I said sky! Oh, all right, leave it there. I'll take care of it. (*Calling*) Hey, electrician, turn off all the other lights and give me a bit of atmosphere... like... moonlight... Blue, blue from the beam balances, and blue on the backdrop, with the spotlight. That's it! Enough! (*A mysterious moonlit scene has been created at command, that induces the Actors to speak and move as they would at night, in a garden, in the moonlight. To the Stepdaughter*) There we are, look! Now instead of hiding behind the doors of the rooms, the boy could wander here in the garden, hiding behind trees. But you've got to understand, it'll be difficult to find a little girl who's capable of doing the scene where she shows you the little flowers. (*Turning to the boy*) You, come here! Let's see if we can get to something concrete! (*And because the boy does not move*) Come on! Come on! (*Then, pulling him forward, trying to get him to keep his head up – it droops again each time*) Ugh, quite a problem, this boy too.... What is the matter? Good Lord, he must be able to say something... (*going up to him, putting a hand on his shoulder, leads him behind the tree drop*) Come, come and show me, hide here a little... This way... Try to stick out your head just a bit, to spy on them... (*moves away to take in the impression; and as soon as the boy performs the action, amid the dismay of the Actors who are deeply affected by it*) Ah, very good, very good... (*To the Stepdaughter*) Listen, what if the little girl, seeing him spying like that, should run up to him and get a word or two out of him?

STEPDAUGHTER (*getting up*). Don't expect him to talk as long as that one's present! (*pointing to the Son*). You'd have to send him away first.

SON (*moving quickly towards one of the stairs*). Right away! Gladly! Nothing I'd like better!

DIRECTOR (*stopping him immediately*). No! Where are you going? Hold on! (*The Mother rises in panic, anguished at the thought of his actually leaving, and instinctively raises her arms as if to hold him back, though without moving from where she is.*)

SON (*at the footlights, to the Director, who is restraining him*). I really have nothing to do with all this! Please, let me go! Let me go!

DIRECTOR. What do you mean, you have nothing to do here?

STEPDAUGHTER (*calmly, with irony*). Oh, don't hold him back! He's not leaving!

FATHER. He's got to act the horrible garden scene with his mother!

SON (*immediately, firmly, fiercely*). I'm not going to act anything! I told you from the beginning! (*To the Director*) Let me go!

STEPDAUGHTER (*running up to the Director*). Allow me, sir. (*Loosing his grip on the Son*) Let him go! (*Then, turning to the Son, as soon as the Director has let go of him*) Okay, get out! (*The Son strains towards the staircase, but, as if held back by an occult force, he cannot descend the steps; then, to the amazement and distress of the Actors, he moves slowly along the footlights towards the other staircase; but there too he remains straining towards it, unable to go down. The Stepdaughter, whose eyes have followed him challengingly, bursts out laughing.*) He can't, you see? He can't! He's got to stay here, like it or not, bound in a chain that can't be broken. I take off, you know, when what's bound to happen does happen – because I hate him, because I don't want to set eyes on him again – well, if I'm still here, and have to bear the sight of him – imagine if he can leave! He has to, really has to stay here with this charming father, and that poor Mother, who has no other children left but him... (*turning to her mother*)... Come on, Mother, come... (*turning to the Director and pointing to her*)... Look, she was getting up, she was getting up to make him stay (*to her mother, as if drawing her on by magical powers*)... Come, come... (*then to the Director*)... Imagine if

she's got the heart to show what she feels here before your actors, yet
her longing to get close to him is so great that – there, see? – she's
willing to live her scene! (*In fact, the Mother has drawn near, and as soon
as the Stepdaughter has spoken her last words, she indicated that she
consents.*)

SON (*immediately*). Ah, but I'm not! I'm not! If I can't go, I'll stay; but
I repeat that I'm not acting anything!

FATHER (*to the Director, shaking with anger*). You can force him to, sir!

SON. Nobody can force me!

FATHER. I'll force you!

STEPDAUGHTER. Wait, wait! First the little one at the pool! (*She runs to
get the child, falls on her knees before her, takes her little face in her hands.*)
My poor little darling, your beautiful eyes are bewildered... God
knows where you think you are! We're on a stage, my dear! What's a
stage? Well, see? A stage is a place where you play that you're being
serious. People act out plays on it. And we're going to act out a play
now, seriously, you know! You too... (*she embraces her, clasping her tightly
to her breast and swaying a little*). Oh, my little darling, my little darling,
what a bad part you have to perform! What a horrible thing they
have thought up for you! In the garden, the pool... It's make-believe,
of course! That's what's so awful, my dear, that everything here is
make-believe! But maybe, being a child, you like a make-believe pool
better than a real one, so you can play in it, right? No, no, it may be a
game for others, but not for you, unfortunately, you who are real, my
little darling, and are playing for real in a real pool, beautiful, big,
green, with lots of bamboo plants that shade it and are reflected in it,
and lots and lots of ducklings swimming in it, breaking the reflection.
You want to catch one of the ducklings... (*With a shout that frightens
everybody*) No, Rosetta, no! Mother isn't watching you because of that
fiend of a son there! I've got a thousand devils in my head... and that
one... (*leaving the child, she turns with her usual roughness to the boy*)
What are you hanging around here for, like a little beggar all the
time? It'll be your fault too, if that child drowns. It'll be because of
this behaviour of yours, as if by getting you into the house I hadn't
paid for all of us! (*She seizes his arm to force him to pull a hand out of his
pocket*) What've you got there? What're you hiding? Get your hand
out! (*she pulls his hand out of his pocket and, to everybody's horror, discovers
that he is clutching a revolver. She looks at him almost as if she were gratified,
then she says in a low voice*) Where, how did you get it? (*And since the
boy, terrified, always with his eyes wide open and empty, does not answer*) You

little fool, if I were you, instead of killing myself, I'd have killed either of those two, or both, father and son! (*She pushes him back behind the little cypress tree where he had been spying; then takes the child and lowers her into the pool, arranging her so that she remains hidden; finally she collapses there, her face in her arms, which are lying on the edge of the pool.*)

DIRECTOR. Perfect! (*Turning to the Son*) In the meantime...

SON (*rebelliously*). What meantime! It's not true, sir! There's been no scene between me and her! (*pointing to the Mother*). Make her say it herself, exactly how things were. (*The Second Female Lead and the Juvenile Lead have left the group of Actors, the former watching the Mother who stands in front of her very attentively, the latter the Son, so as to play their roles later.*)

MOTHER. Yes, it's true, sir. I had gone into his room...

SON. In my room, did you hear? Not in the garden!

DIRECTOR. But that's not important. The events have to be grouped, I said.

SON (*seeing the Juvenile Lead watching him*). What do you want?

JUVENILE LEAD. Nothing, I'm watching you.

SON (*turning to the other side, to the Second Female Lead*). Ah, and you are over here, to play her role? (*pointing to the Mother*).

DIRECTOR. Right, right! And you should be thankful for the attention they are paying!

SON. Oh, yes! Thank you very much! But haven't you understood yet that you can't perform this play? We're not inside you, and your actors are looking at us from the outside. Would you be able to live in front of a mirror which not only freezes us with our own image but sends it back to us with a grimace that's an unrecognizable distortion of ourselves?

FATHER. It's true, believe me, it's true!

DIRECTOR (*to the Second Female Lead and the Juvenile Lead*). All right, get away from them.

SON. It doesn't work, I'm not taking part in this.

DIRECTOR. Be quiet now, and let me hear your mother! (*To the Mother*) So you'd gone in?

MOTHER. Yes, sir, into his room. I couldn't bear it any longer. To empty my heart of all the anguish that was dragging me down. But as soon as he saw me...

SON. ... No scene. I just went out, I went out to avoid making a scene. Because I've never made scenes. Do you hear?

MOTHER. It's true, it's true. That's how it went.

DIRECTOR. But now that scene between you and him has got to be made. It's indispensable!

MOTHER. As far as I'm concerned, I'm here! I wish you could give me the chance to talk to him for a while, to tell him all that's in my heart.

FATHER (*approaching the Son, violently*). You'll do it! For your mother! Your mother!

SON (*as resolute as ever*). I will not.

FATHER (*seizing him by the front of his shirt and shaking him*). By god, you obey! Obey! Don't you hear how she's speaking to you? Don't you have a son's heart in you?

SON (*seizing him in turn*). No! No! And you stop this, once and for all! (*General excitement. The Mother, terrified, tries to come between them, to separate them.*)

MOTHER. For god's sake! Please!

FATHER (*without letting go*). You've got to obey! You've got to obey!

SON (*wrestling with him and finally throwing him to the ground near the stairs to everyone's horror*). But what the hell is this frenzy that's taken hold of you? He's got no qualms about bringing his shame and ours before everybody! I want no part of this! No part! And this is how I interpret the will of the author who didn't want to bring us onstage!

DIRECTOR. But you came here!

SON (*pointing to the Father*). He did, not me!

DIRECTOR. But aren't you here too?

SON. He's the one who wanted to come, dragging us all along, and lending himself to all this... cooking up with you, not only what really did happen, but – as if that weren't enough – even what didn't happen!

DIRECTOR. But then why don't you tell what really did happen? Tell it to me! Did you leave your room without saying a word?

SON (*after a moment's hesitation*). Not a word. So as not to make a scene!

DIRECTOR (*urging him on*). Well, and afterwards? What did you do?

SON (*all present wait with strained attention; he moves a few steps on the stage*). Nothing... As I was crossing the garden... (*he stops, gloomy, absorbed in thought*).

DIRECTOR (*urging him to say more, impressed by his restraint*). Well? Crossing the garden?

SON (*exasperated, hiding his face with his arm*). Why do you want me to talk about it, sir? It's horrible! (*The Mother, trembling, with half-smothered moans, is looking towards the pool.*)

DIRECTOR (*in a low voice, noticing the direction of the Mother's gaze, turns to the Son with growing apprehension*). The little girl?

SON (*looking straight ahead of him, into the hall*). There, in the pool...

FATHER (*still on the ground, pointing to the Mother with pity*). And she was following him, sir!

DIRECTOR (*to the Son uneasily*). And then you?

SON (*slowly, still looking straight ahead*). I ran. I rushed to pull her out... But all of a sudden I stopped, because behind those trees I saw something that froze me: the boy standing there motionless, his eyes crazy, looking at his drowned sister in the pool. (*The Stepdaughter, who had remained bent over near the pool hiding the child, answers like an echo from the back, sobbing incontrollably. Pause.*) I tried to approach, and then... (*From behind the trees, where the boy has been hiding, the roar of a gunshot is heard.*)

MOTHER (*with a piercing scream, running with the Son and all the Actors, pell-mell*). My son, my son! (*Then, amid the general confusion and the incoherent shouts of the others*) Help! Help!

DIRECTOR (*amid the shouts, trying to push his way through, while the boy is lifted by the head and feet and carried away behind the white drop*). Has he wounded himself? Has he really wounded himself? (*Everyone, except the Director and the Father, still on the floor near the stairs, have disappeared behind the lowered drop that has served as the sky, and remain there for a while talking painfully. Then from both sides of it the Actors come back on the stage.*)

LEADING LADY (*coming in from the right, grief stricken*). He's dead, poor boy! He's dead! Oh, what a thing to happen!

LEADING MAN (*coming in from the left, laughing*). What do you mean, dead? It's all make-believe, fiction, don't you believe it!

OTHER ACTORS (*from the right*). Fiction? Reality! He's dead!

OTHER ACTORS (*from the left*). No! Fiction! Fiction!

FATHER (*rising and shouting above their voices*). What do you mean, fiction? Reality, reality, sir! Reality! (*He too disappears, in despair, behind the backdrop.*)

DIRECTOR (*at his wits' end*). Fiction! Reality! The hell with all of you! Lights! Lights! (*Suddenly the entire stage and hall are flooded with brilliant light, the Director takes a deep breath as if liberated from a nightmare, and the entire company look at each other surprised and confused.*) Oh, nothing like this ever happened to me before! They made me waste a whole day! (*Looking at his watch*) Go, go! What more do you want to do now? Too late to start rehearsing again. See you tonight! (*As soon as the Actors have said goodbye and gone*) Hey, electrician, turn everything off! (*He has not yet finished saying so, when the theatre falls for a moment into the thickest darkness.*) Well, Christ! Leave at least one bulb on, so I can see where I'm going! (*Immediately, behind the backdrop, as if a wrong switch has been pushed, a green spotlight is lit, which projects, large and distinct, the shadows of the Characters, without the boy and the little girl. The Director, seeing them, runs from the stage, terrified. At the same moment the green spotlight behind the backdrop is turned off and the stage is again lit by blue moonlight. Slowly, from the right side of the backdrop, the Son comes forward first, followed by the Mother with her arms stretched out to him; then from the left side, the Father. They stop midstage, remaining there like shapes in a dream. Last the Stepdaughter comes out from the left, running towards one of the stairs. On the first step she stops for a moment to look at the other three and bursts into strident laughter. Then she runs down the steps, runs up the aisle between the seats, stops once more and laughs again, looking at the three who remain up there; she exits the hall, and her laughter is heard again from the lobby. Soon after, the curtain drops.*)

Henry IV

Characters

.... (HENRY IV)

The Marquise   MATILDE SPINA

Her daughter   FRIDA

The young Marquis   CARLO DI NOLLI

The Baron   TITO BELCREDI

The Doctor   DIONISIO GENONI

The Four Sham Privy Councillors:

1ST LANDOLPH (*Lolo*)

2ND ARIALD (*Franco*)

3RD ORDULPH (*Momo*)

4TH BERTHOLDT (*Fino*)

The old house servant GIOVANNI

TWO VALETS *in costume*

In a solitary villa in the Umbrian countryside, in our time.

ACT ONE

(*A salon in the villa meticulously decorated to simulate the throne room of Henry IV in the imperial palace at Goslar. But in the midst of the antique furnishings two large modern oil portraits, life size, stand against the back wall [raised a little from the floor on a wooden shelf that runs the length of the wall, wide enough for people to sit on it as on a bench], one to the right and one to the left of the throne. The imperial throne and its low canopy stand against the wall, dividing the wooden shelf in two. The two portraits represent a gentleman and a lady, both young, dressed in Carnival costumes, one as Henry IV, the other as Mathilda of Tuscany. Doors on the right and left walls.*

As the curtain rises, the two valets, as if caught by surprise, jump up from the wooden shelf on which they were lying and take up positions like statues, one on each side at the foot of the throne, with their halberds. Soon after, through the second right-hand door, Ariald, Landolph, Ordulph, and Bertholdt enter, young

men paid by the Marquis Carlo Di Nolli to play the role of privy councillors, regal
vassals from the lower aristocracy at the court of Henry IV. They dress, therefore,
in the costume of German knights of the eleventh century. This is the first day on
the job for the last one, Bertholdt, whose real name is Fino. His three co-workers
instruct him on his duties, poking some fun at him. The entire scene must be per-
formed in an extremely lively manner.)

LANDOLPH (*to Bertholdt, as if continuing an explanation*). And this is the
   throne room!
ARIALD. At Goslar!
ORDULPH. Or, if you like, in the castle in the Hartz!
ARIALD. Or at Worms
LANDOLPH. According to the event we're performing, it jumps around
   with us, sometimes here, sometimes there.
ORDULPH. In Saxony!
ARIALD. In Lombardy!
LANDOLPH. On the Rhine!
ONE OF THE VALETS (*standing rigidly at attention, moving only his lips*).
   Pssst!!
ARIALD (*turning at the sound*). What is it?
FIRST VALET (*still like a statue, in an undertone*). Is he coming in or not?
   (*referring to Henry IV*).
ORDULPH. No, no. He's sleeping. Make yourselves comfortable.
SECOND VALET (*relaxing his pose with the First; taking a deep breath, and*
   going to lie on the shelf as before). Well, for god's sake, you could have
   told us!
FIRST VALET (*approaching Ariald*). Got a match?
LANDOLPH. Hey, no pipes in here!
FIRST VALET (*while Ariald holds a lit match for him*). No, I'm smoking a
   cigarette (*after lighting it, he too goes to lie down on the bench*).
BERTHOLDT (*who has been watching half-amazed and half-perplexed, looking*
   around the room, then looking at his and his companions' clothing). But,
   pardon me... this room... these costumes... which Henry IV? ... I'm
   lost. Is he or isn't he the French one? (*Landolph, Ariald, and Ordulph*
   burst out laughing.)
LANDOLPH (*still laughing, gesturing towards Bertholdt as if inviting his*
   laughing companions to poke more fun at him). The French one, he says!
ORDULPH (*as above*). He thought it was Henry of France!
ARIALD. Henry IV of Germany, old boy. The Salic dynasty!
ORDULPH. The great tragic emperor!

LANDOLPH. The one who was at Canossa! We fight it here, day in day
   out, the terrible war between Church and State! Ah!

ORDULPH. The Empire against the Papacy! Ah!

ARIALD. Antipopes against Popes!

LANDOLPH. Kings against the Anti-kings!

ORDULPH. And war against Saxony!

ARIALD. And all the rebel princes!

LANDOLPH. Against the Emperor's own sons!

BERTHOLDT (*shielding his head with his hands from this barrage of news*).
   I got you, I got you! No wonder I was lost, seeing myself in this
   costume and coming into this room! I was right: this isn't sixteenth-
   century clothing!

ARIALD. What sixteenth century?

ORDULPH. We're between the year one thousand and eleven hundred
   here!

LANDOLPH. You can count – if on January 25, 1071, we're in front of
   Canossa...

BERTHOLDT (*more confused than ever*). Oh, my god, this is a disaster!

ORDULPH. Well, sure, if you thought you were in the French court!

BERTHOLDT. All my review of history in preparation for this job...

LANDOLPH. Man, we come four hundred years earlier! You're not a kid
   any more!

BERTHOLDT (*getting angry*). But they could have told me, for god's sake,
   that he was Henry IV of Germany, not of France! In the fifteen days
   they gave me to get ready, god only knows how many books I've
   skimmed through!

ARIALD. But didn't you know that poor Tito played Adalbert of Bremen
   here?

BERTHOLDT. What Adalbert? I didn't know a damn thing!

LANDOLPH. No, this is how it was! When Tito died, the Marquis Di
   Nolli...

BERTHOLDT. That's the one, the Marquis! Couldn't he have told me... ?

ARIALD. Maybe he thought you knew!

LANDOLPH. He didn't want to hire a replacement. He thought the three
   that were left were enough. But Henry started shouting: 'Adalbert's
   been forced to leave' – (because – get it? – to him poor Tito wasn't
   dead, but as Adalbert he'd been forced to leave the court by the rival
   bishops of Cologne and Mainz).

BERTHOLDT (*holding his head in both hands*). But I don't know beans
   about all this history!

ORDULPH. Then you're stuck, old boy!

ARIALD. And the bad thing is, *we* don't know who you are, either.

BERTHOLDT. You don't, either? You don't know who I'm supposed to impersonate?

ORDULPH. Uhm! 'Bertholdt.'

BERTHOLDT. But who is Bertholdt? Why Bertholdt?

LANDOLPH. He began to shout: 'They chased Adalbert away? Then I want Bertholdt! I want Bertholdt!'

ARIALD. The three of us looked at each other. Who could this Bertholdt be?

ORDULPH. So here you are, Bertholdt, old man!

LANDOLPH. You'll be great for the part!

BERTHOLDT (*rebelling, starts to leave*). Ah, but I won't do it! Thank you very much! I'm leaving! I'm out of here!

ARIALD (*holding him back with Ordulph, laughing*). No, calm down, calm down!

ORDULPH. You are not to be the Bertholdt of the folk tale, after all!

LANDOLPH. If it's any comfort to you, *we* don't know who *we* are either. He's Ariald, he's Ordulph, I'm Landolph... That's what he calls us... But who are we? – Names of that time! So 'Bertholdt' must be a name of that time too. – Only one of us, poor Tito, got a nice role, the kind you read about in the history books; the Bishop of Bremen. He looked like a real bishop! Oh, he was magnificent, poor Tito!

ARIALD. Of course, he was able to study his role very well in the history books!

LANDOLPH. He even could order His Majesty around: he made him follow his guidance like a guardian, a counsellor. We're 'privy councillors' too, but we're only here to make up the right number, because it's a historical fact that Henry IV was hated by the upper aristocracy for surrounding himself at court with young men from the lesser aristocracy.

ORDULPH. That's us!

LANDOLPH. Yeah, kind of little vassals; loyal, sort of wild, cheerful...

BERTHOLDT. Must I be cheerful too?

ARIALD. Sure, like us!

ORDULPH. And don't think it's easy.

LANDOLPH. Which is a pity! Because, as you see, all the props are here. Our clothing would be good for marvellous appearances in a historical pageant, the type that's so popular in theatres nowadays. And material – oh, material enough not for just one, but many tragedies. It's all right here in the story of Henry IV. Instead, all four of us, and those two poor guys (*pointing to the valets*) when they're standing impaled-stiff at the foot of the throne, we're all... we're like this, we've got no producer who'd hire us to perform some scene. There's – how should I put it? – the form is there, but the content is missing. We're worse off than the real privy councillors of Henry IV, because, though nobody had given them a part to perform either, at least they didn't know they had a role to play, they played it because they were playing it, they didn't know they had to play it; in short, it wasn't a role, it was their life. They looked after their own interests at the expense of the others, they sold investitures, or something. But what are we here for in these fancy clothes, in this beautiful court... to do what? Nothing... Like six puppets hanging from a wall, waiting for somebody to take them down and move them this way and that and give them some words to say.

ARIALD. No, no, dear boy! Pardon me! You've got to answer correctly! You've got to know how to answer correctly! If he talks to you and you're not ready to answer the way he wants, watch out!

LANDOLPH. Yeah, that's true. It's true!

BERTHOLDT. And you say it's nothing!? How can I answer correctly? I studied up for Henry IV of France, and now here comes Henry IV of Germany (*Landolph, Ariald, Ordulph laugh again*).

ARIALD. Well, you've got to fix that right away.

ORDULPH. Never mind, we'll help you.

ARIALD. We've got a lot of books in there. First you need a quick review of the subject matter.

ORDULPH. You must know something about the subject already...

ARIALD. Look (*turning him around and showing him the portrait of the Marquise*) Who's that one, for example?

BERTHOLDT (*looking*). That? Well, first of all it looks to me like something out of place: two modern portraits here in the midst of all these real antiques.

ARIALD. You're right. In fact, they weren't here before. There are two niches behind those two pictures. Two statues were meant to be there, carved in the style of the period. Since they were empty, they were covered by those two canvases.

LANDOLPH (*interrupting and continuing*). ... which would be out of place for sure, if they were real paintings.

BERTHOLDT. And what are they? Aren't they paintings?

LANDOLPH. Yes. If you go and touch them, they're paintings. But for him (*pointing mysteriously to the right, Henry IV*), who doesn't touch them...

BERTHOLDT. He doesn't? What are they for him, then?

LANDOLPH. Oh, I'm interpreting, mind you, but I think I'm basically right. They're images, images like... like a mirror might give back. Understand? There, that one (*pointing to the portrait of Henry IV*) portrays him just as he is now, in this throne room, which also is, as it should be, in the style of the time. Why are you surprised? If they put a mirror in front of you, wouldn't you see yourself in it as you are right now, dressed in these antique rags? Well, it's as if there were two mirrors there that give back living images, here in the midst of a world that – never mind how – you'll see, you'll see, living here with us, how it'll come alive!

BERTHOLDT. Oh, listen, I don't want to go crazy here!

ARIALD. What d'you mean, go crazy?! You'll enjoy yourself!

BERTHOLDT. Oh, but say, how come you've all grown so wise?

LANDOLPH. You don't come back from eight hundred years of history without bringing a bit of experience with you!

ARIALD. Come on, come on! You'll see, in no time we'll draw you into it.

ORDULPH. And you'll grow wise too, at this school!

BERTHOLDT. Yes, please, help me right away. Give me at least the basics.

ARIALD. Leave it to us, I'll do a bit, he'll do a bit...

LANDOLPH. We'll tie your strings on, get you set up, like the best-working marionette ever. Come on, let's go! (*taking him by the arm to lead him away*).

BERTHOLDT (*stopping and looking at the portrait on the wall*). Wait! You didn't tell me who that one is. The emperor's wife?

ARIALD. No. The emperor's wife is Bertha of Susa, sister of Amedeus II of Savoy.

ORDULPH. And the emperor, who wants to be young with us, can't stand her – he's thinking of separating from her.

LANDOLPH. That one is his arch-enemy: Mathilda, the Marquise of Tuscany.

BERTHOLDT. Ah, I see, the one who was the pope's host...

LANDOLPH. At Canossa. Right!

ORDULPH. Pope Gregory VII.

ARIALD. Our bogeyman! Come on, let's go! (*they are moving towards the right-hand door through which they came, when from the left side door the old butler, Giovanni, enters, in a tailcoat*).

GIOVANNI (*hurriedly, anxiously*). Hey! Pssst! Franco! Lolo!

ARIALD (*stopping and turning*). What do you want?

BERTHOLDT (*surprised at seeing him in the throne room in a tailcoat*). Oh, how come? He comes in here?

LANDOLPH. A man of the twentieth century! Off with you! (*He runs up to him with the other two for a joke, threateningly, as if to chase him out.*)

ORDULPH. Away with you, ambassador from Gregory VII.

ARIALD. Away, away!

GIOVANNI (*fending them off, annoyed*). Oh, stop it!

ORDULPH. No! you cannot set foot in here!

ARIALD. Out, out!

LANDOLPH (*to Bertholdt*). It's witchcraft, you know! A devil called up by the Sorcerer of Rome! Draw your swords! (*he too makes as if to draw his sword*).

GIOVANNI (*shouting*). Stop, I say! Don't play the fool with me. The Marquis has arrived with company...

LANDOLPH (*rubbing his hands*). Splendid, splendid! Any ladies?

ORDULPH (*as above*). Old? Young?

GIOVANNI. There are two gentlemen.

ARIALD. But the ladies, who are the ladies?

GIOVANNI. The marquise and her daughter.

LANDOLPH (*surprised*). Oh! How come?

ORDULPH (*as above*). The marquise, you said?

GIOVANNI. The marquise, the marquise!

ARIALD. And the gentlemen?

GIOVANNI. I don't know.

ARIALD (*to Bertholdt*). They're coming to give us the content, understand?

ORDULPH. All ambassadors of Gregory VII! This should be fun!

GIOVANNI. Hey, will you let me speak?

ARIALD. Speak, speak!

GIOVANNI. One of the gentlemen seems to be a doctor.

LANDOLPH. Oh, we get it. One of the usual doctors!

ARIALD. Good, Bertholdt! you bring good luck!

LANDOLPH. You'll see how we handle this doctor!

BERTHOLDT. I think I'm going to be in trouble right from the start!

GIOVANNI. Listen to me. They want to come in here, into this room.

LANDOLPH (*amazed and dismayed*). What? Her? The marquise, here?

ARIALD. So much for 'content,' then!

LANDOLPH. This's going to be a real tragedy!

BERTHOLDT (*curious*). Why? why?

ORDULPH (*pointing to the portrait*). Because she's that one there. Can't
  you understand?

LANDOLPH. The daughter is the marquis's fiancée.

ARIALD. What have they come for? I'd like to know.

ORDULPH. If he sees her, it's going to be awful!

LANDOLPH. But perhaps by now he won't recognize her!

GIOVANNI. If he wakes up, you've got to keep him in there.

ORDULPH. Yeah? Are you joking? How?

ARIALD. You know how he gets!

GIOVANNI. Good Lord, even by force! Those were their orders! Go on,
  go on!

ARIALD. Yes, yes. He might be up already.

ORDULPH. Let's go, let's go!

LANDOLPH (*going off with the others, to Giovanni*). But later you'll explain.

GIOVANNI (*shouting after them*). Lock that door and hide the key! And
  the other door too! (*pointing to the door on the right. Landolph, Ariald,
  Ordulph go out the second door on the right*).

GIOVANNI (*to the two valets*). Off with you too! In there! (*pointing to the
  first door on the right*). Lock the door and hide the key! (*The two valets
  exit through the first door on the right. Giovanni goes to the door on the left
  and opens it to let the Marquis Di Nolli in.*)

DI NOLLI. Have your orders been clear?

GIOVANNI. Yes, my lord, don't worry. (*Di Nolli goes out for a minute to
  invite the others in. Baron Tito Belcredi comes in first with the doctor, Dionisio
  Genoni, then Lady Matilde Spina and the Young Marquise, Frida. Giovanni
  bows and exits. Lady Matilde Spina is about forty-five, still beautiful and
  shapely, although she does, all too clearly, remedy the inevitable ravages of age
  with boldly but intelligently applied make-up that gives her the fierce aspect of
  a Valkyrie. This make-up contrasts strikingly with her mouth, which is very
  beautiful and sorrowful. A widow for many years, she is a close friend of the
  Baron Tito Belcredi, whom neither she nor anyone else has ever taken seriously, at least outwardly. What Tito Belcredi is to her, basically, only he knows for
  certain; he, therefore, can afford to laugh, if his friend needs to pretend that
  she does not know. He is always laughing in response to the laughter that the
  marquise's mockery of him arouses in others. Slender, prematurely grey, slightly
  younger than she, he has a curious, birdlike head. He would be extremely
  lively, were it not that his agility [which makes him a swordsman to be
  reckoned with] is sheathed, so to speak, in a sleepy Arab indolence, revealed in
  his strange nasal drawl. Frida, the daughter of the marquise, is nineteen.
  Saddened by the shade in which her imperious and striking mother keeps her,*

*she is also offended, in that shade, by the careless gossip the older woman
provokes, which damages the mother not so much as the daughter. Fortunately
she is already engaged to the Marquis Carlo Di Nolli, a stiff young man, very
indulgent towards others, but closed and fixed in that little he believes himself
to be and to be able to do in the world – although, perhaps, he too is not so
sure about it. He is, in any case, dismayed by the many responsibilities he
believes he is burdened by, so that while the others, yes – lucky folks – can talk
and amuse themselves, he cannot; not because he does not want to, but
because he really cannot. He is dressed in very strict mourning because of the
recent death of his mother. Doctor Dionisio Genoni sports the pleasant,
shameless, ruddy face of a satyr, with bulging eyes, a short, witty little beard,
shiny, almost silvery; he has nice manners and is almost bald. They enter,
perturbed, almost fearful, looking around the room curiously [except Di Nolli]
and speaking at first in low voices.*)

BELCREDI. Oh, splendid, splendid!

DOCTOR. Very interesting! the delirium present also in his physical
surroundings, right! Splendid, really splendid!

LADY MATILDE (*who has been looking around for her portrait, sees it and moves
up to it*). Ah, there it is! (*gazing at it from the proper distance, with mixed
feelings*) Yes, yes, look… my god. (*Calling her daughter*) Frida, look…

FRIDA. Your portrait?

LADY MATILDE. No, look! It isn't me, it's *you* there!

DI NOLLI. It's true, I was telling you.

LADY MATILDE. I'd never have thought… (*shaken as if by a shiver down her
spine*) God! What a feeling! (*then looking at her daughter*) But why,
Frida? (*squeezing her close with an arm around her waist*) Come now!
Don't you see yourself in me, there?

FRIDA. Well, I truly…

LADY MATILDE. You don't? But how come you don't? (*turning to Belcredi*)
Tito, you look. Isn't it so?

BELCREDI (*without looking*). Oh, no, I don't look; I say no, a priori,
without looking!

LADY MATILDE. What a fool! He thinks he's paying me a compliment
(*turning to Dr Genoni*) Doctor, what do you think? (*He is moving
towards it.*)

BELCREDI (*with his back turned, pretending to warn him in secret*). Pssst! No,
Doctor, don't get involved.

DOCTOR (*disconcerted, smiling*). Why shouldn't I?

LADY MATILDE. Never mind him! Come! He's impossible!

FRIDA. He's a professional clown. Didn't you know?

BELCREDI (*to the doctor, seeing him moving towards the painting*). Watch out for your feet, watch out for your feet, Doctor! Your feet!

DOCTOR (*as above*). My feet? Why?

BELCREDI. You're wearing iron shoes?

DOCTOR. Me?

BELCREDI. Yes. And you're walking straight into four little glass feet.

DOCTOR (*laughing loudly*). Not at all! After all, it seems to me, there is nothing surprising in the fact that a daughter might resemble her mother...

BELCREDI. Bang! That's it!

LADY MATILDE (*with exaggerated anger, moving towards Belcredi*). Why 'bang'? What is it? What did he say?

DOCTOR (*innocently*). Isn't it so?

BELCREDI (*answering the marquise*). He said there's nothing to be surprised at, while you were utterly amazed. And why, if now the thing seems so natural to you?

LADY MATILDE (*even angrier*). Fool, fool! Precisely because it *is* so natural! Because that's not my daughter! (*pointing to the painting*) That's my portrait! And finding my daughter there instead of myself amazed me, and my amazement, believe me, was sincere, and I forbid you to doubt it! (*After this violent outburst, a moment of general embarrassment.*)

FRIDA (*in a low voice, annoyed*). My god, always the same... a big discussion for every trifle.

BELCREDI (*also in a low voice, in an apologetic tone, like a whipped dog*). I didn't doubt anything! I just noticed that you too, from the beginning, didn't share your mother's amazement; or if anything amazed you, it was the fact that your resemblance to that portrait seemed so great to her.

LADY MATILDE. Of course! Because she can't recognize herself in me as I was at her age, while I can easily recognize myself there, in her, the way she is now.

DOCTOR. Exactly! Because a portrait is there, fixed forever in one moment of time; it's distant and devoid of memories for the young marquise, while all that it can remind the marquise of, movement, gestures, looks, smiles, so many things that in fact are not now there...

LADY MATILDE. That's right!

DOCTOR (*going on, turning to her*). You, of course, can see them again, alive, now, in your daughter.

LADY MATILDE. But he has to spoil it for me, every least little yielding to the most spontaneous feeling, like this, for the pleasure of making me angry.

DOCTOR (*dazzled by the light he has shed, goes on in a professorial tone to Belcredi*). The resemblance, my dear Baron, often comes out of imponderable elements! And that explains the fact...

BELCREDI (*to interrupt the lecture*). That somebody might find some resemblance between me and you, dear professor!

DI NOLLI. Please, drop it, drop it! (*gesturing to the two doors on the right to remind them that somebody might be listening on the other side*). We've gotten a bit too far off the point, we were coming to...

FRIDA. That's the way it goes when he's around... (*pointing to Belcredi*).

LADY MATILDE (*immediately*). That's why I didn't want him to come.

BELCREDI. Thanks. After all the laughing you did at my expense! What ingratitude!

DI NOLLI. Enough of that, Tito, please! The doctor is here, we've come for a very serious reason, and you know how important it is to me.

DOCTOR. Yes! Let's first clarify some important points. Excuse me, my lady, how did this portrait get here? Did you give it to him as a present?

LADY MATILDE. No, no. I had no reason to. I was Frida's age then, and not even engaged. I gave it to him three or four years after the accident, on the insistence of his mother (*pointing to Di Nolli*).

DOCTOR. Who was his sister? (*meaning Henry IV's, pointing to doors on the right*).

DI NOLLI. Yes, Doctor. And our coming here is a debt paid to my mother, who left me a month ago. Instead of being here, she (*pointing to Frida*) and I were supposed to be on our honeymoon...

DOCTOR. And occupied quite differently. I understand!

DI NOLLI. Well! She died in the firm belief that the recovery of her beloved brother was imminent.

DOCTOR. And can you tell me from what signs she inferred that?

DI NOLLI. It seems to have come from a strange talk they had shortly before my mother died.

DOCTOR. A talk? There you are... it would be very useful to know what it was about... very useful!

DI NOLLI. Ah, I don't know. I know that mother came back from her last visit in anguish; because he seemed to have shown unusual tenderness towards her, as if foreseeing her approaching end. From her death bed, she made me promise that I'd never neglect him; that I'd have him seen by a professional...

DOCTOR. There you are. All right. Let's see, let's see, first... Often the least causes... This portrait, then...

LADY MATILDE. Well, Doctor, I don't believe you should give it so much importance. It struck me because I hadn't seen it for so many years.

DOCTOR. Please, please, be patient...

DI NOLLI. Yes, it's been there for some fifteen years...

LADY MATILDE. More! More than eighteen, by now!

DOCTOR. Please, pardon me, you don't know yet what my question is! I attach great significance to these two portraits – painted, I assume, before the famous, and very unfortunate, pageant, right?

LADY MATILDE. Well, of course.

DOCTOR. When he was, therefore, perfectly sane, right? That's what I meant! Was he the one who asked you to have it done?

LADY MATILDE. Oh, no, Doctor! So many of us who took part in the pageant had it done. Just so as to remember the pageant.

BELCREDI. I had it done too. I was Charles of Anjou!

LADY MATILDE. As soon as the costumes were ready.

BELCREDI. Because, you see, the idea was to collect them all, as if in a gallery, in the hall of the villa where the pageant took place, to remember it by. But later each one wanted to keep his own.

LADY MATILDE. And mine, as I said, I gave up without much regret, because his mother... (*again pointing to Di Nolli*).

DOCTOR. You don't know whether he was the one who requested it?

LADY MATILDE. Oh, I don't know. Maybe... Or his sister, to try lovingly to...

DOCTOR. One more thing, one more thing: the idea of the pageant was his?

BELCREDI (*immediately*). No, it was mine, mine!

DOCTOR. Please...

LADY MATILDE. Don't believe him. It was poor Belassi's idea.

BELCREDI. What d'you mean, Belassi?

LADY MATILDE (*to the doctor*). Count Belassi, who died a couple of months later, poor man.

BELCREDI. Belassi wasn't even there when...

DI NOLLI (*annoyed at the prospect of another discussion*). Pardon me, Doctor, is it really necessary to establish whose idea it was?

DOCTOR. It would surely be useful...

BELCREDI. It was mine! Oh, for goodness sake! It's nothing to be proud of, seeing what the results were! Look, Doctor, I remember it perfectly, it was one morning at the club, at the beginning of November.

I was leafing through a German illustrated magazine. (I was only
looking at the pictures, of course, since I don't know German.)
There was one of the Emperor, in some university town where he'd
been a student, I don't remember which one.

DOCTOR. Bonn, Bonn.

BELCREDI. Bonn, all right. On horseback, all dressed up in one of those
strange traditional costumes of the ancient German student societies,
followed by a train of noble students, also on horseback and in
costume. The idea came to me from that picture. Because at the club
we were thinking of putting on a big fancy-dress pageant for the next
Mardi Gras. So I proposed this historical cavalcade – 'historical' so to
speak, a kind of mish-mash. Each of us had to choose a character
to represent from this century or that, a king or an emperor, or a
prince, with his lady, or queen, or empress, beside him, on horseback. The horses too, decked out according to the custom of the
period. And the proposal was accepted.

LADY MATILDE. I got my invitation from Belassi.

BELCREDI. If the invitation said the idea was his, it was an 'inappropriate
appropriation,' if I may say so. He wasn't even there that evening at
the club when I made the proposal. And neither was *he*, for that
matter (*referring to Henry IV*).

DOCTOR. So he chose the character of Henry IV?

LADY MATILDE. Because, prompted by my first name – just so, without
thinking much about it – I said I wanted to go as the Marquise
Mathilda of Tuscany.

DOCTOR. I don't... I don't get the connection.

LADY MATILDE. Well, neither did I at the beginning, when I heard him
answer that then he would be at my feet, as at Canossa, as Henry IV.
Yes, I knew about Canossa, but to tell the truth, I didn't remember
the events that well. And when I reread them to impersonate my
character, I was struck by the fact that I was supposed to be a very
faithful, very zealous friend of Pope Gregory VII, who was locked in a
ferocious struggle with the German emperor. Then I understood
why, when I'd chosen to impersonate his implacable enemy, he
wanted to be at my side, in that cavalcade, as Henry IV.

DOCTOR. Ah! Was it perhaps because...

BELCREDI. Yes, Doctor, because at that time he was courting her relentlessly, and she (*pointing to the marquise*), naturally...

LADY MATILDE (*stung, flaring*). 'Naturally,' of course, of course! And
then, more than ever 'naturally'!

BELCREDI (*pointing to her*). See? She couldn't stand him.

LADY MATILDE. It's not true! I didn't dislike him. On the contrary! But for me, as soon as somebody wants to be taken seriously...

BELCREDI (*continuing*). ... he gives her the most perfect proof of his stupidity!

LADY MATILDE. No, dear! Not in this case. Because he wasn't at all a fool like you.

BELCREDI. I never made anybody take me seriously!

LADY MATILDE. Oh, I know that well! But with him, it was no joke. (*In a different tone, to the doctor*) It's one of the unfortunate things that happen to us women, my dear Doctor, to see before us a pair of eyes gazing at us with a pent-up, fervent promise of eternal love! (*She bursts out laughing shrilly*) There's nothing funnier. If men could see themselves with that 'eternal' in their eyes... It's made me laugh like this every time! And more than ever that time. But I've got a confession to make. I can make it now, after more than twenty years. When I laughed like that at him, it was also out of fear. Because maybe you could have believed a promise from those eyes. But it would have been very dangerous.

DOCTOR (*with great interest, attentively*). There you are, that's it – this is something I'd really like to know – very dangerous, you say?

LADY MATILDE (*lightly*). That's because he wasn't like the others! And since I too... yes, I'm... I'm a little... more than a little, to tell the truth... (*she is looking for an unpretentious word*) intolerant, that's it, intolerant of everything that's deliberate and smothering! But I was too young then – understand? – and a woman. I'd have to bite the bit. It would have taken a courage I knew I didn't have. So I laughed at him too. With remorse; even with annoyance at myself later, because I saw my laughter was getting mixed up with the laughter of all the others – idiots – who mocked him.

BELCREDI. More or less like they mock me.

LADY MATILDE. You make people laugh at you with your affectation of putting yourself down all the time, my dear, while he was the opposite! There's quite a difference. Besides people laugh at you to your face!

BELCREDI. Well, better than behind your back.

DOCTOR. Let's get back to the matter at hand, shall we? So, already a bit over excitable at that time, if I understood correctly!

BELCREDI. Yes but in a very curious way, Doctor!

DOCTOR. How would that be?

BELCREDI. Well, I'd say... pretty cool-headed...

LADY MATILDE. Not at all! He was like this, Doctor. ... A little strange, of course, but because he was full of life, imaginative!

BELCREDI. I'm not saying he faked his excitement. On the contrary, he often got genuinely worked up. But I could swear, Doctor, that he'd see himself right away, at the very moment he was feverish with enthusiasm, that's it. And I believe that must have happened to him with every spontaneous impulse he had. I'll say more: I'm sure he suffered badly because of it. Sometimes he'd explode in really comical fits of anger against himself!

LADY MATILDE. That's true!

BELCREDI (*to Lady Matilde*). And why? (*To the doctor*) In my view, it was because that sudden clarity of seeing himself act cut him off right away from any intimacy with his own emotion, which seemed to him – not faked, because it was sincere – but something to which he had to give on the spot the value – who knows – of an act of intelligence, to replace the warmth of sincere feeling that he felt was lacking in him. And he improvised, exaggerated, let himself go, that's it, to divert his mind and stop seeing himself. So he seemed erratic, silly, and... even ridiculous at times.

DOCTOR. And... would you say, unsociable?

BELCREDI. Not at all! He was into everything! He was for organizing pageants, dances, performances for charities; for fun, of course! But he was a very good actor, you know?

DI NOLLI. And with his madness he became a splendid and terrible actor!

BELCREDI. But from the very beginning! Just think that when the accident happened, after he fell from the horse...

DOCTOR. Striking the back of his head, right?

LADY MATILDE. Oh, how horrible! He was right at my side! I saw him between the hooves of the horse, which had reared...

BELCREDI. But we didn't believe, at first, that he'd hurt himself badly. Yes, there was a delay, some confusion in the cavalcade. People wanted to see what had happened. But he'd already been picked up and taken inside the villa.

LADY MATILDE. Nothing, you know! Not even the slightest wound, not a drop of blood!

BELCREDI. We thought he'd just fainted...

LADY MATILDE. And, a couple of hours later, when...

BELCREDI. Right, he came back into the salon of the villa – that's it, that's what I wanted to say...

LADY MATILDE. Oh, his face! I realized it right away!

BELCREDI. No! Don't say that! None of us realized it, Doctor, understand?

LADY MATILDE. Oh, sure! That's because you were all acting like madmen!

BELCREDI. Everyone was acting his part, for a joke. A real Babel!

LADY MATILDE. You can imagine, Doctor, how frightened we were when we realized *he* was acting *his* part in earnest!

DOCTOR. Oh, because he too, then…?

BELCREDI. Yes, he joined us! We thought he'd recovered and was acting, like the rest of us… better than the rest of us, because – as I told you – he was very good! In a word, we thought he was playing around!

LADY MATILDE. They started to goad him…

BELCREDI. So then – he was armed, you know, as a king would be – he drew his sword and charged two or three people. It was a terrifying moment for all of us!

LADY MATILDE. I'll never forget that scene – all our masked faces, crude, contorted, facing that terrible mask of his – no longer a mask, but madness.

BELCREDI. He was Henry IV! The real Henry IV, in a moment of furious rage!

LADY MATILDE. I think his obsession with the pageant must have affected him, Doctor… he'd been obsessed with it for more than a month. He always put such intensity into everything he did!

BELCREDI. The stuff he studied to get ready! Down to the finest details… the smallest things…

DOCTOR. Ah, it's easy to see: the momentary obsession became a fixation when he fell and struck his head, causing the brain damage. A permanent fixation. In these cases the result can be imbecility, or insanity.

BELCREDI (*to Frida and Di Nolli*). See how absurd things are, my dears? (*To Di Nolli*) You were four or five years old; (*to Frida*) to your mother it seems that you've taken her place in that portrait, where she was never even dreaming she'd give birth to you. I have grey hair already, and he – there he is (*pointing to the portrait*) whack! a hit on the head – and he never moved from there: Henry IV.

DOCTOR (*who had stepped aside to think, gestures to draw everybody's attention, and is about to give his scientific explanation*). Here it is, ladies and gentlemen, here's what we have… (*But suddenly the first door on the right is opened – the one closest to the footlights – and Bertholdt enters looking very upset.*)

BERTHOLDT (*bursting in like a person at the end of his rope*). Excuse me, please… (*but then he stops suddenly, seeing the disarray his appearance has caused in the others*).

FRIDA (*with a cry of fear, drawing back*). Oh god! There he is!

LADY MATILDE (*backing away in consternation, an arm before her eyes so as not to see him*). Is it him? Is it him?

DI NOLLI (*immediately*). No, no, calm down!

DOCTOR (*astonished*). And who is this?

BELCREDI. Someone who escaped from our pageant!

DI NOLLI. He's one of the four young men we keep here to help him in his madness.

BERTHOLDT. I beg your pardon, my lord…

DI NOLLI. What pardon? I gave orders to keep the doors locked and to let nobody come in here!

BERTHOLDT. Yes, sir, but I can't take it, and I'm asking permission to leave!

DI NOLLI. Oh, you're the one who started work this morning!?

BERTHOLDT. Yes, sir, and I'm saying that I can't take it…

LADY MATILDE (*greatly concerned, to Di Nolli*). Then he's not as calm as you said!?

BERTHOLDT (*immediately*). No, no, madam! It's not him! It's my three companions! You say 'help,' my lord? What kind of help! They're not helping! *They*'re the really crazy ones! I come here for the first time and instead of helping me, my lord… (*through the same door enter Landolph and Ariald, in a rush, but they stop at the door before coming forward*).

LANDOLPH. May I come in?

ARIALD. May I come in, my lord?

DI NOLLI. Yes, what is it? What are you doing?

FRIDA. Good Lord! I'm leaving, I'm leaving… I'm afraid! (*starting towards the left-hand door*).

DI NOLLI (*stopping her immediately*). No, Frida!

LANDOLPH. My lord, this moron… (*pointing to Bertholdt*).

BERTHOLDT (*protesting*). Oh, no, thank you, my friends! I'm getting out of here!

LANDOLPH. What do you mean, you're getting out?

ARIALD. He's ruined everything, my lord, rushing in here!

LANDOLPH. He's gotten him into a furious rage! We can't keep him in there any longer. He's given orders for him to be arrested, and he wants to try him from the throne right away! What do we do?

DI NOLLI. Close the door! close it! Go shut that door! (*Landolph goes to shut it.*)

ARIALD. Ordulph won't be able to keep him there alone…

LANDOLPH. Look, my lord, if we could at least announce your visit now, to distract him. If you ladies and gentlemen have already thought of the disguise to present yourselves in…

DI NOLLI. Yes, yes, we've thought it all out. (*To the doctor*) If you think you can see him now, Doctor,…

FRIDA. Not me, not me, Carlo! I'm leaving the room. You too, Mother, please come with me!

DOCTOR. Say… he is not still armed, is he?

DI NOLLI. Of course not, Doctor! (*To Frida*) Sorry, Frida, but this fear of yours is really childish! You wanted to come…

FRIDA. Oh, not me, please, it was mother!

LADY MATILDE (*resolutely*). And I'm ready! What do we have to do?

BELCREDI. Pardon me, is it really necessary to disguise ourselves this way?

LANDOLPH. Indispensable, sir, indispensable! Unfortunately, you see (*pointing to Belcredi's clothes*). Seeing you in those modern clothes would be a disaster!

ARIALD. He'd take it as a diabolical disguise.

DI NOLLI. Just as these men seem in fancy dress to you, that's how we'd seem to him.

LANDOLPH. And the thing wouldn't be so bad, sir, if it didn't look to him like the work of his arch-enemy.

BELCREDI. Pope Gregory VII?

LANDOLPH. That's it. He says he was a pagan!

BELCREDI. The pope? Not bad!

LANDOLPH. Yes, sir. And that he evoked the dead! He accuses him of all sorts of diabolical arts. He's terribly afraid of him.

DOCTOR. It's the persecution complex!

ARIALD. He'd fly into a terrible rage!

DI NOLLI (*to Belcredi*). But you needn't be present. We'll go in there. It's enough for the doctor to see him.

DOCTOR. You mean… by myself?

DI NOLLI. But they'll be there! (*pointing to the three young men*).

DOCTOR. No, I mean, if the marquise…

LADY MATILDE. Yes! I want to be there too! I want to be there, to see him!

FRIDA. Why, Mother? Please, come with us!

LADY MATILDE (*imperiously*). Let me do it! This's what I came for! (*To Landolph*) I'm to be Adelaide, the mother.

LANDOLPH. You are, very good. The mother of Empress Bertha. Then all you have to do is to put on the ducal crown and a cape that covers you entirely. (*To Ariald*) Go on, Ariald, go on!

ARIALD. Wait, what about this gentleman? (*pointing to the doctor*).

DOCTOR. Oh, yes... I think we said, Bishop... Bishop Hugo of Cluny.

ARIALD. You mean the abbot? All right, Hugo of Cluny.

LANDOLPH. He's come here many times already...

DOCTOR (*astonished*). What do you mean, come here?

LANDOLPH. Don't be afraid. I mean, that it's a costume that's easily available...

ARIALD. Used many times before.

DOCTOR. But...

LANDOLPH. There's no danger he might remember. He looks at the clothing more than the person.

LADY MATILDE. That's a good thing for me too, then.

DI NOLLI. We're going, Frida! Come on, come with us, Tito!

BELCREDI. Oh no! If she stays (*pointing to the marquise*), I stay too.

LADY MATILDE. But I don't need you at all!

BELCREDI. I'm not saying you need me. I'd like to see him too. Isn't that allowed?

LANDOLPH. Yes, perhaps three is a better number.

ARIALD. Then the gentleman will be... ?

BELCREDI. Well, try to find an easy disguise for me too.

LANDOLPH (*to Ariald*). Yes... a Cluny Benedictine.

BELCREDI. A Cluny Benedictine?

LANDOLPH. The habit of a Benedictine monk from the Cluny Abbey. You'd be accompanying Monsignor. (*To Ariald*) Go, go! (*To Bertholdt*) You be off too, don't show your face here for the rest of the day! (*but as soon as he sees them move off*) Wait. (*To Bertholdt*) You bring the clothing he gives you back here! (*To Ariald*) And you go in right away to announce the visit of the Duchess Adelaide and Monsignor Hugo of Cluny. Understand? (*Ariald and Bertholdt go out the first stage-right door.*)

DI NOLLI. We'll withdraw, then (*he goes off with Frida stage left*).

DOCTOR (*to Landolph*). He should be glad to see me dressed as Hugo of Cluny, I think.

LANDOLPH. Very much so. Don't worry. Monsignor has always been received here with great respect. You too, Marquise, don't worry. He always remembers that it was thanks to the intercession of you two that, after two days of waiting in the snow, half-frozen, he gained admission to the castle of Canossa and the presence of Gregory VII, who didn't want to receive him.

BELCREDI. And what about me?

LANDOLPH. You might keep yourself at a respectful distance.

LADY MATILDE (*irritated, very nervous*). It would be better if you left!

BELCREDI (*in a low voice, annoyed*). You're very upset...

LADY MATILDE (*haughtily*). I am what I am! Leave me alone! (*Bertholdt comes back with the clothes.*)

LANDOLPH (*seeing him enter*). Here are the clothes! This cape for the marquise.

LADY MATILDE. Wait, let me take off my hat! (*handing it to Bertholdt*).

LANDOLPH. Take it out there. (*To the marquise, starting to put the ducal crown on her*) Allow me, please.

LADY MATILDE. Heavens, isn't there a mirror in here?

LANDOLPH. In there (*pointing to the left-hand door*). If your ladyship wants to put it on by yourself...

LADY MATILDE. Yes, yes, it would be better. Give it to me, it'll just be a moment (*taking her hat and going out with Bertholdt who carries the cape and the crown. Meanwhile the Doctor and Belcredi are putting on the Benedictine habits as well as they can*).

BELCREDI. To tell the truth I never thought I'd become a Benedictine. Hey, you know, this is quite an expensive madness!

DOCTOR. Well, many other kinds of madness are too...

BELCREDI. When to indulge them you've got a fortune at your disposal...

LANDOLPH. Yes, indeed, we've got an entire wardrobe, full of all costumes of the period, tailored to perfection using old patterns. I'm in charge of that. I have it done by theatrical costume shops that know what they are doing. It's very expensive. (*Lady Matilde is back, wearing cape and crown.*)

BELCREDI (*immediately, admiringly*). Oh, splendid! Truly regal!

LADY MATILDE (*seeing Belcredi, bursts out laughing*). Oh, Lord! No, no, take it off! You look like an ostrich dressed up as a monk!

BELCREDI. And the doctor?

DOCTOR. Well, we must be forbearing.

LADY MATILDE. No, no, the doctor's not so bad. But you, you're truly ridiculous!

DOCTOR (*to Landolph*). Do many visitors come here, then?

LANDOLPH. It depends. Often he orders that this or that person be brought to him. Then you've got to look for someone who's willing. Women too...

LADY MATILDE (*wounded, but trying to hide it*). Oh, women too!

LANDOLPH. Well, earlier, yes... a lot of them.

BELCREDI (*laughing*). Nice. In period costume? (*Pointing to the marquise*) Like that?

LANDOLPH. Well, you know, the kind of women who...

BELCREDI. ... who are willing, I get it! (*Maliciously to the marquise*) Watch out, it's getting risky for you! (*The second stage-right door opens and Ariald appears. First he signals secretly for talking in the room to stop, then solemnly announces:*)

ARIALD. His Majesty, the Emperor! (*The two valets enter first and take positions at the foot of the throne. Then Henry IV enters between Ordulph and Ariald, who keep a little behind him, respectfully. Henry IV, close to fifty, very pale, his hair already grey at the back; over his temples and forehead, instead, it seems blond, having been dyed in a childish, all-too-obvious way. On his cheeks, amid the tragic pallor, he has been dabbed with rouge like a doll, very obviously. He is wearing penitential sackcloth, as at Canossa, over his royal robes. In his eyes there is an agonized fixity that is frightening. In contrast with the body posture of repentant humility he affects, the more exaggerated the more he feels that the humiliation is unmerited. Ordulph holds the imperial crown in both hands, Ariald the eagle-crested sceptre and the globe with the cross.*)

HENRY IV (*bowing*). My lady, Monsignor... (*Then looking at Belcredi, about to bow to him too, he turns instead to Landolph who has moved up close to him and asks in a low voice, suspiciously*) Is that Pier Damiani?

LANDOLPH. No, Your Majesty, he is a monk from Cluny accompanying the abbot.

HENRY IV (*still eyeing Belcredi with growing distrust, and, noticing that he turns with anxiety and embarrassment to Lady Matilde and the Doctor, as if looking for advice through eye contact, straightens up and shouts*). He is Pier Damiani! Looking at the duchess does you no good! (*Immediately turning to Lady Matilde as if to avert some danger*) I swear, I swear, milady, that my feelings towards your daughter have changed! I confess that if he (*pointing to Belcredi*) had not come from Pope Alexander to forbid it, I would have divorced her! Yes, there were those who would have sanctioned it – the bishop of Mainz, for a hundred and twenty farms. (*Glances at Landolph, a bit confused, and says immediately*) But I must not speak ill of the bishops at the present

time. (*Speaking humbly to Belcredi again*) Now I'm grateful, believe me,
I'm grateful, Pier Damiani, for that impediment! My whole life is
made up of humiliations – my mother, Adalbert, Tribor, Goslar – and
now this penitential cloth you see me wearing. (*Changing tone abruptly, he says, like one who, in an astute parenthesis, goes over his part*) It's
not important! Clarity of ideas, perspicacity, firm bearing, and
patience in adversity! (*Then turning to them all, he says with repentant
gravity*) I know how to correct the mistakes I made, and I humble
myself before you too, Pier Damiani. (*He bows deeply before him and
remains so, as if bent by an obscure suspicion that is now rising in him and
makes him add, almost against his will, in a threatening tone*) Unless you
were the source of the obscene rumour that my blessed mother,
Agnes, had an illicit relationship with Bishop Henry of Augusta!

BELCREDI (*since HENRY IV is still bent over with a finger threateningly
pointed in his direction, puts his hand to his heart and denies it*). No, not
me...

HENRY IV (*straightening up*). No? Is it true? Infamy! (*eyes him for a while
and then says*) I don't believe you capable of it. (*He goes up to the Doctor
and pulls a bit at his sleeve, winking cunningly*) It's always 'them'! Always
the same, Monsignor!

ARIALD (*low, with a sigh, as if to prompt the Doctor*). Oh, yes, the rapacious
bishops.

DOCTOR (*to play along, turned towards Ariald*). Those, oh yes, those...

HENRY IV. Nothing has been enough for them! A poor boy, Monsignor.
One spends his time playing, even when, without knowing it, one is
king. I was only six and they took me from my mother, and they used
me, unaware, against her, against the very powers of the dynasty,
profaning everything, thieving, thieving, one greedier than the next,
Hanno more than Stephen, Stephen more than Hanno!

LANDOLPH (*in a low voice, to remind him*). Your Majesty...

HENRY IV (*turning around immediately*). Oh, yes! I must not speak ill of
the bishops at present. But this infamy about my mother, Monsignor,
tops them all! (*Looking at the marquise, he softens.*) And I can't even cry
for her, my lady. I'm telling you, since you should have maternal
feelings. She came to visit me from her convent about a month ago.
I was told she died (*a long pause, full of emotion, then, smiling very sadly*)
I cannot cry for her, because if you're here now, and I am so (*pointing
to the sackcloth he is wearing*), it means I'm twenty-six.

ARIALD (*almost whispering, sweetly, to comfort him*). And therefore that she
is alive, Your Majesty.

ORDULPH (*same as above*). Still in her convent.

HENRY IV (*turning to look at them*). Right. And I can put off grieving to another time. (*Showing the marquise, almost coquettishly, his dyed hair*) Look, still blond, (*then in a low voice, as if confidingly*) I did it for you! I really don't need it. But some exterior sign helps. Marks of time, right, Monsignor? (*He turns to the marquise, looking at her hair*) Oh, but I see that you too, Duchess... (*winking and making an expressive gesture*) Eh, Italian... (*as if to say 'fake,' without disdain, indeed with sly admiration*) God forbid I should show disgust or surprise! All these unreasonable desires! No one is willing to recognize that mysterious and inevitable power which limits our will. But I mean, if we're born and we die! Did you ask to be born, Monsignor? I didn't! And between the two events, both independent of our will, how many things happen that we all would like not to happen, and to which we become resigned reluctantly.

DOCTOR (*just to say something while he studies him attentively*). Ah, yes, most unfortunate!

HENRY IV. Yes. Here's how it is – when we don't resign ourselves, our whims surface. A woman wants to be a man... an old man wants to be young... None of us lies or pretends! It's all too clear – we've all locked ourselves into a fine concept of ourselves, and in good faith too. And yet, Monsignor, while you keep yourself steady, clutching your saintly habit with both hands, from right here, from your sleeves, something that you're not aware of slips, slithers like a snake – your life, Monsignor! And it's quite a surprise when you see it suddenly standing in front of you. Spite and anger against yourself, or remorse. Remorse too. Oh, if you knew how much remorse I found myself facing! With a face that was my own, but so horrible, I couldn't look at it... (*Moving to the marquise again*) Has it never happened to you, my lady? Do you really remember always having been the same? Oh god! But one day – how was it, how was it you could do such a thing... (*staring so acutely into her eyes that she almost faints*) yes... 'that one'! ... You know what I'm talking about. (Oh don't worry, I won't tell anyone.) And that you, Pier Damiani, could be a friend of that...

LANDOLPH (*as above*). Your Majesty...

HENRY IV (*immediately*). No, no, I won't speak his name! I know it displeases you greatly! (*Turning to Belcredi as if in an aside*) What an opinion, eh? ... what an opinion you had of him... Yet we all continue to hold on to our idea of ourselves all the same, just as those who get old dye their hair. What does it matter that this colour of mine is not, for you, the true colour of my hair? Surely you, my lady, colour it not to fool others, nor yourself… only just a bit, a tiny bit, your image in the mirror. I do it as a game. You do it in earnest. But I assure you – no matter how in earnest you are – you too are wearing a disguise, my lady, and I'm not talking about the venerable crown that circles your forehead, to which I bow, nor your ducal cape, I'm talking only about this memory you want to fix in yourself artificially – of your blond hair, which at one time you were so proud of – or of your dark hair, if it was dark: the vanishing image of your youth. Instead, to you, Pier Damiani, the memory of what you've been, of what you've done, now seems like the recognition of past realities, that stay within you like a dream – am I right? And to me too – like a dream – and many of them inexplicable, when I think about it… Well! no wonder, Pier Damiani… our life today will be that way tomorrow! (*All of a sudden he falls into a rage and grabs hold of the sackcloth he is wearing*) This sackcloth! (*with almost ferocious glee; threatening to tear it off, while Ariald and Ordulph, frightened, run up to him to restrain him*) Ah, by God! (*Pulling away, he tears off the cloth and shouts to the two 'councillors'*) Tomorrow at Bressanone, twenty-seven German and Lombardy bishops will sign with me the dismissal of Pope Gregory VII: not a pope, just a false monk!

ORDULPH (*with the other two, begging him to be silent*). Your Majesty, Your Majesty, in the name of God!

ARIALD (*gesturing to him to put the sackcloth back on*). Be careful what you say!

LANDOLPH. The Monsignor is here, along with the Duchess, to intercede in your favour! (*secretly he signals the Doctor urgently to say something right away*).

DOCTOR. Ah, that's it… We're here to intercede…

HENRY IV (*immediately, repentant, almost frightened, letting the three put the sackcloth back on his shoulders and pressing it on himself with shaking hands*). Please, pardon, yes, pardon, Monsignor; pardon, my lady… I feel, I swear, I feel the full weight of the excommunication! (*Bending down, he takes his head between his hands, as if waiting for something about to crush him, and stays that way for a while, but then in a changed tone, but without changing his position, he whispers in confidence to Ariald and Ordulph*) I don't know why today I cannot be humble before that guy! (*pointing secretly to Belcredi*).

ORDULPH (*in a low voice*). Because Your Majesty continues to believe that he's Pier Damiani, while he's not!

HENRY IV (*eyeing him with fear*). He's not Pier Damiani?

ARIALD. Why, he's a humble monk, Your Majesty!

HENRY IV (*sorrowfully sighing with exasperation*). Well, none of us can weigh what we do, when we do it instinctively... Perhaps you, my lady, can understand me better than anyone else, being a woman. This is a solemn, decisive moment. Right now, even while I'm talking to you, I could accept the help of the Lombard bishops, hold the pope, by besieging this castle; run to Rome to elect an antipope; reach out to Robert Guiscard to form an alliance. – Gregory VII would be finished! – But I resist the temptation and, believe me, it's wise. I can feel the spirit of the times, and the majesty of a man who knows how to be a pope! Maybe you feel like laughing at me now, seeing me like this? You'd be fools to laugh, because you've got no idea of the political wisdom that tells me to wear this sackcloth now. I tell you that tomorrow the parts could be changed around! And what would you do then? Would you laugh at the pope dressed as a prisoner? No. We'd be even. Today I'm disguised as a penitent, tomorrow he is, as a prisoner. But woe to him who's not able to wear his disguise, either as king or pope! Perhaps he's being a little too cruel right now – yes, I think so. Think, my lady, that Bertha, your daughter, towards whom, I repeat, my feelings have changed (*turning suddenly to Belcredi, he shouts at him as if he had said no*), changed, changed, because of the love and devotion for me she was capable of in that terrible moment! (*He stops, shaken by his angry outburst and tries to restrain himself, with a suppressed groan of exasperation, then turns again to the marquise in a tone of tender, grieving humility*) She's come with me, my lady. She's down in the courtyard – she wanted to follow me like a beggar, and she's frozen, frozen from two nights outdoors, in the snow! You are her mother! The deepest pity should move you to implore, with him (*pointing to the Doctor*) the pope's pardon – implore him to let us see him!

LADY MATILDE (*trembling, in a whisper*). Yes, yes, at once...

DOCTOR. We'll do it, we'll do it!

HENRY IV. And another thing... (*drawing them close and speaking in a low voice, with great secrecy*) It's not enough for him to receive me. You know he can do anything – I mean anything! He even raises the dead! (*Beating his chest*) Look at me! Here I am! There's no magic he doesn't know. Well, Monsignor, my lady, my real penalty is this – or that – look! (*pointing to his portrait on the wall, almost in fear*) I cannot separate myself from that act of magic! – I am a penitent now, and I'll remain so, I swear to you, until he has received me. But then the two of you, after the excommunication has been lifted, should implore the pope, who can do it, to separate me from that (*pointing to the portrait again*), and let me live it all, this poor life of mine, from which I am excluded… One can't go on being twenty-six forever, my lady. And I'm asking you this for your daughter too, that I may love her as she deserves to be loved, so drawn to her as I am now, so tender as her pity has made me. There it is. I am in your hands (*bowing*). My lady! Monsignor! (*He starts to withdraw, bowing, through the door by which he had come in. But when he sees Belcredi, who had drawn close in order to hear, look towards the back, Henry takes it into his head that Belcredi wants to steal the imperial crown placed on the throne. To everyone's amazement and dismay, he runs to snatch it and hide it under his sackcloth; then, smiling slyly, he resumes his repeated bowing, and exits. The marquise is so deeply moved that she drops suddenly into a chair, half fainting.*)

⋅ ACT TWO

(*Another room in the villa, next to the throne room, furnished with austere antiques. On the right there is a kind of platform about one foot high, with a railing in front, with openings on the sides and in the middle for access to the steps; on the platform there are a table and five heavy period chairs, one at the head and two on each side of the table. The main entrance is at the rear. Two windows on the left look into the garden. A door on the right leads into the throne room. Same day, late afternoon.*

Lady Matilde, the Doctor, and Tito Belcredi are having a discussion. Lady Matilde aloof, sombre, evidently annoyed by what the two are now saying, although she can hardly avoid listening in, for in her agitation everything interests her against her will, keeping her from concentrating and making a decision on a powerful idea that has come to her in a flash and draws her strongly. The words of the other two attract her attention because she instinctively feels the need to be restrained from reaching that decision.)

BELCREDI. You may be right, Doctor. But that was my impression.

DOCTOR. I'm not saying you're wrong, only that it was just… an impression.

BELCREDI. But he said it himself, and clearly! (*Turning to the marquise*) Isn't it true, Marquise?

LADY MATILDE (*distracted, turning towards him*). What did he say? (*Then disagreeing*) Oh yes... But not for the reason you think.

DOCTOR. He was referring to the clothing we'd put on: your cape (*pointing to the marquise*), our Benedictine habits. It's all so childish.

LADY MATILDE (*abruptly, turning, angry*). Why childish? What are you saying?

DOCTOR. On the one hand, yes! Please let me finish, Marquise. On the other hand, much more complicated than you can imagine!

LADY MATILDE. To the contrary, it's very clear to me.

DOCTOR (*with the expert's patronizing smile towards those unable to comprehend*). Oh yes! One must understand this particular psychology of the insane, by which one can be quite sure that a madman has noticed the disguise before him and perceived it as such, and yet – yes – believes in it, as children do, for whom it's make-believe and reality at the same time. That's why I said childish. But it's very complicated, in the sense that he is, must be, perfectly aware that he is for himself, looking at himself, an image – that image of his there! (*He is referring to the portrait in the throne room, and therefore pointing to the left.*)

BELCREDI. He said so!

DOCTOR. There you are, very well. An image, before which other images have come: ours, right? Now in his delirium – sharp and extremely lucid – he was able to detect right away a difference between his and ours: that is, that our images were make-believe. And he distrusted us. All mad people are always armed with a vigilant distrust. But that's all. Of course, he couldn't perceive the pity in our game, the game we played around his. And his seemed to us even more tragic, the more he defiantly – do you follow me? – prompted by his distrust, wanted to reveal it to us as a game – yes, even his coming before us with a bit of hair dye and rouge and saying he'd put it on on purpose, for laughs!

LADY MATILDE (*abruptly*). No! That's not it, Doctor! That's not it!

DOCTOR. What do you mean, that's not it?

LADY MATILDE (*decisively quivering with intensity*). I'm very sure he recognized me!

DOCTOR. That's impossible, impossible...

BELCREDI (*at the same time*). Of course not!

LADY MATILDE (*even more sharply, almost hysterical*). He recognized me, I tell you! When he came up close to talk to me, looking into my eyes, right into my eyes... he recognized me!

BELCREDI. But he was talking about your daughter…

LADY MATILDE. It's not true! He was talking about me! about me!

BELCREDI. Yeah! perhaps when he was referring to…

LADY MATILDE (*immediately, breaking in with no effort to be polite*). My dyed hair! But didn't you notice that he added at once: 'or the memory of your dark hair, if it was dark'? – He remembered perfectly that I had dark hair then.

BELCREDI. Surely not, surely not.

LADY MATILDE (*ignoring him, turning to the Doctor*). In fact, Doctor, my hair *is* dark, like my daughter's. That's why he started talking about her!

BELCREDI. But he doesn't know her, your daughter! He never saw her!

LADY MATILDE. That's just it! You don't understand a thing! When he spoke of my daughter he meant me, as I was then!

BELCREDI. Can insanity be infectious?!

LADY MATILDE (*in a low voice, scornfully*). What do you mean, infectious? Fool!

BELCREDI. Excuse me, were you ever his wife? In his madness your daughter is his wife – Bertha of Susa.

LADY MATILDE. Exactly! Because no longer dark – the way he remembered me – but blond, I seemed to him to be Adelaide, the mother. My daughter doesn't exist for him, he's never seen her, as you said. Then how does he know whether she's blond or dark?

BELCREDI. But he said 'dark' in general, good Lord, speaking of people who try to fix the memory of youth in the colour of their hair – blond or dark! And you, as usual, begin to imagine things! – She says that I shouldn't have come, Doctor, but *she*'s the one who shouldn't have come!

LADY MATILDE (*taken aback for a moment by Belcredi's observation, seems rapt in thought, then starts up again, uneasy, because now she is uncertain*). No… no… he was talking about me… He talked to me, with me, and about me all the time…

BELCREDI. For God's sake! He didn't leave me one moment to catch my breath, and you say he talked about you all the time? Don't tell me you thought he was referring to you even when he was talking to Pier Damiani?

LADY MATILDE (*defiantly as if breaking all the restraints of civility*). Who's to say? Can you explain why right away, from the very beginning, he felt such enmity towards you, and you alone? (*From the tone of the question the answer is clear: 'Because he understood that you are my lover!' Belcredi realizes this so well that then and there he is left speechless, smiling foolishly.*)

DOCTOR. The reason may be that only the visit of the Duchess Adelaide and the Abbot of Cluny had been announced to him. Seeing an unannounced third person before him, suspicion set in at once...

BELCREDI. That's it, exactly! Suspicion made him see me as an enemy – Pier Damiani! But she's taken it into her head that he recognized her...

LADY MATILDE. There's no doubt about it! – His eyes told me, Doctor: you know when a person looks at you in a way that... no doubt is possible! Perhaps it was a question of just one second. What can I say!

DOCTOR. It can't be ruled out: a moment of lucidity...

LADY MATILDE. Perhaps that! And then what he said seemed so filled with regret for my youth and his own – for this horrible thing that's happened to him, which has fixed him there, in that disguise he's been unable to free himself from and which he wants to free himself from, he does!

BELCREDI. Sure! So he can fall in love with your daughter. Or you – whichever you prefer – moved by your pity for him.

LADY MATILDE. In fact, my pity is profound, believe me!

BELCREDI. That's quite apparent, Marquise. So much so that a miracle worker could easily see a miracle as possible.

DOCTOR. May I say something now? I don't perform miracles, because I'm a doctor and not a miracle worker. I paid great attention to everything he said, and I repeat that a certain analogical elasticity, typical of every systematized delirium, is evidently in him already very... what should I say? very weakened. The elements of his delirium, that is, no longer keep each other in place. It seems to me that he finds it hard by now to keep his balance in his superimposed personality, because of sudden recollections that tear him (and this is a hopeful sign) – not from a state of incipient apathy, but from an easy yielding to a state of thoughtful melancholy, which suggests – yes, really considerable cerebral activity. Very hopeful, as I said. Now you see, if by this extreme charade we have arranged...

LADY MATILDE (*turning to the window in the tone of a complaining invalid*). How come that car isn't here yet? Three and a half hours...

DOCTOR (*distracted*). What's that?

LADY MATILDE. The car, Doctor, the car. It's been more than three and a half hours!

DOCTOR (*taking out his watch*). Oh, more than four, by mine!

LADY MATILDE. It should have been here at least a half hour ago. But as usual...

BELCREDI. Perhaps they can't find the dress.

LADY MATILDE. I told them precisely where it's kept! (*Very impatient*)
And Frida... where is Frida?

BELCREDI (*leaning slightly out the window*). Perhaps in the garden with
Carlo.

DOCTOR. He might persuade her to overcome her fear...

BELCREDI. Oh, it's not fear, Doctor, she's annoyed.

LADY MATILDE. Do me a favour, don't beg her. I know how she is!

DOCTOR. Let's wait patiently. It'll just take a minute, and it must be
done at night. If we succeed in shaking him, as I said, in shocking
him out of it in one violent wrench, the already slack threads that still
bind him to his fiction, giving him back what he's asking for himself
(he said: 'One cannot go on being twenty-six years old forever, my
lady!'), that is, freedom from this prison sentence, which seems like
one to him too – well, in short, if we can suddenly give him the
sensation of the distance of time again...

BELCREDI (*cutting in rapidly*). He'll be cured! (*Then speaking each syllable
very distinctly, ironically*) We will free him!

DOCTOR. We may hope to get him back, like a watch that 's stopped at a
certain time. There you are, yes, we wait for that hour to come, as if
we're holding our watches in our hands – then one good shake! –
and let's hope that it starts ticking again after being stopped so long.
(*The Marquis Carlo Di Nolli comes in through the main entrance.*)

LADY MATILDE. Oh, Carlo, where has Frida gone?

DI NOLLI. She's coming any moment.

DOCTOR. Has the car come?

DI NOLLI. Yes.

LADY MATILDE. Oh good. Did they bring the dress?

DI NOLLI. Quite a while ago

DOCTOR. Ah, perfect!

LADY MATILDE (*trembling*).. Where is it? Where is it?

DI NOLLI (*shrugging and smiling sadly, like someone taking part unwillingly
in an uncalled-for joke*). Well... now you'll see (*pointing to the main
entrance*) There it is... (*On the threshold of the main entrance Bertholdt
announces solemnly:*)

BERTHOLDT. Her highness, the Marquise Mathilda of Canossa! (*Frida
enters immediately, magnificently beautiful, wearing the gown her mother once
wore as 'the Marquise of Tuscany,' so that the figure in the painting in the
throne room seems to have come to life.*)

FRIDA (*passing Bertholdt, who bows, says with disdainful haughtiness*). Of
Tuscany, of Tuscany, please! Canossa is just one of my castles.

BELCREDI (*admiringly*). Look at her, look at her! She looks like someone else!

LADY MATILDE. She looks like me! – My god, do you see? – Hold still, Frida! – Do you see? she's my portrait come to life!

DOCTOR. Yes, yes. Perfect! The portrait!

BELCREDI. Oh yes, no two ways about it... she's it!

FRIDA. Don't make me laugh or I'll burst. Gosh, what a tiny waist you had, Mother! I had to suck myself in to fit into this!

LADY MATILDE (*in great agitation, adjusting her gown*). Wait... Hold still... These creases... Is it really that tight?

FRIDA. I'm suffocating! We've got to do it soon, please...

DOCTOR. Well, we must wait for it to get dark...

FRIDA. No, no. I can't take it, I can't stay in this thing until night!

LADY MATILDE. But why did you put it on so early?

FRIDA. The minute I saw it! What a temptation! Irresistible...

LADY MATILDE. You could have called me, at least! Let me help you... It's still full of creases, good Lord!

FRIDA. I saw them, mother. But they're old creases... It'll be difficult to get them out.

DOCTOR. It's nothing, Marquise! The illusion is perfect. (*Then, gesturing to her to stand a little in front of her daughter without blocking the view of her*) Please, if you will, stand over here, at a certain distance – a bit forward...

BELCREDI. To give a feeling of the distance in time!

LADY MATILDE (*Turning towards him very slightly*). Twenty years later. A disaster, ha?

BELCREDI. Let's not exaggerate!

DOCTOR (*very embarrassed, trying to make amends*). No, no! I was thinking, rather... I mean, for the dress... I mean, just to see...

BELCREDI (*laughing*). But as for the dress, Doctor, much more than twenty years! It's eight hundred! An abyss! You really want him to make that jump, with one big shove? (*Pointing first to Frida and then the Marquise*) From there to here? You'll have to pick up the pieces in a basket! Ladies and gentlemen, think about it. I'm serious. For us it's twenty years, two dresses, and a pageant. But if for him, as you say, Doctor, time has stopped, if he lives there (*pointing to Frida*) with her, eight hundred years back: I say, the jump will make him so dizzy, that landing in our midst – (*the Doctor signals no, wagging his finger*). You're saying no?

DOCTOR. No, dear Baron, because life starts over! Our life, here, will become real for him too, at once, and will put a stop to all this right away, quickly tearing away the illusion and revealing to him that the eight hundred years you mention are only twenty! It'll be like some of those tricks of the Masonic rite, the jump off a cliff, for instance, which seems such a big thing, but in reality you've only gone down one step.

BELCREDI. Ah, a real discovery! ... But please, Doctor, look at Frida and the marquise! Who is farther ahead? We, the older ones, Doctor! The young believe they're ahead, but it's not true: we're farther ahead, in as much as time is more ours than theirs.

DOCTOR. Yes, if time didn't carry us farther away!

BELCREDI. No! From what? If they (*pointing to Frida and Di Nolli*) still have to do what we've already done, Doctor: getting old, making our own mistakes over again, more or less... This is the illusion, that we exit from life through a door before us! But it isn't true! If as soon as we're born we begin to die, those who've started earlier are farther ahead of all the others. And the youngest one is father Adam! Look there (*indicating Frida*), eight hundred years younger than all of us, the Marquise Mathilda of Tuscany (*he bows to her deeply*).

DI NOLLI. Please, Tito, please stop joking.

BELCREDI. Well, if you think I'm joking...

DI NOLLI. Yes, good Lord, ever since you came...

BELCREDI. What do you mean? I even put on a Benedictine habit...

DI NOLLI. Sure! To do something serious...

BELCREDI. Well, I mean... If it's been serious for the others... there, for Frida now, for instance... (*then, turning to the Doctor*) I swear to you, Doctor, that I still don't understand what you intend to do.

DOCTOR (*annoyed*). You'll see! Leave it to me... Of course, if you see the marquise still dressed like that...

BELCREDI. Ah, because she too must... ?

DOCTOR. Oh, sure! In another dress that's in there, for the moment when he thinks he's standing in front of the Marquise Mathilda of Canossa....

FRIDA (*while talking in a low voice with Di Nolli, noticing the Doctor's mistake*). Of Tuscany! Of Tuscany!

DOCTOR (*as above*). It's all the same!

BELCREDI. Oh, I get it! He'll find himself before two of them... ?

DOCTOR. Two of them, exactly. And then...

FRIDA (*calling him aside*). Please, Doctor, come here, listen.

DOCTOR. Coming! (*He approaches the two young people and expounds his theory.*)

BELCREDI (*in a low voice to Lady Matilde*). Oh, good Lord! So, then...

LADY MATILDE (*turning on him, with determination*). Then what?

BELCREDI. This thing interests you that much? To make you take part in this? It's unheard of, for a woman!

LADY MATILDE. For any common woman!

BELCREDI. No, for all women, darling, in this matter! It's an act of self-denial...

LADY MATILDE. I owe it to him!

BELCREDI. Don't lie, please! You know you're not demeaning yourself.

LADY MATILDE. Then, where is the self-denial?

BELCREDI. Just enough not to demean yourself before the others, but enough to offend me.

LADY MATILDE. But who's worried about you at this moment!

DI NOLLI (*coming forward*). Yes, yes, then! We'll do that... (*To Bertholdt*) You there, go call one of those three.

BERTHOLDT. Right away! (*exits through the main entrance*).

LADY MATILDE. But we must pretend to leave first!

DI NOLLI. Right! I'm calling him in to prepare for your departure. (*To Belcredi*) You may keep out of this – stay here!

BELCREDI (*shaking his head ironically*). Yes, yes, I can stay out of it, of course...

DI NOLLI. That's so we don't arouse his suspicions again, see?

BELCREDI. Yes, yes. *Quantité negligeable!*

DOCTOR. We must make him absolutely, absolutely sure that we've left. (*Landolph, followed by Bertholdt, enters through the right-hand door.*)

LANDOLPH. May I?

DI NOLLI. Come in, come in. There.... – You're Lolo, right?

LANDOLPH. Lolo or Landolph, as you like!

DI NOLLI. Well, look, the Doctor and the marquise are going to leave now...

LANDOLPH. Very good. It's enough for them to say that they've obtained the favour of his being received from the pope. He's in there in his rooms, moaning, sorry for all he's said, and in despair that he won't be granted the favour. If you wouldn't mind, then... be patient and wear the clothing again...

DOCTOR. Yes, yes, let's go, let's go...

LANDOLPH. Wait. Allow me to make a suggestion: please add that the Marquise Mathilda of Tuscany has joined in your plea to the pontiff to receive him.

LADY MATILDE. There, can't you see he's recognized me?

LANDOLPH. No, excuse me, it's just that he's extremely afraid of the displeasure of the marquise who gave hospitality to the pope in her castle. It's strange: in history, as far as I know – but you, I'm sure, know it better than I do – don't they say, ha?, that Henry IV secretly loved the Marquise of Tuscany?

LADY MATILDE (*at once*). No, not at all. They say nothing of the kind! Quite the contrary!

LANDOLPH. There, I thought so! But he says he loved her – he always says so... – And now he is afraid that her anger over this secret love might act against him in the pontiff's estimation.

BELCREDI. He must be convinced that this dislike no longer exists!

LANDOLPH. There you are! Very good!

LADY MATILDE (*to Landolph*). Very good, yes! (*Then to Belcredi*) Because history says explicitly, in case you don't know, that the pope yielded precisely to the pleading of the Marquise Mathilda and the Abbot of Cluny. And I can tell you, dear Belcredi, that at the time of the cavalcade, I intended to use this historical detail to show him that my feelings were no longer as hostile as he thought.

BELCREDI. Oh, that's just splendid, dear Marquise. By all means, follow history...

LANDOLPH. There you are. Then the lady could certainly avoid wearing another disguise, and show up dressed as the Marquise of Tuscany, with Monsignor (*pointing to the Doctor*).

DOCTOR (*immediately, forcefully*). No, no! Certainly not, please! It would spoil everything! The impact of the confrontation must be sudden, one shot. No, no. Marquise, come on, come on. You'll show yourself again as the Duchess Adelaide, mother of the empress. And we'll take our leave. This is essential, above all: that he knows we've gone. Come on, come on, let's not waste any more time, we've a great deal to get ready. (*The Doctor, Lady Matilde, and Landolph exit through the right-hand door.*)

FRIDA. I am beginning to be afraid again.

DI NOLLI. Again, Frida?

FRIDA. It would've been better if I'd seen him earlier...

DI NOLLI. Believe me, there's no reason for it, really!

FRIDA. He's not furious?

DI NOLLI. No, he's quite calm.

BELCREDI (*with ironic sentimental affectation*). Melancholy! Didn't you hear? He loves you!

FRIDA. That's just it! Thank you very much!

BELCREDI. So he won't want to hurt you...

DI NOLLI. Anyway, it'll just be a matter of a moment...

FRIDA. Sure, but in there with him in the dark...

DI NOLLI. Just for a moment! And I'll be nearby, and all the others will be behind the doors, waiting, ready to come to your aid. As soon as he sees your mother in front of him, your role will be over...

BELCREDI. I'm afraid of something else: that all of this will be futile...

DI NOLLI. Don't start that again! I think the remedy's going to be very effective!

FRIDA. Me too, me too! I feel it inside... I'm trembling all over!

BELCREDI. But crazy people, my friends – (unfortunately they don't know it) – have this one felicity which we don't take into account...

DI NOLLI (*interrupting him, annoyed*). What 'felicity,' now? What are you talking about?

BELCREDI (*forcefully*). They don't reason!

DI NOLLI. But what's reasoning got to do with it?

BELCREDI. What! Don't you think it's reasoning he's supposed to do – according to us – when he sees her (*pointing to Frida*) and her mother? But we've planned it all out! The entire thing!

DI NOLLI. No, not at all. What reasoning? We're setting before him a double image of his own invention, as the Doctor says.

BELCREDI (*with a sudden outburst*). Listen, I've never understood why they take a degree in medicine!

DI NOLLI (*astonished*). Who?

BELCREDI. Psychiatrists.

DI NOLLI. Oh, nice idea, what degree should they get?

FRIDA. If they're psychiatrists!

BELCREDI. They should take law degrees, darling! It's all talk! And the better the talker, the better the psychiatrist. 'Analogical elasticity,' 'the sensation of the distance of time'! Meanwhile the first thing they say is that they don't perform miracles – when exactly what's needed is a miracle! But they know the more they tell you they are not miracle workers, the more serious you believe they are – they don't perform miracles – so they always come out all right! It's gorgeous!

BERTHOLDT (*who has been looking through the keyhole of the door on the right*). They're coming, they're coming this way...

DI NOLLI. Oh, yes?

BERTHOLDT. It looks as if he means to come with them. Yes, yes, here he comes!

DI NOLLI. Let's withdraw, then! Quick! (*Turning to Bertholdt before exiting*) You stay here!

BERTHOLDT. I've to stay? Me? (*Without answering him, Di Nolli, Frida, and Belcredi rush out through the main door, leaving Bertholdt anxious and confused. The right-hand door opens and Landolph enters first, bowing with alacrity; then Lady Matilde enters, wearing the cape and the ducal crown, as in the first act, then the Doctor wearing the cassock of the Abbot of Cluny; Henry IV is among them, wearing royal robes; finally Ordulph and Ariald enter.*)

HENRY IV (*continuing a speech supposedly started in the throne room*). And I ask you: how can I be shrewd, if they think I'm obstinate…

DOCTOR. No, why obstinate, for heaven's sake!?

HENRY IV (*smiling, pleased*). Then you think I'm really shrewd?

DOCTOR. No, no, neither obstinate nor shrewd!

HENRY IV (*stopping and exclaiming in the tone of one who wants to observe, kindly, but also ironically, that this cannot be so*). Monsignor, if obstinacy is not a vice that can go with shrewdness, I was hoping that, since you deny me my obstinacy, you would at least allow me a bit of shrewdness. I assure you I need it very much! But if you want to keep it all for yourself…

DOCTOR. Oh, me? Do you think I'm shrewd?

HENRY IV. No, Monsignor! What are you saying? You don't seem so at all! (*Ending the conversation to turn to Lady Matilde*) With your permission, I'd like to have a word in private with my lady the Duchess. (*Leading her aside and asking her anxiously, with care not to be overheard*) Is your daughter really dear to you?

LADY MATILDE (*disconcerted*). Yes, of course…

HENRY IV. And you want me to repay her with all my love, all my devotion, for the grave wrongs I did her? Although you mustn't believe all the accusations of debauchery my enemies accuse me of.

LADY MATILDE. Oh, no. I don't believe them. I never did…

HENRY IV. Well, then, do you want me to?

LADY MATILDE (*as above*). What?

HENRY IV. To love your daughter again? (*Looking at her and adding immediately in a mysterious tone of mingled admonition and dismay*) Don't be friends with the Marquise of Tuscany! Don't do it!

LADY MATILDE. Yet I repeat, that she begged, that she pleaded no less than we did, to obtain your admission…

HENRY IV (*immediately, in a low voice, trembling*). Don't tell me, don't tell me! For God's sake, my lady, don't you see what effect it has on me?

LADY MATILDE (*looking at him, then in a very low voice, as if confiding in him*). Do you still love her?

HENRY IV (*dismayed*). Still? What do you mean, still? Do you know, perhaps? Nobody knows! Nobody must know about it!

LADY MATILDE. But perhaps she knows, if she's pleaded so hard for you!

HENRY IV (*looks at her for a while, then says*). And you love your daughter? (*After a brief pause he turns to the Doctor, in a humorous tone*) Oh, Monsignor, how true it is that I knew I had this wife only later – too late, too late. And even now, I must have her, there's no doubt I have her – but I could swear I very rarely think of her. It may be a sin, but I don't feel close to her; I don't feel close to her in my heart. It's amazing, though, that even her mother doesn't feel close to her in her heart! Confess, my lady, that you care very little about her! (*Turning to the Doctor, with exasperation*) And she speaks of the other one (*becoming increasingly excited*) with an insistence, an insistence I cannot explain to myself.

LANDOLPH (*humbly*). Perhaps, Your Majesty, to correct the contrary opinion you may have conceived of the Marquise of Tuscany. (*Then, dismayed at having dared express this observation, immediately adds*) I mean, of course, at this particular time…

HENRY IV. Why? Do you also believe she's been a friend to me?

LANDOLPH. Yes, in this particular instance, Your Majesty!

LADY MATILDE. Yes, it was just for this reason…

HENRY IV. I see. It means you don't believe I love her. I see, I see. Nobody ever believed it; nobody even suspected it! All the better this way! Enough, enough. (*Breaking off, he turns to the doctor, his mood and face completely changed.*) Monsignor, do you see? The conditions on which the pope has based the revocation of the excommunication have nothing to do – not a single thing – with the reasons why he had excommunicated me! Tell Pope Gregory we'll meet again at Bressanone. And you, my lady, if you're lucky enough to meet your daughter down in the courtyard of the castle of your friend the marquise – what should I say? Tell her to come up; we'll see if I'm capable of keeping her close to me, as wife and empress. Many have come here before, assuring me that they were she – the one I, knowing I had a wife, yes, sometimes I even tried to (nothing shameful – my wife, after all!) – But all of them, telling me that they were Bertha, that they were from Susa – I don't know why – burst out laughing! (*Confidentially*) You understand? – in bed – me without this robe – She too… Yes, good Lord, without clothes on… a man and a woman… It's natural… You stop thinking about who we are. The clothes, hung up, are there, like phantoms! (*In a different tone, still confidentially, to the Doctor*) And I think, Monsignor, that phantoms, in general, are basically nothing more than a little confusion of the soul: images we can't keep in the realm of dreams – they're found in the waking state too, during the day, and they're frightening. I'm always very frightened when I see them before me at night – so many jumbled up images, laughing, thrown off their horses – sometimes I'm even afraid of my blood pulsing in my veins, in the silence of the night, like a gloomy thump of footsteps in faraway rooms… Enough, I've kept you standing here too long. My respects to you, my lady, and to you, Monsignor. (*At the threshold of the main entrance, to which he has led them, he takes leave of them, and they bow. Lady Matilde and the Doctor exit. He closes the door and turns quickly, transformed.*) Fools! Fools! Fools! A regular rainbow of colours! As soon as I spoke to her: white, red, yellow, green… And that other one: Pier Damiani! – Ah, ah! Perfect! I pinned him down! He was afraid to come before me again! (*He says this in a joyful, explosive frenzy, pacing back and forth, rolling his eyes, until suddenly he sees Bertholdt, amazed, frightened by the sudden change. He stops in front of him and points him out to his companions, also lost in amazement*) Just look at this moron here, staring at me with his mouth open… (*shaking him*). Don't you understand? Don't you see how I ward them off? How I demolish them? How I make them appear before me, the terrified fools? And the one thing they're frightened of is that I might tear the mask they're wearing and find them wearing a disguise; as if I hadn't forced them to wear it in the first place, for this pleasure of mine, to play the madman here!

LANDOLPH, ARIALD, ORDULPH (*shaken, befuddled, looking at each other*). What? What are you saying? But then… ?

HENRY IV (*turning to them at their expressions of surprise, and shouting, imperiously*). Enough! Let's cut it out! I'm tired of it! (*Then immediately, as if, thinking about it, he cannot accept or believe it*) By god, the impudence of coming before me, here, now – with her lover… And with that air of going along with it all out of pity, so as not to infuriate a poor devil already out of it, out of the world, of time, of life! – Otherwise that fellow, he'd never have subjected himself to such an imposition! Yet all the time, every moment, they expect everybody to be the way they expect them to be. And isn't that an imposition? Oh, of course not! It's just their way of thinking, of seeing, of feeling: but each one of us has his own! You have your own way too, right? Sure, but what can yours be? The herd's way! Wretched, feeble, uncertain... And they take advantage of it, they make you submit to and accept theirs, so you'll feel and see like them! Or maybe they just believe they do! Because, after all, what do they succeed in imposing on you? Words! Words which everyone understands and repeats in his own way! Yes, but that's how so-called common notions are formed! And woe to whoever one day finds himself stamped with one of these words, which everyone repeats! 'Crazy,' for instance, or 'imbecile.' But tell me, can you sit still when you know that somebody's out there trying to persuade everyone that you're the way *he* sees you, to fix you in everybody's opinion according to his idea of you? 'Crazy,' 'crazy'! I'm not talking about now that I'm playing at being insane! Before, before I hit my head falling from the horse... (*He suddenly stops, seeing the four men agitated, more dismayed and bewildered than ever*) Just look at yourselves! (*mimicking their amazement wryly*) Oh, oh, what a revelation! – Am I, or am I not? – Oh, all right, yes, I'm crazy. (*Terrifyingly imperious*) If so, then down on your knees! On your knees! (*compelling them to go down on their knees, one by one*). I'm ordering you to kneel before me! Like that! And touch the ground three times with your forehead! Down! That's how everyone should behave before mad people! (*Seeing the four on their knees, his ferocious gaiety evaporates and he becomes indignant.*) Come on, you sheep, get up! You obeyed me?! You could've put me in a straight jacket... – Crush a person with the weight of a word? He's nothing! What is he? A fly! – An entire life is crushed this way by the weight of words! The weight of the dead – Here I am: can you seriously believe that Henry IV is still alive? Yet, see, I'm speaking to live ones and ordering you around. I want you to be this way! Does this seem a joke to you too, that the dead continue to live? – Yes, in here it's a joke: but get out of here, into the living world. The sun rises, time is before you. Dawn. This day we have before us – you say – we'll make it ours! Yes? You? Farewell traditions! farewell customs?! Start talking! You'll only repeat all the words that have always been said! You think you're living? You're chewing the life of the dead again! (*He stands in front of Bertholdt, by now totally stupefied.*) You don't understand a thing, do you? What's your name?

BERTHOLDT. Me? ... Uh... Bertholdt...

HENRY IV. What Bertholdt, you idiot! Just between you and me, what's your name?

BERTHOLDT. Act... actually, my... my name is Fino...

HENRY IV (*turning quickly to stop the other three who are trying to warn Bertholdt against acceding to Henry's request*). Fino?

BERTHOLDT. Fino Pagliuca, yessir!

HENRY IV (*turning to the others again*). How many times do you think I heard you call each other by your names? (*To Landolph*) Your name is Lolo. Right?

LANDOLPH. Yessir... (*Then in an outburst of joy*). My god, then...?

HENRY IV (*immediately, curt*). What? .

LANDOLPH (*crestfallen, immediately*). No, I was just saying...

HENRY IV. I'm not crazy any longer? Of course not. Don't you see me? We play a joke on those who believe it (*To Ariald*) I know your name is Franco... (*To Ordulph*) And yours, wait...

ORDULPH. Momo!

HENRY IV. There, Momo! How beautiful, ah?

LANDOLPH (*as above*). But then... good Lord...

HENRY IV (*as above*). What? Nothing! Let's have a nice long big laugh among ourselves... (*Laughing*) ha, ha, ha, ha, ha, ha!

LANDOLPH, ARIALD, ORDULPH (*looking at each other, hesitant, bewildered, between joy and dismay*). He's recovered? Is it really true? How did it happen?

HENRY IV. Sssst! Quiet! (*To Bertholdt*) You're not laughing? Are you still offended? I wasn't talking to you, you know! – It's convenient, you know? It's convenient for everybody to make people believe certain folks are crazy, to have the excuse to keep them locked up. You know why? Because people can't bear to hear them talk. What do I say of those people who just left? That one is a whore, the other a filthy libertine, the other a fraud... It's not true! Nobody can believe it! – But everybody keeps listening to me, terrified. I'd like to know why, if what I say isn't true. – You can't believe what crazy people say! – Yet they go on listening like this, their eyes wide open with fear. – Why? – Tell me why, tell me! I'm perfectly calm, you see?

BERTHOLDT. Well, because... perhaps they think that...

HENRY IV. No, dear boy, no... Look me straight in the eye... I'm not going to say it's true, don't worry! Nothing is true! – But look me straight in the eye!

BERTHOLDT. Yes, okay – and so?

HENRY IV. You see, you see? You yourself! You yourself have fear in your eyes now! Because I seem crazy to you! – There it is! There's the proof! (*laughing*).

LANDOLPH (*irritated, taking courage, expressing the feelings of the others too*). But what proof?

HENRY IV. This dismay of yours, because now, once again, I seem crazy to you! Yet, by god, you know it! You believe me; you've believed until now that I'm crazy! Isn't it true? (*Looking at them for a moment, he sees they are terrified.*) But you see it, right? You feel that this dismay of yours can become terror, as if the ground under your feet might shift and the air you breathe be taken away? Of course! Because do you know what it means to find yourself facing a madman? It means you're facing someone who shakes the foundations of everything you've built within you, around you – the logic, the logic of all your constructions! – After all, madmen build without any logic, bless them! Or with a logic of their own, that floats like a feather! They're fickle, fickle! Today like this and tomorrow who knows how! You hold on tight and they let go! While you say: This can't be, they believe that everything can be. But you say that's not true. And why? Because it doesn't seem true to you, and you, and you (*pointing to three of them*), and a hundred thousand others! Huh, dear boys! you'd have to see then what those hundred thousand others who're not supposed to be mad think is true, and what a spectacle they make of their agreements, what flowers of logic! I know that as a child I thought the moon in the well was real. How many things I thought were real! I believed everything I was told, and I was happy! Because you're in terrible trouble if you don't hold on tightly to what seems true to you today, and what will seem true to you tomorrow, even if it's the opposite of what seemed true to you yesterday! It would be terrible for you to dwell, as I have, on this dreadful thing which can really drive a man insane: you're next to another person and looking into his eyes – as I once looked into certain eyes – you can think of yourself as a beggar before a door you'll never enter. The one who enters will never be you, with the world you have and see and touch inside you, but someone you don't even know, just as the other person, inside his impenetrable world, sees and feels you... (*A sustained pause. The shadows in the hall begin to thicken, increasing the feeling of bewilderment and deeper dismay that has befallen the four disguised men, and that draws them increasingly apart from the central disguised figure, absorbed in his contemplation of a fearful anguish, which is not his alone, but everyone's. Then he shakes himself, looks around for the four men whom he no longer senses around him, and says:*) It's gotten dark in here.

ORDULPH (*quickly, coming forward*). Do you want me to get the lamp?

HENRY IV (*ironically*). Yeah, the lamp... You think I don't know that as
soon as I turn my back with my oil lamp to go to sleep, you turn on
the electric light for yourselves – both in here and in there in the
throne room? – I pretend not to see it...

ORDULPH. Oh! Then would you like...

HENRY IV. No, it would blind me. Let me have my lamp.

ORDULPH. Sure, it's probably ready, here behind the door. (*Going to the
main door, he opens it, goes out, and immediately returns with an antique
lamp, the kind one holds by a ring on the top.*)

HENRY IV (*taking the lamp and pointing to the table on the platform*). There, a
bit of light. Sit down around the table. Not that way! In nice, relaxed
poses... (*To Ariald*) There, like that... (*showing him the right pose, then to
Bertholdt*) You like this (*showing him*) There, that's it. (*Sits down himself*)
And I, here... (*Turning his face towards the window*) We should be able
to order the moon to send a nice, decorative beam towards us... The
moon does us good. I for one feel the need of it, and often lose myself
looking at it from my window. Who can believe, looking at it, that it
knows that eight hundred years have gone by, and I, seated at the
window, could not actually be Henry IV looking at the moon, like any
poor mortal? But look, look, at this marvellous picture: the emperor
among his faithful councillors... Don't you like it?

LANDOLPH (*in a low voice to Ariald, as if not to break the spell*). Well, you
know, if we'd been aware it wasn't true...

HENRY IV. Wasn't true, what?

LANDOLPH (*hesitant, as if to beg pardon*). Well, you see... because, I was
telling him (*pointing to Bertholdt*) this morning, when he began
working here, I said: It's a pity that dressed like this... and with so
many beautiful costumes there in the wardrobe, and a hall like that...
(*pointing to the throne room*)...

HENRY IV. Well, it's a pity, you say?

LANDOLPH. Right, that we didn't know...

HENRY IV. ... That we were performing this comedy, here, as a joke?

LANDOLPH. Because we thought...

ARIALD (*coming to his aid*). Yeah... that it was done in earnest!

HENRY IV. And how is it otherwise? You don't think it's done in earnest?

LANDOLPH. Well, if you're saying that...

HENRY IV. I'm saying that you're fools! You should have been able to
create the deception for your own sake – not to perform it before me
and those who come visiting once in a while, but for the way you are
naturally, every day, with no one watching (*to Bertholdt, seizing his*

arms) for yourself, do you see, so that in this deceit you could find the wherewithal to eat, sleep, even scratch a shoulder if you got an itch there (*turning to all the others*), feeling yourselves alive, really alive in the history of the twelfth century, here at the court of your Emperor, Henry IV! And from here, from this remote time, so colourful and so gloomy, to think that meanwhile, eight centuries downstream, the people of the twentieth century are scuffling, scrambling in constant anxiety to know how their affairs will end up, to see how the events that are unsettling and agitating them so much will eventually work out. While you, instead, are already in history, with me! Though my case is sad, the facts horrible, the struggles harsh, the events painful, they are history already, they won't change, they can't change, do you see? Fixed forever: you can settle back on them, admiring how each effect obediently follows its cause, with perfect logic, how each event unfolds, precise and coherent in every detail. The pleasure, the pleasure of history, I mean, which is so magnificent!

LANDOLPH. Yes! Wonderful! Wonderful!

HENRY IV. Wonderful, but enough now! Now that you know it, I couldn't play it anymore myself! (*Taking the lamp to go to sleep*) And neither could you, if you haven't understood the reason for it until now. Now it revolts me! (*Almost to himself, with violent, restrained anger*) By god, I've got to make her sorry she came here! Disguised as a mother-in-law... Ah! And he as an abbot... and bringing a doctor with them. To study me... And perhaps they even hope to cure me... The fools! I want to have the pleasure of slapping at least one of them in the face: that one! – He's a famous fencer! Will he run me through? We'll see, we'll see... (*A knock is heard from the main entrance*) Who is it?

GIOVANNI'S VOICE. Deo gratias!

ARIALD (*delighted at the joke that can still be played at Giovanni's expense*). Oh, it's Giovanni, who comes every night to play the humble friar!

ORDULPH (*as above, rubbing his hands*). Yes, yes, let's let him go on doing it!

HENRY IV (*quickly, severely*). Fool! Why? Just to play a joke at the expense of a poor old man, who does it for my sake?

LANDOLPH (*to Ordulph*). It must look like the real thing! Right?

HENRY IV. Right, like the real thing! Because only then is the real thing no longer a joke! (*Going to open the door, he lets in Giovanni, dressed like a humble friar, with a parchment scroll under his arm*) Come in, father, come in! (*Then, assuming a tone of tragic gravity and dark resentment*) All the documents of my life and reign favourable to me have been deliberately destroyed by my enemies: only this story of my life escaped destruction, written by a humble friar faithful to me – and you dare laugh at him? (*Turning affectionately to Giovanni, he invites him to sit down at the table*) Sit, father, sit here near the lamp (*setting the lamp he is still holding near him*). Write, write.

GIOVANNI (*unrolling the parchment and getting ready to write from dictation*). I'm ready, Your Majesty!

HENRY IV (*dictating*). The peace treaty of Mainz favoured the poor and the righteous, while it was unfavourable to the evil and the powerful. (*The curtain begins to fall*) It brought riches to the former, hunger and poverty to the latter...

ACT THREE

(*The throne room, dark. In the darkness the back wall is barely discernible. The canvases of the two portraits have been removed and in their place, inside the frames that still enclose the niches, Frida, dressed as the 'Marquise of Tuscany,' as she was in the second act, and Carlo Di Nolli, dressed as 'Henry IV,' have taken up the exact same poses as the portraits.*

As the curtain rises, for a moment the stage looks empty. The left-hand door opens and Henry IV enters holding the lamp by its ring; turned towards the room he has left, he is speaking to the four young men who are supposedly there with Giovanni, as in the previous act.)

HENRY IV. No, stay there, stay there. I'll take care of myself. Good night. (*Closing the door, very sad and tired, he starts to cross the room towards the second right-hand door, which leads to his private apartments.*)

FRIDA (*as soon as he has passed the throne, she whispers from the niche, as if about to faint with fear*). Henry...

HENRY IV (*stopping at the sound, as if struck in the back by a traitor's blade. turns his terrified face to the back wall, instinctively raising his arms to protect himself*). Who's calling me?! (*It is an exclamation rather than a question, a shudder of terror that expects no answer from the darkness and terrifying silence of the room, which are suddenly filled for him with the suspicion that he actually is mad.*)

FRIDA (*No less frightened, at that terrified reaction, by what she has consented to do, repeats a little louder*). Henry... (*As though she wants to carry out the part assigned to her, she cranes her neck towards the other niche.*)

HENRY IV (*cries out and lets the lamp fall, to protect his head with his arms, and makes as if to run away*).

FRIDA (*jumping from the niche to the shelf below it and shouting as if she has gone mad*). Henry... Henry... I'm so frightened... so frightened... (*While Frida continues to shriek convulsively, on the verge of fainting, everybody bursts in from the left-hand door – the Doctor, Lady Matilde also dressed as the 'Marquise of Tuscany,' Tito Belcredi, Landolph, Ariald, Ordulph, Bertholdt, Giovanni. One of the latter immediately turns on the lights – a strange light, from bulbs hidden in the ceiling, so that only the upper portion of the stage is illuminated. Paying no attention to Henry IV, who stands there looking on, astounded by this unexpected rush of people, after the moment of terror from which he is still trembling all over, the others run to anxiously support and comfort Frida, who is still trembling and wailing and writhing convulsively in the arms of her fiancé. They all talk in confusion.*)

DI NOLLI. No, no, Frida. I'm here, I'm right here with you!

DOCTOR (*arriving with the others*). That's enough! That's all! Your task is over...

LADY MATILDE. He's cured, Frida. Do you see? He's cured!

DI NOLLI (*astounded*). Cured?

BELCREDI. Calm down! It was a joke!

FRIDA (*as above*). No! I'm so frightened! I'm so frightened!

LADY MATILDE. Of what? Look at him! He wasn't mad! It isn't true!

DI NOLLI (*as above*). It isn't true? What are you saying? Cured?

DOCTOR. It seems so! Though, as far as I'm concerned...

BELCREDI. Yes, he is! They told us (*pointing to the four young men*).

LADY MATILDE. Yes, for a long time! He let them in on the secret!

DI NOLLI (*now more angry than astonished*). What? If only a little while ago...

BELCREDI. Ha! He was acting, to play a joke on you, and on us too, while we, in good faith...

DI NOLLI. Is it possible? On his sister too? Right up to her death?

HENRY IV (*has kept apart, observing now one, now the other, under the accusations and the derision for what everybody takes as a cruel joke – now discovered – on his part, showing by his flashing eyes that he is planning a revenge that for the moment his tumultuous interior scorn keeps him from seeing clearly. He now rises up, deeply wounded, to assume as real the fictitious role they have treacherously prepared for him, shouting at his nephew*). Go on, go on!

DI NOLLI (*dumbfounded at his cry*). What do you mean, go on?

HENRY IV. Not only 'your' sister has died, you know?!

DI NOLLI (*as above*). My sister? I mean yours, whom you forced up to her last visit to come before you here as your mother, Agnes!

HENRY IV. And wasn't she your mother?

DI NOLLI. My mother, of course she was my mother!

HENRY IV. But your mother died to me 'old and far away'! You've just come down from there, young and fresh! (*pointing to the niche*) And how do you know I haven't cried a long time for her, in secret, even dressed like this?

LADY MATILDE (*dismayed, looking at the others*). But what is he saying?

DOCTOR (*very absorbed, observing him*). Easy, take it easy, please!

HENRY IV. What am I saying? Ask everybody if Henry IV's mother wasn't Agnes! (*Turning to Frida as if she were actually the Marquise of Tuscany*) You, Marquise, ought to know, I think!

FRIDA (*still frightened, clinging closer to Di Nolli*). No, not me! not me!

DOCTOR. There, he's raving again... Please, ladies and gentlemen, take it easy!

BELCREDI (*riled*). What raving, Doctor? He's starting to act a role again!

HENRY IV (*immediately*). Me? You've emptied out those two niches; he's standing before me as Henry IV...

BELCREDI. Enough of this joke already!

HENRY IV. Who said it was a joke?

DOCTOR (*to Belcredi, loudly*). Don't provoke him, for God's sake!

BELCREDI (*ignoring him, louder*). But they've said it! (*pointing to the four young men*). They did! they did!

HENRY IV (*turning to look at them*). *You* did? You said it was a joke?

LANDOLPH (*timidly*). No... Really, we said you had recovered!

BELCREDI. So, that's enough! Let's go! (*To Lady Matilde*) Don't you find the very sight of him unbearably childish (*pointing to Di Nolli*), Marquise? And of you, dressed up like this?

LADY MATILDE. Oh, shut up! Who cares about the dress now, if he's really recovered?

HENRY IV. Yes, recovered! I've really recovered! (*To Belcredi*) Ah, but not to put an end to it at once, as you would like to think! (*Attacking him*) Do you know that in twenty years nobody's ever dared come before me like you and this man here? (*pointing to the Doctor*).

BELCREDI. Yes, I know! And in fact this morning I too came before you dressed...

HENRY IV. As a monk, oh yes!

BELCREDI. And you took me for Pier Damiani! And I didn't laugh, thinking, in fact…

HENRY IV. That I was crazy! Does it make you laugh now, seeing her in that get-up, now that I've recovered? Yet you might have thought that, in my eyes, her appearance, now (*interrupts himself with a gesture of scorn*) Oh! (*and turns angrily to the Doctor*) Are you a physician?

DOCTOR. Yes, I am…

HENRY IV. And you dressed her up as the Marquise of Tuscany? Do you know, Doctor, that you risked pushing me back in a moment into my mind's darkness? My god, making portraits talk! Making them jump from their frames alive… (*Contemplating Frida and Di Nolli, then the marquise, finally his own clothing*) Ah, a very nice arrangement… Two couples… Very good, very good, Doctor… for a madman… (*Indicating Belcredi with a slight movement of his hand*) He sees it as a Mardi Gras parade out of season, right? (*Turning to look at him*) I should get out of these masquerade clothes too! In order to come away with you, right?

BELCREDI. With me! With us!

HENRY IV. Where? To the club? In tuxedo and white tie? Or to the marquise's house, both of us, together?

BELCREDI. Wherever you like! Would you want to stay on here, pardon me, to keep up all alone what was simply the unfortunate trick of a Mardi Gras? It's really incredible, just incredible, that you could do it, once you recovered from your unfortunate accident!

HENRY IV. Sure. But see, falling from the horse and striking my head, I really was out of my mind for I don't know how long…

DOCTOR. Ah, there you are! And did it last a long time?

HENRY IV (*very quickly, to the Doctor*). Yes, Doctor, a very long time; about twelve years. (*Immediately turning to speak to Belcredi*) And seeing not one thing of everything that took place after that Mardi Gras, for you and not for me; how things changed; how friends betrayed me; my place taken by others, for instance… say… in the heart of the woman you were in love with; and who had died; and who had disappeared… all this, you know, wasn't a joke for me, as you seem to think!

BELCREDI. No, please, I'm not talking about that! I mean afterwards!

HENRY IV. Ah, yes? Afterwards! One day… (*Stopping and turning to the Doctor*) A very interesting case, Doctor. Study me, study me attentively! (*He trembles visibly as he speaks*) By itself, God knows how, one day, the malfunction up here… (*touching his forehead*), who knows, it was cured. I open my eyes gradually, I don't know at first if I'm dreaming

or awake; yes, I *am* awake. I touch this thing and that... I see them all
clearly... Ah, then, as he says (*pointing to Belcredi*), off then, off with
this masquerade clothing! this nightmare! Let's open the windows!
Let's breathe life in! Off, off, let's run outside! (*Checking his passion
abruptly*) Where? To do what? To be pointed at by everyone, secretly,
as Henry IV, no longer like this, but arm in arm with you, among
life's dear friends?

BELCREDI. No! What are you saying? Why?

LADY MATILDE. Who could, now... ? No one would dream of it! It was
just an accident!

HENRY IV. But they all were calling me crazy before! All of them! (*To
Belcredi*) And you know it! You more than anyone else, you came
down hard on those who came to my defence!

BELCREDI. Oh come on, it was all in jest!

HENRY IV. And look here at my hair! (*showing him the hair at the back of
his head*).

BELCREDI. But mine is grey too!

HENRY IV. Yes, but with this difference: that mine got grey in here,
while I was Henry IV, do you see? And without my realizing it!
I realized it all in just one day, suddenly, when my eyes opened
again, and I was shocked, because at once I realized that not only
my hair but everything must have become grey like this, everything
crumbled, everything: and that I would arrive hungry as a wolf at a
banquet already cleared away.

BELCREDI. But, pardon me, the others too...

HENRY IV (*quickly*). I know, they couldn't stand around waiting for me
to recover, not even those who, behind me, pricked my horse until
they drew blood...

DI NOLLI (*shocked*). What? What?

HENRY IV. Yes, the traitors, to make it rear on its haunches and throw
me off!

LADY MATILDE (*quickly, horrified*). This is the first I've heard of it!

HENRY IV. That too was probably done in jest!

LADY MATILDE. But who was it? Who was riding behind us?

HENRY IV. It doesn't matter who! All those who went on with the
banquet and would have left me their scraps, Marquise, some scraps
of pity, lean or fat, or in the dirty dish some fishbone of remorse.
Thank you! (*Turning abruptly to the Doctor*) So, Doctor, see if this case
isn't really something new in the annals of madness! I preferred to
remain mad... finding here everything ready and laid out for this

new kind of delight: to live my madness in perfectly lucid awareness, and take vengeance on the brutality of a stone that had bruised my head! To clothe this solitude – so squalid and empty, as it seemed to me when I opened my eyes again – to clothe it at once with all the colours and splendour of that faraway Mardi Gras when you (*looking at Lady Matilde and pointing to Frida*) – there you are, Marquise – had your triumph! – and compel all those who came before me to carry on, by god, for my own enjoyment now, that famous old parade which had been – for you, not for me – the game of a single day! To make it become forever – no longer a game, no, but a reality, the reality of an actual madness – here, everybody masqueraded, and the throne room, and these four councillors of mine, secret councillors, and – of course – betrayers! (*Turning to them quickly*) I'd like to know what you've gained by revealing my recovery! If I've recovered, you won't be needed any more, you'll be dismissed! ... Letting somebody into your secrets, that's really a crazy thing to do! Ah, but now it's my turn, I'll accuse *you*! Do you know what? They thought that now they could start playing the joke on you too, together with me. (*He bursts out laughing. Though disconcerted, the others laugh too, except Lady Matilde.*)

BELCREDI (*to Di Nolli*). Do you hear? Not bad...

DI NOLLI (*to the four young men*). You?

HENRY IV. They must be forgiven! This (*pulling at his clothes*), this costume, which is for me the clear and intentional caricature of that other masquerade – continual, minute by minute – in which we are the involuntary clowns (*pointing to Belcredi*), when unwittingly we take on the disguise of what we think we are – they don't see it yet – their clothing – as what they actually are, and we must forgive them. (*Turning to Belcredi again*) You know, one gets used to things easily, and strolls, with ease, like a tragic character (*he does it*) in a room like this! – Look, Doctor! – I remember a priest – most certainly from Ireland – a handsome man – sleeping in the sun, a November day, leaning his arms on the back of a bench, in a public garden, drowned in the golden delight of that warmth that for him must have been almost summerlike. One can be sure that in that moment he no longer knew he was a priest, nor where he was. He was dreaming! And God knows what he was dreaming! An urchin came by who had picked a flower with a long stem. As he went by, he tickled the sleeper's neck, right here. I saw him open his smiling eyes, his entire mouth stretched in the blessed smile of his dream. Oblivious. But at

once, I tell you, he stiffened in his priestly habit, and the same
seriousness you have seen in my eyes returned to his; because Irish
priests defend the seriousness of their Catholic faith with the same
zeal I put into defending the sacrosanct rights of the hereditary
monarchy. – I am cured, ladies and gentlemen, because I am perfectly aware that I am playing the madman here. And I do it quietly!
Your situation is much worse, who live your madness in so much
agitation, without knowing or seeing it.

BELCREDI. You see the conclusion we've come to? that *we're* the crazy
ones now!

HENRY IV (*with a start that he tries to restrain*). But if you weren't mad, you
and she together (*pointing to the marquise*) would have come here?

BELCREDI. To tell the truth, I came thinking you were the madman.

HENRY IV (*at once, loudly, pointing to the marquise*). And she?

BELCREDI. I don't know about her... I see she is almost spellbound by
what you're saying... fascinated by this 'conscious' madness of yours!
(*Turning to her*) Dressed up as you are, you might even stay here to
live it, Marquise...

LADY MATILDE. You are insolent!

HENRY IV (*at once, placatingly*). Never mind him, never mind! He keeps
on provoking me, although the Doctor has warned him against it.
(*Turning to Belcredi*) But why do you think I should be troubled now
about what happened between us? The part you had in my misfortune with her (*pointing to the marquise; then talking to her and pointing to
Belcredi*), the role he now represents for you! This is my life! It isn't
yours! – Yours, the life you grew old in, I have not lived! (*To Lady
Matilde*) Is this what you wanted to tell me, to show me, through your
sacrifice, dressing yourself up like this on the Doctor's advice? Oh,
very well done, I've told you, Doctor: – 'What we were then, eh? and
how we are now.' But I'm not a madman in the sense you mean,
Doctor! I know very well that he (*pointing to Di Nolli*) cannot be me,
because I am Henry IV; I myself, right here, for twenty years, see?
Fixed in this eternal mask! *She's* lived them (*pointing to the marquise*),
she's enjoyed these twenty years, to become – there she is – someone
I can't recognize any longer; because I know her like this (*pointing to
Frida and coming up to her*), for me she's always this. You seem to me
like a bunch of children I can frighten. (*To Frida*) And you were
really frightened, child, by the trick they'd persuaded you to play,
without understanding that for me it could not have been the trick
they intended, but this terrible, fantastic thing: the dream that comes

alive in you, more than ever! There you were an image; they made you into a living person – you are mine! mine! mine! I've a right to you (*He takes her into his arms, laughing like a madman, while all cry out in terror; but as they rush to tear Frida from his arms, he grows even more menacing, and shouts to his four young men*) Hold them back, hold them back! I order you to hold them back! (*The four young men, confused, almost spellbound, automatically attempt to hold back Di Nolli, the Doctor, and Belcredi.*)

BELCREDI (*breaking loose at once, hurls himself on Henry IV*). Leave her alone! Leave her alone! You are not mad!

HENRY IV (*in a flash, drawing the sword from the sheath of Landolph, who is standing near him*). I'm not mad? Take this! (*He wounds him in the belly. All cry out in horror and rush to support Belcredi, shouting confusedly.*)

DI NOLLI. Are you wounded?

BERTHOLDT. He's wounded him! He's wounded him!

DOCTOR. I told you!

FRIDA. My God!

DI NOLLI. Frida, come here!

LADY MATILDE. He's mad! He's mad!

BELCREDI (*while he is carried away to the other room through the left-hand door, fiercely protests*). No! You're not mad! He's not mad! He's not mad! (*They all exit through the left-hand door, shouting, and continuing to shout until above the other cries, a louder one is heard from Lady Matilde, followed by silence.*)

HENRY IV (*left on the stage with Landolph, Ariald, and Ordulph, his eyes open wide, shocked by the life of his own fiction which has suddenly driven him to commit a crime*). Now, yes… it must be so… (*calling them around him, as if for protection*) here together, here together… and forever!

CURTAIN

Each in His Own Way

Foreword

The performance of this play should begin in the street, or, more exactly, under the marquee of the theatre, with two or three shouting newsboys selling an Evening News, *consisting of a single sheet made to look like an 'extra'; in the centre of this, in large, very visible characters, the following 'indiscretion' in exemplary journalese appears:*

THE SUICIDE OF THE SCULPTOR LA VELA

AND TONIGHT'S PLAY AT THE

.... THEATRE

In theatre circles news has suddenly spread which is destined to provoke an enormous scandal. It is said that Pirandello has taken the topic for his new play, *Each in His Own Way,* to be performed tonight at the .... Theatre, from the very dramatic suicide of the young sculptor Giorgio La Vela that took place in Turin a few months back. Our readers will remember that La Vela, upon discovering his fiancée, A.M., in his studio in Via Montevideo, engaged in intimate relations with Baron N., instead of shooting the guilty lovers, turned the weapon on himself and died.

It also emerged that Baron N. was to marry La Vela's sister. The shock caused by the tragic event is very much alive, not only because of the fame La Vela had achieved at such a young age, but also because of the social standing and the celebrity of the other two figures in the tragedy. It is very likely that some unpleasant repercussions may occur tonight at the theatre.

In addition, the theatregoers entering the theatre to buy their tickets shall see near the ticket booth the actress designated as A.M. in the paper, that is, Amelia Moreno, in person, surrounded by three gentlemen in evening dress, who are trying to persuade her to give up her intention of entering the theatre to see the play. They would like to take her away. But at least, they beg, she should be good and remove herself from the sight of so many people who might recognize her. Her place is not there. She should, for god's sake, let herself be led away. Does she want to make a scene? Pale, convulsed, she shakes her head, saying no. She wants to stay, to watch the play, to see how far the arrogant writer has gone. She tears her little handkerchief to shreds between her teeth. People notice her, and when she realizes this, she feels like either hiding or screaming at them. She keeps repeating to her friends that she wants a box in the third row. She will sit in the back so as not to be seen. They should go, go buy her a ticket. She promises she will not make a scene; she will leave the theatre if she proves unable to stomach it. A third-row box; are they going to make her go get it herself?

This improvised, but very realistically performed scene should begin a few minutes before the time set for the start of the play and last – arousing the surprise, the curiosity, and even maybe a certain apprehension in the real theatregoers who are about to enter – until the bells inside the theatre indicate that the curtain is about to rise.

At the same time, the members of the audience who have entered or are just entering the lobby will find there, or in the corridor leading to the auditorium, another surprise, another reason for curiosity and perhaps apprehension, in another scene, performed by Baron Nuti and his friends.

'Calm down, calm down; I'm calm, see? absolutely calm. And I assure you I'd be even calmer if you'd go away. It's you who are attracting everybody's attention by crowding around me! Leave me alone and nobody will look at me any more. I'm nothing but a spectator like everybody else, after all. What do you expect me to do inside the theatre? I know she's going to come, if she hasn't already; I just want to see her, just to see her – yes, yes, from a distance. I'm not after anything else, believe me. Will you get out of here now? Don't force me to make a spectacle of myself in front of the people who are coming here to enjoy themselves at my expense. I want to be alone. How can I convince you? Calm – yes I 'm calm. How much calmer can I be?'

And he will continue to pace up and down, his expression wild, his whole body shaking, until the whole audience has gone in.

All this will explain to the audience why, on the posters announcing this evening's performance, the theatre management has deemed it prudent to print the following caveat:

Please note. It is impossible to say whether this play will have two or three acts, because certain incidents may well prevent the completion of the performance.

Characters

In the play to be performed on stage:

DELIA MORELLO

MICHELE ROCCA

The old lady
The old house servant FILIPPO
LADY LIVIA PALEGARI *and her guests, her women friends and old friends*
of the family
DORO PALEGARI, *her son, and* DIEGO CINCI, *his young friend*
FRANCESCO SAVIO, *Doro's opponent, and his friend* PRESTINO, *other friends,*
the FENCING TEACHER *and a waiter*

In the theatre lobby:
MISS MORENO ('EVERYONE KNOWS WHO SHE IS')
BARON NUTI
THE DIRECTOR OF THE PLAY
ACTORS AND ACTRESSES
THE THEATRE MANAGER
THE MANAGER OF THE THEATRICAL COMPANY
THE THEATRE USHERS
THE POLICE
FIVE DRAMA CRITICS
AN ELDERLY, UNSUCCESSFUL AUTHOR
A YOUNG AUTHOR
A MAN OF LETTERS WHO DISDAINS THE ACT OF WRITING
AN AMIABLE SPECTATOR
AN ANNOYED SPECTATOR
A FEW SPECTATORS FAVOURABLY DISPOSED TO THE AUTHOR OF THE PLAY
MANY SPECTATORS UNFAVOURABLY DISPOSED TO THE AUTHOR
THE WORDLY SPECTATOR
OTHER SPECTATORS, MALE AND FEMALE

ACT ONE

(We are in the old palace of Lady Livia Palegari, a noblewoman, during her reception hours, which are almost over. To the rear, through three arches and two columns, we see a large, richly decorated salon, brightly lit up and full of guests, men and women. At the front of the stage, much less brightly lit, there is a smaller drawing room, rather sombre, its walls covered in damask, and decor-

*ated with old paintings of great value, most of them of religious subjects; thus
we have the feeling of being in the chapel of a church, of which the salon in the
background is the nave – a sacred chapel of a worldly church. This drawing
room is furnished with only a bench and a few straight chairs for the convenience of whoever wants to look at the pictures on the walls. No door. From the
salon some of the guests will come here, two or three at a time, to exchange
confidences away from the others. As the curtain rises we find in this drawing
room an Old Friend of the Family and a Thin Young Man, discussing something privately.)*

THIN YOUNG MAN (*his small, misshapen head is that of a plucked bird*). But
  what's *your* opinion?

OLD FRIEND OF THE FAMILY (*handsome, authoritative, but also somewhat sly,
  sighing*). My opinion? (*Pause*) I don't know. (*Pause*) What do the
  others think?

YOUNG MAN. Well… some one thing, some another.

OLD FRIEND. Of course, of course! Everyone has their own opinion.

YOUNG MAN. But to tell the truth, nobody seems to stick to it very firmly,
  since everybody, like you, wants to know what the others think,
  before they say anything.

OLD FRIEND. Listen, I stick to mine all right. But since I don't want to
  talk lightly, it obviously makes sense to find out if other people
  know something I don't, which might change my opinion to some
  degree.

YOUNG MAN. But as far as you know?

OLD FRIEND. My dear friend, one never knows everything!

YOUNG MAN. Well, opinions then…

OLD FRIEND. Oh Lord! I stick to mine, but – there you are – only until
  I'm proven wrong!

YOUNG MAN. But, pardon me, sir – by admitting that we never know
  everything, you're already foreseeing the likelihood that you might
  be wrong.

OLD FRIEND (*looks at him, pensively, then smiles and asks*). And so you've
  drawn the conclusion that I have no opinion?

YOUNG MAN. Because, judging from what you're saying, nobody can
  have firm opinions!

OLD FRIEND. And don't you think that that's already having an opinion?

YOUNG MAN. Yes, but a negative one!

OLD FRIEND. Better than nothing, eh? better than nothing, my friend!

  (*He takes him by the arm and the two start off to the salon in the rear, where*

*we see young ladies offering tea and cake to the guests. Pause. Two Young
Ladies enter the smaller room circumspectly.*)

THE FIRST (*impetuously*). You're giving me a whole new lease on life! Tell
me more, more!

THE SECOND. But, look, it's nothing more than my personal impression!

THE FIRST. If you got it, it means there's some truth in it! Was he pale?
Was he smiling sadly?

THE SECOND. It seemed that way to me.

THE FIRST. I shouldn't have let him leave. I knew it in my heart! I held
his hand all the way to the door. He was already a step outside the
door and I was still holding his hand. We had kissed, separated, but
our hands – no, they didn't want to part. When I got back in, I fell
down, as if the tears had sapped my strength. – But tell me, tell me:
no allusion?

THE SECOND. Allusion to what?

THE FIRST. Well, I mean, if – just speaking in general – as often
happens…

THE SECOND. No, he wasn't talking; he was listening to what the others
were saying.

THE FIRST. Of course, because he knows! He knows how much we hurt
each other because of this damned need to talk. As long as there is a
shred of uncertainty in us, we should keep our mouths shut. We talk
and talk, and don't even know what we're talking about… But did he
look sad? Did he smile sadly? Do you remember what the others were
saying?

THE SECOND. No, I don't. I wouldn't like you to build up any illusions,
darling. You know how it is, don't you? We fool ourselves. Maybe he
was indifferent and he looked to me as if he were smiling sadly. Wait,
yes – when someone said…

THE FIRST. Said?

THE SECOND. Wait, he said – 'Women, like dreams, are never the way
you want them to be.'

THE FIRST. *He* didn't say that?

THE SECOND. No, no.

THE FIRST. Good Lord! – In the meantime I don't know if I'm doing
the right thing or not. And I'm the one who used to boast that I
always did my own thing! – I'm a nice person, but I can turn mean –
and if I do, he'd better watch out!

THE SECOND. My dear, I wouldn't like to see you give up being who you
are.

THE FIRST. And who am I? And how do I feel? I swear I don't know any
more! Everything's shifting, changing, insubstantial. I turn this way,
that way, I laugh, I go into a corner to cry. Always restless! In anguish!
Constantly hiding from myself, ashamed of seeing myself changing
every minute! (*Other guests enter at this point: two bored young men,
elegantly dressed, and Diego Cinci.*)

FIRST YOUNG MAN. Are we disturbing you?

SECOND YOUNG LADY. No, no. 'Course not. Come in.

SECOND YOUNG MAN. This is the chapel where they hear confession.

DIEGO. Right! Lady Livia should keep a priest and a confessional here
for the benefit of her guests.

FIRST YOUNG MAN. What confessional! One's conscience! One's
conscience!

DIEGO. Great, great! and what's that?

FIRST YOUNG MAN. What d'you mean? My conscience?

SECOND YOUNG MAN (*solemnly*). 'Mea mihi conscientia pluris est quam
hominum sermo.'

SECOND YOUNG LADY. What? What? You speak Latin?

SECOND YOUNG MAN. It's Cicero, Miss. I remember it from high school.

FIRST YOUNG LADY. And what does it mean?

SECOND YOUNG MAN (*as before*). 'I care more for the witness of my
conscience than for the talk of the entire world.'

FIRST YOUNG MAN. We all say, modestly: 'I have my conscience and that
is enough for me.'

DIEGO. If we were alone.

SECOND YOUNG MAN. What d'you mean, 'If we were alone'?

DIEGO. That it would be enough. But then even conscience would cease
to exist. Unfortunately, my dear friends, I exist, and you exist too.
Unfortunately!

FIRST YOUNG LADY. Why unfortunately?

SECOND YOUNG LADY. That's not nice!

DIEGO. Because we must always take the others into consideration, my
dear ladies!

SECOND YOUNG MAN. Not at all! When I have my conscience!

DIEGO. Why can't you understand that your conscience actually means
'the others inside you'?

FIRST YOUNG MAN. The usual paradoxes!

DIEGO. What paradoxes! (*To the second young man*) Listen, what does it
mean that 'you have your conscience and that's enough for you'?
That the others can think of you and judge you as they please, even

unjustly; that you're absolutely sure, and easy in your mind that you haven't done anything wrong. Right?

SECOND YOUNG MAN. Sure!

DIEGO. Good! And who gives you that security, if not the others? Who gives you that sense of ease?

SECOND YOUNG MAN. No, I do! My conscience itself! Of course!

DIEGO. Only because you think that the others, in your place and under the same circumstances, would have done exactly what you did! That's why, dear boy! And also because, besides the concrete, particular situations in life... yes, there are abstract and general principles on which we can all agree (it doesn't cost much!). But in real life, look: if you shut yourself up disdainfully in yourself and state that 'you have your own conscience, and that's enough for you,' it's because you know that everybody condemns you and disapproves of you, and even laughs at you. Otherwise you wouldn't say it. The fact is that principles remain abstract; nobody can see them the way you see them in the situation you're involved in, nor see himself in what you did. And if that's how it is, can you tell me to what end your conscience is good enough for you? To feel alone? Of course not! Solitude frightens you. What do you do then? You imagine many heads, all like yours, many heads which are in fact your own head; which, in a given case, pulling their strings, will say yes or no, no or yes, as you like. And this eases your mind and reassures you. Come on, come on, this game of your conscience which is enough for you... it's certainly a marvellous game!

FIRST YOUNG LADY. It's getting late, you know. We must leave.

SECOND YOUNG LADY. Yes, of course. Everyone's going. (*To Diego, feigning indignation*) What morbid things you talk about!

FIRST YOUNG MAN. We must go too. Let's go. (*They go back into the salon to take leave of their hostess and depart. In the salon by now the guests remaining to take leave of Lady Livia are very few. She then moves forward to the front of the stage, visibly troubled, detaining Diego Cinci. She is followed by the Old Friend of the Family we have met at the beginning, and by a Second Old Friend.*)

LADY LIVIA (*to Diego*). No, no, my dear, please don't go. You're my son's closest friend. I'm all upset. Please, tell me, tell me if it's true, what these old friends of mine have just told me.

FIRST OLD FRIEND. Please, Lady Livia, don't forget, they are only suppositions!

DIEGO. About Doro? What's happened to him?

LADY LIVIA (*surprised*). What? You don't know anything about it?

DIEGO. No. Nothing important, I hope. Or I would know about it.

SECOND OLD FRIEND (*lowering his eyes as if to attenuate the gravity of what he is saying*). Last night's scandal...

LADY LIVIA. ... at the Avanzis! In defence of that... what's her name? ... that infamous woman!

DIEGO. Scandal? What infamous woman?

FIRST OLD FRIEND (*same as above*). Huh! Miss Morello.

DIEGO. Ah. It's Delia Morello?

LADY LIVIA. So you know her?

DIEGO. My dear lady, who doesn't?

LADY LIVIA. Doro too? So it's true! He knows her!

DIEGO. Good Lord, he might. But what scandal?

LADY LIVIA (*to the first old friend*). And you were denying it! ...

DIEGO. ... the way everybody knows her, dear lady. But what happened?

FIRST OLD FRIEND. There, you see! As I said: 'maybe without ever having spoken to her'!

SECOND OLD FRIEND. Right! By hearsay.

LADY LIVIA. And he took up her defence? To the point where he almost got into a fight...

DIEGO. ... with whom? ...

SECOND OLD FRIEND. ... with Francesco Savio...

LADY LIVIA. ... it's incredible! Letting it go that far! In a respectable house! For a woman like that!

DIEGO. Well, perhaps, in the course of a discussion...

FIRST OLD FRIEND. ... sure, in the heat of discussion...

SECOND OLD FRIEND. ... as often happens.

LADY LIVIA. Please, don't try to mislead me! (*To Diego*) Tell me, *you* tell me, dear! You know everything about Doro...

DIEGO. ... don't upset yourself so much, dear lady...

LADY LIVIA. ...no! It's your duty, if you're a real friend of my son's, to tell me all you know!

DIEGO. But I don't know anything! And I'm sure it's probably nothing! Why be so upset about words?

FIRST OLD FRIEND. No, that's not so...

SECOND OLD FRIEND. ... you can't deny it, this thing has made a great impression on everybody.

DIEGO. But what, for God's sake?

LADY LIVIA. ... this scandalous defence! You think it's nothing?

DIEGO. But you know yourself, dear lady, that everybody's done nothing for the last twenty days but talk about Delia Morello! Awful things have been said about her everywhere people meet, in drawing rooms, cafés, press rooms. You must have read something in the papers yourself.

LADY LIVIA. Yes. That a man killed himself over her!

FIRST OLD FRIEND. ... a young painter, Salvi...

DIEGO. ... yes, Giorgio Salvi...

SECOND OLD FRIEND. ... who seems to have been a very promising artist...

DIEGO. ... and it seems that he wasn't the first one.

LADY LIVIA. What? Someone else too?

FIRST OLD FRIEND. ... yes, that's what one newspaper said...

SECOND OLD FRIEND. ... that somebody else had killed himself before, over her? ...

DIEGO. ... a Russian, a few years ago, in Capri.

LADY LIVIA (*becoming hysterical, burying her face in her hands*). Oh, my God! my God!

DIEGO. Please, don't worry that Doro's going to be the third one! Believe me, dear lady, the unfortunate death of an artist like Giorgio Salvi must be mourned by everybody; but then... if you know how the various events of that case evolved... you can really even find excuses for that woman.

LADY LIVIA. You too?

DIEGO. Me too, yes. Why not?

SECOND OLD FRIEND. Defying everyone's indignation?

DIEGO. Yes! Yes, it can be done!

LADY LIVIA. My Doro! My Lord, always so earnest!

FIRST OLD FRIEND. Reserved.

SECOND OLD FRIEND. Dignified.

DIEGO. It's possible that someone took issue with him and he reacted a little too strongly, let himself go.

LADY LIVIA. No, no. You don't fool me! you don't fool me! Is she an actress, this Delia Morello?

DIEGO. She'a madwoman, dear lady.

FIRST OLD FRIEND. But she was a dramatic actress.

DIEGO. She's been fired from every company because of her immoderate behaviour, to the point where she can't find a job any more. 'Delia Morello' might be a stage name. Who knows what her name is, who she is, where she's from!

LADY LIVIA. Is she beautiful?

DIEGO. Very!

LADY LIVIA. They all are, these damned women! Could Doro have met
her at the theatre?

DIEGO. Maybe. He could have talked to her a few times in her dressing
room, if at all. Anyway, she's not as terrible as everyone imagines,
dear lady. No reason to be upset.

LADY LIVIA. After two men have killed themselves because of her?

DIEGO. I wouldn't have.

LADY LIVIA. She must have driven both of them wild.

DIEGO. She wouldn't have driven me wild.

LADY LIVIA. But I don't fear for you, I fear for Doro!

DIEGO. You needn't fear, dear lady. And believe me, if that unlucky
woman has brought trouble to others, she's always brought the worst
trouble on herself. She's one of those strange women, always over-
reacting, always running away from something, who never know
where they'll end up. Yet she often seems like a poor scared child
looking for help.

LADY LIVIA (*badly shaken, seizing Diego's arm*). Diego, these are things
Doro told you!

DIEGO. No, dear lady!

LADY LIVIA (*insistently*). Please be candid, Diego. Doro's in love with this
woman!

DIEGO. But I've told you no!

LADY LIVIA (*as above*). Yes, *yes* – he is! The words you just said are the
words of a man in love!

DIEGO. But those were my words, not Doro's!

LADY LIVIA. It's not true! Doro said them to you! Nobody can convince
me otherwise!

DIEGO (*feeling her insistence*). My God... (*suddenly finding his way: with a
clear voice, light, inviting*) Dear lady, can't you imagine... let's see, a
small carriage on a country road – really out in the country – on a
beautiful sunny day?

LADY LIVIA (*taken aback*). A small carriage? What's that got to do with it?

DIEGO (*angrily, truly moved*). Dear lady, do you know what happened to
me the night I watched by my dying mother's bedside? There was an
insect before me, with flat wings and six legs, which had fallen into a
glass of water on the night table. And I missed my mother's last
breath, absorbed as I was in watching the faith that insect was putting
in the agility of its two last and longest legs, the ones he used for

taking off. It was swimming desperately, fixed on the idea that those
two legs were capable of taking off even from a liquid surface except
for some little thing attached to their extremities that made the jump
difficult. As each effort failed, it kept drying them against its front
legs and repeating the attempt. I kept watching it for half an hour.
I saw it die and not my mother. Do you understand? Please let me
alone!

LADY LIVIA (*confused, bewildered, glancing at her two friends, who are equally
bewildered*). I'm really sorry, but I don't see what connection...

DIEGO. Does it seem absurd to you? Tomorrow you'll laugh – I assure
you – at all this useless consternation about your son, thinking of this
small carriage I ran by you to distract you. Consider that I myself
cannot laugh, however, thinking of that insect my eyes lighted on
while I was watching at my dying mother's bedside.

(*A pause. Lady Livia and the two old friends, after this sudden diversion,
turn to look at each other, more bewildered than ever, unable, no matter how
they try, to fit that small carriage and that insect into the subject of the
conversation. On the other hand, Diego Cinci is truly moved by the memory of
his mother's death. Thus Doro Palegari, now entering, finds him in a
thoroughly changed mood.*)

DORO (*surprised, looking at the four of them*). What is it?

LADY LIVIA (*coming out of her daze*). Oh, here you are! Doro, darling boy,
what've you done? These friends just told me...

DORO (*reacting with great irritation*). ... about the scandal, right? that I'm
head over heels in love with Delia Morello, huh? All the friends I pass
in the street wink at me: – 'Delia Morello, eh?' – Good god, where
are we? What kind of world are we in?

LADY LIVIA. But if you...

DORO. ... if I what? I swear it's incredible! It's already become a scandal!
In no time!

LADY LIVIA. You defended...

DORO. ... I defended nobody! ...

LADY LIVIA. ... at the Avanzis' last night...

DORO. ... at the Avanzis' last night I heard Francesco Savio express an
opinion on the tragic death of Salvi which is on everybody's tongue.
It didn't seem correct to me, and I spoke against it. That's all!

LADY LIVIA. But you said things...

DORO. ... I might have said a lot of stupid things too, I don't know what
I said! When you get started talking... But can a person have an
opinion of his own on things that happen or can't he? It seems to me

we can interpret an event one way or another, as we see it – today one way, and tomorrow maybe differently! If I see Francesco Savio tomorrow, I'm perfectly ready to admit that he was right and I was wrong.

FIRST OLD FRIEND. Oh, very good, then!

LADY LIVIA. Yes, please, do so, Doro darling.

SECOND OLD FRIEND. ...to put an end to all this talk!

DORO. That's not why! I don't give a damn about the talk! It's to put an end to the irritation I feel...

FIRST OLD FRIEND. ... right, right! ...

SECOND OLD FRIEND. ... seeing yourself so misunderstood!

DORO. No! Because of all the exaggerations I let myself indulge in, seeing Francesco Savio so damned insistent on certain false arguments, which after all – it's true – were substantially correct. Now that I've cooled off, I repeat, I'm ready to admit it. And I'll do it, I'll do it in front of everybody, so that they stop making this famous discussion into such a big deal! I'm fed up with it!

LADY LIVIA. Good, good, Doro darling! And I'm glad you're admitting already, and in front of this friend of yours, that one can't defend a woman of that kind!

DORO. Why? He too said she could be defended?

FIRST OLD FRIEND. Yes, he did, but just... he was just saying it...

SECOND OLD FRIEND. ... academically, to calm your mother...

LADY LIVIA. Oh, yes, nice way to calm me! Good thing you've done it now. Thank you, Doro darling.

DORO (*reacting angrily to her thanks*). Are you serious? You're getting me more upset, don't you see?

LADY LIVIA. Because I've thanked you?

DORO. Of course! Why are you thanking me? If not because you too have believed that...

LADY LIVIA. No, no!

DORO. ....then why are you thanking me and saying that you're calm now? That drives me crazy!

LADY LIVIA. Please, Doro. Forget the whole thing.

DORO (*turning to Diego*). And how do *you* think Delia Morello can be defended?

DIEGO. Forget it! Now that your mother 's no longer upset.

DORO. No, I'd like to know, I'd like to know.

DIEGO. In order to start an argument with me?

LADY LIVIA. That's enough, Doro!

DORO (*to his mother*). No, just to know! (*to Diego*) To see if your reasons
are the same as the ones I brought up to refute Francesco Savio's.

DIEGO. And in that case, you'd change your mind again?

DORO. Do you think I'm a weathervane? – I claimed you couldn't say
Delia Morello wanted to ruin Salvi, for this reason: practically the day
before their wedding, she went with the other guy, because Salvi's
real ruin would have been his marriage to her.

DIEGO. Right! But you know what a lit torch in the sun at a funeral looks
like? You don't see the flame. What do you see? That it sends up smoke!

DORO. What d'you mean?

DIEGO. That I agree with you. That Miss Morello knew it, and that
because she knew it, she didn't want the marriage to take place! But
all this isn't clear, perhaps even to herself, and all the others see is
the smoke of her so-called treachery.

DORO (*immediately, impetuously*). No, no, my friend! Yes, the treachery
was there, undeniably, and of a very sophisticated kind! I've thought
it out carefully all day today. She went with the other fellow – with
Michele Rocca – to pursue her vendetta against Salvi to the very end,
as Savio insisted last night.

DIEGO. Okay! Then set your mind at ease with Savio's opinion now, and
forget about the whole thing.

FIRST OLD FRIEND. There! It's the best thing to do with such a subject!
And we're leaving, Lady Livia... (*he kisses her hand*).

SECOND OLD FRIEND (*following the other*)... very happy that the whole
matter has been cleared up! (*He kisses her hand and turns to the two
young men*) Good night, dear boys.

FIRST OLD FRIEND. Goodbye, Doro. Good night, Cinci.

DIEGO. Good night. (*Takes him aside a little and says in a low voice, maliciously*) Congratulations!

FIRST OLD FRIEND (*bewildered*). For what?

DIEGO. I notice with pleasure that there's always something more in
you, underneath it all, that luckily never comes to the surface.

FIRST OLD FRIEND. In me? No! What?

DIEGO. Come on! What you really think you keep to yourself, and don't
let people notice. But we're in agreement, you know!

FIRST OLD FRIEND. Uhm! What can I say if I don't get you!?

DIEGO (*pulling him even further aside*). I'd even marry her! But I hardly
have enough for me, not a penny more. It would be like getting
somebody else under your umbrella when it's raining, both of you
get wet.

LADY LIVIA (*who has been conversing, reassured, with Doro and the other old friend, turns to the first one, who is laughing*). Well, then, my friend... What are you laughing about?

FIRST OLD FRIEND. Nothing, just something very naughty.

LADY LIVIA (*goes on talking as she moves, arm in arm with him, towards the large salon in the back, into which they disappear stage right as she talks*). ... if you go to Cristina's house tomorrow, please tell her to be ready at the time we've agreed on... (*After Lady Livia and the old friends have gone, Doro and Diego remain silent for quite a while. The large room behind them, empty and brightly lit, arouses a strange feeling.*)

DIEGO (*opening the fingers of both hands like fans, interweaving them to form a grid or net, and coming close to Doro to show it to him*). It's like this, see? just like this.

DORO. What is?

DIEGO. The conscience we were talking about before. An elastic net. If you just loosen it a bit, that's it! the madness that lurks in each of us slips out.

DORO (*after a brief silence, dismayed and suspicious*). Are you referring to me?

DIEGO (*almost to himself*). The images that have accumulated in you through the years drift in front of you, disconnected, fragments of a life that perhaps you've lived and that has remained unknown to you because you didn't want to or couldn't project it within you in the light of reason; ambiguous actions, shameful lies, deep resentments, crimes meditated in your own shadow down to the last details – unconfessed desires – all of it, all of it pours out, vomits out of you, and you're left bewildered, terrified by it.

DORO (*as before*). Why are you saying this?

DIEGO (*his eyes staring into the void*). After nine sleepless nights... (*Interrupts himself and turns to Doro suddenly*) Try it! Try not sleeping for nine nights in a row! – That porcelain bowl on the night table, with just one blue line around it. And tan-tan, the chime, what a death! Eight, nine... I was counting every hour: ten, eleven – the chime of the clock – twelve, and then waiting for the quarter hour chime! There's no loving feeling left, when you've neglected the primary needs that must be satisfied. In revolt against the brutal fate that kept the body there, no feeling left – the death rattle going on and on – only the body by then, almost unrecognizable, the body of my mother – do you know what I was thinking? I was thinking – oh God, could she stop that rattling at last!

DORO. But she died more than two years ago, didn't she, your mother?

DIEGO. Yes. Do you know how I caught myself during a momentary suspension of that death rattle, in the horrible silence that overtook the room, when I turned my head, I don't know why, towards the mirror of the armoire? Bent over the bed, intent on watching very closely, to see whether she was dead. Exactly as if to show itself to me, my face in the mirror was still set in the expression it had as I watched, in a terror that was almost gay, for its liberation. The return of the death rattle aroused in me such a revulsion from myself that I hid my face as if I'd committed a crime, and I started crying – like the baby I had been for my mother, whose pity – yes! – I was still expecting because of how tired I was feeling, dropping with fatigue – although I'd just been desiring her death, my poor mother who had watched over me so many nights when I was small and sick...

DORO. Can you tell me why, all of a sudden, this memory of your mother?

DIEGO. I don't know why. Do *you* know why you got so touchy when your mother thanked you for having calmed her fears?

DORO. Because she too had supposed, even for a moment...

DIEGO. Come on. We understand each other even just by looking at each other!

DORO (*shrugging his shoulders*). What do you understand!

DIEGO. If it weren't true, you would have laughed instead of getting angry.

DORO. Why now? You too seriously think that...

DIEGO. Not me! *You're* thinking it!

DORO. But now I'm saying Savio was right...

DIEGO. See? From this to this. And you've even gotten irritated with yourself, because of your 'excesses'!

DORO. Because I recognize...

DIEGO. ... no, no! read, read yourself clearly!

DORO. What do you want me to read, for pity's sake?

DIEGO. Now you say Savio was right. Do you know why? In reaction to a feeling you've been harbouring without your knowing it.

DORO. Nothing of the sort. Don't make me laugh!

DIEGO. Yes! yes!

DORO. I told you you make me laugh!

DIEGO. In the heat of yesterday's argument it came to the surface and it stunned you, and it made you say things you didn't know you felt. Of course! You think you never thought about them! But you have, you have!

DORO. How, when?

DIEGO. Hiding them from yourself! Just as there are illegitimate children, my friend, so there are bastard thoughts!

DORO. Yours certainly are!

DIEGO. Mine too! Each one of us means to marry for life only one soul, the most convenient one, the one who brings us as a dowry whatever's most conducive to our aspirations. But then, beyond the honest conjugal walls of our conscience, we have affairs, fall into no end of error with all our other, ostracized souls that live down in the cellars of our being, and from whom actions, thoughts, are born which we don't want to recognize – or that, if we're forced to, we adopt and legitimize with many adjustments and reservations and precautions. This thought of yours you now reject, poor foundling thought! But look it straight in the eye – it's your own! You've really fallen in love with Delia Morello! Like a fool!

DORO. Hah, hah, hah, hah! You make me laugh, you really make me laugh (*Filippo, the butler, comes in while Doro is laughing.*)

FILIPPO. Excuse me, sir. There is a Mr Francesco Savio to see you.

DORO. Oh, here he is! (*to Filippo*) Show him in.

DIEGO. I'm going.

DORO. No, wait, and I'll show you how I've fallen in love with Delia Morello! (*Francesco Savio enters.*) Come in, come in, Francesco.

FRANCESCO. Doro, dear! Good evening, Cinci!

DIEGO. Good evening.

FRANCESCO (*to Doro*). I've come to tell you how sorry I am about our squabble last night.

DORO. Look at that! I meant to come to see *you* tonight to tell you how sorry I am too.

FRANCESCO (*embraces him*). My friend, you've lifted a great weight from my chest.

DIEGO. I swear, what a picture, the two of you!

FRANCESCO (*to Diego*). Do you know that we almost wrecked our old friendship?

DORO. Oh, come on. Of course we didn't!

FRANCESCO. We didn't? I felt awful all night, thinking that I'd failed to understand the generous feeling…

DIEGO (*bursts out*). … perfect! … that pushed him to defend Delia Morello, right? …

FRANCESCO. … in front of everybody,… courageously… while everybody was blaming her for everything.

DIEGO. And you first of all!

FRANCESCO (*heatedly*). Yes! Because I'd never given much thought to the reasons – one more right, more convincing than the other – that Doro brought out!

DORO (*disappointed, astounded*). Oh yes? Now you...

DIEGO (*as above*). Perfect! Taking that woman's side now, right?

FRANCESCO. ... not giving a damn about the scandal! Undaunted by all those idiots' dirty laughter at his cutting rejoinders!

DORO (*as above, exploding*). Listen here! You're a weathercock!

FRANCESCO. What? I came to say you were right!

DORO. Exactly, that's why! A weathercock!

DIEGO (*to Francesco*). He wanted to tell you *you* were right!

FRANCESCO. Me?

DIEGO. You, you! Right about everything you said against Delia Morello!

DORO. And now he has the gall to come here and tell me *I* was right!

FRANCESCO. Because I thought about what you said last night!

DIEGO. Sure, exactly as he thought about what *you* said last night!

FRANCESCO. And now he says *I* was right?

DIEGO. The way you're saying *he* was right!

DORO. Yeah, now! After he made me everybody's laughingstock last night, the object of all kinds of nasty ideas, and upset my mother...

FRANCESCO. ... I did?

DORO. ... you! Yes you! egging me on, compromising me, getting me to say things that had never crossed my mind! (*comes up to him aggressively, shaking with anger*). Don't you dare go around now saying I was right!

DIEGO (*insistently*). ... because now you've recognized the generosity of his feeling...

FRANCESCO. ... but it's true!

DORO. You are a damn weathercock!

DIEGO. Because, if you do, you'll make people believe that he's in love with Delia Morello, and that's the reason why he defended her!

DORO. Damn it, Diego, either you stop this or next I'll be starting with you! (*to Francesco*) A weathercock, a weathercock!

FRANCESCO. That's the fifth time you've shouted it in my face! Watch yourself!

DORO. And I'll do it a hundred times – now, tomorrow, always!

FRANCESCO. May I remind you that I'm your guest here!

DORO. Here, outside, wherever you like, I'll shout it to your face: weathercock!

FRANCESCO. Oh, yeah? All right. If that's the way you want it, see you later! (*he exits*).

DIEGO (*starts after him*). Hey, let's not be silly about this!

DORO (*holding him back*). Let him go!

DIEGO. But are you serious? You'll end up in a lot of trouble!

DORO. I don't give a damn!

DIEGO (*pulling free*). You are crazy! ... Let me go! (*He hurries off attempting to catch up with Francesco.*)

DORO (*shouts after him*): I forbid you to interfere! (*Losing sight of him, he starts pacing the drawing room up and down, muttering between his teeth*) Look at that! Now! *Now* he has the nerve to come and tell me to my face that I was right! ... Weathercock... After he got everyone to believe... (*At this point Filippo enters, a bit confused, holding a calling card.*)

FILIPPO. Excuse me...

DORO (*stopping, sharply*). What is it?

FILIPPO. There's a lady to see you.

DORO. A lady?

FILIPPO. Here (*he hands him the calling card*).

DORO (*reading the name on the calling card, visibly disturbed*). Here? Where is she?

FILIPPO. She's waiting in the other room.

DORO (*looks around, perplexed; then asks, trying to hide his anxiety and distress*). And... has my mother gone out?

FILIPPO. Yes, sir. Not long ago.

DORO. Show her in, show her in. (*He goes towards the salon to receive Delia Morello. Filippo withdraws and returns soon after, accompanying Delia Morello as far as the columns. She is wearing a veil, quietly dressed, but extremely elegant. Filippo bows again and withdraws.*)

DORO. Delia! you here?

DELIA. To thank you, to kiss your hands, my friend!

DORO. No, why? What are you saying?

DELIA. Yes! Here... (*she bends as if really meaning to kiss his hand, which she is still holding in hers*) really, really!

DORO. No, no! I'm the one who owes *you*...

DELIA. For the good turn you did me!

DORO. What good turn? I only...

DELIA. ... no! I don't mean for defending me! What do I care about defences, or offences! I'm always tearing *myself* apart! I'm grateful for what you thought, for what you felt, not because you shouted it in everybody's face!

DORO (*not knowing what to say*). I thought... well, what I... knowing the facts as I did... I... I thought it was right.

DELIA. Right or wrong... it doesn't matter to me! The fact is that I recognized myself, 'recognized,' understand? in everything you said about me, as soon as I heard it!

DORO (*as above, but not wanting to show his bewilderment*). Oh, good. So... I've... I've guessed right then?

DELIA. As if you had lived in me forever. But understanding what I never understood about myself, never, never! I felt constant shivers down my spine. I shouted, 'Yes! yes! that's it! that's it!' You can't imagine with what joy, with what pangs of emotion I saw myself, I felt myself in all the reasons that came to you!

DORO. I'm... I'm happy, believe me. Happy because they seemed so clear to me at that moment when they 'came to me' – really – without much thought, as if... as if by some inspiration that had dawned in me – yes, that's it – by some intuition into your soul – and that – to tell the truth, was all...

DELIA. Oh, that was all?

DORO. Yes. But, if now you tell me that you've recognized yourself in them...

DELIA. My dear friend, ever since this morning I've been living in this insight of yours, which has seemed true to me too! So much so that I've been asking myself how it came to you, since actually you know me so little, while I've been tossed, suffering – I don't know – as if I were literally beside myself! as if I must be condemned forever to pursue the person I am, to restrain her, to ask her what she wants, why she's in pain, what I should do to subdue her, to soothe her, to give her peace!

DORO. Yes, that's it, some peace! You need that badly.

DELIA. He's constantly before my eyes, as I saw him, coming at me suddenly and falling at my feet, pale, heavy; I felt the life in me – I don't know – sputtering out, as I leaned over to look in the abyss of that moment at the eternity of that sudden death, there, on his face, become in a moment devoid of all memories, extinguished. And I alone, I alone knew what life there had been in that head that had shattered there because of me – because of me, I who am nothing! I felt I was out of my mind. Imagine how I feel now!

DORO. Please, calm down, calm yourself.

DELIA. I do calm down. And as soon as I calm down – there, see? – I feel like this – as if I were deafened. Deafened all over my body. Exactly like that. I clutch myself and I don't feel as if I'm there. I look at my hands, and they don't seem mine. And all the things – my god, the

things one must do – I don't know any more why they have to be
done. I open my bag, I take out my mirror, and in the horror of this
empty coldness that comes over me, you can't imagine how they
make me feel, in the oval of that mirror – my painted lips, my
painted eyes, this face I have ruined turning it into a mask.

DORO (*emotionally*). Because you don't look at them with other people's
eyes.

DELIA. You too? Am I really condemned to hate like enemies everyone
I come closer to, so they can help me to understand myself? Dazzled
by my eyes, my mouth... And nobody who really cares about what
I need most!

DORO. About your soul, yes.

DELIA. And that's why I punish them right where they lust after me.
First I provoke them, these desires that disgust me; so I can take my
revenge better later on – giving my body to those they'd least expect
me to. (*Doro nods his head affirmatively, as if to say: 'unfortunately!'*)
Just to show them how I despise what they most appreciate about
me (*Doro again assents with a motion of his head.*) Have I hurt myself
by such behaviour? Yes, I always did. Oh, but I'd rather deal with
scoundrels, scoundrels who don't pretend to be anything else –
who, even though they make you sad, don't disappoint you. And
who may even have some good qualities, a certain naïveté at times,
which is all the more cheering and refreshing because we don't
expect it from them!

DORO (*surprised*). That's exactly what I said...

DELIA (*feverishly*). ... yes, yes...

DORO. ... that's exactly how I explained the strange...

DELIA. ... the strange things I did, yes! – the wild leaps, somersaults...
(*she is suddenly transfixed, staring into space, as if absorbed in a faraway
vision*). Look! ... (*Then, as if talking to herself*) It seems impossible...
Of course... Somersaults... (*absorbed again*). That little girl the gypsies
were teaching to do somersaults, in a green field next to my little
country house, when I was a child... (*as above*). It seems impossible
that I was ever a child... (*she imitates, without explaining, how her mother
used to call her*) – 'Lilí, Lilí' – How afraid she was of those gypsies: that
they might suddenly pick up their tents and carry me off! (*Returning
to herself*) They didn't carry me off. But I did learn to do somersaults,
by myself, coming from the country to the city – here – among all
this pretence, all this falsity, that gets worse all the time – and we
can't get free of it, because if we try to reconstruct it in ourselves,

around us, simplicity looks false – looks? no, it *is*, it's false, it's fake. Nothing is true any more! And I want to see, I want to feel – to feel at least one thing, at least one single thing that is true, really true, in myself!

DORO. But this goodness that is in you, hidden, as I tried to make the others see...

DELIA. ...yes, yes! and I'm so grateful, yes – but that too, it's so complicated – complicated, so much so that you've brought down on yourself the anger and the laughter of everybody, to explain it. You've explained it for me too. Yes, I was disliked by everybody, as you said, treated with suspicion by everybody, there at Capri. (I believe some people even thought I was a spy). I made quite a discovery there, my friend. I discovered that 'loving humanity' only means being satisfied with oneself. When one is satisfied with oneself, he 'loves humanity.' He must have been full of this love – oh, gloriously full! – when, after the last show of his paintings in Naples, he came to Capri...

DORO. ... Giorgio Salvi? ...

DELIA. To do some landscape studies... And finding me in that state of mind...

DORO. ... there you are! exactly as I said! Completely wrapped up in his art, with no room for any other feeling.

DELIA. Colour! For him feelings were nothing but colours!

DORO. He asked you to sit for a portrait...

DELIA. ... yes, at first. Then... He had quite a way of asking for what he wanted, quite a way... He was impudent, like a child. And I was his model. You said it perfectly: nothing hurts us more than to feel shut out from a joy...

DORO. ... a living joy, present before us, around us, which we don't see or intuit the reason for...

DELIA. Exactly! I was a joy... a pure joy... only for his eyes... but that showed me that he too, basically, didn't value, and didn't want from me, anything but my body. Not like the others, of course, for low purposes, no!

DORO. But that in the long run could only hurt you even more...

DELIA. ... that's it! Because if getting no help for anxiety and uncertainty from those others had always angered and nauseated me, then my disgust for someone who also wanted my body, and nothing else, but only to get from it a joy...

DORO. ... an ideal joy...

DELIA. ... exclusively for himself! ...

DORO. ... must have been even stronger, since there was no reason for revulsion...

DELIA. ... and made it impossible for me to take the sudden revenge that at least I was able to take on the others! – To a woman an angel is always more irritating than a beast!

DORO (*beaming*). Listen! My words exactly! Exactly what I said!

DELIA. But I'm repeating your words, just as they were related to me. They've shed so much light...

DORO. ... ah, yes! ... so you could see the real reason...

DELIA. ... for what I did! Yes, yes, it's true, to be able to take my revenge, I made my body gradually become alive before him, no longer for the pleasure of his eyes alone...

DORO. ... and when you saw him conquered and enslaved like all the others, to better enjoy your revenge, you forbade him to take from it any other joy than the one he'd been content with up to that point...

DELIA. ... as the only one he should get, the only one worthy of him!

DORO. So, having taken your revenge, you didn't want him to marry you at all, right?

DELIA. No, no. I had to struggle so hard, so hard to try to change his mind! When he got angry, exasperated at my obstinate rejection, and threatened to do crazy things, I wanted to get away, to disappear.

DORO. And then you imposed the conditions you knew were the hardest for him to accept... on purpose...

DELIA. ... on purpose, yes, on purpose...

ORO. ... that is, that he introduce you as his future bride to his mother and sister...

DELIA. ... yes, yes, of whose reserve and purity he was very proud and jealous... on purpose, so that he would refuse! Oh, how he talked about that little sister of his!

DORO. Exactly! Then it was just as I maintained! – and please tell me the truth, here – when the sister's fiancé, Mr. Rocca...

DELIA (*horrified*). ... no, please! Don't talk about him to me, for god's sake!

DORO. But this is the major evidence for all the ideas I brought out, and you've got to tell me, you've got to tell me that it's true, what I maintained...

DELIA. ... yes. That I gave myself to him in desperation, pure desperation, when I saw no other way out...

DORO. ...right! exactly! ...

DELIA. ... to let him catch me, to make him catch me, and so prevent that marriage...

DORO. ... that would have meant unhappiness for him...

DELIA. ... and for me too! for me too! ...

DORO (*triumphant*). ... exactly! just what I maintained myself! That's what I said in your defence! ... And that imbecile kept saying, no! that all the rejections, the struggle, the threats, the attempt to disappear, were all deceitful schemes...

DELIA (*struck*). ... he said that? ...

DORO. ... yes! well thought out, and devised to reduce Salvi to desperation, after you seduced him...

DELIA. ... ah, so! I... seduced? ...

DORO. ... exactly! ... and that the more he despaired, the more you denied yourself to him, to get a lot of things, which he'd never have granted you otherwise...

DELIA (*increasingly shaken and increasingly bewildered*). ... like what? ...

DORO. ... well, first of all, that introduction to the mother, to the little sister, and her fiancé...

DELIA. ... oh, and not because I was hoping to find a pretext in his refusal to scrap the promise of marriage? ...

DORO. ... no, not at all, it was another one of your wicked schemes, he maintained...

DELIA (*totally confused*). ... and that was? ...

DORO. ... for the pleasure of showing yourself, appearing victorious, before everybody in society, side by side with the purity of that little sister of his – you – the despised one, the contaminated one...

DELIA (*stabbed to the heart*). ... that's what he said? ... (*Her eyes have gone blank, she is crushed.*)

DORO. ... that's it, that's what he said! and that when you found out that the reason for the prolonged postponement of that introduction you'd set as a condition was the fierce opposition of Mr Rocca, the sister's fiancé...

DELIA. ... again to take revenge, right? ...

DORO. ... yes, and wickedly,...

DELIA. ... for that opposition? ...

DORO. ... yes, then, you lured and swept Mr Rocca off like a straw in a whirlwind, without a thought for Mr Salvi, just for the pleasure of showing that sister what the pride and the honesty of such virtuous defenders of morality as her fiancé really are! (*Delia remains silent for a long time looking in front of her, as if she has lost her senses, then suddenly*

covers her face with her hands, and remains motionless. After looking at her
for a while, Doro, perplexed and surprised:) What is it?

DELIA (*remains still for a while, with her face hidden; then uncovers it and*
stares in front of her for a while; finally lifts her arms in a desolate gesture).
And who knows, my friend, if that's not really why I did it?

DORO (*bursts out*). What? But then? (*At this point Lady Livia arrives, very*
upset and agitated, shouting, while still in the inner room.)

LADY LIVIA. Doro, Doro!

DORO (*rising immediately in a very troubled voice*). My mother!

LADY LIVIA (*bursting into the room*). Doro, I was out for my walk and they
told me that last night's scandal will have a chivalrous sequel!

DORO. No, who told you that?

LADY LIVIA (*turning to Delia, disdainfully*). ... Oh yes? And I even find
this lady in my house?

DORO (*firmly, stressing the words*). Yes, in your house, Mother!

DELIA. I'm going, I'm going. Oh, this won't happen. It won't. You can
be calm, madam. I'll prevent it. I'll see to preventing it! (*She exits*
quickly, violently agitated.)

DORO (*following her for a few steps*). Please, madam, don't take the risk of
interfering. (*Delia has disappeared.*)

LADY LIVIA (*shouting, to stop him*). So it's actually true?

DORO (*turning and shouting in exasperation*). True? What? ... That I'll
fight a duel? ... maybe. ... But why? For something nobody understands – nobody knows what it is, how it is! neither he nor I... and
not even she herself! not even she herself!

CURTAIN

FIRST CHORAL INTERMEZZO

(*Very soon after the curtain has been lowered, it is raised again to show the part of*
the theatre lobby that leads to the orchestra-level seats and boxes – and eventually
to the stage, seen way in the back. The spectators are seen gradually filing out, after
seeing the first act of the play. [Many others are coming out through other exits that
are unseen; quite a number of them, in fact, arrive from time to time from the left.]

With this representation of the theatre lobby and of an audience that has seen
the first act of the play, what during the act on stage had been in the foreground
and appeared to be the representation of an event in real life, now reveals itself to
have been an artistic invention, and is therefore more or less distanced, pushed

into the background. Later, when this choral intermezzo is about to end, this theatre lobby and the spectators will also, in turn, be pushed even further into the background, when it is learned that the play presented on the stage is a comédie à clef, *based by the author, that is, on an event that is actually supposed to have taken place and has been reported recently in the newspapers: the case of Miss Moreno [*'everybody knows who she is'*] and Baron Nuti and the sculptor Giacomo La Vela who committed suicide because of them. The presence of Miss Moreno and Baron Nuti in the theatre, among the spectators, establishes a first plane of reality, closer to life, leaving the uninvolved spectators, who discuss and grow passionate about a mere invention of art, in the middle. Later, in the second choral intermezzo, all three planes of reality will come into conflict, when, moving from one plane to the other, the real characters of the drama attack the fictional ones of the play, and the spectators try to intervene. Then it will not be possible to complete the performance of the play.*

Meanwhile, for this first intermezzo, a voluble naturalness and fluid liveliness are strongly recommended. It is common knowledge by now that at the end of each act of Pirandello's irritating plays arguments and antagonisms arise. Those who defend them must show to their unyielding adversaries that smiling humility which usually has the marvellous effect of stirring things up even further.

First a number of groups should form, with someone seen moving from one to the other now and then in search of enlightenment. It is useful, as well as amusing, to see opinions visibly change, two or three times, after two or three opposing opinions are heard above the din. Some peace-loving spectator may smoke, smoking away his boredom, if he is bored; his doubts, if he has doubts; for the vice of smoking, like any other vice that has become a habit, has this sad characteristic, that it no longer, except very rarely, gives pleasure in itself, but takes its quality from the moment in which it is being satisfied and the state of mind in which it is satisfied. Thus those who are simply irritated can also smoke, if they want to, and get their irritation to vanish into smoke.

Above the crowd the plumes of the hats of two carabinieri are seen. A few usherettes and doormen; two or three private box attendants, dressed in black with white aprons. A few newspaper boys shout the headlines of the papers. In the groups an occasional woman here and there. I wish these women would not smoke. But perhaps more than one is smoking. Others are seen visiting from one box to another.

The five drama critics are very cautious at first, especially when asked, about expressing their views. They are gradually drawn together, to exchange their first impressions. The indiscreet friends who draw close to them in order to hear immediately attract many curious spectators, so the critics stop talking or move to another place. It is not out of the question that one or the other of them who is blasting the work and its author here in the lobby will say good things about them tomorrow in his newspaper. For the profession is one thing, quite another the man who professes it for reasons of convenience, which compel him to sacrifice his sincerity [this applies, of course, when the sacrifice is possible: I mean, if he has any sincerity to sacrifice]. Similarly, those same spectators who have applauded the first act of the play inside, may prove to be harsh denigrators here in the lobby.

This first intermezzo could easily be improvised, since the statements made indiscriminately about all the plays of this author are well known and often repeated: 'cerebral,' 'paradoxical,' 'obscure,' 'absurd,' 'impossible.' However, here are some of the most important lines for one or another of the occasional actors of this intermezzo, which do not exclude others that can be improvised to keep the confused animation of the lobby alive.

First the brief exclamations, questions, and answers of indifferent spectators, who are exiting first, while the dull hubbub of the audience is still heard from inside.)

BETWEEN TWO EXITING HURRIEDLY. I'm going up, I'm going up to see him! / Second row, number eight! But tell him, tell him, please! (*Going off to the left*) / For sure. Leave it to me!

SOMEONE COMING IN FROM THE LEFT. Oh, so you got a seat?

SOMEONE WHO IS LEAVING HURRIEDLY. As you can see! See you later. (*He is off.*) (*Now others come in from the left, where many voices are also heard; others come out through the wide centre door; others come out of the small individual doors of the boxes.*)

ONE SPECTATOR. What a roomful, eh?

ANOTHER. Great, really great!

A THIRD. Have you seen whether the ladies have come?

A FOURTH. No, I don't believe so. (*Greetings exchanged here and there: 'Good evening! Good evening!' – Nothing to do with the play. Some introductions. Meanwhile spectators favourably inclined to the author, their faces aglow and their eyes sparkling, seek each other out and keep together for a while to exchange their first impressions, then scatter around, approaching this group or that to defend the play and the author, petulantly and with irony, from the criticism of their unyielding adversaries who, in the meantime, have also sought each other out.*)

THE FAVOURABLY INCLINED SPECTATORS. – Ah! here we are!

– All set!

– It's going really well, isn't it?

– Ah! fresh air at last!

– That last scene with the woman!

– And she, the woman!

– And the scene with those two switching from one side to the other!

THE SPECTATORS WHO ARE NOT FAVOURABLY INCLINED (*at the same time*).
- The usual word games! Go figure what they mean!
- They 're pulling our legs!
- It seems to me he's beginning to feel a bit overconfident!
- I didn't understand a thing!
- A bunch of riddles!
- Heck, if the theatre has to be torture!

ONE OF THE NOT FAVOURABLY INCLINED SPECTATORS (*to the other group*).
Oh you people understand everything, don't you?

ANOTHER NOT FAVOURABLY INCLINED ONE. Of course, of course! All
geniuses, those guys!

ONE OF THE FAVOURABLY INCLINED GROUP (*approaching*). Are you
talking to me?

THE FIRST OF THE NOT FAVOURABLY INCLINED GROUP. Not to you, to
him! (*pointing to another of the approving spectators*).

THE ONE WHO HAS BEEN POINTED AT (*approaching*). To me? Are you
talking to me?

THE FIRST OF THE NOT FAVOURABLY INCLINED GROUP. To you! To you!
You wouldn't understand even a school play, my friend!

THE ONE WHO HAS BEEN POINTED TO. Yeah! And *you* understand that
this is stuff to shove aside with a kick, right? like a stone in the
street!

VOICES FROM A NEARBY GROUP.
- But what do you think there is to understand? Haven't you heard?
Nobody knows anything!
- Just listen to them – It is, it isn't – they say one thing, and then they
say the opposite!
- It seems like a joke to me!
- And all that dialogue at the beginning?
- It didn't lead to any conclusion!

ONE WHO PRETENDS TO KNOW (*moving to another group*). Yeah, it seems
like a joke. Nobody knows anything!

VOICES OF ANOTHER GROUP
- One thing's sure, it's interesting!
- All right, but this constant turning on the same pivot!
- That's not what it is! I don't think so!
- It's all a certain way of understanding, of conceiving things!
- And has he shown that? Then enough already!
- Yes, enough! enough! I can't stand it any more!
- But you were applauding! Yes, you were, I saw you!

– But you know, a conception of life, if it's a total conception, can
have so many different sides to it!

– What conception? Can you tell me what this act was all about?

– Well! That's smart! And what if it doesn't try to be 'about' anything? If it tries to show the continual reversals of our convictions
and feelings?

THE ONE WHO PRETENDS TO KNOW (*moving to another group*). That's it!
That's what it is! Perhaps it doesn't try to be about anything. On
purpose! on purpose, understand? It's the play about turn-abouts!

VOICES OF A THIRD GROUP (*around the drama critics*).

– All this is crazy! What's going on here?

– You are the professional critics, *you* enlighten us.

FIRST CRITIC. Well, the act has various motifs. Perhaps too many.

ONE OF THE GROUP. All that stuff about conscience!

SECOND CRITIC. Gentlemen, this is only the first act.

THIRD CRITIC. But let's tell the truth! Do you think it's right, to destroy
the nature of characters in this way? to move the action so casually,
with no logical order? to pick up the story, in such an offhand way,
after an argument?

FOURTH CRITIC. But the argument is about this play. It *is* the play!

SECOND CRITIC. And it appears live after all, in the end, in the woman!

THIRD CRITIC. Well, I'd like to see the drama played out and nothing
else!

ONE OF THE APPROVING SPECTATORS. And the woman is perfectly drawn!

ONE OF THE DISAPPROVING SPECTATORS. What you're saying, rather, is
that Miss (*he names the actress who plays the part of Miss Morello*) has
played her to perfection.

THE ONE WHO PRETENDS TO KNOW (*returning to the first group*). The
drama is live, live in the woman! That can't be denied! Everybody
says so!

ONE OF THE FIRST GROUP (*answering him indignantly*). Oh go on! It's a
tangled mess of contradictions!

ANOTHER (*also indignant*). It's the usual sophistry! I can't stand it any
more!

A THIRD ONE (*as above*). It's all dialectical traps! Cerebral acrobatics!

THE ONE WHO PRETENDS TO KNOW (*leaving to move to the second group*).
Ah yes, of course, the usual sophistry! It can't be denied. Everybody
says so!

FOURTH CRITIC (*to the third*). But what characters, at this point, if you
don't mind! Where do you find characters in life any more?

THIRD CRITIC. Oh, come on, by the simple fact that words exist!

FOURTH CRITIC. Words, of course, words, and the author wants to show
how they can be turned about!

FIFTH CRITIC. Here's the thing: if the theatre, I'm asking, which, unless
I'm mistaken, is supposed to be art...

ONE OF THE DISAPPROVING SPECTATORS. ... right, right! poetry, poetry!

FIFTH CRITIC. ... should instead be controversy – admirably done, I don't
deny it – disagreements, quarrels, clash of opposing arguments!

ONE OF THE APPROVING SPECTATORS. But it's you who're doing the
arguing here! I didn't realize that any was going on on the stage!
Unless for you unreasoning passion is reasoning...

ONE OF THE DISAPPROVING SPECTATORS. Here we have a famous author:
you tell us, *you* tell us!

THE OLD, UNSUCCESSFUL AUTHOR. Ah, as far as I am concerned, if you
want him, you can have him! You know what I think of him.

VOICES. No, no! Tell us, tell us!

THE OLD, UNSUCCESSFUL AUTHOR. Well, they're tiny intellectual con-
cerns, gentlemen, the kind of... the kind of... – how shall I put it – of
trivial philosophical problems you can buy four for a penny!

FOURTH CRITIC. Oh no, you can't say that!

THE OLD, UNSUCCESSFUL AUTHOR (*grandiosely*). And no profound
spiritual travail that's born of simple and truly convincing forces!

FOURTH CRITIC. Oh, yes, we know, we know these 'simple and truly
convincing forces'!

A MAN OF LETTERS WHO DOES NOT STOOP TO WRITING. What in my
opinion is most offensive is the lack of courtesy, that's all.

SECOND CRITIC. No, no! On the contrary, I think this time there's more
air than usual blowing through the act!

THE MAN OF LETTERS WHO DOES NOT STOOP TO WRITING. Go on! But there
is no real artistic judgment! We'd all be good at that kind of writing!

FOURTH CRITIC. As far as I'm concerned, I don't want to make a
judgment this early, but I see flashes, flickers of light. I have the
impression of a mirror gone crazy, giving off sparks. (*A violent clamour
is heard at this point, from the left. Shouts of: 'Yes, a madhouse, a madhouse!'
'Machine! Tricks! Tricks!' 'A madhouse! a madhouse!' Many people run in,
shouting: 'What's going on over there?'*)

THE ANNOYED SPECTATOR. Why does the end of the world have to come
at every debut of a Pirandello play?

THE PEACEFULLY INCLINED SPECTATOR. Let's hope they don't beat each
other up!

ONE OF THE APPROVING SPECTATORS. Well, this is really something! When you come to see a play by another author, you sink into your chair and get ready to take in the illusion the scene tries to create for you, if it succeeds in creating one! When you come to see a Pirandello play, you grab the arms of your chair with both hands, this way, you sit up this way, with your head ready to butt, to reject at all costs what the author's telling you. You hear a word, any word – let's say 'chair' – Oh, my God, did'ya hear? he said 'chair.' But he doesn't fool me! God knows what's under that chair!

ONE OF THE DISAPPROVING SPECTATORS. Yes, yes, granted, all of it – but there's not one bit of poetry!

OTHER DISAPPROVING SPECTATORS. Right! Right! And we want a bit of poetry! Some poetry!

ANOTHER APPROVING SPECTATOR. Yeah, sure! Go and look under the chairs of other writers for poetry!

THE DISAPPROVING SPECTATORS.
   – Enough, enough of these fits of nihilism!
   – And this wallowing in destruction!
   – Negating is not building!

THE FIRST OF THE APPROVING SPECTATORS. Who's negating? You're negating!

ONE OF THE ADDRESSEES. *We* are? *We* never said that reality doesn't exist!

THE FIRST OF THE APPROVING SPECTATORS. And who's negating it, your reality? – that is, if you've ever succeeded in creating it?

A SECOND ONE. You yourselves negate it, by saying that there's only one…

THE FIRST. … the one that seems to you to be it, today…

THE SECOND. … forgetting that yesterday you thought it was something different!

THE FIRST. Because you get it from others, like any convention, an empty word – mountain, tree, road – you believe there's a 'given' reality; and you think there's been fraud if someone reveals to you the fact that it's an illusion! Fools! Here we're taught that each of us must build the ground under our feet by ourselves, each time, for every step we try to take, making everything that doesn't belong to you crumble, because you hadn't built it yourself and were walking on it as parasites, parasites, lamenting for the lost, ancient poetry!

BARON NUTI (*coming in from the left, pale, beside himself, shaking, in the company of two* spectators *who try to restrain him*). But it's another thing they're teaching here, sir: to trample on the dead and to slander the living!

ONE OF THE TWO WHO ACCOMPANY HIM (*taking him immediately by the arm
to lead him away*). No, no, come away! come away!

THE OTHER MAN WHO ACCOMPANIES HIM (*at the same time, doing the same*).
Let's go, let's go! For goodness sake, let it be!

BARON NUTI (*as he is being led away towards the left, turns around to repeat
violently*). To trample on the dead and slander the living!

VOICES OF CURIOUS BYSTANDERS (*in the general surprise*).

– Who was that?
– Who is he?
– What a face!
– He looks like a corpse!
– Crazy!
– Who could he be?

THE WORLDLY SPECTATOR. It's Baron Nuti! Baron Nuti!

VOICES OF CURIOUS SPECTATORS.

– And who knows him?
– Baron Nuti?
– Why did you say that?

THE WORLDLY SPECTATOR. What? Hasn't anybody understood yet that
the play is a *comédie à clef?*

ONE OF THE CRITICS. *À clef?* What do you mean?

THE WORLDLY SPECTATOR. Yes, yes! The case of Miss Moreno! The exact
same one! Taken entirely from life!

VOICES.

– Of Miss Moreno?
– And who's she?
– Oh, come on! The actress who was in Germany for such a long time!
– Everybody in Turin knows who she is!
– Oh, yes! The one mixed up in the suicide of the sculptor, La Vela,
that happened a few months ago!
– Oh, look at that! And Pirandello?
– What? Pirandello has started writings *comédies à clef* now?
– It looks that way!
– And it isn't the first time!
– But is it legitimate to take the subject of a work of art from life!?
– Sure, at least if when you do it, you don't – as the gentleman
said – trample on the dead and slander the living!
– But who's that Nuti?

THE WORLDLY SPECTATOR. The one who La Vela killed himself over!
Who was going to be his brother-in-law!

ANOTHER OF THE CRITICS. Because he was caught with Miss Moreno? Right before the wedding?

ONE OF THE DISAPPROVING SPECTATORS. But then, the facts are exactly the same! It's horrible, for god's sake!

ANOTHER. So we have in the theatre two actors from the real-life drama?

A THIRD ONE (*meaning Baron Nuti and pointing towards the left*). And there's one of them!

THE WORLDLY SPECTATOR. And Miss Moreno is upstairs, hidden in a third-row box! She recognized herself in the play immediately! They're holding her there, they're restraining her, because she seems really crazy! She's shredded three handkerchiefs between her teeth! She's going to shout, you'll see! She's going to make a scene!

VOICES

    – Of course, she's right!

    – Seeing herself put in a play!

    – The staging of her own case!

    – And the other guy too! My god, he really scared me!

    – It's going to end badly, it's going to end badly! (*The bells announcing the resumption of the performance are ringing.*)

    – They're ringing the bells, they're ringing the bells!

    – Act Two's beginning!

    – Let's go and see! Let's go and see!

(*A general movement towards the entrance to the hall, with subdued voices, confused comments on the news that is spreading gradually. Three of the favourable spectators remain a little behind, in time to see, in the lobby already emptied of spectators, Miss Moreno rushing in from the left; she has come down from her third-row box and is restrained by three friends who would like to get her out of the theatre to prevent her from making a scene. The theatre ushers, stunned at first, gesture to them to keep quiet so that the performance is not disturbed. The three favourable spectators draw back a little to listen, surprised and alarmed.*)

MISS MORENO. No, no! Let me go, let me go!

ONE OF HER FRIENDS. But it's crazy! What d'ya want to do?

MISS MORENO. I want to go on the stage!

THE OTHER. But for what? Are you mad?

MISS MORENO. Let me go!

THE THIRD FRIEND. Let's get out of here, instead!

THE OTHER TWO, Yes, out! out! Listen to us!

MISS MORENO, No, I want to punish, I have to punish this disgraceful thing!

THE FIRST. But how? Before the entire audience?

MISS MORENO. On the stage!

THE SECOND. Absolutely not! We won't let you do this crazy thing!

MISS MORENO. Let me go, I said. I want to go out on the stage.

THE THIRD. But the actors are on stage already!

THE FIRST. The second act has already started!

MISS MORENO (*changing her mind suddenly*). Has it started? I want to see, then! I want to see! (*She turns to the left to re-enter.*)

HER FRIENDS. No, let's go! Listen to us! Let's go away!

MISS MORENO (*dragging them along*). No, let's go up! Let's go back to the box, immediately! I want to see! I want to see!

ONE OF HER FRIENDS (*while they disappear to the left*). But why do you want to go on tormenting yourself?

ONE OF THE USHERS (*to the three favourable spectators*). Are they crazy?

THE FIRST OF THE APPROVING SPECTATORS (*to the other two*). Do you understand?

THE SECOND. Was that Miss Moreno?

THE THIRD. Tell me, is Pirandello backstage?

THE FIRST. I'm running up to tell him to get away. This evening is not going to end peacefully, that's for sure!

CURTAIN

ACT TWO

(*We are at the home of Francesco Savio, the next morning, in a narrow hallway that opens to a spacious veranda, which serves Savio as a fencing hall. Through the large glass wall at the back of the narrow hallway we see a platform, a long bench for friends and spectators, masks, gloves, quilted fencing jackets, foils, sabres. A green cloth curtain, on rings this side of the glass wall, when drawn from either side of the central door, can conceal the veranda and make the narrow hallway a private space. Another curtain of the same material, running on iron rods at the rear end of the veranda cuts off the veranda from the view of the garden beyond, a bit of which can be seen when anyone, to get down into the garden, separates the two halves of the curtain in the middle, above the steps. The furniture of the hallway consists only of a few wicker chairs painted green, two love seats, and two coffee tables also of wicker. There is a window on the left-hand side and a door on the right, – in addition to the door to the veranda.*

As the curtain rises, Francesco Savio and his fencing master are seen on the veranda in masks, jackets, and gloves, fencing at epée. Prestino and two Friends are watching.)

THE FENCING MASTER. Open up! Open up your invitation! Watch out
for this disengage! Good! Very good inquartata! Careful now! Stop
thrust! Opposition! Cut out the invitations and feints now! Watch out
for the riposte! Stop! (*They stop fencing.*) Very good! A good counter-
attack. (*They lift their masks.*)

FRANCESCO. Enough. And thank you, Maestro. (*He shakes his hand.*)

PRESTINO. Enough, yes, enough!

THE FENCING MASTER (*taking off his glove and jacket*). But you'll see, it's
not going to be easy with Palegari, because when he opens himself to
attack, he foresees...

THE FIRST FRIEND. ... and his parrying is perfect, be careful!

THE OTHER FRIEND. All his moves are very fast! Very!

FRANCESCO. Yes, I know, I know! (*He too takes off his glove and jacket.*)

FIRST FRIEND. You've got to keep moving, all the time!

THE FENCING MASTER. And engage his weapon constantly.

FRANCESCO. All right, all right!

OTHER FRIEND. The thing to do, if you get a chance, is to give him a
good direct hit!

FIRST FRIEND. No. A stop thrust, a stop would be best. Listen to me.
You'll see, you'll slip one in!

THE FENCING MASTER. My compliments, in any case, your disengage is
magnificent.

PRESTINO. Take my advice: leave yourself open to anything. You both
get out of it with the usual scratch on the wrist. Give us something to
drink to your health with, why don't you? (*He comes into the hallway
with the others.*)

FRANCESCO. Right, right (*presses an electric bell on the wall, then turns to the
fencing master*): You, Maestro, would you like a drink?

THE FENCING MASTER. No, nothing for me, I never drink in the morning.

FRANCESCO. I have some excellent beer.

PRESTINO. Good, yes!

FIRST FRIEND. Let's have a beer! (*A servant appears at the door on the right.*)

FRANCESCO. Bring us a few bottles of beer, right away. (*The servant
withdraws and returns soon after with a bottle and several glasses on a tray:
he pours, serves, and withdraws.*)

THE FIRST. It's going to be the funniest duel in the world, you can boast
about it!

OTHER FRIEND. Yeah! I don't think there's ever been a case of two
people duelling because each one insisted the other was right.

PRESTINO. But of course! Very natural!

FIRST FRIEND. No. Why very natural?

PRESTINO. They were moving in opposite directions; they both turned at the same time to go in the other direction, so they had to meet, to clash with one another...

THE FENCING MASTER. ... of course! Since the former accuser now wants to be the defender, and vice versa – each one using the other's reasoning...

FIRST FRIEND. ... are you sure of this?

FRANCESCO. Believe me, I went to him with my heart in my hand, and...

FIRST FRIEND. ... and not because you felt...

FRANCESCO. ... no, no, without...

FIRST FRIEND. ... no, I mean, that you had inadvertently made a big mistake, accusing Miss Morello so furiously... ?

FRANCESCO. ... no, no, I...

FIRST FRIEND. ... let me finish, for god's sake! I mean without realizing what was so plain to everybody, that night... ?

OTHER FRIEND. ... that he was defending her because he was in love with her... ?

FRANCESCO. ... not at all! And that's exactly why the two of us clashed! because I didn't take that into consideration, either before or after. You're made to look like an imbecile... And then they call you one, for letting yourself get caught in a moment... in a spontaneous act... which now is having all these ridiculous consequences. I was planning to go relax with my sister and brother-in-law in the country today. They're waiting for me!

PRESTINO. The night before, he'd discussed the thing objectively, coolly...

FRANCESCO. ... without seeing anything else, I swear, beyond my own arguments, and without the least suspicion that he might have secret feelings!

OTHER FRIEND. But does he really?

FIRST FRIEND. Oh yes! oh yes!

PRESTINO. He must, it's clear he does!

FRANCESCO. If I'd suspected it, I wouldn't have gone to his house to admit that he was right, I'd have known for sure that I'd irritate him!

OTHER FRIEND. I wanted... wait a moment... I wanted to say, for one thing... (*he remains confused, lost, all look at him in anticipation*).

FIRST FRIEND (*after waiting for a while*). ... what? ...

OTHER FRIEND. ... something... Gosh! I've forgotten.

DIEGO CINCI (*he has just appeared at the door stage right*). May I?

FRANCESCO (*surprised*). Oh, Diego, it's you?

PRESTINO. Did anybody send you?

DIEGO (*with a shrug*). Who would have sent me?! ... Good morning, Maestro.

THE FENCING MASTER. Good morning, dear Cinci. But I'm on my way out (*he shakes hands with Savio*). See you tomorrow morning, dear Savio. And keep calm, right?

FRANCESCO. Very calm, don't worry. Thank you.

THE FENCING MASTER (*to the others, waving his hand*). Gentlemen, I'm sorry to leave you all, but I have to go. (*The others respond to his salutation.*)

FRANCESCO. Maestro, if you like, you can get out this way (*points to the veranda door*). Open the curtain there, go down the steps, and you're right in the garden.

THE FENCING MASTER. Thanks, I'll do that. Goodbye, everybody. (*He leaves.*)

FIRST FRIEND (*to Diego*). We expected you to act as Doro Palegari's second.

DIEGO (*first wagging his finger in denial*). I didn't want to. I found myself in the middle, last night. I'm friends with both, I wanted to keep out of it.

OTHER FRIEND. And why did you come now?

DIEGO. To say that I am very happy that you're going to fight.

PRESTINO. Very happy is going a bit too far! (*the others burst out laughing*).

DIEGO. And I'd like both of them to jab each other, without serious consequences. A little bloodletting would be healthy. And, you know, a nice little wound; it's a thing you can be sure of: two, three centimetres, maybe five... (*he takes Francesco's arm and lifts the sleeve a bit*). Let's see your wrist. Nothing's there. But tomorrow morning you'll have a nice little wound here you can admire.

FRANCESCO. Thanks for the nice comforting thought! (*The others burst out laughing again.*)

DIEGO (*immediately*). He too, hopefully, he too... we musn't be selfish! Want to hear something amazing? Guess who paid Palegari a visit after you left and I ran after you?

PRESTINO. Delia Morello?

OTHER FRIEND. She probably went there to thank him for defending her!

DIEGO. Yeah. Except that when she heard what you said in your accusation – do you know what she did?

FRANCESCO. What?

DIEGO. She said you were right.

FRANCESCO, PRESTINO, AND FIRST FRIEND (*together*). Oh, yes? ... How nice! ... And he, Doro?

DIEGO. You can imagine how he felt.

THE OTHER. He mustn't know any more why he is fighting a duel!

FRANCESCO. No, that he does know! He's going to fight because he has insulted me, in your presence; while I – as I was saying to my friends here, and as you yourself were able to see – had gone to him to admit in all sincerity that he'd been right.

DIEGO. And now?

FRANCESCO. Now, what?

DIEGO. Now that you know that Delia Morello says you are right?

FRANCESCO. Well, now... if she herself...

DIEGO. No, old man, no! Maintain your position, because now more than ever Delia Morello needs defending! And *you* must defend her, you who were her accuser!

FRANCESCO. Against herself, who now accuses herself to the one who wanted to defend her before?

DIEGO. That's why, that's why! My admiration for her multiplied a hundred times when I heard this! (*Turning to Francesco suddenly*) Who are you? (*To Prestino*) Who are you? Who am I? All of us here? Your name is Francesco Savio, mine Diego Cinci, yours Prestino... We've got mere specks of certainty about ourselves and about each other today, and they're as different from yesterday's as they are from tomorrow's... (*to Francesco*) You live on the income from your property and are bored...

FRANCESCO. No, who says that? ...

DIEGO. No, you don't get bored? That's good. I have reduced my soul to a mole's den by digging, digging away. (*To Prestino*) And you? What d'you do?

PRESTINO. Nothing.

DIEGO. A nice profession! ... But even those who work, the serious people, all of us, all of us: life, inside and outside of us – go, go and look into it! – is such a constant thief that, if even the most steady affections do not have the strength to resist it, imagine mere opinions, the fictions we're capable of creating for ourselves, all the ideas that, in this incessant flight, we're barely able to intuit! It's enough to get to know something contrary to what we knew – a certain guy was white? Now he's black – or merely to have a different impression from one hour to the other; sometimes a single word is sufficient, spoken in this or that tone. And then there are the images of a hundred things that are constantly crossing our minds, suddenly changing our mood. We walk sadly down a street already darkened by evening shadows; it's enough to raise our eyes to a little balcony still lit up by the sun, with a red geranium burning in that sun, and... god knows what faraway dream moves us suddenly...

PRESTINO. And where are you taking us with all of this?

DIEGO. Nowhere. Where do you want to get, if that's the way it is? In order to grasp something and keep your balance, you fall back into the affliction and boredom of today's small certainty, of that little bit you succeed in knowing about yourself, anyway: your name, your income, your home; your habits, your affections – all the routine things of your existence – and your poor body that still moves and can still follow the flow of life, until the motion, which gradually becomes slower and more rigid with old age, ceases altogether, and then goodnight!

FRANCESCO. But weren't you talking about Delia Morello? ...

DIEGO. ... Oh, yes... to describe my profound admiration... to tell you that it's at least a joy... a lovely, terrifying joy... when, swept up by strong feelings in a tempestuous moment, we see the crumbling of all those inauthentic forms in which our fatuous daily life has congealed; and, below the levees, beyond the limits that had allowed us to form a sort of consciousness, to construct some kind of personality, we see even that part of the flow that wasn't running unperceived within us, but was clear to us because we'd channelled it carefully into our feelings, into the duties we'd undertaken, into the habits we'd adopted, overflow in a swift, marvellous flood, upsetting and sweeping away everything. Then, at last! The hurricane! ... The eruption! ... The earthquake!

ALL THE OTHERS (*together*). And you think it's nice? ... Oh, thank you, no! ... Not for me! ... God save us!

DIEGO. Dear friends, after the farce of our endless chatter, of all our ridiculous changes of mind, behold the tragedy of a soul in disarray, who no longer knows how to get herself together! And she's not the only one! (*to Francesco*) You'll see, they'll come swooping down on you here, like the wrath of God twice over, both of them, she and he...

FRANCESCO. ... he? who? Michele Rocca?

DIEGO. Yes, him! Michele Rocca.

FIRST FRIEND. He got here last night from Naples!

OTHER FRIEND. Ah, there you are! I heard he was looking for Palegari to slap him. I meant to tell you about it a little while ago! He was looking for Palegari to slap him!

PRESTINO. Of course, we already knew it! (*to Francesco*) I told you about it.

FRANCESCO (*to Diego*). And why would he come here to my house, now?

DIEGO. Because he wants to fight a duel with Doro Palegari, before you do. But now – oh, of course! he should fight with you instead – now...

FRANCESCO. ... with me? ...

THE OTHERS TOGETHER. What? What does he mean?

DIEGO. ... oh, yes! if you've sincerely changed your mind, and so adopted as your own all the insults Palegari hurled at him at the Avanzis' house – it's clear! – the sides have been swapped – so Rocca should slap *you* now.

FRANCESCO. Slow down! What the hell are you saying?

DIEGO. Excuse me – you're fighting a duel with Doro only because he insulted you, right? Now why did Doro insult you?

FIRST AND OTHER FRIEND (*not letting him finish*). Of course! Sure! It's true! Diego is right!

DORO. The sides have been swapped, so you're left to defend Delia Morello, holding Michele Rocca responsible for everything.

PRESTINO (*offended*). Don't joke around!

DIEGO. Who's joking? (*to Francesco*) As far as I'm concerned, you may very well boast that you're on the side of reason.

FRANCESCO. And do you want me to challenge Michele Rocca too?

DIEGO. Oh no. The situation would really turn serious then. The desperation of that poor soul...

THE FIRST FRIEND. ... with Salvi's corpse lying between him and Salvi's sister, his fiancée...

THE OTHER FRIEND. ... and the marriage plans cancelled...

DIEGO. ... and Delia Morello, who's sent it up in smoke!

FRANCESCO (*exploding with irritation*). What d'you mean? How, 'sent up in smoke'? Oh, now you say, 'sent up in smoke'?

DIEGO. It's undeniable that she used him...

FRANCESCO. ... treacherously, then, as I said in the first place!

DIEGO (*disapprovingly, to stop him*). Ah, ah, ah, no, listen: the anger you're feeling because of the embarrassing situation you got yourself into mustn't make you change sides again!

FRANCESCO. Not at all! didn't you say yourself she went to confess to Doro Palegari that I'd guessed right in accusing her of treachery!

DIEGO. See? See?

FRANCESCO. What should I see? Listen: if I hear that she accuses herself and says I'm right, of course I'm going to change and go back to my earlier opinion of her! (*Addressing the others*) Aren't I right? Aren't I?

DIEGO (*forcefully*). But I tell you that she used him – even treacherously, as you put it, only to save Giorgio Salvi from the danger of marrying her! Do you understand? There's no way you can say absolutely that she acted treacherously against Salvi too – you can't! – And I'm ready to stand up for her, even if she accuses herself – against herself, yes, yes,...

FRANCESCO (*conceding angrily*). ... for all the reasons – okay – for all the reasons Doro Palegari found...

DIEGO. ... which made you...

FRANCESCO... change my mind, all right, I changed my mind. But the fact remains that what she did to Rocca was real treachery!

DIEGO. Come on... she did what women do! When he went to her, he seemed to be playing a trick on her, and she played it on him! That's what's burning Michele Rocca up: the mortification of his male ego! He can't yet confess that he was a foolish toy in the hands of a woman: a stupid little puppet that Delia Morello tossed into a corner, smashing it to pieces, after she'd enjoyed making him raise his joined hands like a beggar, by touching with her finger the wound-up spring of passion on his chest. The puppet has pulled himself upright now, the little porcelain face and hands a pitiful mess – fingers gone from the little hands, the little face missing its nose, all cracked and chipped: the spring on his chest has poked through the red satin vest, has jumped out of it, broken – and yet, no, look! the little puppet's shouting, no, it isn't true that that woman made him raise his joined hands in order to laugh at him, and that after she laughed, she smashed him to pieces. He says, no! no! I ask you, can there be a spectacle more touching than this!

PRESTINO (*flying into a rage, approaching Diego with hands raised as if to strike him*). And why are you trying to make a joke of it then, you fool?

DIEGO (*dumbfounded, like the others who are all staring at Prestino*). Me?

PRESTINO. Yes, you, you! You've been acting like a clown ever since you came in here, trying to make him, me, everybody seem ridiculous!

DIEGO. But myself too, you fool!

PRESTINO. You're the fool! It's easy to laugh at everything like that! making us out to be a bunch of weathercocks who turn the other way as soon as a bit of breeze comes up! I can't stand hearing him talk any more! I don't know, he seems to me to be burning his very soul when he talks, the way certain bad dyes burn cloth.

DIEGO. No, dear boy, I laugh because...

PRESTINO. ... you laugh because you've hollowed out your heart like the den of a mole – you've said it yourself – and there's nothing in it any more. That's why!

DIEGO. That's what you think!

PRESTINO. I think so because it's true! And even if what you say were true, that that's the way we are, I think it should make you sad, compassionate...

DIEGO (*furious himself, now, aggressively seizing Prestino's shoulders and staring into his eyes, steadily, at close range*). ... yes... if you let us look at you this way...

PRESTINO (*surprised*). ... how?

DIEGO. ... this way, straight in the eye, this way! ... no... look at me... this way... naked as you are, with all the nasty, ugly stuff you have inside... you and me both... the fears, the remorse, the contradictions! ... Tear out of you the puppet you create by your false interpretation of your actions and your feelings, and you'll discover right away that it has nothing to do with what you really are or can be, with what's in you that you don't know, and that it's a terrible god, mind you, if you even dream of opposing him, yet he immediately shows compassion for every one of your faults if you let yourself go and refuse to find excuses for yourself. Oh, but letting ourselves go seems to us a denial of ourselves, a thing unworthy of a real man; and it will always be this way as long as we believe that our humanity consists of our so-called conscience – or of the courage we've shown once, instead of the fear that's persuaded us so many times to play it safe. You've agreed to be Savio's second in this stupid duel with Palegari. (*Abruptly, to Francesco*) And you believed that Palegari was calling you a weathervane last night, in that moment? He was calling himself that! You didn't understand. He was saying it to the little puppet he couldn't see in himself, but saw in you who were holding up a mirror to him! ... I laugh... But I laugh in this way; and my laughter hurts me first of all. (*There is a pause during which all are absorbed in thought, each one thinking about himself. Each man, then, between one pause and the next, speaks as if only to himself.*)

FRANCESCO. Of course, I bear no real grudge towards Doro Palegari. He dragged me into it...

PRESTINO (*after another pause*). Often you have to give the impression that you believe. But you've got to feel more pity, not less, if lying makes us cry all the more.

FIRST FRIEND (*after another pause, as if he were reading the mind of Francesco Savio*). The countryside must be beautiful right now...

FRANCESCO (*spontaneously, showing no surprise, as if he were uttering an excuse*). I'd even bought toys to take to my little niece!

THE OTHER FRIEND. Is she still as pretty as when I saw her?

FRANCESCO. Even prettier! A darling child... So pure! A real beauty! (*While saying this he has taken a teddy bear out of a box and wound it up. Now he puts it down on the floor to make it jump, while his friends laugh. After the laughter, a sad pause.*)

DIEGO (*to Francesco*). Listen, if I were you... (*He is interrupted by the butler who appears at the side door stage right.*)

BUTLER. Excuse me.

FRANCESCO. What is it?

BUTLER. I must talk to you...

FRANCESCO (*goes up to him, listens to what the butler whispers to him, then, displeased*). No! Right now? (*turning to look at his friends, hesitant, perplexed*).

DIEGO (*immediately*). It's her?

PRESTINO. You can't receive her. You musn't!

FIRST FRIEND. Of course not, not while the challenge is still standing...

DIEGO. ... no! The challenge has nothing to do with her!

PRESTINO. Why not? She's the cause! As your second I'm telling you, no, you mustn't receive her!

OTHER FRIEND. But a lady can't be dismissed that way, without even finding out what she's come here for!

DIEGO. I'm not saying anything any more.

FIRST FRIEND (*to Francesco*). You could ask what she's here for.

OTHER FRIEND. ... right, and if by any chance...

FRANCESCO. ... she indicates that she'd like to talk about the duel? ...

PRESTINO. ... cut her short, immediately!

FRANCESCO. I want nothing better than to send her packing, you can imagine!

PRESTINO. Good! Go, go! (*Francesco exits, followed by the butler.*)

DIEGO. I think it would be a good thing if he were to advise her to... (*At this point, pushing the veranda curtain aside furiously, Michele Rocca bursts in from the garden, prey to a dark agitation he can barely restrain. He is about thirty, dark haired, consumed by remorse and passion. It is clear from his distorted face, his gestures, his entire behaviour that he is capable of any imaginable excess.*)

ROCCA. May I come in? (*surprised to find himself among so many unexpected people*). Is she here? Have I come to the right place?

PRESTINO (*dumbfounded like the others*). You can start by telling us who you are.

ROCCA. Michele Rocca.

DIEGO. Ah, here he is!

ROCCA (*to Diego*). Are you Mr Francesco Savio?

DIEGO. Not me. Savio's in there (*points to the right-hand door*).

PRESTINO. But excuse me, how did you get in here? Just like that?

ROCCA. I was shown this entrance.

DIEGO. The doorkeeper, probably thinking he was one of Francesco's friends...

ROCCA. Didn't a lady come in here, just before me?

PRESTINO. Why, were you following her perhaps?

ROCCA. Yes, I was following her! I knew she'd be coming here.

DIEGO. Me too! And I foresaw your coming too!

ROCCA. Horrible things have been said about me. I know that Mr. Savio has defended me, though he doesn't know me. Now he must not, *must not* listen to that woman, without first hearing from me how things really stand!

PRESTINO. But it's useless now, my dear sir.

ROCCA. No! Why useless?

PRESTINO. Yes, useless. Any interference is useless now!

FIRST FRIEND. There's a challenge standing and accepted...

OTHER FRIEND. ... the conditions have all been established...

DIEGO. ... and souls radically changed.

PRESTINO (*very irritated, to Diego*). Please don't get mixed up in this – stop it, once and for all, damn it!

FIRST FRIEND. You like to make things more complicated, don't you?

DIEGO. No, on the contrary! He's come here thinking that Savio had defended him... and I'm telling him that now Savio doesn't defend him any more

ROCCA. Oh yes? Now he accuses me too?

DIEGO. Not just him, believe me!

ROCCA. You too?

DIEGO. Me too, yes. And everyone here, as you can see.

ROCCA. Of course! So far you've talked only to that woman!

DIEGO. Certainly not. None of us. Not even Savio, who's in there now, listening to her for the first time.

ROCCA. And why you are accusing me then? Even Mr Savio, who was defending me before? And why is he fighting a duel with Mr Palegari, then?

DIEGO. My dear sir, in you… I understand… it takes a really striking form, but believe me – as I was just saying – madness is really present to some degree in everybody. He's fighting, if you must know, because he's changed his mind in your regard.

FIRST FRIEND (*bursting out, with the others*). No, no! Don't pay any attention to him! …

OTHER FRIEND. … he's fighting because, after the fracas of the night before last, Mr Palegari got very upset…

FIRST FRIEND (*following quickly*). … and insulted him…

PRESTINO (*as above*). … and Mr Savio has taken up the insult and challenged him…

DIEGO (*raising his voice over the others*). … although everyone is now of one accord…

ROCCA (*immediately, forcefully*). … in judging me, without having heard me? But how was this infamous woman able to draw everyone over to her side?

DIEGO. Yes, everyone… except herself.

ROCCA. Except herself?

DIEGO. Ah, ah. Don't believe that she has taken this side or that side. She doesn't know which side she's on. … And if you take a good look at yourself, Mr Rocca, you'll see that maybe you haven't taken any side yet, either.

ROCCA. You're joking! Please tell Mr Savio – one of you, please – tell him I'm here to see him.

PRESTINO. But what do you want to tell him. I assure you that it's all useless.

ROCCA. What do you know? If he's against me too now, all the better!

PRESTINO. But he's in there with the lady now…

ROCCA. … that's all the better too! I followed her in here just for that. Perhaps it's lucky for her that I meet her in the presence of others – of a stranger that chance has drawn between us, so that… My god, I was ready for anything, like a blind man, and… and for the simple reason that I find myself here among you, unexpectedly, and have to speak, to answer… I feel… I feel as if my spirit has loosened its manacles… grown lighter…. I haven't talked to anybody for days and days! And you, gentlemen, don't know what a hell is burning within me! – I wanted to save my future brother-in-law, whom I already loved like a brother!

PRESTINO. Save him? Good! ...

FIRST FRIEND. ... by taking away his fiancée? ...

OTHER FRIEND. ... on the eve of his wedding?

ROCCA. No, no! Please, listen to me! Taking away his fiancée! What fiancée! ... It didn't take much to save him! It was enough to show him, make him see with his own eyes, that the woman he wanted to make his own by marrying her could be his the same way she'd been others', as she could be any of yours, with no need to marry her!

PRESTINO. All the same, you took her from him!

ROCCA. I was challenged to! challenged!

FIRST FRIEND. In what way?

OTHER FRIEND. Challenged by whom?

ROCCA. Challenged by him. Let me tell you! With the knowledge of his mother and sister... after he introduced her to the rest of the family, doing violence to all his purest feelings... I... with the knowledge of his mother and sister, as I said... followed them to Naples on the pretext of helping them to get their apartment ready (they were going to get married in a couple of months)... There was one of those little misunderstandings that often take place between engaged people. In a huff, she went away from him for a few days. (*Suddenly, as if before a horrifying vision, he covers his eyes*) My god. ... I can see her, how she left... (*uncovers his eyes, more upset than ever*)... because I was present at their quarrel. (*Regaining control*) So then I took advantage of the moment that I thought was opportune to show Giorgio what madness he was about to commit. It's incredible, incredible! ... Using a tactic that's very common with this kind of woman, she'd never allowed him even the least liberty...

FIRST FRIEND (*listening very intently, as are all the others, to the story*). Of course! ...

ROCCA. ... and at Capri she'd shown herself so disdainful of everybody, so reserved and proud! So he challenged me – *he* did, do you understand? – he challenged me to prove what I was saying, promising that, once he had proof, he would leave her, break things off. – And instead he killed himself!

FIRST FRIEND. But how did it happen? You offered to do it yourself? ...

ROCCA. ... I'd been challenged to! To save him! ...

OTHER FRIEND. ... But then, the betrayal...

ROCCA. ... horrible, horrible! ...

OTHER FRIEND. ... *he* did it to her? ...

ROCCA. ... *he* did it! ...

OTHER FRIEND. ... by killing himself! ...

PRESTINO. ... It's incredible! incredible! ...

ROCCA. ... that I offered to do it myself? ...

PRESTINO. ... No! – that he allowed you to offer to prove such a thing! ...

ROCCA. ... on purpose! because he'd realized at once, you know, that from the very first moment she saw me at my fiancée's side, she'd maliciously set out to attract me, to attract me to her, enveloping me in her charm. And he'd pointed it out to me... he himself, Giorgio! So it was easy for me – understand? – to make my proposal at that moment, to tell him: 'But if you know very well that she'd even sleep with me!'

PRESTINO. So then... oh god... then he almost wanted to challenge himself?

ROCCA. He should have shouted at me, made me understand that he'd already been poisoned for good, and that it would be useless for me to try to rip the venomous fangs out of that viper!

DIEGO (exploding). No, come on, what viper!

ROCCA. A viper! a viper!

DIEGO. Too ingenuous for a viper, my dear sir! Turning them on you so soon – no, instantly – those fangs!

PRESTINO. Unless she did it on purpose to cause the death of Giorgio Salvi!

ROCCA. Maybe!

DIEGO. But why? If she'd already succeeded in forcing him to marry her! Do you think it was to her advantage to let her fangs be ripped out before she'd reached her goal?

ROCCA. But she didn't expect that to happen!

DIEGO. Then she was no viper! Come on! A viper would certainly have suspected it. A viper would have bitten afterwards, not before! If she bit before, it means that either she was no viper, or she wanted to lose those fangs for Giorgio Salvi's sake.

ROCCA. But then you believe that...

DIEGO. It's you who lead me to believe it, you who think that woman is treacherous! To stick with your version, it's illogical for a treacherous woman to do what she did! A treacherous woman who's after marriage, and before the marriage gives herself to you so easily...

ROCCA (starting). ... gives herself to me? Who told you that she gave herself to me? I didn't have her, I didn't! Do you believe I could think of having her?

DIEGO (dumbfounded, as are the others). Oh, no?

THE OTHERS. What? What then?

ROCCA. All I needed was the proof that she'd be willing! some proof to show him… (*At this point the right-hand door opens and Francesco Savio, who has been detained by Delia Morello, appears in a state of extreme distress and agitation. In order to prevent him from fighting with Doro Palegari, Delia Morello has infatuated him. He immediately addresses Michele Rocca, very firmly.*)

FRANCESCO. What is this? What do you want here? What do you mean by all this shouting in my house?

ROCCA. I came to tell you…

FRANCESCO. You have nothing to tell me!

ROCCA. You are wrong! I must speak, and not only to you…

FRANCESCO. Don't you dare threaten me, damn it!

ROCCA. I'm not threatening you! I just asked to be allowed to speak…

FRANCESCO. You've been following a lady all the way to my house…

ROCCA. I've explained to your friends here…

FRANCESCO. What the hell do I care about your explanations! You've followed her, don't deny it!

ROCCA. Yes! Because if you want to fight Mr Palegari…

FRANCESCO. … what fight? I'm not fighting anybody any more!

PRESTINO (*astounded*). What? What're you saying?

FRANCESCO. I'm not fighting any more!

FIRST FRIEND, DIEGO, OTHER FRIEND (*together*). Are you crazy? Are you serious? This is wild!

ROCCA (*at the same time, raising his voice above the others, jeeringly*). Of course! She's seduced him! She's seduced him!

FRANCESCO (*moving towards him as if to attack him*). You shut up, or I…

PRESTINO (*getting in front of him*). No! Answer me first! You're not going to fight Palegari any more?

FRANCESCO. No. Because I can't make a woman even more desperate than she is now, over such a foolish thing!

PRESTINO. But the scandal will get worse if you don't fight! The conditions of the duel have been set down and signed already!

FRANCESCO. But it's ridiculous for me to fight Palegari now!

PRESTINO. What do you mean, ridiculous?

FRANCESCO. Ridiculous, ridiculous! We agree with each other! And you know damn well we do! You just love to get mixed up in this kind of stupid farce, don't you?

PRESTINO. But it was *you* who challenged Palegari, because he insulted you!

FRANCESCO. Pure stupidity! Diego said it himself! Enough!

PRESTINO. I can't believe this! I just can't believe it!

ROCCA. He's promised her not to fight with her gallant defender!

FRANCESCO. Yes! And now that I've got you in front of me...

ROCCA. ... I who have been the cause of your promise not to fight? ...

FRANCESCO. ... no! you've come all the way to my house to infuriate me! What do you want here from that lady?

PRESTINO. Stop it!

FRANCESCO. He's been following her since last night!

PRESTINO. But you can't fight him!

FRANCESCO. Nobody'll be able to say I've chosen a less dangerous adversary!

PRESTINO. No, dear boy! Because if I go, now, to propose myself to Palegari... as your substitute...

FIRST FRIEND (*shouting*). ... you'd be disqualified!

PRESTINO. ... disqualified!

ROCCA. But I can ignore any disqualification!

FIRST FRIEND. No! Because you'd have to face us who've disqualified him!

PRESTINO (*to Francesco*). And you won't find anybody to be your second! ... You've still got the whole day to think it over! I can't stay here any longer, I'm going!

DIEGO. Of course he'll think it over! He will!

PRESTINO (*to the other two*). Let's go, let's get out of here! (*The three of them go out through the garden.*)

DIEGO (*moves a few steps in their direction, advising*). Please stay calm, stay calm, gentlemen! Don't do anything rash! (*then turning to Francesco*) And you, watch what you're doing!

FRANCESCO. You go to hell too! (*then attacking Rocca*) And you, get out of here! out of my house! I'm at your service whenever and however you wish!

(*At this point Delia Morello appears on the threshold of the right-hand door. As soon as she sees Michele Rocca so changed from what he was, become another person, she suddenly feels the lie she has armed herself with until now fall from her eyes and from her hands: the lie she has armed herself with to defend herself against the secret, violent passion which seized them both from the first moment they saw each other. The frenzied passion they have tried to hide from themselves, to mask with pity, with concern for Giorgio Salvi, shouting that they wanted, each in their own way and one opposing the other, to save him. Now stripped of this lie, one facing the other, by the pity they suddenly feel for each other, pale and trembling, they look at each other for a moment.*)

ROCCA (*almost moaning*). Delia... Delia... (*goes to embrace her*).

DELIA (*letting him embrace her*). No... No... How you've punished yourself! (*they embrace frantically, bewildering and horrifying the other two*).

ROCCA. Delia! My love!

DIEGO. That's how they hate each other! Was that it? Do you see? do you see?

FRANCESCO. But it's absurd! It's monstrous! There's a man's corpse between them!

ROCCA (*turning like a feeding beast, without letting go of her*). Yes, it *is* monstrous! But she must stay with me! She must suffer with me! With me!

DELIA (*seized with horror, wildly tearing herself away*). No, no! Go away, go away! Leave me alone!

ROCCA (*still holding her, as above*). No! Here with me, with my desperation! Here!

DELIA (*as above*). Leave me alone, I tell you! Let me go! Assassin!

FRANCESCO. You let go of her, damn it! Let her go!

ROCCA. Don't come near me!

DELIA (*succeeding in tearing herself away*). Let me go! (*While Diego and Francesco restrain Michele Rocca, who is trying to hurl himself upon her*) I'm not afraid of you! No! I'm not! No harm can come to me from you, even if you kill me!

ROCCA (*restrained by the two men, shouts*). Delia! Delia! I've got to hold on to you! I can't be alone any more!

DELIA (*as above*). I don't feel anything. I fooled myself into thinking I was feeling pity, fear – no! It isn't true!

ROCCA (*as above*). I'm going crazy. Let go of me!

DIEGO AND FRANCESCO. They're two wild animals! It's appalling!

DELIA. Let him go! I'm not afraid of him. I was quite cold when I let him embrace me! It wasn't fear, or pity.

ROCCA. The bitch! I know she isn't worth a damn! ... But I want you! I want you!

DELIA. Any evil – even if you kill me – will be a lesser evil! Another crime, prison, death itself! I want to go on suffering this way!

ROCCA (*continuing, to the two who are holding him*). She isn't worth a damn, but all the suffering I went through for her sets her cost high now. It's not love, it's hatred! Hatred!

DELIA. Hatred, yes. Mine too! Hatred!

ROCCA. It's the very blood that was shed for her! (*he succeeds in freeing himself with a violent wrench*). Have pity, have pity... (*follows her across the room*).

DELIA (*moving away from him*). No, no! Don't you dare!

DIEGO AND FRANCESCO (*seizing him again*). Just be still, for God's sake! You're at our mercy!

DELIA. He'd better not try to make me feel pity, either for myself or for him! I don't feel any! If you have any for him, make him go, make him go away!

ROCCA. How can I go away? You know that my life's been drowned in that blood forever!

DELIA. And you didn't want to save your fiancée's brother from dishonour?

ROCCA. You bitch! It isn't true! You know that both mine and yours are lies!

DELIA. Two lies, yes! Two lies!

ROCCA. You wanted me, just as I wanted you, from the first moment we saw each other!

DELIA. Yes, yes! To punish you!

ROCCA. Me too, to punish you! But your life too, it was drowned in that blood forever!

DELIA. Yes, mine too! Mine too! (*she runs to him like a flame, pushing aside those who try to restrain her*). It's true! It's true!

ROCCA (*embracing her quickly, frantically*). So, now we've got to stay deep in it, holding each other like this! like this! Not alone – me, you, alone – both of us together, like this!

DIEGO. If it would only last!

ROCCA (*leading her away by the stairs to the garden, leaving the other two dumbfounded and terrified*). Come, come away, come away with me…

FRANCESCO. Those two are really crazy!

DIEGO. Because you don't see yourself.

CURTAIN

SECOND CHORAL INTERMEZZO

(*Again the curtain, which has just been lowered at the end of the second act, is raised to show the same section of the corridor that leads to the stage. This time, however, the public will be slow leaving the auditorium. In this hallway, the ushers, the usherettes, and the box attendants are apprehensive, because at the end of the act they have seen Ms Moreno, despite the efforts of her three friends to restrain her, run across the hallway and break onto the stage. Now a clamour of shouts and applause comes from the auditorium, gradually increasing, both because the actors called to the stage to take their bows have not yet come out to thank the public, and because strange screams and upsetting noises are heard from the stage through the curtain, and they are heard even more loudly here in the hallway).*

ONE OF THE USHERS. What the hell is going on?

ANOTHER USHER. Isn't this an opening night? The usual uproar, then.

AN USHERETTE. No, they're applauding and the actors aren't coming out.

A BOX ATTENDANT. But there are shouts from the stage. Don't you hear?

SECOND USHER. And in the auditorium too.

A SECOND BOX ATTENDANT. Could it be because of the lady who just ran across here?

THE FIRST USHER. It must be her! They were trying to restrain her as if she were possessed by the devil.

THE FIRST BOX ATTENDANT. She ran straight onto the stage.

THE FIRST USHER. She wanted to go up there after the first act too.

A THIRD BOX ATTENDANT. All hell's breaking loose, listen.

(*Two or three box doors are flung open at the same time and some dismayed spectators come out, while the noise from the auditorium is heard much more loudly.*)

THE PEOPLE FROM THE BOXES (*either coming out of the doors or just peering out*).

– Yes, it's on the stage!

– What is it? Are they hitting each other?

– They are shouting! shouting!

– And the actors aren't coming out!

(*Other ladies and gentlemen, more and more appalled, come out of the boxes into the hallway and look towards the rear at the small stage door. Soon after, a stream of spectators from the left runs out. All are shouting: 'What is it? What is it? What's going on?' Other spectators are coming out of the orchestra entrance, nervous and upset.*)

A CONFUSION OF VOICES

– They're fighting on the stage!

– Oh, yes, listen!

– On the stage?

– Why? Why?

– Who knows?

– Let me through!

– What happened?

- Oh, for god's sake, what are things coming to?
- What a mess!
- Let me through!
- Is the play over?
- What about the third act?
- There must be a third act!
- Make room, make room!
- Yes, at four o'clock, see you!
- Listen, what an uproar on the stage!
- Let me through, I want to go to the cloakroom!
- Oh, oh, d'you hear?
- This is a scandal!
- It's indecent!
- What's all this uproar about?
- Well… it seems that…
- It's impossible to figure out!
- What the hell…
- Oh, oh, down there!
- The door's opened!

(*At the rear of the hallway the small stage door has been flung open, and immediately the confused voices of the actors and actresses, the Director, Ms Moreno, and her three friends are heard, echoed by the shouts of the spectators, who gradually crowd around the stage door, amid the angry protestations of somebody who, annoyed, indignant about the whole thing, is trying to break through the crowd to leave the theatre.*)

VOICES FROM THE STAGE.

- (*of the actors*) Get out! Out of here! – Throw her out! – Insolent witch! – Shrew! – Shameless bitch! – You'll pay for this! – Go on! Get out!
- (*of Ms Moreno*) It's a disgrace! No! No!
- (*of the company director*) Get lost!
- (*of one of the three friends*) She's a lady, after all!
- (*of Ms Moreno*) It revolted me!
- (*of another friend*) Show some respect for a lady!
- (*of the actors*) What lady?! – She came up here to attack us! – Out, out!
- (*of the actresses*) Shrew! Shameless bitch!
- (*of the actors*) She can be thankful she's a lady! She got what she deserved! Get out! Out!
- (*of the director*) Clear out, all of you!

VOICES OF THE CROWD OF SPECTATORS (*all at the same time, accompanied by booing and applause*).
  – Miss Moreno! Miss Moreno!
  – Who's Miss Moreno?
  – They've slapped the leading lady in the face!
  – Who? Who slapped who in the face?
  – Miss Moreno, Miss Moreno!
  – And who's Miss Moreno?
  – The leading lady?
  – No, no, they 've slapped the author in the face!
  – The author? Slapped in the face?
  – Who? Who slapped whom?
  – Miss Moreno!
  – No, the leading lady!
  – The author's slapped the leading lady?
  – No, no, the other way around!
  – The leading lady slapped the author in the face!
  – No, certainly not! Miss Moreno's slapped the leading lady!
VOICES FROM THE STAGE. Enough, enough! – Get out of here! – Bastards! – Shameless bitch! – Out, out! – Please, make room! – Let people through!
VOICES OF SPECTATORS.
  – Throw the bastards out!
  – Enough, enough!
  – Is it really Ms Moreno?
  – Enough! Out!
  – No, the play must go on!
  – Throw the bastards out!
  – Down with Pirandello!
  – No, long live Pirandello!
  – Down, down!
  – He's the troublemaker!
  – Enough, enough!
  – Let them through! Let them through!
  – Make room! Make room!
(*The crowd of spectators opens up to let through some actors, actresses, the manager of the company and the theatre manager, who are trying to convince them to stay. In the confusion of this passage, the crowd of spectators first falls silent to hear what is going on, then breaks in from time to time with loud comments.*)

THE THEATRE MANAGER. For heaven's sake, don't be reckless. Do you want to wreck the play?

ACTORS AND ACTRESSES (*all together*). No, no! – I'm going! – We're all going! – This is too much, for God's sake! – It's a disgrace! – We protest! We protest!

THE MANAGER OF THE COMPANY. Protest what? Against whom are you protesting?

ONE OF THE ACTORS. Against the author! And rightly so!

ANOTHER. And against the theatre manager who agreed to stage such a play!

THE THEATRE MANAGER. But you can't protest like this, going away and leaving the play half done! It's anarchy!

OPPOSING VOICES OF THE SPECTATORS. Fine! Fine! – Who are they? – The actors, don't you see? – No, not at all! – They're right! They're right!

THE ACTORS (*all together*). Yes, we can!

THE CHARACTER ACTOR. When we're compelled to play a *comédie à clef!*

VOICES OF SOME UNINFORMED SPECTATORS. À clef? – Where? Why *à clef*? – A *comédie à clef*?

THE ACTORS. Yessir! You bet we can!

VOICES OF INFORMED SPECTATORS. Oh, yes! – It's well known! – It's a scandal! – Everyone knows about it! – The case of Miss Moreno! – She's here! She's been seen in the theatre! – She ran onto the stage! – She slapped the leading lady in the face!

THE UNINFORMED SPECTATORS AND THOSE FAVOURABLY DISPOSED TO THE AUTHOR (*all at the same time, in a great confusion*). But nobody realized it. – We liked the play. It was good. – We want to see the third act. – We've paid for it! – Fine! Fine! – What about the rights of the audience who buys the tickets?

ONE OF THE ACTORS. But we have a right to some respect too!

ANOTHER. We're going! I'm going!

THE CHARACTER ACTRESS. After all, the leading lady's already left!

VOICES OF SOME SPECTATORS. She's left? – How? Through what? Through the stage door?

THE CHARACTER ACTRESS. Because a spectator attacked her on the stage.

CONFLICTING VOICES OF SOME SPECTATORS. Attacked her? – Yessir! Miss Moreno! – And she was right! – But who? who? – Miss Moreno! – And why did she attack her? – The leading lady?

ONE OF THE ACTORS. Because she recognized herself in the character of the play.

ANOTHER ACTOR. And she thought we were accomplices with the author in this slander.

THE CHARACTER ACTRESS. Let the public decide whether this should be the reward for our efforts.

BARON NUTI (*restrained as in the first intermezzo by two friends, more violently agitated than ever, coming forward*). It's true! It's an unheard-of disgrace! And you've got every right to rebel!

ONE OF HIS FRIENDS. Don't get yourself into trouble! Let's go, let's go!

BARON NUTI. It's truly wicked, gentlemen. Two hearts held up to public contempt! Two hearts, still bleeding, being pilloried!

THE THEATRE MANAGER (*desperate*). Now the play from the stage to the hallway!

VOICES OF SPECTATORS UNFAVOURABLY DISPOSED TO THE AUTHOR. He's right, he's right! – It's disgraceful! – It's not allowed! – The actors are right! – It's slander!

VOICES OF FAVOURABLY DISPOSED SPECTATORS. What? What? – Who says? – Where's the slander? – Nothing defamatory about it!

THE THEATRE MANAGER. Please, gentlemen, are we in a theatre or in a public square?

BARON NUTI (*seizing one of the favourably disposed spectators by the lapels, while the others, terrified by the fury in his face and manner, fall silent*). You say they're allowed to do this? To take me, a living person, and put me on the stage? Make me see myself there, with my living torment, in front of everybody, saying words I never said? doing things I never thought of doing?

(*From the rear, in front of the little stage door, in the following silence, are heard as if in reply the words the director now speaks to Miss Moreno, who is being dragged away, crying, dishevelled, almost unconscious, by her three escorts. As the first words are uttered, everybody turns in that direction, making room, and Nuti lets go of the spectator and turns that way too, asking, 'What is it?'*)

THE DIRECTOR. But you've been able to ascertain that neither the author nor the actress have ever known you!

MISS MORENO. My own voice! My exact gestures! All my mannerisms! I saw myself! I saw myself up there!

THE DIRECTOR. Only because you wanted to recognize yourself!

MISS MORENO. No, no! It's not true! Because it was the horror, the horror I felt of seeing myself represented there, doing that! What nerve! Me, me, embracing that man? (*She sees Nuti suddenly almost in front of her and utters a cry, raising her arms to hide her face.*) Oh, my god! There he is, there he is!

BARON NUTI. Amelia, Amelia…

(*General agitation among the spectators who can hardly believe their eyes, finding before them the very characters and the same scene they have just witnessed at the end of the second act. They show their emotions both by the expressions on their faces and by some brief subdued comments and exclamations.*)

SPECTATORS' VOICES. Look, look! – There they are, over there! – Oh, oh! – Both of them! – They're playing the scene! – Look, look!

MISS MORENO (*to her escorts, wildly*). Get him away from me! Get him away from me!

THE ESCORTS. Yes, let's go, let's go!

BARON NUTI (*lunging at her*). No, no! You must come with me! Come with me!

MISS MORENO (*trying to break loose*). No! Let me go, let me go! Murderer!

BARON NUTI, Don't repeat what they put in your mouth up there!

MISS MORENO. Leave me alone! I'm not afraid of you!

BARON NUTI. But it's true, it's true, we've got to punish ourselves together! Didn't you hear? Everyone knows by now! Come, come away! Come!

MISS MORENO. No! Leave me alone, damn you! I despise you!

BARON NUTI. We're drowned, really drowned in the same blood! Come! Come!

(*He drags her away, disappearing on the left, followed by many spectators, among loud comments: 'Oh, oh! Who'd believe it! – It's incredible! – Frightening! – Look at them! – Delia Morello and Michele Rocca!' The other spectators, who stay on in the hallway, follow them with their eyes and more or less the same kind of comments.*)

A FOOLISH SPECTATOR. Imagine – first they objected so violently, and then they did the same thing as in the play!

THE DIRECTOR. Right! She had the nerve to come and attack the leading lady right on the stage! 'Me, embracing that man?!'

MANY. It's incredible, incredible!

AN INTELLIGENT SPECTATOR. No, no, gentlemen. That was the most natural thing! They saw themselves as if in a mirror and they objected violently, especially to that last gesture of theirs!

THE DIRECTOR. But they repeated that very gesture!

THE INTELLIGENT SPECTATOR. Right! Exactly so! They did, as they had to, before our eyes, against their will, what art had foreseen! (*Some spectators approve, some applaud, some laugh.*)

THE BRILLIANT ACTOR (*who's just come forward from the small stage door*). Don't believe it, sir. Those two? Look, I'm the brilliant actor who played the role of Diego Cinci in the play with great conviction. As soon as they're out the door, those two... – You people haven't seen the third act.

THE SPECTATORS. Oh, yes! The third act! What was going to happen in the third act? Tell us, tell us!

THE BRILLIANT ACTOR. Well, stuff like... and afterwards... after the third act... stuff, what stuff! (*He walks out as he says this.*)

THE THEATRE MANAGER (*to the director*). My dear director, pardon me, but do you think you can hold a public meeting here with the audience?

THE DIRECTOR. I've got nothing to do with it. Have the place cleared out.

THE MANAGER OF THE COMPANY. In any case the show can't go on. All the actors are gone.

THE DIRECTOR. So you turn to me too? Put up a sign and send people home!

THE THEATRE MANAGER. But some spectators might still be in the auditorium!

THE DIRECTOR. All right. I'll go out there and send off the people who are still in their seats with a couple of words!

THE THEATRE MANAGER. Yes, yes! Please, do so. (*While the director goes towards the small stage door*) Gentlemen, time to leave. Clear out, please. The performance is over. (*The curtain falls, and immediately the director pushes aside a corner of it to get to the footlights.*)

THE DIRECTOR. I regret to have to announce to the audience that, on account of the unpleasant incidents which occurred at the end of the second act, the third act cannot be performed.

CURTAIN

The Mountain Giants

A Myth

Characters

The Countess's Theatre Company:

ILSE *still called the Countess*

THE COUNT *her husband*

DIAMANTE *the Supporting Actress*

CROMO *the Character Actor*

SPIZZI *the Juvenile Lead*

BATTAGLIA *the General Actor, playing any role, including women*

SACERDOTE

LUMACHI *with the cart*

The people of La Scalogna:

COTRONE *called the Magician*

QUACQUÉO *a dwarf*

DUCCIO DOCCIA

SGRICIA

MILORDINO

MARA-MARA *with a parasol, also called the Scotswoman*

MADDALENA

PUPPETS

APPARITIONS

THE ANGEL ONEHUNDREDANDONE *with his cohort*

Time and place undetermined: at the borders between fable and reality

I

(A villa called 'La Scalogna,' where Cotrone lives with his Scalognati.
Almost in the centre of the stage, on a little rise, is a tall cypress reduced in its old age to a mere trunk, like a pole. At its top a tuft of lights, like a brush.

The plaster of the villa is a faded red. On the right only the entrance is visible; the four steps leading to it are set between two projecting small round porches, with balustrades and pillars supporting their domed roofs. The door is old and still retains some traces of its original green paint. To the right and left of the door, and level with it, two french doors open onto the round porches.

This villa, once majestic, is in a state of neglect and decay. It is totally isolated in the valley in which it stands. A small lawn stretches before it with a bench on the left. A path leading to it goes down steeply towards the cypress, and continues to the left, passing over a small bridge above an invisible stream.

This bridge on the left must be very visible, and usable, with two parapets.

The wooded slopes of the mountain can be seen beyond it.

As the curtain rises, it is almost evening. From inside the villa a song is heard, with the accompaniment of strange instruments, a song that rises and falls, now bursting into odd shrill cries, now flinging itself into reckless glissandi, drawing towards a vortex, and suddenly freeing itself, fleeing like a horse spooked by its own shadow. This song must give the impression that some impending danger is about to be overcome, a danger one yearns to be done with so that everything can be calm again and in its proper place, as after certain evil moments of madness which come over us without our knowing why. Through the glass of the two french doors to the porches one can see that the interior of the villa is lit by strange coloured lights that give the appearance of mysterious apparitions to La Sgricia, who sits calm and motionless on the porch to the right of the main entrance, and to Doccia and Quacquéo, who sit on the left one, the former with his elbows on the railing and his head between his hands, the latter sitting on the railing with his shoulders against the wall. La Sgricia is a little old woman wearing a bonnet awkwardly tied under her chin and a short, violet cape, a pleated black-and-white-checked dress, and fingerless cotton gloves. When she speaks, she always appears to be slightly irritated and blinks her eyelids continuously over her cunning, restless eyes. From time to time she runs a finger quickly under her turned-up nose.

Duccio Doccia is short, of uncertain age, totally bald, with solemn oval eyes, a heavy, drooping lip, in a long, pale face, which reveals the skull; he has long, soft hands, and his legs are bent when he walks as if he intended to sit down after every step.

Quacquéo is a fat dwarf, dressed like a child, with red hair, and a broad face, the colour of terracotta; the foolish smile on his lips is malicious in his eyes. As the singing inside the villa ends, Milordino, a sickly young man of thirty, with an unhealthy, struggling beard on his cheeks, a derby on his head, and a waistcoat green with age, which he refuses to discard so as not to lose his civilized appearance, comes out from behind the cypress, badly frightened, shouting:)

MILORDINO. Oh, oh! People coming! Quick, quick! Lightning!
Thunder! and the green flashing strip! the green flashing strip on
top of the roof!

LA SGRICIA (*getting up, opening the french doors and calling into the interior of
the villa*). Help, help! People coming! (*then leaning over the railing*)
What kind of people, Milordino? what people?

QUACQUÉO. At night? If it were day, I'd understand… must be somebody
who's lost. They'll go back. You'll see.

MILORDINO. No, no! They're coming forward! They're down here! Lots
of them! More than ten!

QUACQUÉO. Hm! that many! They must be brave, then (*he jumps over the
railing onto the doorsteps and goes over to the cypress to look with Milordino*).

LA SGRICIA (*shrieking into the villa*). The lightning! The lightning!

DOCCIA. Hey, slow down! The lightning's expensive!

MILORDINO. They've got a cart too; they're pulling it themselves: one
between the shafts and two pushing from the back.

DOCCIA. They must be people heading for the mountain.

QUACQUÉO. No, no! They really seem to be heading for us. Oh, oh!
they've got a woman on the cart! Look, look! the cart's full of hay
and the woman's lying on it!

MILORDINO. Send Mara to the bridge with the parasol at least!

MARA-MARA (*rushes out of the front door of the villa shouting*). Here I am!
Here I am! They'll be afraid of the Scotswoman! (*She is a small
woman who can be got up as a swollen, stuffed little bale, wearing a very
short Scotch plaid skirt over the stuffed part, bare legs with wool stockings
rolled down over her calves; she has a little green oilcloth hat, with a straight
brim and a rooster feather on one side on her head, a small parasol in her
hand, a haversack and a flask hanging across her chest.*) Hey, give me
some light from the roof! Or I'll break my neck! (*She runs to the little
bridge, climbs on one of the parapets and, lit by a green floodlight from the
top of the villa that gives her the appearance of a ghost, she starts walking
back and forth on it, simulating an apparition. From time to time large
flashes of light are seen from behind the villa, like heat lightning, followed by
peals of thunder made by chains.*)

LA SGRICIA (*to the two men who are watching*). Are they stopping? Are they
turning back?

QUACQUÉO. Someone call Cotrone!

DOCCIA. Cotrone, Cotrone!

LA SGRICIA. He's got an attack of gout! (*Both La Sgricia and Doccia have
come down from the porches and are standing on the lawn in consternation.*

From the door emerges Cotrone, a huge, bearded man, with a handsome open
face, large, serene, shining eyes, a fresh, gleaming mouth with a healthy set of
teeth between the blond of his unkempt moustache and beard. His feet are a bit
flat. He dresses carelessly: a large black jacket, wide, light-coloured trousers, an
old Turkish fez on his head, a pale blue shirt partly open, showing his chest.)

COTRONE. What's this? Aren't you ashamed? Scared to death and trying
to scare others?!

MILORDINO. They're coming in droves! There are more than ten!

QUACQUÉO. No, there are eight! there are eight! I counted them,
including the woman!

COTRONE. Cheer up then! Even a woman? Maybe she's a dethroned
queen! Is she naked?

QUACQUÉO (*shocked*). Naked? No, she didn't seem to be naked.

COTRONE. Naked, you fool! On a haycart, a naked woman. Breast up
and red hair spreading out like blood in a tragedy! Her banished
ministers pull her, in short sleeves, not to sweat too much. Come on,
wake up, where's your imagination? You're not turning rational on
me, are you? Just think, we're in no danger, and down with reason!
By god, the night is almost here! The night is our kingdom!

MILORDINO. Sure, but if these guys don't believe in that sort of thing...

COTRONE. Why, do you really need others to believe in you, to believe in
yourself?

LA SGRICIA. Are they still coming up this way?

MILORDINO. Neither our lightning nor Mara seem to be stopping them.

DOCCIA. Well, if it isn't working, then we're wasting the stuff; turn them
off!

COTRONE. Yes, turn the things off up there! Enough of this lightning!
You, Mara, come here! If they're not frightened, they must be our kind
of folks; we'll understand each other and communicate easily. The villa
is large enough. (*Struck by a new thought*) Oh, wait. (*To Quacquéo*) Did
you say there are eight of them?

QUACQUÉO. Eight, yes. I thought so...

DOCCIA. You thought... But you counted them!

QUACQUÉO. Eight, yes, eight.

COTRONE. Then they're very few.

QUACQUÉO. Eight and a cart. Is that few?

COTRONE. Unless the others've left the band.

LA SGRICIA. Bandits?

COTRONE. No, what kind of bandits! Keep quiet. With crazy people
anything's possible. Maybe it's them!

DOCCIA. Who, them?

QUACQUÉO. Here they are!

(*Since the lightning and the spotlight that lit Mara-Mara on the parapet of the bridge have been turned off, the stage has been left bathed in a delicate twilight slowly turning to the light of a rising moon. From the path behind the cypress the Count, Diamante, Cromo, and Battaglia, of the Countess's company, appear.*

The Count is a young man, pale, blond, with a bewildered, exhausted look. Although extremely poor by now, as his clothing indicates – a formal evening suit, now discoloured, very worn and even torn in places, a white waistcoat, and an old straw hat – he retains in his features and in his demeanour the disappointed misery of great nobility.

Diamante is close to forty. Above a buxom, rather over-endowed chest, she holds her hard head high, with a certain swagger. Violently made up, she is armed with tragic brows over two deep grave eyes, and an imperious, disdainful nose. Two inverted commas of black hair curl at the corners of her mouth, and some more hair curls on her chin. She always seems about to explode with benevolence for the poor unfortunate young Count, and with indignation towards Ilse, his wife, whose victim she believes him to be.

Cromo is oddly bald, front and back; his remaining carrot-coloured hair forms two triangles whose points join at the top of his head. He is pale, freckled, with pale-green eyes. He speaks in a deep voice, with the tone and gestures of one who gets angry at every small incident.

Battaglia, though a man, has the horse face of a wicked old maid, and all the affected mannerisms of a sick monkey. He plays male and female roles, the latter in a wig, of course. He is also a prompter. Though his face bears the marks of his vices, his eyes are imploring and mild.)

CROMO. Oh, thank you, friends, you were really good! We were nearly exhausted!

DOCCIA (*surprised*). Thanks for what?

CROMO. What do you mean, for what? For the signals you gave us to let us know we'd finally reached our destination.

COTRONE. Ah, that's it, then! It's really them!

BATTAGLIA (*pointing at Mara*). What courage the lady has!

CROMO. Yeah! on the railing of the bridge! Marvellous! With the parasol!

DIAMANTE. And the lightning! Beautiful! And that green flame on the roof!

QUACQUÉO. Ugh, look at that! They took it for a performance! We're creating ghosts…

MILORDINO. ... and they enjoyed them!

DIAMANTE. Ghosts? What ghosts?

QUACQUÉO. You know, the apparitions, to scare people and keep them away!

COTRONE. Be quiet! (*To Cromo*) The Countess's company? Just as I was saying...

CROMO. Here we are!

DOCCIA. The company?

BATTAGLIA. ... the last remains of our company...

DIAMANTE. Not at all! Its pillars! Say, its pillars, fortunately, and first of all the Count here. (*Takes the Count's hand, holding the other behind his shoulder as with a child*) Come forward, come, please.

COTRONE (*holding out his hand*). Welcome, Count!

CROMO (*declaiming*). A Count with neither a county nor a bank account.

DIAMANTE (*indignant*). When will you finally stop belittling yourselves, humiliating...

THE COUNT (*displeased*). No, my dear, they do not humiliate me...

CROMO. Let's keep calling you Count, all right. But don't you think at this point we should start toning things down?

BATTAGLIA. ... when I said 'the last remains' I was talking only about myself...

CROMO (*to quiet him*). You're modest, we know that.

BATTAGLIA. No, I'd say my mind's wandering, rather, from fatigue and hunger.

COTRONE. But you'll find a chance to rest here and... yes, something to eat too, I believe...

SGRICIA (*quickly, cold, definite*). The kitchen fire's out.

MARA-MARA. We can light the fire again. But tell us at least...

DOCCIA. ... yes, who these people are...

COTRONE. Of course, right away (*To the Count*) But what of the Countess?

THE COUNT. She's here. But she's so tired...

BATTAGLIA. She can't stand up any more.

QUACQUÉO. The woman on the cart? A Countess? (*Clapping his hands and raising a foot*) Ah, we get it! You've arranged to surprise us with a performance!

COTRONE. No, my friends, let me explain...

QUACQUÉO. Yes, yes. And they took ours for a performance, too!

COTRONE. Because they too belong more or less to our family. You'll understand! (*To the Count*) Does the Countess need some help?

DIAMANTE. She could make the effort to walk up by herself!

THE COUNT (*angry, curt, shouts in her face*). No, she can't!

CROMO. Lumachi is gathering his strength...

BATTAGLIA. ... his last ounce of strength...

CROMO. ... for this last effort.

COTRONE (*solicitous*). But I can give a hand too...

THE COUNT. No, there are two more people down there with Lumachi. I'd rather you told us... (*he looks around, confused*) I can see, we are in a valley, here, at the foot of a mountain...

CROMO. And where would the hotels be?

BATTAGLIA. ... and the restaurants? ...

DIAMANTE. The playhouse where we'll be acting?

COTRONE. Yes, well, if you let me speak, I'll explain both to my people and to you. We're all mistaken, my friends. But we mustn't get upset over such a small thing.

OFFSTAGE VOICES OF THE YOUNG ACTOR, SACERDOTE, AND LUMACHI, WHO ARE PULLING THE HAYCART ON WHICH THE COUNTESS IS LYING.

– Come on! Push!

– We're there!

– Hey, slow down! Take it easy! Don't push so hard!

CROMO. Here's the Countess!

THE COUNT. Watch out for the cypress! Watch out! (*He runs to help, together with Cotrone. As the cart reaches the lawn, Lumachi lowers the props so that it can stand upright on them and its wheels without any additional support. He moves out from the shafts and steps aside. All the others look with consternation at the Countess, who lies on the green hay with her copper-coloured hair in disarray; she wears a sad, shabby dress of purple voile, low necked, rather worn, with long, wide sleeves, that slide back up easily, leaving her arms bare.*)

MILORDINO. My god, how pale she is!

MARA-MARA. She looks dead!

SPIZZI. Silence!

ILSE (*after a moment, sits up in the cart and recites with deep emotion*).
If you would hear
This new tale,
Give credence then
To this poor woman's dress;
But yet more credence
To these my tears,
A mother's tears
For a tragic destiny,
A tragic destiny.

(*At this point, as if on an agreed-upon signal, the Count, Cromo, and all the other members of the Countess's company burst into different sorts of laughter, all expressing disbelief, then suddenly stop, and Ilse continues.*)
Thus do they all laugh,
All the educated folk
Who see my tears unmoved,
Who feel no pity...

COTRONE (*recovering from his amazement*). Oh, you're performing!

MILORDINO. Terrific!

MARA-MARA. They're performing!

SACERDOTE. Silence! When she's begun, she needs to be encouraged!

ILSE (*continuing*).
Indeed, they feel annoyance;
'Fool! Fool!' they shout
Into my face,
Refusing to believe
That my own son,
My own flesh and blood...
But you must give me credence,
I'll bring you witnesses:
All poor women,
Poor mothers like myself,
My own neighbours;
We know each other, all of us,
We all know it is true...
(*gestures as if to call them*).

THE COUNT (*leaning over her, gently*). No, stop now, my dear...

ILSE (*gesturing impatiently*). The women, the women...

THE COUNT. But the women, don't you see? They aren't here right now...

ILSE (*as if awakening*). They're not? Why? Where have you taken me?

THE COUNT. We've arrived... now we'll inquire...

MILORDINO. She was really good!

SGRICIA. What a shame! I was enjoying it so much!

DOCCIA. ... to hear them laugh like that, together?

QUACQUÉO (*to Cotrone*). See? I told you! Isn't it true?

COTRONE. Of course it is! They're performing. What else should they do? They're in show business!

THE COUNT. Please, don't use that expression in front of my wife!

ILSE (*getting off the cart, some threads of hay still in her hair*). Why not? Say it, say it! I like it!

COTRONE. Forgive me, madam. I meant no offence…

ILSE (*speaking as if in delirium*). Yes, show business, yes! Not him (*points to her husband*). But I am, since birth. It's in my blood! – Now he has sunk to my level…

THE COUNT (*trying to stop her*). No, what are you saying?

ILSE. Yes, down to my level, from his marble palaces, into wooden sheds! Into the public squares, even, the public squares! Where are we now? Lumachi, where are you? Lumachi? Try the trumpet! Let's see if we can gather a few people together. (*Looks around, lost in delirium, horrified.*) Oh god, where are we now? Where are we? (*Spizzi has drawn near; she takes refuge on his chest.*)

COTRONE. Among friends, Countess, don't worry!

CROMO. She's feverish, delirious.

QUACQUÉO. Is she really a Countess?

THE COUNT. Of course. She is my wife!

COTRONE. Quacquéo, keep quiet!

MARA-MARA. But you haven't told us anything yet…

DOCCIA. They seem crazy to us!

THE COUNT (*to Cotrone*). We have been directed to you…

COTRONE. Yes, Count. Please forgive my friends; I forgot to inform them. I used that expression for their benefit, but I know that…

SPIZZI (*barely twenty, pale, flashing eyes, blond hair, perhaps bleached once, now faded; a rosebud mouth, but a long nose hanging above rather detracts from it; pathetically elegant in his faded sporting outfit, with calf-length knickers and woollen socks, interrupting*). You know nothing and can know nothing of the heroic martyrdom of this woman!

ILSE (*resentful and impetuous, detaching herself from his chest*). Spizzi, I forbid you to speak of this! (*Then, trembling with contempt, addressing Cromo*) If I only hadn't been born an actress, understand? … My disgust is that *you* had to be the first to believe it and get others to believe it… 'You want a good contract – sell yourself!' 'Dresses, jewels? – Sell yourself!' Even for a filthy flattering review!

CROMO (*dumbfounded*). What are you saying? Why to me?

ILSE. Because you said it!

CROMO. *I* did? When did I say it? What did I say?

THE COUNT (*pleading with his wife*). Don't demean yourself, talking about these things – you! – it's horrible!

ILSE. No, my dear; we must talk about them, now that we've reached the end! When we are reduced to this, shadows of what we used to be… (*to Cotrone for a second, then to all the others too*) You know, we sleep all together… in stables…

THE COUNT. It's not true...

ILSE. Not true? What about yesterday?

THE COUNT. It wasn't a stable, darling. You slept on a bench in a railroad station.

CROMO. Third-class waiting room..

ILSE (*to Cotrone, continuing*). ... when you stretch and turn over, words just come out, you say things you shouldn't... (*to Cromo*) Do you think one can't hear them in the dark because one can't see? I heard you!

CROMO. Heard what?

ILSE. Something that, buried as I was in those... I'm not sure whether they were spiderwebs...

THE COUNT. Certainly not, Ilse. How could that be?

ILSE. ... rags of darkness, then, which were flapping cold against my feverish face... yes... yes, as I was trying to breathe... (*to Cromo*) When I heard you, eeeh, eeeh! I laughed like that, but at once I shivered, felt a chill, and clenched my teeth. I had to hug myself tight, tight, not to start whining like a beaten dog... (*abruptly, again to Cromo*) Didn't you even hear me laughing?

CROMO. No.

ILSE. Yes, you did. In the dark you thought it was somebody else – you didn't believe it could be me – someone else agreeing with you...

CROMO. I don't remember a thing!

ILSE. I remember everything!

SPIZZI. But what did he say?

ILSE. That so as not to undergo this heroic martyrdom, as you call it, and not have you all undergo it too, how much better it would have been if... – he said...

CROMO (*understanding at last, and protesting*). Oh, yes, now I get it! But this is something all of us have said, not just me! And whoever hasn't said it has thought of it; he too, I bet! (*pointing to the Count*).

THE COUNT. Me? What?

ILSE. That I, my dear (*takes his head in her hands*), on this noble forehead (*turns to Cromo*) 'without much ado,' that's what you said, right?

CROMO. Yes, without much ado, and we wouldn't be starving now!

ILSE. ... I should have planted two magnificent horns... (*she is about to stick her fingers out like horns on her husband's forehead, but is seized by an uncontrollable fit of contempt and revulsion*) Ah! (*She abruptly changes her obscene gesture into a loud slap on Cromo's cheek, reels, and falls in a violent convulsion of laughter and tears. Cromo, stunned, nurses his cheek. Surprised by the sudden event, all start talking simultaneously, some commenting, some rushing to help. Four groups form: one trying to help the Countess – the*

Count, Diamante, Cotrone; the second – Quacquéo, Doccia, Mara-Mara,
Milordino; the third – Sacerdote, Lumachi, Battaglia, La Sgricia; the fourth
– Spizzi and Cromo. The four groups speak the four sentences assigned to
each, at the same time.)

THE COUNT. Oh, my god, she's losing her mind! Ilse, please, we can't go
on like this!

DIAMANTE. Please, Ilse, calm down. At least for your husband's sake!

COTRONE. Countess, Countess... Come on, let's carry her over there, it's
better...

ILSE. No, leave me alone! Leave me alone! Everyone must hear...

QUACQUÉO. What a performance! And then she wants to deny it!

DOCCIA. Oh, she's good! She goes straight to the point!

MARA-MARA. She really let him have it!

MILORDINO. Where on earth have these people escaped from?

BATTAGLIA. Dig, dig, it's our own grave...

LUMACHI. I can't understand, why such a fuss over nothing!

SACERDOTE. It's true though, we've all said it!

LA SGRICIA (*crossing herself*). It's like being with a bunch of infidels!

SPIZZI (*pushing up close to Cromo*). Coward! How dare you...

CROMO (*pushing him back*). Out of my way! It's time to put an end to it!

SPIZZI. 'Without much ado' to keep the show going... You'd have sold
your own wife!

CROMO. What show business, you fool?! I was talking about the one who
killed himself.

THE COUNTESS (*freeing herself from those who are trying to restrain her, and
coming forward*). Is it true that you've all said it?

SPIZZI. No, absolutely untrue!

DIAMANTE. I never said such a thing!

BATTAGLIA. And neither did I.

ILSE (*to her husband*). Is it true you've thought of it too?

THE COUNT. Certainly not, Ilse. You're raving! And in front of
strangers...

COTRONE. Don't mind us, Count...

ILSE. That is just why! We've come like this...

COTRONE. Don't mind us, we're on holiday here, open-hearted, dear
Countess.

ILSE. Countess? I'm an actress – and I had to remind him (*points to Cromo*) that it's an honourable title – he's an actor too, like the others.

CROMO. And I'm not proud of it, no! And you shouldn't be either, in front of me, because I've always been an actor, and done it honourably, and I've followed you this far. While you at a certain point wanted to give up acting! Remember?

THE COUNT. Not true! I was the one who forced her to give up the stage.

CROMO. And you were right! I wish you'd kept it up – you a Count, me a beggar – I wouldn't be on such familiar terms with you now. (*To the Countess*) You'd married a Count... (*to the others, as if parenthetically*) He was rich! (*to the Countess again*) You weren't an actress any more, to keep yourself chaste as you kept yourself so proudly until then (I know, I've realized that's what you meant to say).

ILSE. Yes, that's it, yes!

CROMO. But you, my dear, wanted to boast too much about your chastity! By then you were a Countess, good Lord! And as a Countess you could have given him those horns! Countesses are more generous. They do it. That unlucky fellow wouldn't have killed himself, and you, and he, poor guy, and all of us, wouldn't be at this pass now!

ILSE (*straight, stiff, as if rigidified; then, in a convulsion that surges from her very entrails, shaking, starts laughing again as she said she had laughed before*). Huh huh huh, huh huh huh... (*raises her hands to her head and with her index fingers makes two exaggerated horns, saying, convulsively, in a harsh voice*) The butterflies' horns are called feelers...

THE COUNT (*with restrained anger, facing Cromo*). Get out! Go away! You can't stay with us any longer!

CROMO. Go away? Where do you expect me to go now? What do you pay me with?

ILSE. (*quickly, to her husband*) Yes, what do you pay him with? Do you hear him? (*then turning to Cotrone*) That's the problem, sir; we can't earn enough to pay any more.

SPIZZI. No, Ilse. You can't say that of us!

ILSE. I'm talking about him, not you.

CROMO. It's not true! You can't say that of me either! The pay? I would have left long ago, like the others. I am still here because of my esteem for you. I'm talking because you make me so angry, even now...

ILSE (*with a desperate cry*). What else can I do?

CROMO. Nothing now, of course! But before! Before the guy killed himself and became for you and all of us the cancer that's gnawed us to the bone. Look at us: like mangy, famished, stray dogs, kicked away by everyone... and she there, with that head of hers high and her wings fallen, like a strung-up sparrow, the kind that are sold in bunches, tied together through the nostrils in their beaks...

QUACQUÉO. Who killed himself? (*The question is lost in the deep emotion Cromo's words have excited among his companions. Nobody answers.*)

LA SGRICIA. One of you?

ILSE (*noticing her, has a sudden impulse of sympathy*). No, dear grandma. Not one of them. One who was superfluous in the human race. A poet.

COTRONE. No, signora, not a poet, please.

SPIZZI. The countess is speaking of the author of *The Tale of the Changeling*, which we've been performing for two years now.

COTRONE. Exactly, that's what I guessed...

SPIZZI. And you dare say he wasn't a poet?

COTRONE. If he was, he didn't kill himself because of it!

CROMO. He killed himself because he was in love with her! (*pointing to the Countess*).

COTRONE. Ah, that was it? And because the signora, I imagine, faithful to her husband, chose not to respond to his love. Poetry has nothing to do with it. A poet writes poetry, he doesn't kill himself.

ILSE (*pointing to Cromo*). Didn't you hear? He said I should have re-sponded to his love! Since I was a Countess! As if the ability came with the title.

THE COUNT. ... rather than from the heart!

CROMO. Oh, be quiet. She loved him too!

ILSE. Me?

CROMO. Yes, yes, you! You too! And that does you credit in my eyes! Otherwise I couldn't begin to explain any of this. And he (*points to the Count*) now pays for your heroic refusal to surrender! For one must never go against the heart's dictates!

THE COUNT. Will you stop making everything public?

CROMO. Since we were talking about it... *I* didn't start all this.

THE COUNT. You did start it!

QUACQUÉO. So much so that you got yourself a slap in the face! (*This provokes some laughter.*)

ILSE. Right, dear. A slap in the face (*goes up to Cromo and caresses his face*), which I now erase. You are not the enemy, even if you're making a public spectacle of me.

CROMO. Not me!

ILSE. Yes, you're stabbing me, before all these people.

CROMO. *I'm* stabbing you?

ILSE. It seems that way to me... (*to Cotrone*), but it's natural... When you go out in public... (*to the Count*) Poor, dear man, you'd like to keep your dignity intact... Don't worry, it will end. I have a feeling that we're near the end...

THE COUNT. No, Ilse! You only need to rest awhile...

ILSE. What are you still trying to hide? and where? If you're free of sin, you can display your soul like a naked child or one in rags. Even sleep I feel torn in rags from my eyes... (*looks around, looks ahead*) We are facing the countryside... and the evening darkness... and these people before us... (*to her husband*) Do you understand? I loved him. And I made him die. This can be said now, my dear, of a dead man who has received nothing from me. (*Approaches Cotrone*) Dear sir, it feels almost like a dream, or another life, after death... This sea we've crossed... My name was Ilse Paulsen then...

COTRONE. I know, Countess...

ILSE. I had left a good name on the stage...

THE COUNT (*glancing angrily at Cromo*). A pure one!

CROMO (*impetuously*). Who's ever denied it? She was always a fanatic. Before he married her, she wanted to become a nun, imagine!

SPIZZI. You can say that? and expect that once she was a Countess...

CROMO. I've explained exactly why I said it!

ILSE. For me it was a sacred debt! (*To Cotrone again*) One day a young man, a friend of his (*points to her husband*), a poet, came to read me a work he was writing – for me – he said, – though with no hope, since I was no longer acting. The work seemed so beautiful to me that (*turning to Cromo*), yes, I became enthusiastic about it at once. (*To Cotrone again*) But I clearly understood (a woman quickly realizes these things – I mean when somebody has gotten ideas about her); he wanted to draw me back to my former profession with the lure of his work. But not for the sake of the work, but to have me for himself... I felt that if I rejected him outright, he would never finish his work. And because of the beauty of his work, not only did I not reject him outright, but I fed his illusion to the end. When the work was finished, I withdrew – though all ablaze by then – from that fire. If I am reduced to this, how can you not understand? He's right (*pointing to Cromo*), I'd never be free of it. The life I denied him, I had to give to his work. He himself realized it (*points to her husband*) and allowed me to return to the theatre in order to pay this sacred debt. For this one work alone!

CROMO. Consecration and martyrdom! Because he (*pointing to the Count*) was never jealous, even afterwards.

THE COUNT. I had no reason to be!

CROMO. But don't you see that for her he's not dead? She wants him to live! There she is, ragged as a beggar, dying, making us all die, so that he – yes, he – may go on living!

DIAMANTE. He's the one who's jealous, instead.

CROMO. Brava, you've guessed right!

DIAMANTE. Come on, you're all in love with her!

CROMO. No, it's spite and compassion!

ILSE (*at the same time as Spizzi*). He tries to humiliate me! but he praises me even more!

SPIZZI. He enjoys acting spiteful, even though he's not!

BATTAGLIA (*at the same time*). Such an upheaval in my soul... I'm all shook up...

LUMACHI (*at the same time, folding his arms*). I ask you, is this situation conceivable?

ILSE (*to Cromo*). Sure, I'm dying of it! I accepted it, like an inheritance! Although I must say, at the beginning I had no idea he would make me suffer all this pain with his work, the pain he had in him, and I found...

COTRONE. So this work – played before ordinary people – because it's the work of a poet – has been your ruin? Oh, how well I understand!

BATTAGLIA. From our very first performance...

COTRONE. No one wanted to hear of it?

SACERDOTE. All of them were against it!

CROMO. Booed so loud the walls shook!

COTRONE. That's how it was, eh?

ILSE. You're pleased about it?

COTRONE. No, Countess, it's because I understand it so well! A poet's work...

DIAMANTE. Nothing worked! Not even the fantastic scenery, stuff never seen before! The dogs!

BATTAGLIA (*sighing as usual*). And the lighting! What lighting!

CROMO. Marvellous, spectacular staging! There were forty-two of us, between actors and extras...

COTRONE. And you've shrunk to so few?

CROMO (*pointing to his clothing*). And in such rags! ... The work of a poet...

THE COUNT (*bitterly indignant*). You too!

CROMO (*pointing to the Count*). And an entire estate eaten up!

THE COUNT. I don't regret it. I wanted to do it!

ILSE. Beautiful! Worthy of you!

THE COUNT. No, I'm not an enthusiast. I really believed in the work...

COTRONE. Believe me, dear lady, when I say 'the work of a poet' it's not to disparage it – quite the contrary! – It's to disparage the people who turned their backs on it!

THE COUNT. For me, belittling the work is belittling her (*pointing to his wife*), belittling the price I put on what she has done! I paid for it with all I possessed, and I don't regret it, I don't care! As long as she holds the high ground and this condition to which I've been reduced is at least ennobled by the beauty and greatness of the work; otherwise... otherwise, all these people's contempt... you see... and the laughter... (*he is almost choked by his emotion*).

COTRONE. My dear Count, I hate such people! That's why I live here! See the proof? (*points to the fez he has been holding in his hand since the arrival of the guests, and presses it on his head*) I was a Christian, now I've become an infidel!

SGRICIA. Leave religion alone! ah, leave it alone!

COTRONE. No, my dear, it has nothing to do with Mohammed! Infidel because the Christian world has rejected poetry. But, my god, was the hostility really that great?

THE COUNT. Not really. We did find friends, occasionally...

SPIZZI. ... full of enthusiasm...

DIAMANTE (*gloomy*). ... but very few!

CROMO. ... and the impresarios have cancelled our contracts and ruled out performances in the major cities with the excuse that our company has dwindled, we've no more props or costumes.

THE COUNT. It's not true! We still have with us everything necessary for the performance!

BATTAGLIA. The costumes are there in their bags...

LUMACHI. ... under the hay...

SPIZZI. ... and they're not really necessary, after all!

CROMO. And the scenery?

THE COUNT. We've always managed, so far!

BATTAGLIA. The roles can be doubled. I play either male or female parts...

CROMO. Even offstage!

BATTAGLIA (*with a feminine gesture*). Wicked thing!

SACERDOTE. In a word, we are jacks of all trades!

DIAMANTE. And we don't skip anything! What we cannot act out, we read.

SPIZZI. And the beauty of the work is such that nobody minds the actors or the props that are missing!

THE COUNT (*to Cotrone*). But nothing is missing. Believe me, nothing is missing! It's this same damned tendency to belittle ourselves!

COTRONE. I admire your spirit, Count; but, believe me, with me you don't need to praise the beauty of the work and the excellence of the performance. You've been directed to me by an old friend of mine, who probably was too late, or couldn't find a way to pass on to you the advice I gave him, to prevent you from making the journey way out here.

THE COUNT. Oh yes? Why?

SPIZZI. Nothing for us here?

CROMO. I told you so.

LUMACHI. Yeah, I thought so too! Off in the mountains!

COTRONE. Be patient, don't lose hope. We'll arrange something!

DIAMANTE. But where, if there is nothing here?!

COTRONE. Not in town, that's for sure! If you've left anything there, you'd better retrieve it.

THE COUNT. But isn't there a theatre in town?

COTRONE. Yes, there is, but just for the rats, Count. It's always closed, and even if it were open, nobody would go there.

QUACQUÉO. They're thinking of tearing it down...

COTRONE. They want to replace it with a little stadium...

QUACQUÉO. ... for racing and wrestling.

MARA-MARA. No, no, I heard they want to make a movie house out of it!

COTRONE. So, don't even think of using it!

THE COUNT. Where, then? There are no houses near here...

DIAMANTE. Where did we end up?

SPIZZI. They referred us to you...

COTRONE. ... and I am here, entirely at your disposal, together with these friends of mine. Don't be discouraged, we'll see, we'll think it over, we'll find something. In the meantime, if you'd like to come into the villa... You must be tired. We will try to accommodate you as best we can tonight. The villa is quite large.

BATTAGLIA. And maybe a bit of supper...

COTRONE. But it would be good for you to follow our example a bit...

BATTAGLIA. That is...

DOCCIA. To do without everything and to need nothing.

QUACQUÉO. Please, don't scare them!

BATTAGLIA. And what if we need everything?

COTRONE. Please, come in, please!

BATTAGLIA. How does one do without everything?

COTRONE. Please, Countess... (*Ilse, slumped on the bench shakes her head*)... you won't?

QUACQUÉO (*to Doccia*). See that? Now she doesn't want to go in any more!

THE COUNT. She will later. (*To Cotrone*) Please, attend to the others for now.

DIAMANTE. But you think we should accept?

CROMO. Well, at least we'd have a roof over our heads! You don't want to stay here in the damp of the night, do you?

BATTAGLIA. We've got to have something to eat! ...

COTRONE. Of course, of course. We'll find something. Will you take care of it, Mara-Mara?

MARA-MARA. Sure, come, come.

LUMACHI. We surely can't go back all the way to the town. I have a cart, but I have to pull it!

SACERDOTE (*to Battaglia, starting to enter the villa*). If you eat only a little, you'll sleep better.

BATTAGLIA. At first, yes! But then such a tormenting hunger sets in, that gnaws at your stomach as well as your sleep!

COTRONE (*to Lumachi*). The cart can stay outside. (*To Doccia*) You, Duccio, take care of assigning the rooms.

SPIZZI. For the Countess!

CROMO. But there will be enough for everybody, we hope.

MILORDINO. Sure, sure! We've got rooms to spare.

LA SGRICIA. Not mine, though. I won't give up mine for anybody!

COTRONE. Yours, of course not! Calm down! The organ's in her room: it's the chapel.

QUACQUÉO (*pushing them, playfully*). Come on, come on! We'll enjoy ourselves! I play the child! I dance like a cat on the organ keyboard! (*All enter the villa, except Ilse, the Count, and Cotrone.*)

A BRIEF PAUSE

II

(*The last glow of twilight is waning, and the light on the stage dims. Then gradually moonlight brightens the stage. Cotrone waits for all the others to enter the villa, then, after a brief pause, begins to speak in a calmer tone.*)

COTRONE. For the Countess the bedroom of the former masters of
the villa is still as it was: the only one that still has a key, and I have
it.

ILSE (*still sitting, is silent, absorbed; then begins to speak in a remote voice*).
Five tom cats for a single female:
Five ready toms encircling her,
Waiting to spring, they burn
To see the anguish of her longing.
But let one barely stir,
And all the others pounce upon him;
They fight, they scratch, they bite,
They flee, and fly in hot pursuit...

COTRONE (*whispering to the Count*). Is she rehearsing her lines?

THE COUNT (*whispering to Cotrone*). No, this is not her role. (*Then loudly
in a spiteful tone*) 'Yes, yes, yes...'

ILSE.
And are the cats then
That play such tricks
On children's heads? Look!
Oh look!

THE COUNT. What is it I'm to look at?

ILSE.
Here, this little braid
Of twisted hair
(*Then, in a different tone, the tone of a mother protecting the head of her
child, pressing it against her breast*)
No, my treasure!
(*In the previous tone*)
See? A comb
Must not touch it;
A scissors
Must not cut it;
Or the child
Would die...

COTRONE.. The Countess surely has an enchanting voice... I think if she
were to enter the villa for a while, she would quickly feel better.

THE COUNT. Come, Ilse. Come on, dear. You'll rest a little, at least.

COTRONE. We may lack the necessities, but we have such an abundance
of all superfluities... Just look. Even outdoors. Take this facade. All
I have to do is shout... (*He cups his hands around his mouth and shouts*)

Hey there! (*Instantly the facade of the villa is lit by a wonderful dawn light*) And the walls give off light!

ILSE (*amazed like a little girl*). Oh, how beautiful!

THE COUNT. How did you do it?

COTRONE. They call me Cotrone the Magician. I live modestly on these magical effects. I create them. And now watch (*Cups his hands around his mouth again and shouts*) Darkness! (*The tenuous moonlight returns as the glow of the facade vanishes.*) The night seems to create this darkness just for the fireflies, which, as they fly – god knows where – blaze out for a moment, now here, now there, in their faint flash of green. Now look, there… there…. there… (*as he speaks and points in three different directions, three green apparitions, like evanescent larvae, appear for a moment, even as far away as the foot of the mountain*).

ILSE. My god, how did you do that?!

THE COUNT. What are they?

COTRONE. Fireflies! My fireflies! A magician's fireflies! It's like being at the very borderlines of life here, Countess. The borderlines come undone at will; the invisible enters; phantoms take on shapes of air. It's a natural phenomenon. Things happen here that usually happen only in dreams. I make them happen while we are awake. That's all. Dreams, music, prayer, love… All that man is, you will find within and around this villa. (*At this point an extremely irritated Sgricia comes to the threshold.*)

LA SGRICIA. Cotrone, you'll see that the Angel Onehundredandone will no longer want to visit us, I'm warning you!

COTRONE. No, he'll come, Sgricia. Don't be afraid! Come here…

LA SGRICIA (*approaching*). It's the talk that's going on in there, by all those devils!

COTRONE. But you know one needn't fear words. (*Introducing her*) This is the person who prays for all of us. La Sgricia of the Angel Onehundredandone. She came to live with us here, since the church wouldn't recognize the miracle the Angel they call Onehundredandone performed for her.

ILSE. Onehundredandone?

COTRONE. Yes. Because he's in charge of a hundred souls from purgatory, whom he leads every night on holy enterprises.

ILSE. Oh yes? And what was the miracle?

COTRONE (*to La Sgricia*). Come on, Sgricia. Tell it to the Countess.

LA SGRICIA (*frowning*). You won't believe it, anyway!

ILSE. Oh, yes, yes, I will.

COTRONE. No one may be more inclined to believe it than the Countess. It was during a trip she had to make to a nearby village, where one of her sisters lived… (*At this point a voice high up in the air – monotone, echo-like, but clear – says:*)

VOICE. A village with a bad reputation, as unfortunately there are still on this wild island. (*The Countess and the Count, amazed, look above in every direction.*)

COTRONE (*quickly, to reassure them*). Nothing to fear, just voices. I'll explain…

VOICE (*from the cypress tree*). A man is killed like a fly.

ILSE (*frightened*). Oh my god! Who's speaking?

THE COUNT. Where do these voices come from?

COTRONE. Don't be upset, Countess! Don't be upset! They take shape in the air. I'll explain.

LA SGRICIA. They are the murdered ones! Listen, listen! (*Cotrone, smiling, gestures surreptitiously to the Countess, as if to say, behind La Sgricia's back: 'Don't believe it. We're doing it for her!' But La Sgricia sees him and gets angry.*) What do you mean by denying it? What about the baby?!

COTRONE (*obligingly, playing the part*). Oh, the baby, yes. (*To Ilse*) The story's told of a cart driver, Countess, who, having given a lift to a small boy he met on the road at night around here, killed him in his sleep when he heard a couple of pennies jingling in his pocket, to buy some tobacco when he reached the village. He threw the body over a hedge, and gee-up, went on his way singing under the starry sky…

LA SGRICIA (*in a terrifying voice*). … under the eyes of God, who was watching him! And He watched him so closely that do you know what the murderer did? When dawn came, instead of going to his master's farm, he stopped at the local police and with the child's pennies in his bloody hand he accused himself as if another person were speaking through his mouth. Do you see what God can do?

COTRONE. Armed with this kind of faith, she had no fear starting off at night…

LA SGRICIA. What do you mean, at night! I wasn't supposed to start off at night, I was supposed to start off at dawn. It was my neighbour, whom I'd asked to lend me his little donkey.

COTRONE. That farmer had once asked her to marry him.

LA SGRICIA. That's got nothing to do with it! He woke up in the middle of the night worried about getting the little donkey ready by daybreak.

He mistook the moonlight for daybreak. I realized at once, as I
looked at the sky, that it was moonlight, not daylight. I'm an old
woman, I crossed myself, I got in the saddle, and left. But on the
road... at night... amid the open fields... and fearful shadows...
and the silence that muffled even the sound of the donkey's
hooves... and that moon... and the long white road... I pulled my
shawl over my eyes, and covered up like that, maybe from weakness,
or the journey's slow pace, or whatever, the fact is, I found myself at
a certain point, as if I were waking up, between two long lines of
soldiers...

COTRONE (*as if to draw attention to the coming miraculous event*). Here it
comes now...

LA SGRICIA (*continuing*). Those soldiers were moving along both sides of
the road, and at their head, in front of me, in the middle, on a
majestic white horse, was their captain. I felt so comforted at that
sight, and I thanked God for fixing it that on the very night of my
trip those soldiers too had to go to Favara. But why in such silence?
Young men of twenty... An old woman in the midst of them on that
little donkey... Yet they weren't laughing. You couldn't even hear
them walking, they didn't raise even a speck of dust... Why? How
could it be? I realized how as dawn came, in sight of the village. The
captain stopped on his huge white horse, waited for me to come up
to him on my little donkey. 'Sgricia, I am the Angel
Onehundredandone,' he told me, 'and these who have escorted you
this far are souls of Purgatory. When you reach your destination,
make your peace with God, for you shall die before noon.' Then he
disappeared with his holy escort.

COTRONE (*quickly*). Now comes the best part! When her sister saw her
coming, pale, wildly upset...

LA SGRICIA. 'What's wrong with you?' she shouted. And I: 'Send for a
confessor.' 'Are you sick?' 'I shall die before noon.' (*She stretches out
her arms.. And in fact... (she bends down to look into the Countess's eyes
and asks:*) Maybe you believe you are still alive? (*She motions 'no' with
her index finger before Ilse's face.*)

VOICE (*from the cypress*). Don't you believe it! (*The old lady with an
approving smile gestures to the Countess as if to say 'Did you hear that?' and
thus, smiling and satisfied, goes back into the villa.*)

ILSE (*looks first at the cypress, then at Cotrone*). Does she believe she's dead?

COTRONE. In another world, Countess, with all of us...

ILSE (*shaken*). What world is this? And these voices?

COTRONE. Accept them! Don't try to explain them! I could…

THE COUNT. But are they contrived?

COTRONE (*to the Count*). If they help you to enter another truth, far from your own, even one so transient and mutable as this… (*to the Countess*) stay, stay in that far distance and try to look at things with the eyes of this little old lady who has seen the Angel. One must stop reasoning. That is the basis of our life here. Lacking everything, but with all the time in the world: an incalculable treasure, a welling up of countless dreams. The things around us speak and have meaning only in the arbitrary forms into which our desperation happens to change them. Our kind of desperation, of course! We are serene and rather lazy. Sitting here, we contrive, how shall I say, mythological enormities, very natural ones, given the quality of our existence. One cannot live on nothing, so it's a continual heavenly intoxication. We breathe the air of fable. Angels can very easily come down among us. And all the things that arise within us are a wonder even to ourselves. We hear voices, laughter. We see enchanted figures rise from every shaded corner, created by the disordered colours that are left in our eyes dazzled by the excessive sun of our island. We can't bear voiceless shadows. The images are not invented by us, they are the desires of our own eyes. (*He listens*) There, I hear her coming. (*He shouts*) Maddalena! (*He points*) There, on the bridge. (*Maddalena appears on the bridge in the reddish light of a small lamp she carries in her hand. She is young, with red hair and golden skin; dressed in red, peasant-style, she seems a moving flame.*)

ILSE. My god, who's she?

COTRONE. The 'Red Lady.' Don't be afraid! She's flesh and blood, Countess. Come, Maddalena, come. (*While Maria Maddalena approaches, he adds*). A poor idiot, who can hear but cannot speak. She's alone, no family left, and roams the countryside. Men take her, and she is oblivious to the end of what has happened to her many times already. She leaves her babies on the grass. Here she is. On her lips and in her eyes you always find the smile of the pleasure she gives and receives. She comes to take shelter with us in the villa almost every night. Go in, go in, Maddalena. (*Maria Maddalena, with a sweet smile on her lips, a veil of pain in her eyes, nods repeatedly and enters the villa.*)

ILSE. And who does the villa belong to?

COTRONE. To us and to no one. To the ghosts!

THE COUNT. What do you mean, the ghosts?

COTRONE. Yes. The villa is widely believed to be inhabited by ghosts. That's why it was abandoned by its old owners, who were so terrified they even fled the island, a long time ago.

ILSE. But you don't believe in ghosts...

COTRONE. How can I not? We create them!

ILSE. Ah, you create them...

COTRONE. Pardon me, Countess. I wasn't expecting such a question from you. It's not possible for you not to believe in them. You actors give flesh to visions so they may live – and they do live! We do the opposite: we make visions out of our flesh, and we too make them live as well. We don't have to seek them far away – we need only make them emerge from ourselves. You called yourself only a shadow of what you once were?

ILSE. Well, just look at me...

COTRONE. Well, whatever you once were, you've only to let her out. Don't you think she's still alive inside you? Isn't the spirit of the young man who killed himself for you alive still? You have him inside you.

ILSE. Inside me...

COTRONE. And I could make him appear for you. Look, he's in there (*points to the villa*).

ILSE (*getting up, horrified*). No!

COTRONE. There he is! (*On the threshold Spizzi appears costumed as a young poet resembling the one who killed himself for the Countess, with clothing found in the strange wardrobe of the villa used for the many apparitions: a black cape of the sort once worn over formal dress; a white silk scarf around his neck; a top hat on his head. His hands within the cape hold it out in an elegant bell shape and conceal an electric lantern that lights his face from below, like a ghost. As soon as the Countess sees him, she utters a cry and falls back on the bench, hiding her face.*)

SPIZZI (*running up to her*). No, Ilse, no,... my god, it was just a joke...

THE COUNT. Oh, it's you, Spizzi. Ilse, it's Spizzi.

COTRONE. Come out of himself, to show himself as a ghost!

THE COUNT (*angry*). What are you saying now?

COTRONE. The truth!

SPIZZI. I was only joking!

COTRONE. And I have always invented truths, my dear sir! And people have always taken them for lies. One is never more truthful than when one invents truth. Here's the proof! (*points to Spizzi*). You say you were joking? No. You obeyed. Masks are not chosen by pure chance. And here are more proofs... More proofs... (*Through the door of the villa Diamante, Battaglia, Lumachi, and Cromo, in the order Cotrone will present them, come back on stage, all in costume, and each lit by the different-coloured lamps they hold hidden in their hands. All the others follow them.*) You (*he takes Diamante's hand*), of course, dressed as a countess... (*to the Count*). Did you by chance have any function at court, Count?

THE COUNT (*in a disconcerted voice*). No, why?

COTRONE (*pointing to Diamante's dress*). Because this is definitely a lady-in-waiting's dress. (*Turning to Battaglia*) And you, like a turtle in its shell, felt comfortable in this costume of a sanctimonious old bigot. (*Then pointing to Lumachi, who has put on a donkey's hide with a cardboard head*) And you went for the donkey that you miss... (*then goes to shake hands with Cromo*). And you've dressed up as a Pasha. Congratulations! You must be a kind-hearted man...

THE COUNT. What is this? Mardi Gras?

CROMO. Inside there (*points to the villa*) there's an entire arsenal of things for the apparitions!

LUMACHI. You should see what costumes! A costume shop can't have that many!

COTRONE. And each of you went for the mask that fitted you the best!

SPIZZI. No, no, I did it...

THE COUNT (*irritated*). ... as a joke? (*Pointing to Spizzi's suit*) Do you think such a costume makes a good joke?

ILSE. He obeyed...

THE COUNT. Whom?

ILSE (*pointing to Cotrone*). Him. He's a magician. Didn't you hear?

COTRONE. No, Countess...

ILSE. Oh, be quiet, I know! ... You invent truth?

COTRONE. I've never done anything else all my life! Without meaning to, Countess. All those truths which we refuse to recognize consciously, I make them emerge from the secret places of our senses, or – in other cases, the more frightening ones – from the recesses of our instincts. I invented so many of them in my village, that I had to flee, pursued by scandal. Now, in this place, I endeavour to dissolve them into evanescent visions, passing shadows. With these friends of mine I contrive to diffuse even exterior reality into a soft glow, by pouring the soul, like wisps of painted clouds, into the dreaming night.

CROMO. Like fireworks?

COTRONE. But without the noise. Silent enchantments. Foolish people fear them and stay away, so we are masters here. Masters of nothing and of everything.

CROMO. And what do you live on?

COTRONE. Again, on nothing and everything.

DOCCIA. You can't have everything except when you've got nothing any more.

CROMO (*to the Count*). Do you hear? That's just our case! So we've got everything?

COTRONE. Well, no, because you still want something. When you no longer want anything, then, yes.

MARA-MARA. You can sleep with no bed...

CROMO. ... poorly...

MARA-MARA. ... but you sleep!

DOCCIA. Who can deny you your sleep, when God who wants you to be healthy sends it to you, as a gift, when you're tired? Then you sleep, even without a bed!

COTRONE. And you need hunger too, right, Quacquéo? For a piece of bread to give you the pleasure of eating, the way the rarest foods can never give you if you're full or have no appetite. (*Quacquéo, smiling and nodding, rubs his stomach the way children do to show they are enjoying some food.*)

DOCCIA. And only when you've got no home any more is the whole world yours. You walk and walk, then throw yourself down on the grass under the silence of the sky, and you're everything and nothing, nothing and everything.

COTRONE. This is how beggars talk, Countess, refined people with rare tastes, who have been able to reduce themselves to the condition of exquisite privilege that a beggar has. There are no mediocre beggars. Mediocre people are all sensible and thrifty. Doccia is our treasurer. For thirty years he accumulated those extra coins with which importuned men pay for the luxury of giving alms, and he's come here to offer it to the freedom of dreaming. He pays for everything here.

DOCCIA. Yeah, but if you don't go easy...

COTRONE. He plays the miser, to make it last longer.

THE OTHER SCALOGNATI (*laughing*). It's true, it's true.

COTRONE. I too, perhaps could have become an important man, Countess. But I resigned. I resigned from everything: decorum, honour, dignity, virtue, all things animals know nothing of, thank god, in their blessed innocence. Freed from all these fetters, our soul remains as great as the air, full of sunlight or clouds, open to all lightning, abandoned to all winds, a superfluous and mysterious substance for wonders that lift us and send us off to fairy-tale distances. We look at the earth, what a sad thing! Maybe there's someone down there who thinks he lives our life, but it isn't true. None of us is in the body that others see, but in the soul that speaks from god knows where. Nobody can know: appearances behind other appearances, with the funny names Cotrone... Doccia, Quacquéo... A body is death: darkness and stone. Woe to him who sees himself in his body and his name. We make phantoms, all those that cross our minds. Some are compulsory. See, for instance, the Scotswoman with the parasol (*points to Mara-Mara*), or the dwarf with the turquoise cape (*Quacquéo gestures to mean that it is his distinguishing attribute*). Specialties of the villa. All the others are fruits of our imagination. With the divine prerogative of children who take their games seriously, we pour into the things with which we play the wonder that is in us, and we let ourselves be enchanted by it. It's no longer a game, but a marvellous reality in which we live, cut off from everything, to the excess of madness. Well, ladies and gentlemen, I extend to you the greeting that used to be proffered to pilgrims: unlace your sandals, set down your staff. You have reached the end of your quest. For years I have been waiting for people like you to bring to life other phantoms I've thought of. But we will perform your *Tale of the Changeling*, too, like a marvel sufficient in itself, asking nothing from anyone any more.

ILSE. Here?

COTRONE. Just for ourselves.

CROMO. He's inviting us to stay forever, don't you hear?

COTRONE. Yes! What are you still looking for from people? Can't you see what you've gotten from them so far?

QUACQUÉO AND MILORDINO. Yes, stay! Here with us, here with us!

DOCCIA. Hey, there's eight of them!

LUMACHI. I'm for it!

BATTAGLIA. The place is beautiful!

ILSE. That means I shall go on alone, giving readings of *The Tale*, if no more performances.

SPIZZI. No, Ilse – let whoever chooses to, stay – I'll follow you forever!

DIAMANTE. So will I! (*to the Count*). You can always count on me.

COTRONE. I understand that the Countess cannot give up her mission.

ILSE. To the end.

COTRONE. Not even you want the work to live by itself – in the way it could only here.

ILSE. It lives in me, but that is not enough! It must live among people!

COTRONE. Poor poem! As the poet did not win her love, so this work will not win glory from men. But enough now. It's quite late, and it would be good if we all went to rest. Since the Countess declines, I have an idea which I'll share with you tomorrow at dawn.

THE COUNT. What idea?

COTRONE. Tomorrow at dawn, Count. Daylight blinds, the night belongs to dreams, and only twilight enlightens us. Dawn looks towards the future, sunset towards the past. (*He raises his arm to show the way to the villa's entrance.*) Till tomorrow!

CURTAIN

III

(*The storeroom of the apparitions: a large room in the centre of the villa with four doors, two on each side, as if access were from two parallel corridors. The back wall, smooth and empty, becomes transparent when indicated, and beyond it will be visible, as in a dream, first a dawn sky, with some white clouds; then the foot of a gently sloping mountain, of an extremely tender green, with trees surrounding an oval fountain; finally, during the following general rehearsal of* The Tale of the Changeling, *a beautiful seascape with a harbour and a lighthouse. The large room seems to be cluttered with apparently the strangest kind of props, furniture that is not real furniture but large, shabby, dusty toys; but everything has been set up to create at a single command the scenes of* The Tale of the Changeling. *Musical instruments, a piano, a tuba, a drum, and five colossal bowling pins with human heads are visible. And, propped awkwardly on chairs, many stuffed dolls: three sailors, two streetwalkers, a little old man with long hair in a frock coat, a grim-faced female housekeeper.*

As the curtain rises, the stage seems lit by an unnatural light, though how or from what point is uncertain. In this light the dolls in the chairs take on a human appearance that is disturbing, although the immobility of their masks betrays their nature as dolls. From the first door on the left Ilse enters, fleeing from something, followed by the Count, who tries to stop her.)

ILSE. No, I want to go out, I told you (*she stops suddenly, surprised and almost frightened*). What place is this?

THE COUNT (*also surprised*). Well, perhaps it's what they were calling the storeroom of the apparitions.

ILSE. And this light. Where is it coming from?

THE COUNT (*pointing at the stuffed dolls*). Look at those chaps. Are they stuffed dolls?

ILSE. They look real…

THE COUNT. … Right, and they seem to be pretending not to see us. But look, you'd think they were made just for us, to fill the vacancies in our company: 'the old man at the little piano,' and that one, look: 'the cafè owner,' and the three 'little sailors' we could never find.

ILSE. *He* must have prepared them.

THE COUNT. *He* did? What does he know about it?

ILSE. I gave him the *Tale* to read.

THE COUNT. Ah, that explains it. But stuffed dolls? What do we do with stuffed dolls? They don't speak. I still don't understand where we've ended up. And in this uncertainty I'd like at least to feel that you… (*he goes up to her and reaches out to touch her, timidly and tenderly*).

ILSE (*in a sudden rage, fuming*). Good lord, how do we get out of here?

THE COUNT. Do you really want to get out?

ILSE. Yes, yes! Out, out!

THE COUNT. Out where?

ILSE. I don't know. Out in the open.

THE COUNT. At night? It's the middle of the night. Everyone's asleep. Do you want to expose yourself to the cold at this hour?

ILSE. That bed makes me shudder.

THE COUNT. I understand. It's horrible. So high…

ILSE. With that moth-eaten purple cover.

THE COUNT. But it's a bed, after all.

ILSE. You go sleep there. I can't.

THE COUNT. And you?

ILSE. There's a bench outside, near the entrance.

THE COUNT. But you'll be even more afraid outside, alone. Up there at least you're with me.

ILSE. It's you I'm afraid of, my dear. Only you. Can't you understand?

THE COUNT (*taken aback*). Of me? Why?

ILSE. Because I know you. And I see you. You follow me like a beggar.

THE COUNT. Shouldn't I stay near you?

ILSE. But not this way! Not looking at me this way! I feel all… I don't know, all sticky. Yes, yes, by this soft, imploring timidity of yours. It's in your eyes, in your hands.

THE COUNT (*mortified*). Because I love you…

ILSE. Thanks a lot, my dear! You've got a knack for bringing it up in all the wrong places, or just when I feel utterly dead. The least I can do is run away from it. I feel like screaming like a madwoman. Do you realize there's a kind of horrible usury in what you do?

THE COUNT. Usury?

ILSE. Yes, yes! Usury! Are you trying to get back with me everything you've lost?

THE COUNT. How can you think of such a thing, Ilse?

ILSE. Oh yes! Now force me to ask your pardon, too.

THE COUNT. Me? What are you saying? I haven't lost a thing, I don't feel I've lost a thing, if I still have you. Do you call that usury?

ILSE. It's horrible, unbearable. You're always searching my eyes. I can't stand it!

THE COUNT. I feel you're remote. I would like to call you back…

ILSE. … always the same thing…

THE COUNT (*offended*). … No! To what you once were for me…

ILSE. … ah, once! When? In which other life, can you tell me? Can you really still see in me what I was?

THE COUNT. Aren't you still, always, my Ilse?

ILSE. I don't even recognize my voice any more. I speak, and my voice – I don't know – other people's voices, all noises, I feel as if – I don't know, I don't know – there's a deafness in the air, so that all words become cruel for me. Please, spare me them!

THE COUNT (*after a pause*). It's true, then.

ILSE. What's true?

THE COUNT. That I'm alone. You don't love me any more.

ILSE. What do you mean, I don't love you any more? What are you saying, you fool? When I can't see myself without you any more? I'm only telling you not to *expect it*, because you know, good lord, you know it's possible for me only one way, when you're not thinking about it. You've got to feel it, my dear, without thinking about it. Come on, come on, be reasonable.

THE COUNT. Yes, I know that I should never think of myself.

ILSE. You always say you want other people's happiness!

THE COUNT. But mine too, sometimes! If I'd ever imagined…

ILSE. I can't even think of anything that I regret any more.

THE COUNT. No, I'm talking about your feelings for me…

ILSE. But they're the same, always the same!

THE COUNT. No, it isn't true. Before…

ILSE. Are you really sure about before? That my feelings would have remained unchanged in that different situation? This way they last, at least, as best they can. But don't you see where we are? It's a miracle if, when we touch ourselves, we don't feel even the certainty of our own bodies vanish under our hands.

THE COUNT. That's just why...

ILSE. Why what?

THE COUNT. ... I'd like to feel you near me.

ILSE. Aren't I here with you?

THE COUNT. Maybe it'll pass. But I really feel lost. I don't know any more where we are or where we're going.

ILSE. We can't turn back now.

THE COUNT. And I don't see the road ahead.

ILSE. This man says he invents the truth.

THE COUNT. Oh yes. Easy. He invents it...

ILSE. The truth of dreams, he says, truer than ourselves.

THE COUNT. Oh, dreams, sure.

ILSE. And in truth, look, there is no dream more absurd than this truth: that we are here tonight, and that this is true. If you think of it, if we let it get hold of us, it is madness.

THE COUNT. I am afraid we let it get hold of us a long time ago. We went on and on, and there we were. I'm thinking about the last time we came down the staircase of our palace, treated so deferentially. I was holding Riri, poor little thing. You never think of her. I always do. All that silky white hair!

ILSE. We can't think about all we've lost!

THE COUNT. The lights, the chandeliers above that marble staircase! Coming down, we were so happy and confident, with no thought of the cold, the rain, the dark fog we would find outside...

ILSE (*after a pause*). Yet, believe me, in the end we lost very little, even if it was a lot in material terms. If our wealth has served to buy us this poverty, we shouldn't be discouraged!

THE COUNT. Are you telling me this, Ilse? I've always been the one to tell you, don't be discouraged!

ILSE. Yes, yes! Let's go now. You're a kind man. Let's go up. Perhaps I'll be able to rest a little now. (*They go out through the same door they came in. As soon as they are gone, the stuffed dolls bow, brace their hands on their knees, and break into scornful laughter.*)

THE STUFFED DOLLS.

– How they complicate things. Good lord, how they complicate things!

– ... and then end up doing...

– ... what they would have done naturally...

– ... without all the complications!

(*The tuba, all by itself, with three short rumbling notes, makes an ironical comment; the drum, by itself, without the sticks, shaking itself like a sieve, rattles approvingly; and, as it does so, the five bowling pins with the crude heads jump up straight. Then the stuffed dolls fall back, a derisive 'heh, heh, heh' replacing their sneering 'ho, ho, ho.' Suddenly they stop and rearrange themselves in their earlier positions, when the right rear door opens and La Sgricia comes in, joyfully announcing:*)

LA SGRICIA. The Angel Onehundredandone, the Angel Onehundredandone! He's coming to get me with his entire entourage! There he is! Kneel down, all of you! Kneel down! (*At her command the stuffed dolls kneel by themselves, while the large back wall lights up and becomes transparent. The souls of Purgatory are seen filing past in two rows as winged angels, the Angel Onehundredandone in their midst on a majestic white horse. A soft soprano choir accompanies the procession.*)

With the weapons of peace,

In the still of night,

With faith and love,

It is God who brings help,

To those who struggle

And those who wander.

(*When the procession is almost over, La Sgricia rises to follow it, and exits through the second left door, which remains open after she leaves. Behind the last pair of spirits, as they go forth, the back wall becomes opaque. The music continues a little longer, growing fainter, and the stuffed dolls get up, one by one, and throw themselves again into their chairs, where they sprawl. A moment later, through the door which was left open, Cromo backs in, his figure changing as in dreams: at first his face is his own, then he assumes the mask of the 'Customer' and the nose of the 'Prime Minister' in* The Tale of the Changeling. *Though walking backwards in fear, he seems to be searching for a thread of sound whose source he can no longer find: he is sure he heard it, he thought it came from the well at the end of the corridor. Meanwhile, from the first door on the right enters Diamante, dressed as the witch 'Vanna Scoma,' with her mask raised above her face; she sees Cromo and calls out to him.*)

DIAMANTE. Cromo! (*and, as Cromo turns*) My, what kind of a face is that?

CROMO. Me? What kind of a face? What about you? You're dressed as Vanna Scoma and you've forgotten to lower your mask over your face.

DIAMANTE. Don't make me laugh: *I'm* dressed as Vanna Scoma? But you, you're dressed as the Customer and sporting the nose of the Prime Minister. I'm still dolled up as the Lady-in-Waiting and I was just about to change, but you know what? I'm afraid I've swallowed a pin.

CROMO. Swallowed a pin? That's bad!

DIAMANTE (*pointing to her throat*). I feel it here!

CROMO. But you really think you're still dressed as a lady-in-waiting?

DIAMANTE. I was changing, I said, and while I was changing…

CROMO. Oh, sure, changing. Look at yourself. You're dressed as 'Vanna Scoma'! (*As she inclines her head to look at her dress, with a finger he quickly lowers her mask over her face*) And this is her mask!

DIAMANTE (*lifting her hand to her throat*). My god, I can't speak any more!

CROMO. Because of the pin? Are you really sure you swallowed it?

DIAMANTE. It is here, right here!

CROMO. Were you holding it between your teeth as you were changing?

DIAMANTE. No! I think I swallowed it just now. In fact, I think there were two of them.

CROMO. Two pins?

DIAMANTE. Pins, pins! Although the second one… I don't know… Maybe I just imagined it! Or maybe it happened before the dream? The fact is that I feel it right here!

CROMO. I get it. You must have dreamed about it because you feel a prickling in your throat. I bet you've got sore tonsils, a bit of an infection.

DIAMANTE. It's possible. The humidity, the stress.

CROMO. You may have a fever.

DIAMANTE. Maybe.

CROMO (*short, compassionate, in the same tone*). Drop dead!

DIAMANTE. Drop dead yourself!

CROMO. It's the best solution, my dear, considering the kind of life we lead.

DIAMANTE. Pins in my dress, yes; there was one, all rusted; but I remember I tore it out and tossed it away; I didn't put it between my teeth. Besides, if I am no longer dressed as a lady-in-waiting… (*from the front left door Battaglia enters, terrified*).

BATTAGLIA. My god, my god, I saw it… I saw, I saw…

DIAMANTE. What did you see?

BATTAGLIA. In the wall out there! Terrifying!

CROMO. Well, if you say 'I saw it,' then it's true! Me too, me too, 'I've heard it'!

DIAMANTE. What? Don't scare me like that! I've got a fever!

CROMO. Down there, at the end of the corridor, where the well is: what music! what music!

DIAMANTE. Music?

CROMO (*taking them both by the hand*). Here, come.

DIAMANTE AND BATTAGLIA (*holding back, together*). No, you're crazy! What music?

CROMO. Beautiful! Come with me! Music... what are you afraid of? (*They tiptoe to the back*) But you've got to find the right spot. It must be here. I heard it. Like from another world. It comes from the bottom of that well, see? (*He points beyond the second left door.*)

DIAMANTE. What music?

CROMO. A concert from paradise. Here, wait. That's how it was before: I moved away and I couldn't hear it any more; I got too close and I couldn't hear it any more; then, all of a sudden, at just the right spot... Here it is, stop! Do you hear it? Do you? (*In fact, soft, sweet music is heard, but the sound is muffled. The three, in a line, lean forward to listen, ecstatic and frightened.*)

DIAMANTE. Good lord, it's true!

BATTAGLIA. Could it be La Sgricia playing the organ?

CROMO. Oh, no! This isn't an earthly thing. And if we move a step, there, you can't hear it any more. (*In fact, as they move, the music stops.*)

DIAMANTE. No, again, again! Let's listen again! (*They return to the previous spot and the music resumes*).

CROMO. There it is again. (*They remain there for a while listening, then he comes forward with the other two, and the music stops.*)

BATTAGLIA. Fear has split me wide open.

CROMO. In this villa you really see and hear such amazing things!

BATTAGLIA. I tell you I saw it! The wall over there, it was opening up!

DIAMANTE. Opening up?

BATTAGLIA. Yes, and you could see the open sky through it!

DIAMANTE. Was it a window, maybe?

BATTAGLIA. No, the window was on this side, closed. There was no window in front of me. And it opened up: oh! moonlight like nobody's ever seen, behind a long stone bench, and tufts of grass – you could count the blades one by one. That idiot in the red dress who smiles and doesn't talk came and sat on the bench, and then a little simpering dwarf came.

CROMO. Quacquéo?

BATTAGLIA. Not Quacquéo. A real one, with a dove-grey cape down to his feet, swinging like a bell, and above it, his funny-size head, and his face stained as if with grape juice. He offered the lady a shiny jewellery box; then he jumped over the bench as if to leave, but hid himself behind there, and every now and then raised his head slyly to see if she gave in to the temptation. But she sat there, motionless, smiling, with her head bowed, staring, the jewel box in her hands. You know, I could even see her teeth between her lips as they opened in a smile?

CROMO. Sure you didn't dream all this?

BATTAGLIA. Certainly not! I saw her just as I'm seeing you two now.

DIAMANTE. Good lord, Cromo, I'm afraid I actually swallowed that pin.

CROMO (*struck by a sudden idea*). Please wait, wait here: I have an idea. I'm going to my room, I'll be back! (*he goes out through the door he came in by*).

DIAMANTE (*confused, to Battaglia*). Why is he going to his room?

BATTAGLIA. I don't know. I'm shaking all over... don't leave me... Oh! don't you think those stuffed dolls have moved?

DIAMANTE. Have you seen them move?

BATTAGLIA. One! I thought I saw one move...

DIAMANTE. No, they're just lying there! (*Cromo comes back in, excited, like a boy on vacation.*)

CROMO. That's it! I thought so! I suspected as much! We're not ourselves here, really. We're not ourselves!

BATTAGLIA. What do you mean, we're not ourselves?

CROMO. Cheer up! Cheer up! It's nothing! Keep quiet. Go, go take a look in your rooms, too, and convince yourselves!

DIAMANTE. Of what? That we're not ourselves?

BATTAGLIA. What did you see in your room?

DIAMANTE. And who are we then?

CROMO. Go and see! It's really funny. Go and see! (*As soon as the two leave by the door through which they had come in, the stuffed dolls straighten up, stretching themselves, and exclaim:*)

THE STUFFED DOLLS.

– Oh, at last!

– Thank god, you've understood, at last!

– It's taken forever!

– We couldn't stand it any more!

CROMO (*at first amazed to see them straighten up, then accepting the fact*). Oh, you too? But of course, of course! It's right, you too, why not?

ONE OF THE STUFFED DOLLS. Shall we stretch our legs a bit? (*Two others take Cromo by the hands and they join the circle the rest have made. The musical instruments start playing by themselves again, an out-of-tune accompaniment to the 'Ring around the Roses' of the dolls with Cromo. Meanwhile Battaglia and Diamante come back in, unhinged. Battaglia seems unaware that he is dressed as a 'trollop,' with a rag of a hat on his head.*)

DIAMANTE. I'm going mad! So then this (*she touches her body*) is not my body? Yet I can touch it!

BATTAGLIA. You saw yourself in there too?

DIAMANTE (*pointing to the dolls*). And all of these, standing up? Good lord, what's going on, I'll scre...

CROMO (*immediately putting a hand over her mouth*). Be quiet! What d'ya want to shout for? I too found my body in there, sleeping beautifully. We've awakened outside. Get it?

DIAMANTE. What do you mean, outside? Outside of what?

CROMO. Outside of ourselves! We're dreaming. Understand? We're ourselves, but in a dream, outside our bodies that are sleeping in there!

DIAMANTE. And are you sure our bodies in there are still breathing, that they're not dead?

CROMO. Dead? Mine is snoring! Blissful as a pig! Belly up, and the chest up and down like a bellows!

BATTAGLIA (*sorrowful*). Mouth wide open – mine, which has always slept like a little angel!

ONE OF THE STUFFED DOLLS (*sneering*). Like a little angel, fabulous!

ANOTHER. With spit drooling down one side!

BATTAGLIA (*pointing fearfully at the dolls*) What's this... ?

CROMO. It is all part of the dream, they are too, don't you understand? And you've become a streetwalker, haven't you looked at yourself? Here's a little sailor for you. Here, give him a hug! (*He throws him into the arms of one of the stuffed dolls dressed as a sailor.*) Let's dance! let's dance! gaily, in our dream! (*New music from the instruments. They dance, but with strange, angular, movements, like those made by dolls that cannot bend well. From the front left door Spizzi enters, who elbows his way through the dancing couples to get past. He holds a rope in his hands.*)

SPIZZI. Make way! Make way! Let me through!

CROMO. Oh, Spizzi! you too! What are you carrying? Where are you going?

SPIZZI. Leave me alone! I can't take it any more! I'll put an end to it!

CROMO. What do you mean, an end? With this rope? (*He raises the arm that holds the rope. All burst out laughing when they see the rope. Then Cromo*

shouts to him) Fool, you're dreaming that you're hanging yourself!
You're hanging yourself in a dream!

SPIZZI (*tearing himself away and running towards the second right-hand door,
through which he disappears*). Yeah, sure, now you'll see if I'm hanging
myself in a dream!

CROMO. The poor guy! His love for the Countess! (*In great distress and
dismay Lumachi and Sacerdote enter through the right and left front doors.*)

LUMACHI. Good lord, Spizzi's hanging himself!

SACERDOTE. Spizzi's hanging himself! He's hanging himself!

CROMO. No, no! You're dreaming it too!

BATTAGLIA. Spizzi's sleeping in his bed.

DIAMANTE. And you too, if you take the trouble to go to see yourself!

LUMACHI. What do you mean, sleeping! There he is! He's right there,
he's really hanged himself! Look!

(*The rear wall becomes transparent again, revealing the figure of Spizzi hanging
from a tree. They all scream with horror and run towards the rear of the stage. The
scene darkens immediately and in the dark, while the actors disappear like figures
in a dream, the sneering laughter of the stuffed dolls returning to their chairs and
immobility is heard. As light returns, nobody is on the stage except the dolls in their
former positions. A little later the Countess, Cotrone, and the Count enter from the
front left door.*)

ILSE. I saw him, I saw him! I tell you! Hanging from a tree, here behind
the villa!

COTRONE. But there are no trees behind the villa.

ILSE. What do you mean? There are no trees? Around a pool!

COTRONE. No pool either, Countess. You can go out and see.

ILSE (*to her husband*). Is this possible? You saw him too!

THE COUNT. Yes, I did too!

COTRONE. Please, Countess, don't be frightened. It's the villa. It comes
alive like this every night, spontaneously, in music and in dreams.
And dreams take on a life of their own outside us, without our
knowing it, such dreams as we can make, incoherent dreams. Only
poets can give coherence to dreams. Here is Signor Spizzi, see? in
flesh and blood, who certainly was the first to dream of having
hanged himself. (*Spizzi has come in through the first left door, very gloomy.
Hearing Cotrone, he is shaken, astounded, offended.*)

SPIZZI. How do you know?

COTRONE. We all know it, my dear.

SPIZZI (*to the Countess*). You too?

ILSE. Yes, I dreamed of it too.

THE COUNT. And so did I.

SPIZZI. All of you? How can it be?

COTRONE. It's clear that you can't keep secrets from anybody, even
when you dream. I was explaining to the Countess that this is a
prerogative of our villa. Always, when the moon is out, everything
begins to turn to dreams on the earth, as if life were to vanish and
only a melancholy larva of it remained in our memory. Then dreams
come out, and the passionate ones sometimes decide to pass a rope
around their necks and hang themselves from an imaginary tree. My
dear young man, we all talk, and after we've talked we recognize
almost always that it has been in vain, and withdraw disappointed in
ourselves like a dog to his lair at night after barking at a shadow.

SPIZZI. No, it's these damn words I've been repeating for two years, with
the feeling their writer put into them!

ILSE. But those words are addressed to a mother!

SPIZZI. Of course, I know that! But he who wrote them wrote them for
you, and he certainly did not see you as his mother!

COTRONE. My friends, speaking of the blame he now puts on the words
of his role, you see that dawn is almost here, and last night I promised you that I would share with you an idea I had regarding your
work – where you might be able to go to perform your *Tale of the
Changeling* – if, that is, you really don't want to stay here with us.
Today a union between two families called 'the mountain giants' is
being celebrated with a colossal wedding feast.

THE COUNT (*being short and therefore puzzled, raising his arm*). Giants?

COTRONE. Not actually giants, Count. They're called that because they're
tall people of powerful build, who live on the mountain nearby. I
suggest that you go to them. We'll come with you. One must know
how to deal with them. The work they've undertaken up there, the
constant exercise of their strength, the courage they had to build up
against all the risks and perils of such enormous enterprises – excava-
tions, foundations, reservoirs, factories, roads, farms – have not only
developed their muscles enormously but have also, naturally, made
them thick-skulled and somewhat bestial in behaviour. However,
swollen by their success, they easily offer the handle by which to get
to them, their pride. Properly stroked, it quickly becomes soft and
malleable. Let me handle this side of the business, while you take care
of yours. For me, taking you up the mountain for the marriage of
Uma Dornio and Lopardo D'Arcifa is a cinch; we'll ask for a big sum
too, because the bigger it is, the greater the importance of our offer in

their eyes. But now the problem to solve is a different one. How will you perform your *Tale?*

SPIZZI. Don't the giants have a theatre up there?

COTRONE. It isn't the theatre. A stage can easily be set up anywhere. I'm thinking of the work you want to perform. I've been reading your *Tale of the Changeling* all night with my friends, until a short time ago. How can you say, my dear Count, that you've got all you need and will leave nothing out? There are only eight of you, and you need a huge crowd to perform it.

THE COUNT. Yes, we lack the silent extras.

COTRONE. What silent extras? They all have speaking roles!

THE COUNT. We do have all the main characters.

COTRONE. The difficulty's not in the main characters. What's important is, above all, the magic – creating, I mean, the power of the fable.

ILSE. That's true.

COTRONE. And how can you create it? You lack everything! This is a choral work... Now I understand why you, my dear Count, have consumed your entire estate. Reading it, I was swept off my feet. It's meant to come alive here, Countess, among us who believe in the reality of phantoms more than in that of bodies.

THE COUNT (*pointing to the stuffed dolls in the chairs*). We've already seen those dolls, ready for it...

COTRONE. Ah, yes, already! They've been very quick, I didn't know.

THE COUNT (*amazed*). What do you mean, you didn't know? Didn't you get them ready?

COTRONE. Not I. But it's simple. As I was reading, they were getting ready here, by themselves.

ILSE. By themselves? But how?

COTRONE. I've told you the villa is inhabited by spirits. That wasn't a joke. We're not amazed by anything any more. Human pride is really foolish, if you pardon my saying so. Other beings, my dear Count, live natural lives on earth, of whom we human beings have no perception, but that's only because of our defects; we have only five very limited senses. Well then, at times, in abnormal conditions, those beings reveal themselves to us, and fill us with fear. Of course! We knew nothing of their existence! Non-human inhabitants of this earth, my friends, spirits of nature, of all kinds, who live among us, invisible, in rocks, woods, air, water, fire. The ancients knew it very well; the common people have known it all along; we here know it well who are competing with them and often overcome them,

compelling them to give our marvels, with their help, a meaning they
don't know or don't care about. If you, Count, still see life within the
limits of the natural and possible, I'm warning you that you'll never
understand anything here. Thank God, we're beyond those limits.
It's enough for us to imagine something, and immediately the images
come alive by themselves. It's enough for a thing to be fully alive
within us, and it stages itself by the spontaneous virtue of its own life.
It is the free realization of any necessary birth. At most, we facilitate
that birth somewhat. Those stuffed dolls, for instance. If the spirit of
the characters they represent is embodied in them, you'll see them
moving and talking. And the true miracle is never the performance,
believe me, but always the imagination of the poet in which those
characters were born alive, so alive that you can see them although
they don't exist bodily. Translating them into a fictive reality on the
stage is what is commonly done in theatres. It's your job.

SPIZZI. So you put us on the same level as those stuffed dolls of yours!

COTRONE. Not on the same level, pardon me; a little below, my friend.

SPIZZI. Ah, even below!

COTRONE. If the spirit of the characters is embodied so deeply in the
dolls as to make them move and talk...

SPIZZI. I'm curious to see that miracle.

COTRONE. Ah, you're 'curious,' are you? But you know, one cannot
make these marvels happen out of mere curiosity! One must believe
in them, my friend, as children do. Your poet has imagined a Mother
who believes that her child has been exchanged by those witches of
the night, witches of the wind, what common people call 'The
Women.' Educated people laugh at the idea, of course, and you do
too, perhaps; instead I'm telling you that they do really exist! We've
heard them scream here so many times during stormy winter nights,
with piercing voices, fleeing with the wind, in these valleys. Listen, we
can evoke them if we want to.
They enter our homes at night
Through the chimneys' throat
Like
Black
Smoke.
What does a poor mother know?
She sleeps weary from her day's work,
And they, bending in the dark
Stretch out their thin fingers...

ILSE (*amazed*). Oh, you already know the lines by heart?

COTRONE. Already? We could perform it here and now, *The Tale*, from
   beginning to end, Countess, to go over all the things *you* need, not
   us. Try, Countess, try for a moment to live your role as the Mother,
   and I'll show you, give you a taste of it. When was your child
   exchanged?

ILSE. When? You mean in the *Tale?*

COTRONE. Of course, where else?

ILSE.

   One night, as I slept,
   I hear a wail, and I awake,
   I grope in the dark, in the bed, at my side:
   He's not there;
   Where is that wailing coming from?
   By himself,
   In swaddling bands, my child
   Could not move...

COTRONE. Why do you stop? Go on, ask, ask, as it says in the text: 'Isn't
   that true? Isn't that true?' (*He has not yet finished speaking the lines,
   when the stage darkens for a second and lights up, as by a magic touch, with
   a new brightness, like an apparition, and the Countess finds beside her two
   real women, the Two Neighbours, as in the first act of* The Tale of the
   Changeling, *who immediately answer.*)

THE ONE.

   It's true, it's true.

THE OTHER.

   A child of six months,
   How could he?

ILSE (*looking at them, listening to them, is frightened, as are Spizzi and the
   Count, who draw back*). My god! And these?

SPIZZI. Where've they come from?

THE COUNT. How's it possible?

COTRONE (*shouting at the Countess*). Go on, go on! Why are you amazed?
   You've called them here! Don't break the spell and don't ask for
   explanations! Say: 'When I picked him up...'

ILSE (*obeying, in a daze*).

   When I picked him up,
   Thrown... there... under the bed...
   (*From above, from nowhere in particular, a powerful, derisive voice
   shouts.*)

VOICE.

    Fallen! fallen!

    (*The Countess, terrified, looks up, like the others.*)

COTRONE. Don't lose your place! It's in the text! Go on!

ILSE (*letting herself be swept up in the wonder of it*).

    Yes! I know!

    That's what they say: fallen.

FIRST WOMAN.

    But fallen how? Only

    Those who didn't see him

    There under the bed,

    As he was found,

    Only they can say so

ILSE.

    That's it. *You* tell

    How he was found,

    You who were first

    To come running when I cried out:

    How was he found?

FIRST WOMAN.

    Turned around.

SECOND WOMAN.

    With his little feet

    Towards the headboard.

FIRST WOMAN.

    The swaddling bands untouched,

    Tightly wound

    Around the little legs.

SECOND WOMAN.

    And tied with the tapes…

FIRST WOMAN.

    Perfectly untouched…

SECOND WOMAN.

    So he'd been taken,

    Taken by someone's hands,

    From his mother's side

    And put there for spite,

    Under the bed.

FIRST WOMAN.

    Oh, if it'd been only for spite!

ILSE.

When I picked him up...

FIRST WOMAN.

How much crying!

(*From offstage, all around, loud, incredulous laughter erupts. The Two Neighbours turn around and shout, as if to stop the laughter.*)

THE TWO NEIGHBOURS.

It was another!

It was no longer the same one!

We can swear to it!

(*For a moment darkness returns, followed by the laughter, which ceases the moment the original light returns. From the various doors enter Cromo, Diamante, Battaglia, Lumachi, Sacerdote, all talking at once.*)

CROMO. What? What? Are we performing? Rehearsing?

DIAMANTE. I can't, I have a sore throat!

LUMACHI. My dear Spizzi! Thank god!

BATTAGLIA and SACERDOTE. What is it? What is it?

COTRONE. You've performed, Countess, with two characters come alive from the poet's imagination!

ILSE. Where've they gone?

COTRONE. They've disappeared!

CROMO. Who are you talking about?

BATTAGLIA. What happened?

THE COUNT. The Two Neighbours of Act One have appeared to us!

DIAMANTE. Appeared? What d'you mean, appeared?

THE COUNT. Right here, all of a sudden, and they started performing with her (*points to the Countess*).

CROMO. We heard the laughter!

SPIZZI. These are all tricks, friends, set-ups. Let's not be dazzled like dummies, we who know our craft!

COTRONE. Oh, no, dear boy. If you say such things, you don't know your craft! You're giving importance to something else that's more important to you! If you knew your craft, you'd let yourself be dazzled, you yourself, first of all, because *that*'s the true sign that one knows his craft! Learn from the children, as I said before, who make up a game and then believe in it, and live it as if it were real!

SPIZZI. But we're not children!

COTRONE. If we were children once, we can always be children! And in fact, you were dazzled too, when those two figures appeared here!

CROMO. But how did they appear? How?

COTRONE. On cue! And they said on cue what they were supposed to say – isn't that enough? All the rest, how they appeared, were they real or not, that's not important. I wanted to show you, Countess, that your *Tale* can live only here, but you insist on taking the play out to mankind. So be it! Away from here, though, I have no more power to come to your aid except with these friends of mine; and I put them and myself at your service.

(*At this point the powerful rumble of the cavalcade of the Mountain Giants is heard from outside. They are coming down into the town to celebrate the wedding of Uma Dornio and Lopardo D'Arcifa, with wild, almost savage music and shouting. The walls of the villa shake. Quacquéo, Doccia, Mara-Mara, Sgricia, Milordino, and Maddalena burst onto the stage in great excitement.*)

QUACQUÉO. The Giants, the Giants are coming!

MILORDINO. They're coming down the mountain!

MARA-MARA. On horseback, all of them! All dressed up!

QUACQUÉO. Do you hear them? They sound like the kings of the world!

MILORDINO. They're going to the church for the wedding!

DIAMANTE. Let's go, let's go and see!

COTRONE (*in an imperious, powerful voice stopping all who are already running off at Diamante's suggestion*). No! Nobody move! Nobody shows himself, if we want to go up there and offer a performance! Let's all stay here to rehearse it!

THE COUNT (*drawing the Countess aside*). But aren't you afraid, Ilse? Listen to them!

SPIZZI (*terrified, drawing closer*). The walls are shaking!

CROMO (*also drawing closer in fear*). It sounds like the cavalcade of a horde of barbarians!

DIAMANTE. I'm afraid! I'm afraid!

(*They all stay there listening, arrested in fear, while the music and the rumbling fade in the distance.*)

CURTAIN

IV

(*This is the action of the third act [fourth 'time frame'] of* The Mountain Giants, *as well as I can reconstruct it from what my father told me, and with the meaning that he wanted it to have. This is all I know about it, and I have set it down, unfortunately, without the effectiveness it deserves; but, I hope, without arbitrary alterations. Yet I cannot know whether, in the end, my father's imagination, which was occupied with these images during the entire next-to-last night of his life – in fact, the following morning he told me that he had had to endure the extremely fatiguing task of composing the entire third act in his mind, and that now, having resolved every obstacle, he hoped to be able to rest a bit, happy that, as soon as he recovered, he would be able to set down in a few days the entire act he had composed during those night hours – I cannot know, that is, nor will anybody ever know, whether or not in that final conception, the material had taken on a different configuration, nor whether he had found other developments for the action to take, or higher meanings for the myth. I received from him, that morning, only this further piece of information, that he had imagined a Saracen olive tree. 'There is,' he said, smiling, 'a Saracen olive tree, a huge one, in the middle of the stage: that solved all my difficulties.' And since I did not really understand, he added: 'To draw a curtain from…' Thus I realized that he had been occupied, perhaps for several days, with solving some practical detail like this. He was surely happy to have found a solution.)*

STEFANO PIRANDELLO

The third act was to take place up on the mountain, in an open space before one of the houses of the 'Giants.'

It began with the arrival of the actors, tired out by their journey, with the cart, and in the company of some of the Scalogna people, all led by Cotrone.

The arrival of these strange and unexpected visitors excited the curiosity of the inhabitants (not of the 'Giants,' who were never to appear on stage, but of their servants and the crews of workers they employ for their enormous projects), who were now all seated at a huge banquet at the back of the stage; their tables were to be imagined as reaching beyond the view of the audience, over an enormous area. Some of the banqueters, the closest ones, were to get up and come forward to ask questions, astonished and attracted, as though before beings dropped from another planet. Cotrone would have informed a supposed overseer in a position of authority of the purpose of his friends' visit: they are actors, and have everything at the ready to offer a first-class artistic performance to the ladies and gentlemen, on the occasion of the wedding, to add lustre to the festivities in progress.

This first scene, taking place among the shouting and orgiastic songs of the Rabelaisian banquet, the dancing, and the noisy setting in motion of the fountains of wine that were to bring cheer to it, was to evidence the kind of entertainments the 'Giants' were providing for their people, and that were actually enjoyed by their people. The actors are, then, deeply discouraged, realizing that these people have no notion of what a theatrical performance is. Even worse, when someone who has heard about it comes forward to tell the others that the theatre is great fun, they realize that he is talking about Punch-and-Judy shows, with the usual blows raining on head and shoulders, or the buffoonery of clowns, or the exhibitions of the chorus girls and 'chanteuses'of nightclubs. But they take comfort while Cotrone is led off by the overseer to talk to the 'Giants' about the performance, in the hope – which they try in their minds to turn into a certainty – that the masters before whom they will perform will not be, cannot be, as uncouth as their servants and workers; and that even if they may not entirely understand the beauty of *The Tale of the Changeling*, they will be listening politely. In the meantime, it is difficult for them to shield themselves from the chattering curiosity and the crude compliments of the surrounding mob, and they are anxious for Cotrone to return with an answer.

But Cotrone's answer is that, unfortunately, the 'Giants,' while accepting the proposed performance and ready to pay for it liberally, have no time for such things, so extensive and so many are the projects they must attend to even on such a festive day. The performance must be for their people, who need from time to time some means of spiritual elevation. And the people are frenetically clamouring for the new kind of entertainment that is being offered to them.

The actors' feelings are divided. Some, led by Cromo, say they feel as if they are being thrown to the lions, nothing can possibly be done before such abysmal ignorance, better give up the attempt. Others, following the Countess, drawing their courage from the very spectacle of bestiality that disheartens and frightens the others, affirm that the power of Art must be tested before precisely such ignorant people, and feel quite certain that the beauty of the *Tale* will conquer their unformed souls. Spizzi, elated, already preparing for this extraordinary performance as for an enterprise worthy of a knight of old, drags along those who are hesitating, shaming them by his example. The Count, disgusted and embittered by the surrounding vulgarity, would like at least to shield the Countess from it.

Cotrone tries to make them aware of the unbridgeable distance separating the two worlds that have so strangely come into contact. On the one hand, the world of the actors, for whom the voice of the poet is not only the highest expression of life, but the only certain reality in which and for which it is possible to live; on the other, the world of the people, intent, under the Giants' leadership, on vast works aimed at possessing the forces and riches of the earth, who find in this incessant and vast common labour the very reason for their life, and in which each individual, together with all the others, but also within himself, takes enormous pride. But Ilse is so happy and so ready for the task that Cotrone must admit that anything is possible, even that she may win, so thrilled is she.

Quick, quick, she says, where is the performance going to be held? Right here, before the people already gathered for the banquet. Only a curtain needs to be stretched to shield the actors while they put on their greasepaint and dress for the play.

There is an old Saracen olive tree in the middle of the stage; a cord is stretched between it and the front to hold up the curtain.

While the actors anxiously get ready, continually interrupted by those who peek in and jeeringly call others over to do the same, Cotrone thinks that it would be good to give this unschooled audience some information about the play and steps outside the curtain to speak to them. But at once jokes and catcalls, shouts and coarse laughter burst out, and the Magician comes back in disappointment. They have not let him open his mouth.

'Don't be discouraged by such a little thing, we're used to it,' Cromo tries to comfort him drily. 'Wait till you hear what happens in a little while!'

And they explain to Cotrone that he was hissed because he has no experience with an audience. But now one of them will go out there, Cromo, who is already dressed, with the Prime Minister's nose, to improvise this preparatory clarification. Cromo will get their attention by cracking some joke. Immediately, in fact, loud approving laughter, applause, and encouraging calls from the audience are heard.

The reception accorded to Cromo raises the spirits of the actors a bit, so that Ilse, with Spizzi and Diamante, the most eager and enthusiastic, are able to argue against the fears of Cotrone, who has by now realized that it is going to end badly and tries for the last time to persuade them to desist; passionately he reminds them of the happiness they are turning their backs on, the night of enchantment at the villa, when all the spirits of poetry had come so naturally to life in them, and could continue to live, if they would only return and remain there forever.

Meanwhile, the hilarity aroused by Cromo is such that he too cannot achieve his purpose, to prepare the mood of the audience for the poetic drama they are going to present. Cromo returns soaking wet because, to enhance the fun, the rowdy spectators have incited each other to turn a hose on him. And now bedlam is unleashed out there: they are calling the actors out on stage, yelling for them to get started. What should they do? Ilse, who is alone on stage at the beginning of *The Tale*, moves away from her husband and Cotrone and goes beyond the curtain, ready as for a supreme sacrifice, determined to fight with all her energy to assert the word of the poet before the mob.

At this point the dramatic contrast, already defined, is about to explode into tragedy. Fatally, the fanatics of Art, who think themselves the sole repositories of the spirit, facing the incomprehension and the derision of these servants, are bound to despise them, as people devoid of any spirituality, and to offend them; while the others, equally fanatic, but about a quite different ideal of life, cannot believe the words of these puppets, as the actors seem to them – not because they are in costume, but because they, the others, feel clearly that these poor devils, so fixated on the seriousness of their gestures and their absurd speeches, have placed themselves, who knows why, completely outside of life. Puppets. But because they are puppets, their business should be to amuse their audience. So, after their initial amazement, drowned out by a huge bellowing of boredom and crass questions – Who the hell is she? What does she want? – they want the Countess to stop declaiming those incomprehensible words so loftily and entertain them with some nice little song and a dance. Thwarted by Ilse's determination, their anger is unleashed. Behind the curtain, the drama in which Ilse is fighting before the audience is reflected in the agitation of the other actors and the panic of Cotrone and the Count. The tempest that grows increasingly threatening suddenly strikes the improvised stage when the Countess hurls insults at the audience, calling them animals, nothing but brutes. Spizzi and Diamante rush to help her. The Count faints. Cromo shouts that all of them better start singing and dancing and goes out to try to divert from Ilse the unleashed fury of the audience. Of the pandemonium exploded beyond it some images are silhouetted on the curtain, of gigantic gestures, enormous bodies wrestling, Cyclopic arms and fists raised to strike. But it is too late now. Suddenly a great silence. The actors re-enter bearing Ilse's body, smashed like a broken puppet, in the throes of death; she dies. Spizzi and Diamante, who entered the melee to protect her, have been torn to pieces: no part of their bodies can be found.

The Count regains consciousness, cries out over his wife's body that men have destroyed Poetry in the world. But Cotrone realizes that nobody is to blame for what has happened. No, it is not that Poetry has been rejected, but only this: that the poor fanatical servants of life, in whom today the spirit is mute but may still speak some day, have innocently broken, like rebellious puppets, the fanatical servants of Art. Artists who do not know how to speak to men because they have cut themselves off from life, though not enough to be content solely with their own dreams, they still insist on imposing them on those who have other things to do than believe in them.

And when the overseer comes backstage, mortified, to offer, with the Giants' apologies, a fair reparation, Cotrone persuades the weeping Count to accept it. The Count, close to frenzy, says that he will accept it, and use that blood money to raise a noble and imperishable tomb to his bride. But the feeling will be clear that, though weeping and protesting his noble feelings of fidelity to dead Poetry, it is as if he has suddenly lifted a burden from himself, freed himself of a nightmare; it seems the same with Cromo and the other actors.

And they depart, carrying Ilse's body on the cart with which they came.

Selected Bibliography

Master editions of Pirandello's Works

Maschere nude. 2 vols. Ed. Manlio Lo Vecchio Musti, Milan: Mondadori (Classici Italiani), 1958, 1971, 1978; ed. Alessandro D'Amico, Milan: Mondadori, 1986, 2007.

Novelle per un anno. 3 vols. Ed. Mario Costanzo, Milan: Mondadori (I Meridiani), 1956–7, 1973, 1985, 1990, 1998.

Saggi, poesie, scritti varii. Ed. Manlio Lo Vecchio Musti, Milan: Mondadori, 1960, 1965, 1977, 1993.

Tutti i romanzi. 2 vols. Ed. Corrado Alvaro, Milan: Mondadori (I Meridiani), 1957; ed. Giovanni Macchia, Milan: Mondadori, 1973; ed. Mario Costanzo, Milan: Mondadori, 1993.

Works of Pirandello in English

Theoretical Writings

'The New Theater and the Old.' Tr. Herbert Goldstone. In Haskell M. Blok and Herman Saliger, eds, *The Creative Vision. Modern European Writers on Their Art.* New York: Grove Press; London: Evergreen Books, 1960.

On Humor. Intr. and tr. Antonio Illiano and Daniel P. Testa. Chapel Hill: University of North Carolina Press, 1974.

'Theater and Literature.' Tr. A.M. Webb. In Haskell M. Blok and Herman Saliger, eds, *The Creative Vision. Modern European Writers on Their Art.* New York: Grove Press; London: Evergreen Books, 1960.

Theatre

As You Desire Me. Tr. Samuel Putnam, New York: Dutton, 1931; tr. Marta Abba, New York: Samuel French, [1959]; tr. Marta Abba, in J. Gassner, ed., *Twenty Best European Plays on the American Stage,* New York: Crown, 1957.

To Clothe the Naked and Two Other Plays [*The Rules of the Game, The Pleasure of Honesty*].Tr. William Murray. New York: Dutton; Toronto: Irwin, 1962.

Collected Plays [Vol. 1: *Henry IV, The Man with the Flower in His Mouth, Right You Are (if You Think You Are), Lazarus;* vol. 2: *Six Characters in Search of an Author, All for the Best, Clothe the Naked, Limes from Sicily;* vol. 3: *The Rules of the Game, Each in His Own Way, Grafted, The Other Son*]. London: John Colder; New York: Riverrun Press, 1987, 1988, 1992.

Diana and Tuda. Tr. Marta Abba. New York: Samuel French, [1960].

'Doctor's Duty.' Tr. O.W. Evans. *Poet Lore* (1942): 291–304.

'Dream, but Perhaps Not.' Tr. S. Putnam. *This Quarter* 2, 4 (June 1930).

Each in His Own Way and Two Other Plays [*The Pleasure of Honesty, Naked*]. Tr. A. Livingston. New York: Dutton; London: Dent, 1924.

The Emperor. Tr. Eric Bentley. In *The Genius of the Italian Theater.* New York: Mentor, 1964.

'The Festival of Our Lord of the Ship.' In M. McKlintock, ed., *The Nobel Prize Treasury.* Garden City, NY: Doubleday, 1948.

To Find Oneself. Tr. Marta Abba. New York: Samuel French, [1959].

Henry IV. Tr. Edward Storer. In B. Ulanov, ed., *Makers of the Modern Theater.* New York: McGraw Hill, 1961.

Lazarus. Tr. Phyllis H. Raymond. Sydney: Dante Alighieri, 1952.

Limes from Sicily and Other Plays. Tr. Robert Rietti. Leeds: S.J. Arnold, 1967.

'The Man with the Flower in His Mouth.' Tr. Eric Bentley, *Tulane Drama Review* 1, 3 (June 1957): 65–22; tr. F. May, *New Troy* 1, 1 (June 1957).

The Mountain Giants and Other Plays [*The New Colony, When Someone Is Somebody*]. Tr. Marta Abba. New York: Crown, 1958.

The Mountain Giants: A Myth. Tr. Felicity Firth. *Yearbook of the British Pirandello Society* 10 (1990).

Naked Masks [*Liolà*, tr. Eric Bentley and G. Guerrieri; *It Is So (if You Think So)*, tr. A. Livingston; *Henry IV*, tr. E. Storer; *Six Characters*, tr. E. Storer; *Each in His Own Way*, tr. A. Livingston]. Ed. Eric Bentley. New York: Dutton, 1952, 1958. [Now in Penguin Meridian]

No One Knows How. Tr. Marta Abba. New York: Samuel French, [1961].

The One Act Plays of Luigi Pirandello ['Chee-Chee,' 'Sicilian Limes,' 'By Judgment of the Court,' 'The Vise,' 'The House with the Column,' tr. Elizabeth Abbott; 'At the Gate,' 'The Imbecile,' 'Our Lord of the Ship,' 'The Doctor's Duty,' tr.

Blanche Valentine Mitchell; 'The Jar,' 'The Man with the Flower in His Mouth,' tr. Arthur Livingston]. New York: Dutton, 1928.

Pirandello's Major Plays [*Right You Are, Six Characters, Emperor Henry, The Man with the Flower in His Mouth*]. Tr. Eric Bentley. Evanston, IL: Northwestern University Press, 1991.

Pirandello's One Act Plays ['Bellavita,' 'Cecè,' 'I'm Dreaming, but Am I?' 'The Jar']. Tr. William Murray. Garden City, NY: Doubleday, 1964.

Pirandello's One Act Plays ['The Vise,' 'Sicilian Limes,' 'The Doctor's Duty,' 'The Jar,' 'The License,' 'Chee-Chee,' 'At the Exit,' 'The Imbecile,' 'The Man with the Flower in His Mouth,' 'The Other Son,' 'The Festival of Our Lord of the Ship,' 'Bellavita,' 'I'm Dreaming, but Am I?']. New York: Funk and Wagnalls, 1970.

'The Rest Is Silence.' Tr. Frederick May. Leeds: The Pirandello Society, 1958.

Right You Are! (if You Think So) [*All for the Best*]. Tr. Henry Reed. Harmondsworth: Penguin, 1962.

Right You Are. A stage version. Tr. Eric Bentley. New York: Columbia University Press, 1954.

'Sicilian Limes.' Tr. Isaac Goldberg. In *Plays of the Italian Theater.* Boston: J.W. Luce, 1921. Also in *Theater Arts Magazine* 6, 4 (1922).

Six Characters in Search of an Author. Tr. Edward Storer. In J. Gassner, ed., *A Treasury of the Theater,* vol. 2. New York: Simon and Schuster, 1951.

Six Characters in Search of an Author. Tr. Frederick May. London: Heinemann, 1954, 1958.

Six Characters in Search of an Author, The Emperor. Tr. Eric Bentley. In Robert Corrigan, ed., *The Modern Italian Theater.* New York: MacMillan, 1964, 1965.

Six Characters in Search of an Author. Adapt. Paul Avila Mayer. In R.W. Corrigan, ed., *Masterpieces of the Modern Italian Theater.* New York: Collier, 1967.

Three Plays [*Six Characters, Henry IV,* tr. Edward Storer; *Right You Are,* tr. Arthur Livingston]. New York: Dutton, 1922, 1932; London: Dent, 1923, 1925, 1929.

Three Plays [*Six Characters, Henry IV, It Is So*]. New York: Dutton; London: Dent, 1922.

Three Plays [*The Rules of the Game,* tr. R. Rietty; *The Life I Gave You, Lazarus,* tr. Frederick May]. Harmondsworth: Penguin, 1959.

Three Plays [*The Rules of the Game, Six Characters, Henry IV*]. London: Methuen, 1985.

Tonight We Improvise. Tr. Samuel Putnam, New York: Dutton, 1932, 1938; tr. Marta Abba, New York: Samuel French, [1960].

The Wives' Friend. Tr. Marta Abba. New York: Samuel French, [1959].

Novels

Her Husband. Tr. Martha King and Mary Ann Frese Witt. Durham, NC, and
  London: Duke University Press, 2000.
The Late Mattia Pascal. Tr. Arthur Livingston, London: Dent, 1923; New York:
  Dutton, 1923, 1934; tr. William Weaver, New York: Doubleday, 1964; Los
  Angeles: Eridanos, 1988; tr. Nicoletta Simborowski, London: Dedalus,
  1987.
The Old and the Young. Tr. C.K. Scott Moncrieff. New York: Dutton, 1928, 1933;
  London: Chatto and Windus, 1928, 1930.
One, No One, One Hundred Thousand. Tr. Samuel Putnam. New York: Dutton,
  1933; New York: Howard Fertig, 1982; tr. William Weaver, New York: Marsilio
  Press, 1990.
The Outcast. Tr. Leo Ongley. New York: Dutton, 1925, 1935; London: Dent,
  1925.
Shoot: The Notebooks of Serafino Gubbio Cinematograph Operator. Tr. C.K. Scott
  Moncrieff. New York: Dutton, 1926, 1934; London: Chatto and Windus,
  1927, 1930; Chicago-London: University of Chicago Press, 2005.

Short Stories

Better Think Twice about It and Twelve Other Stories. Tr. Arthur Mayne and Henrie
  Mayne. London: Lane, 1933, 1940; New York: Dutton, 1934, 1935.
'The Blessing,' 'The Starling and the Angel One Hundred and One.' Tr. F.M.
  Guercio. In Anthology of Contemporary Italian Prose. London: Scholastic Press,
  1931.
A Character in Distress [A collection of nineteen short stories by Pirandello]. Tr.
  Michele Pettina. London: Duckworth, 1938. Published in the United States
  as His Medals and Other Stories. New York: Dutton, 1939.
'The Dinner Guest.' Tr. anon. The Golden Book (July 1934).
'Diploma.' Tr. J. Redfern. The Fortnightly Review (July 1939).
'A Dream of Christmas.' Tr. Frederick May. Leeds: The Pirandello Society,
  1959.
'A Finch, a Cat, and the Stars.' Tr. J. Redfern. The Listener (Sept. 1934).
'Fly.' Tr. R. Wellman. The Forum (24 Feb. 1924).
'Goy.' Tr. Arthur Livingston. Menorah Journal (Feb. 1924).
'Here's Another!' Tr. J. Redfern. The Fortnightly Review (Nov. 1933).
The Horse in the Moon: Twelve Short Stories. Tr. Samuel Putnam. New York: Dutton,
  1932.
'Mere Formality.' Tr. anon. The Golden Book (Sept. 1925).

The Merry Go Round of Love and Selected Stories. Tr. Frances Keene and Lily Duplaix. New York: New American Library, 1964.

'The Miracle of Two Bears.' Tr. anon. *Living Age* (30 Jan. 1936).

'Miss Holloway's Goat.' Tr. J. Redfern. *The Golden Book* (May 1934). Also published as 'The Little Black Kid.' *The Listener* (21 Nov. 1934).

The Naked Truth and Eleven Other Stories. Tr. Arthur Mayne and Henrie Mayne. New York: Dutton, 1934; London: Lane, 1934, 1940, 1947.

'Portrait.' Tr. anon. *Living Age* (1 Nov. 1929).

'Reserved Coffin.' Tr. J. Harry. *The Golden Book* (Jan. 1926).

'Shoes at the Door.' Tr. anon. *Living Age* (15 Nov. 1924).

Short Stories. Tr. Lily Duplaix. New York: Simon and Schuster, 1959.

Short Stories. Tr. Frederick May. New York: Oxford University Press, 1964; London: Oxford University Press, 1965; London: Quartet, 1978.

'Sicilian Limes.' Tr. anon. *The Golden Book* (Jan. 1934).

'The Starling and the Angel One Hundred and One.' Tr. F.M. Guercio. *The Bermondsey Book* (June 1927).

Tales of Madness. Tr. and intr. Giovanni Bussino. Brookline Village, MA: Dante University of America Press, 1984.

Tales of Suicide. Tr. and intr. Giovanni Bussino. Brookline Village, MA: Dante University of America Press, 1988.

'Through the Other Wife's Eyes.' Tr. J. Redfern. *The Fortnightly Review* (April 1933). Also published as 'With Other Eyes,' in *The Armchair Esquire*. New York: Putnam's Sons, 1958.

'To the Hoe.' Tr. Ben Johnson, In *Stories of Modern Italy*. New York: The Modern Library, 1960.

'Truth.' Tr. J. Redfern. *The Fortnightly Review* (June 1934).

'Two Double Beds.' Tr. anon. *The Spectator* (24 Nov. 1933).

Major Criticism in English on Pirandello

Abba, Marta. 'Introduction' to *The Mountain Giants and Other Plays by L. Pirandello*. New York: Crown, 1958.

Auger, Helen. 'Pirandello's New Play for Duse.' *New York Times Magazine* (4 Mar. 1923).

Balakian, Anne. 'Pirandello's *Six Characters* and Surrealism.' In John L. Di Gaetani, ed., *A Companion to Pirandello Studies*. Westport, CT: Greenwood Press, 1991.

Bassanese, Flora A. *Understanding Luigi Pirandello*. Columbia, SC: University of South Carolina Press, 1997.

Bassnet-McGuire, Susan. 'Art and Life in Luigi Pirandello's *Questa sera si recita a soggetto*.' In J. Redmond, ed., *Themes in Drama* 2 (1980): 81–102.

– *File on Pirandello*. London: Methuen, 1989.

– *Luigi Pirandello*. London: Macmillan, 1983.

Bassnet, Susan, and Jennifer Lorch, eds. *Luigi Pirandello in the Theater: A Documentary Record*. Reading: Harwood Academic Publishers. 1993.

Bentley, Eric R. 'Father's Day.' *The Drama Review* 13, 1 (Fall 1968): 57–72.

– 'Il tragico imperatore.' *Tulane Drama Review* 10, 3 (Apr. 1966): 60–75.

– 'Introduction' to Luigi Pirandello, *Naked Masks*. New York: Dutton, 1952.

– 'Introduction' to Luigi Pirandello, *Pirandello Major Plays*. Evanston, IL: Northwestern University Press, 1991.

– 'Pirandello: Joy and Torment.' In *In Search of Theater*. New York: Knopf, 1953.

– *The Pirandello Commentaries*. Evanston, IL: Northwestern University Press, 1991.

– *The Playwright as Thinker: A Study of Drama in Modern Times*. New York: Harcourt, Brace and World, 1967; New York: World Publishing Co., Meridian Books, 1986.

– *Theater of War*. New York: Viking, 1973.

Bentley, Eric, ed. *The Genius of Italian Theater*. New York: New American Library, 1964.

– *The Theory of the Modern Stage: An Introduction to Modern Theater and Drama*. Harmondsworth: Penguin, 1992.

Biasin, Gian Paolo, and Manuela Gieri, eds. *Luigi Pirandello: Contemporary Perspectives*. Toronto: University of Toronto Press, 1999.

Biasin, G.P., and N.J. Perella. *Pirandello 86*. Rome: Bulzoni, 1987.

Bini, Daniela. 'Enacting the Dissolution of the Self. Woman as One, No One, and One Hundred Thousand.' In Biasin and Gieri, eds, *Luigi Pirandello: Contemporary Perspectives*. Toronto: University of Toronto Press, 1999.

– *Pirandello and His Muse. The Plays for Marta Abba*. Gainesville, FL: University of Florida Press, 1998.

Bishop, Thomas. *Pirandello and the French Theater*. New York: New York University Press, 1960.

– 'Pirandello's Influence on French Drama.' In Glauco Cambon, ed., *Pirandello: A Collection of Critical Essays*, 34–46. Englewood Cliffs, NJ: Prentice Hall, 1966.

Brose, Margaret. 'Structures of Ambiguity in Pirandello's *Liolà*.' *Yale Italian Studies* 2, 3 (Spring 1978): 115–41.

Brustein, Robert S. 'Luigi Pirandello.' In *The Theater of Revolt. An Approach to Modern Drama*, 279–317. Boston: Little Brown, 1964.

– 'Pirandello's Drama of Revolt.' In Glauco Cambon, ed., *Pirandello: A Collection of Critical Essays*. Englewood Cliffs, NJ: Prentice Hall, 1967.

– *Seasons of Discontent: Dramatic Opinions 1959–1965*. New York: Simon and Schuster, 1965.

Büdel, Oscar. *Pirandello*. New York: Hillary House; London: Bowes and Bowes, 1966.

Caesar, Ann Hallamore. 'The Branding of Women: Family, Theatre and Female Identity in Pirandello.' *Italian Studies* 45 (1990): 48–63.

– *Characters and Authors in Luigi Pirandello*. Oxford: Clarendon Press; New York: Oxford University Press, 1998.

Cambon, Glauco, ed. *Pirandello: A Collection of Critical Essays*. Englewood Cliffs, NJ: Prentice Hall, 1967.

Caputi, Anthony. *Pirandello and the Crisis of Modern Consciousness*. Urbana, IL: Urbana University Press, 1988.

Carrabino, Victor. 'Pirandello's Characters in Search of a Mask.' In Anne Paolucci, ed., *Pirandello*, 123–35. *Review of National Literatures* 14 (1987).

Caute, David. *The Illusion: An Essay on Politics, Theater, and the Novel*. New York: Harper and Row, 1972.

Charney, Maurice. 'Shakespearean and Pirandellian: *Hamlet* and *Six Characters in Search of an Author.*' *Modern Drama* 24 (1981): 323–7.

Chiaramonte, Nicola. 'Pirandello and Humor.' In *The Worm of Consciousness and Other Essays*, 80–3. New York: Harcourt, 1976.

Cincotta, Madeleine. *Luigi Pirandello: The Humorous Existentialist*. Wollongong: University of Wollongong Press, 1989.

Corrigan, Beatrice. 'Pirandello and the Theater of the Absurd.' *Cesare Barbieri Courier* 8, 1 (1961).

Craig, Edward Gordon. *On the Art of the Theatre*. London: Chelsea, 1911.

Dashwood, Julie, ed. *Luigi Pirandello: The Theatre of Paradox*. Lampeter: Edward Mellen Press, 1996.

Di Gaetani, John L., ed. *A Companion to Pirandello Studies*. Westport, CT: Greenwood Press, 1990.

Dombroski, Robert S. 'Laudisi's Laughter and the Social Dimension of *Right You Are (if You Think So).*' *Modern Drama* 16 (1973): 337–64.

Dukore, Bernard F., and Daniel C. Gerould. 'Explosions and Implosions: Avant-Garde Drama between World Wars.' *Educational Theater Journal* 21 (1969): 1–16.

Esslin, Martin. 'Pirandello: Master of the Naked Masks.' In *Reflections: Essays on Modern Theater*. New York: Doubleday, 1969. Also in *Brief Chronicles: Essays of Modern Theatre*, 59–67. London: Temple Smith, 1970.

Feng, Carol B. 'Reconciliation of Movement and Form in *Diana e la Tuda.*' *Modern Drama* 10, 4 (1968): 410–15.

Fido, Franco. 'The Overbearing Author in the Stage Directions of *Maschere Nude.*' In Gian Paolo Biasin and Nicolas J. Perella, eds, *Pirandello 86*, 45–58. Rome: Bulzoni, 1987.

Firth, Felicity. 'The Mask as Face and the Face as Mask: Some of Pirandello's Variations on the Theme of Personal Appearances.' *Yearbook of the British Pirandello Society* 2 (1982): 1–27.

Frese Witt, Mary Ann. 'Modes of Narration in *Sei Personaggi*.' In W. Geerts, F. Musarra, and S. Vanvolsem, eds, *Luigi Pirandello: Poetica e Presenza*, 607–16. Rome: Bulzoni, 1987.

– 'Woman or Mother? Feminine Condition in Pirandello's Theatre.' In John L. Di Gaetani, ed., A *Companion to Pirandello Studies*, 57–72. Westport, CT, and London: Greenwood Press, 1991.

Gieri, Manuela. *Contemporary Italian Filmmaking. Strategies of Subversion. Pirandello, Fellini, Scola, and the Directors of the New Generation.* Toronto: University of Toronto Press, 1995.

Gilman, Richard. *The Making of Modern Drama.* New York: Farrar, Straus, 1974.

Giudice, Gaspare. 'Ambiguity in *Six Characters in Search of an Author*.' In *Theater Three* 7 (Fall 1989): 69–88.

– *Pirandello. A Biography.* London: Oxford University Press, 1975.

Gordon, Jan B. '*Sei personaggi in cerca d'autore:* Myth, Ritual, and Pirandello's Anti-Symbolist Theater.' *Forum Italicum* 6 (1972): 333–55.

Gunzberg, Maggie. *Patriarchal Representations. Gender and Discourse in Pirandello's Theater.* Oxford: Berg, 1994.

Harrison, Thomas. *Essayism. Conrad, Musil, and Pirandello.* Baltimore: Johns Hopkins University Press, 1992.

Heffner, Hubert C. 'Pirandello and the Nature of Man.' In Travis Bogard and William Oliver, eds, *Modern Drama: Essays in Criticism.* New York: Oxford University Press, 1965.

Hodess, Kenneth M. 'In Search of the Divided Self: A Psychoanalytic Inquiry into the Drama of Pirandello.' In Mario B. Mignone, ed., *Pirandello in America*, 133–45. Rome: Bulzoni, 1988.

Hoover, Clark. 'Existentialism in Pirandello's *Sei Personaggi*.' *Italica* 43, 3 (Sept. 1966): 276–84.

Illiano, Antonio. 'Pirandello in England and the United States: A Chronological List of Criticism.' *Bulletin of the New York Public Library* (Feb. 1967).

– '*Six Characters, An American Opera*.' In Anne Paolucci, ed., *Pirandello*, 136–59. *Review of National Literatures* 14 (1987).

– 'A View of the Italian Absurd from Pirandello to Eduardo De Filippo.' *Proceedings of the Comparative Literature Symposium* 3. Lubbock, TX: Texas Tech University, 1970.

Kennedy, Andrew K. '*Six Characters:* Pirandello's Last Tape.' *Modern Drama* 12 (1960): 1–9.

Kligerman, Charles. 'A Psychoanalytic Study of Pirandello's *Six Characters in Search of an Author.' Journal of the American Psychoanalytic Association* 10 (Oct. 1962): 731–44.

Kroha, Lucienne. 'Behind the Veil: A Freudian Reading of Pirandello's *Cosí è (se vi pare).' The Yearbook of the British Pirandello Society* 12 (1992): 1–23.

Kuprel, D.A. 'The Hermeneutic Paradox: Pirandello's *Cosí è se vi pare.' Pirandello Studies* 17 (1997): 46–57.

Lawrence, Kenneth. 'Luigi Pirandello: Holding Nature up to the Mirror.' *Italica* 47 (1970): 61–77.

Leo, Ulrich. 'Pirandello between Fiction and Drama.' In Glauco Cambon, ed., *Pirandello: A Collection of Critical Essays*, 83–90. Englewood Cliffs, NJ: Prentice Hall, 1967.

Lorch, Jennifer. 'The 1925 Text of *Sei Personaggi in cerca d'autore* and Pitoëff's Production of 1923.' In *Yearbook of the British Pirandello Society* 2 (1982): 32–47.

– *Pirandello. Six Characters in Search of an Author. Plays in Production.* Cambridge: Cambridge University Press, 2005.

– 'Theories of Theater in Two Plays by Pirandello.' In W. Geerts, F. Musarra, and S. Vanvolsem, eds, *Luigi Pirandello. Poetica e Presenza*, 191–200. Rome: Bulzoni, 1987.

Loriggio, Franco. 'Life and Death: Pirandello's "Man with the Flower in His Mouth." ' *Italian Quarterly* 47–8 (1969): 151–60.

Lucas, F.L. *The Drama of Chekhov, Synge, Yeats, and Pirandello.* London: Cassell, 1965.

Lumley, F. 'The Mask and the Face of Luigi Pirandello.' In *New Trends in Twentieth Century Drama.* London: Oxford University Press, 1967.

McDonald, David. 'Derrida and Pirandello: A Post-Structuralist Analysis of *Six Characters.' Modern Drama* 20 (1976): 421–36.

MacKlintock, Lander. *The Age of Pirandello.* Bloomington, IN: Indiana University Press, 1951.

Mariani, Umberto. *Living Masks. The Achievement of Pirandello.* Toronto: University of Toronto Press, 2008.

Matthaei, Renate. *Luigi Pirandello.* New York: Ungar, 1973.

Mignone, Mario. 'The Theater of Pirandello and Brecht: Some Points of Contact.' *NEMLA Italian Studies* 2 (1978): 63–85.

Mignone, Mario, ed. *Pirandello in America.* Rome: Bulzoni, 1988.

Moestrup, Jorn. *The Structural Pattern of Pirandello's Work.* Odense: Odense University Press, 1972.

Nagy, Moses M. 'A Quest for Truth through Love and Reason: Marivaux and Pirandello.' *Review of National Literatures* 14 (1987): 47–57.

Newberry, Wilma. *The Pirandellian Mode in Spanish Literature from Cervantes to Sastre*. Albany: State University of New York Press, 1973.

Nolan, David. 'Theory in Action: Pirandello's *Sei personaggi*.' *Forum for Modern Language Studies* 4 (1968): 269–76.

Nulf, Frank. 'Pirandello and the Cinema.' *Film Quarterly* 24, 2 (1970): 40–8.

O'Keefe Bazzoni, Jana. 'Seeing Double: Pirandello and His Audience.' In Anne Paolucci, ed., *Pirandello*, 160–90. *Review of National Literatures* 14 (1987).

Oliver, Roger W. *Dreams of Passion. The Theater of Luigi Pirandello*. New York: New York University Press, 1972.

Paolucci, Anne. 'Pirandello as the "Seminal" Innovator of Our Time.' In Mario Mignone, ed., *Pirandello in America*, 35–40. Rome: Bulzoni, 1988.

– 'Pirandello: Experience as Expression of Will.' *Forum Italicum* 7, 3 (1973): 404–14.

– *Pirandello's Theater. The Recovery of the Modern Stage for Dramatic Art*. Carbondale, IL: Southern Illinois University Press, 1974.

– 'Theater of Illusion: Pirandello's *Liolà* and Machiavelli's *Mandragola*.' *Comparative Literature Studies* 9, 1 (1972): 44–57.

Poggioli, Renato. 'Pirandello in Retrospect.' *Italian Quarterly* 1, 4 (Winter 1958): 19–47. Also in *The Spirit of the Letter*. Cambridge, MA: Harvard University Press, 1965.

Radcliff-Umstead, Douglas. *The Mirror of Our Anguish. A Study of Pirandello's Narrative Writings*. Madison, NJ: Fairleigh Dickinson University Press, 1978.

Ragusa, Olga. 'Correlated Terms in Pirandello's Conception of Umorismo.' In Americo Bugliani, ed., *The Two Hesperias*. Madrid: Turanzas, 1978.

– *Luigi Pirandello*. Columbia University Press, 1968.

– *Pirandello. An Approach to His Theater*. Edinburgh: Edinburgh University Press, 1980.

– 'Pirandello's Haunted House.' *Studies in Short Fiction* 10 (1973): 235–42.

Ray, John B. 'A Case of Identity: The Source of Pirandello's *As You Desire Me*.' *Modern Drama* 15 (1973): 433–9.

Sinicropi, Giovanni. 'The Metaphysical Dimension of Pirandello's Theater.' *Modern Drama* 20 (1997): 353–81.

Sogliuzzo, Richard A. *Luigi Pirandello, Director. The Playwright in the Theater*. New York and London: Scarecrow Press, 1982.

– 'The Use of the Mask in "The Great God Brown" and *Six Characters in Search of an Author*.' *Educational Theater Journal* 18 (1966): 224–9.

Starkie, Walter. *Luigi Pirandello*. London: Dent, 1926; Berkeley: University of California Press, 1965.

Stocchi-Perrucchio, Donatella. *Pirandello and the Vagaries of Knowledge. A Reading of* Il fu Mattia Pascal. Stanford, CA: Anma Libri, 1991.

Stone, Jennifer. *Pirandello's Naked Prompt: The Structure of Repetition in Modernism.* Ravenna: Longo, 1989.
– 'Pirandello's Scandalous Docile Bodies.' In Anne Paolucci, ed., *Pirandello*, 79–92. *Review of National Literatures* 14 (1987).
Styan, J.L. *The Dark Comedy: The Development of Modern Comic Tragedy.* Cambridge: Cambridge University Press, 1948.
– 'Pirandello and the teatro grottesco.' In *Modern Drama in Theory and Practice*, vol. 2. Cambridge: Cambridge University Press, 1981.
Szondi, Peter. *Theory of Modern Drama.* Oxford: Blackwell, 1987.
Tilgher, Adriano. 'Life versus Form.' In Glauco Cambon, ed., *Pirandello: A Collection of Critical Essays*, 19–34. Englewood Cliffs, NJ: Prentice Hall, 1967.
Tindemans, Carlos. 'Characters in Search of an Actor. Luigi Pirandello's *Henry IV*.' In W. Geerts, F. Musarra, and S. Vanvolsem, eds, *Luigi Pirandello: Poetica e Presenza.* Rome: Bulzoni, 1987.
Uwah, Godwin O. *Pirandellism and the Plays of Samuel Beckett.* Potomac, MD: Scripta Humanistica, 1991.
Vittorini, Domenico. *The Drama of Luigi Pirandello.* New York: Russell and Russell, 1969.
William, Herman. 'Pirandello and Possibility.' *Tulane Drama Review* 10, 3 (Spring 1966): 91–111.
Williams, Raymond. *Modern Tragedy.* Palo Alto, CA: Stanford University Press, 1966.

Issues of Journals Mostly or Entirely Devoted to Pirandellian Topics

Canadian Journal of Italian Studies 12, 38–9 (1989); 13, 40–1 (1990).
Forum Italicum 1, 4 (Dec. 1967).
Il Veltro 12, 1–2 (1968).
Italica 44, 1 (March 1967); 52, 2 (Summer 1975).
Modern Drama 6, 4 (Feb. 1964); 20, 4 (1977).
Pirandellian Studies (all issues).
Pirandello Studies (Journal of the Society for Pirandello Studies, U.K., all issues).
P.S.A. (The Pirandello Society of America, all issues).
Review of National Literatures 14 (1987).
Rivista di studi pirandelliani (all issues).
Tulane Drama Review 10, 3 (Spring 1966).
World Theater 16, 3 (1967).